LEAN WORK

lean production

toyota production system

fordism

team concept

flexible specialization

group work

co-determination

high performance systems

reengineering

employee involvement

management by stress

post-fordism

neo-fordism

modern operating agreement

socio-technical systems

LEAN WORK

EMPOWERMENT AND

EXPLOITATION IN THE

GLOBAL

AUTO INDUSTRY

Edited by Steve Babson

Wayne State University Press   Detroit

Library of Congress Cataloging-in-Publication Data

Lean work: empowerment and exploitation in the global auto industry /

edited by Steve Babson.

p.   cm.

Includes bibliographical references and index.

ISBN 0-8143-2535-1 (pbk.: alk. paper)

1. Automobile industry workers—Congresses.   2. Automobile

industry and trade—Management—Congresses.   3. Trade-unions—

Automobile industry workers—Congresses.   4. Employee empowerment—

Congresses.   5. Comparative management—Congresses.   6. Comparative

industrial relations—Congresses.   I. Babson, Steve.

HD8039.A8L43   1995

331.7'6292—dc20   95-2863

DESIGNER
S. R. Tenebaum

Contents

CONTENTS

Contributors

ANDY ADCROFT is a lecturer at the East London Business School, University of London.

PAUL ADLER is a professor of management in the School of Business Administration, University of Southern California.

STEVE BABSON is a labor program specialist at the Labor Studies Center, Wayne State University.

CHRISTIAN BERGGREN is an associate professor in the Department of Work Science, the Royal Institute of Technology, Stockholm.

IRVING BLUESTONE is a University Professor of labor studies at Wayne State University.

ADRIENNE EATON is an assistant professor of labor studies at Rutgers University.

LAURIE GRAHAM is an assistant professor of labor studies at Indiana University.

WILLIAM GREEN is professor of government at Morehead State University.

COLIN HASLAM is a subject leader in business policy at the East London Business School, University of London.

SUSAN HELPER is an assistant professor of economics at Case Western Reserve University.

CHRIS HUXLEY is an associate professor of sociology at Trent University.

CANDACE HOWES is an assistant professor of economics at Notre Dame University.

JAMES JACOBS is an associate vice president for business and community relations at Macomb Community College.

SUKHDEV JOHAL is an associate lecturer at the East London Business School, University of London.

ULRICH JÜRGENS is a research fellow at the International Institute for Comparative Social Research, Science Center, Berlin.

JOHN PAUL MACDUFFIE is a researcher for the International Motor Vehicle Program at MIT, and is an assistant professor at the Wharton School of Business, University of Pennsylvania.

MIKE PARKER is a researcher and skilled trades instructor in Detroit, Michigan.

JOHN PRICE is a research associate at the Center for Japanese Research, University of British Columbia.

FRITS K. PIL is a doctoral student at the Wharton School, the University of Pennsylvania.

JAMES RINEHART is a professor of sociology at the University of Western Ontario.

DAVID ROBERTSON is a staff member of the Research Department, Canadian Auto Workers.

GARY SAGANSKI is director of corporate training at Henry Ford Community College.

HARLEY SHAIKEN is a professor in the Graduate School of Education at the University of California, Berkeley.

JANE SLAUGHTER is director of *Labor Notes*, located in Detroit, Michigan.

HIDEO TOTSUKA is a professor of economics at Saitama University.

JOHN WILLIAMS is a professor of economics at the University of Wales.

KAREL WILLIAMS is professor on the Faculty of Social Sciences and Economics, University of Manchester.

Acknowledgments

This volume is based on the selected and revised proceedings of a conference entitled "Lean Production and Labor: Critical and Comparative Perspectives" held at Wayne State University, Detroit, Michigan, 20–22 May 1993. The conference was organized and sponsored by the Labor Studies Center of the College of Urban, Labor, and Metropolitan Affairs. The views expressed in these essays represent the range of debate at the conference, and I owe a debt of thanks to each author for agreeing to disagree in that public forum and in this volume. In addition, there were many individuals who participated in the conference, facilitated the case-history research, and/or reviewed portions of the manuscript. Nancy Brigham's support was especially important. Among the many others to whom I owe thanks are Ron Alpern, Al Benchich, Ron Blum, Bill Bryce, Felicia Calvo, Bill Cooke, Greg Drudi, Carol Haddad, Frank Hammer, Geri Hill, Robert Hulot-Kentor, Charlie Hyde, Phil Keeling, Charles E. Keys, Jr., Bob King, Gerry Lazarowitz, Tom Lonergan, Brad Markell, Jim Martin, Sean McAlinden, Jim McNeil, Mike Oblak, Onzell Patty, Bernie Ricke, Gil Rodriguez, Maureen Sheahan, Sue Smock, Hal Stack, Josh Stulberg, Lois Tetrick, Jeff Washington, and Steve Wyatt. Arthur Evans and Kathy Wildfong of Wayne State University Press kept the book on schedule, and copy editor Mary Gillis helped congeal the manuscript's many parts into a more consistent whole. The help of all these individuals made the book possible. They are exempted, of course, from all errors of commission or omission.

1

Lean Production and Labor: Empowerment and Exploitation

STEVE BABSON

> Our conclusion is simple: Lean production is a superior way for humans to make things. . . . It provides more challenging and fulfilling work for employees at every level, from the factory to headquarters. It follows that the whole world should adopt lean production, and as quickly as possible.
>
> James Womack, Daniel Jones, and Daniel Roos,
> *The Machine that Changed the World*

Their message has an evangelical urgency: just as the auto industry was "the machine that changed the world" in the opening decades of the twentieth century, so will "lean production" bless our lives in the coming millennium. Reporting the research results of MIT's International Motor Vehicle Program (IMVP), James Womack and his fellow authors have proclaimed the second coming of American manufacturing, revived by lean production methods learned from the Japanese auto industry.

Their book has achieved a singular prominence, selling more than 150,000 copies in the U.S. in its first two years, and becoming a national bestseller. Subsequent studies and reports have further amplified the book's message. According to the IMVP, the old exploitative methods of mass production, with narrowly specialized, low-skill jobs and repetitive tasks dictated by top-down engineering, will give way in the lean factory to teams of multi-skilled, empowered workers who rotate jobs and take responsibility for building the car right the first time. Corporate managers now claim the book and its message as their own. In 1992, *Forbes* reported that Chrysler president Robert Lutz "tells his people to read it and quizzes them on it later." That same year, *The Machine that Changed the World* was a best selling business book in Germany. *Automotive News* pronounced it a study "of great understanding, and of hope. It shows how to create an industrial world in which workers share the challenges and satisfactions of the business."[1]

Workers and their unions, however, are often wary of these claims, even as they also oppose traditional top-down management. The preamble to the United Auto Workers' constitution condemns the "authoritarian climate of the workplace" that makes the worker "an adjunct to the tool rather than its master." But while endorsing reforms that bring "Economic Democracy" to the workplace, the union has also raised a cautionary note. "Working men and women . . . are often in the best position to participate in making intelligent, informed decisions," the UAW resolved at its 1989 convention; "at the same time, we oppose efforts by companies to use democratic sounding programs as a smokescreen designed to undermine collective bargaining and workers' rights." Skepticism on this score has grown with each new round of plant closings that accompanies management's simultaneous call for "worker participation" and lean production. In this real-world context of forced downsizing, where surviving workers are told that their plant's future depends on their willingness to make local contract concessions, where GM chairman Robert Stempel publicly announced in 1992 that "We're working on [each plant] one at a time . . . to see what that plant wants to do and how they're going to do it," and where the work rules and seniority rights that protect workers are defined as obstacles to the required "flexibility" of lean production—in this rocky soil, rosy scenarios of worker empowerment lose much of their bloom. To many workers, the management version of teamwork threatens a new form of exploitation, with greater demands on their mental as well as physical energies, but with no real control of the pace or content of their work. Bill Green, elected shop chairman of UAW Local 2308 at Miller Brewing and an advocate of genuine worker empowerment, articulates the misgivings he felt on his previous job in the auto industry: "Having worked at General Motors for many years, I am aware of management's attempt to use fear and intimidation to try to force individuals into programs that tout 'flexibility' and 'worker participation' with no more 'participation' than to assist in deciding what color to paint the restroom walls. . . . What do these people at MIT know anyway?"[2]

Lean Work measures that question against the available evidence from auto companies around the world. The contributors are drawn from Japan, Germany, Sweden, Britain, and North America, representing a spectrum of research and analysis that is rarely considered in partisan forums, pro or con. Compared with the promotional bias that usually characterizes the mainstream media and much of the business press, the tenor of this collection is more critical and cautious, with a variety of perspectives on how the promise of worker empowerment might actually be realized in the auto factory's contested terrain.

There is also a contrast in research methods. Anyone who studies work organization has difficulty gathering reliable information about the workplace: more often than not, managers concerned for their own job security and the public image of their company permit access to this restricted realm only under conditions that bias the investigation. As a result, researchers are often relying on superficial evidence and one-sided interviews with individuals (usually managers) who have a personal stake in projecting images of an efficient workplace and happy workers. A salient feature of the MIT study is that it goes beyond these impressionistic accounts by using quantifiable data to measure factory performance in a variety of settings. The authors in this volume offer conflicting perspectives on the methodology and conclusions of the MIT study, but they share a concern for widening the debate to include evidence that is usually ignored in standard reporting of "the new factory." In particular, many of the studies collected here present new and important research concerning the experience of workers in these production systems, with evidence drawn from in-depth case studies, surveys, structured interviews, and participant-observer data.

From a critical and comparative perspective, these essays address the primary questions of what a lean-flexible production system is, and how it affects work and workers. A host of related questions follow. What, for example, are the performance outcomes of lean production in terms of productivity and quality, and how can these be measured? Does lean-flexible production empower workers and enhance their skills? Is it a "fragile" system that depends on voluntary worker participation? Or can the system exploit workers and strengthen management control? If the latter, what specific conditions give lean-flexible production the potential for intensifying work and compelling commitment, and does organized resistance by an independent union nullify or rescue the system's promised benefits? Finally, given all of the above, what are the appropriate goals of public policy in guiding work restructuring?

Empowerment and Exploitation

Few of these questions permit the kind of unqualified yes-no answers that predominate in partisan debate. The very terms "empowerment" and "exploitation" can easily lend themselves to categorical assessments in which lean production is deemed to be either one *or* the other. In fact, empowerment and exploitation are more likely to coexist in any production system, with the range of possibilities marked by degrees rather than categories. Calibrating such a spectrum is no easy matter, however, since the concept of power—what it is and how it's distributed—is the subject of contentious debate.

One commonly held definition equates power with responsibility: production workers are therefore said to be "empowered" when they take on new responsibilities—such as monitoring quality, maintaining machinery, and troubleshooting problems—that were previously performed by supervisors or skilled trades. Since this definition fails to account for those cases where workers are given additional responsibility without matching resources to get the job done, it can just as easily serve as a formula for stress. A more discriminating definition of power must also specify the distribution of authority within the workplace. Empowerment is relative on such a scale, defined in relation to the conflicting claims that groups of workers and managers make on limited resources of people, time, skills, tools, materials, energy, information, and money. In this formulation, power means the authority to use or withold such *enterprise resources.* In allocating overtime, for example, supervisors in some plants have the authority to assign the extra hours to favored employees, or make the assignment mandatory for the unwilling; alternatively, workers in union plants may have the right to decline overtime assignments and "equalize" the extra hours offered to co-workers. In some cases (notably, Germany), elected worker representatives may also have the authority to veto overtime and bargain for additional hiring to cover expanded production.[3]

The authority to allocate or withold enterprise resources may be formalized in work rules and titles, but the day-to-day exercise of authority is predicated on a group's *capacity to mobilize* in defense of these formal claims. Assembly line workers who are "responsible for quality" are not highly empowered if, for example, they lack the authority to stop the line when changes in model mix (the sequence of different car models on the line) require rebalancing of workloads. But even when workers have the formal authority to pull the stop cord, they must also have the collective capacity to defend themselves against supervisors who badger and "disfavor" workers for stopping the line. Power, then, not only entails *responsibility* and formal *authority*, but also the *capacity to mobilize* a group's internal resources (member loyalty, organization, symbols of unity, leadership skills) for actions that defend or extend the group's claim to enterprise resources. Workers will retain the authority to pull the stop cord and thereby gain additional time, people, and/or tools to meet quality standards only if their mobilization can impose the appropriate sanctions on contrary supervisors.[4]

This "capacity to mobilize" is a crucial—and often ignored—determinant of power. Most accounts of the "empowered workplace" assume that management's delegation of responsibility and authority to workers constitutes a transfer of power; in fact, managers often retain the power to unilaterally cancel such an entrustment if they subsequently experience a change of heart, "circumstances," or owners. Rather than a gift bestowed, power devolves to those who have the capacity to hold or take it. That "capacity to mobilize" differs in key respects for managers and workers, defined by their unequal position in our corporate economy. As owners or representatives of capital, managers have greater access to material resources and the institutional backing that accrues to holders of private property. Ultimately, this institutional backing can take the form of legally sanctioned force: as in layoffs, plant closings, or permanent replacement of strikers. For workers, on the other hand, the capacity to mobilize depends on the degree to which reliable mechanisms of due-process protect their formal rights, and the degree to which an oppositional "culture of solidarity" unifies workers for mutual protection.[5]

This suggests a straight-line progression from empowerment, where workers (white or blue collar) exercise a high degree of discretion and control of enterprise resources, to exploitation, where workers are passive objects upon which managers unilaterally force their will. Yet even this scale of relative power can misrepresent the actual complexity of environments where "empowerment" includes something like its opposite: as when the delegation of power to subordinates is conditioned on their conformance to, if not internalization of, goals that primarily serve the dominant party. Power, then, may also require a definition of what *goals* are served by empowered workers, and this entails the additional complexity of specifying which social actors define these goals. Certainly, management defines the organization's financial goals. But at each level of the corporate hierarchy, power is hedged by superiors who dictate strategy, by investors who demand short-term profits, and by government officials who enforce public policy. Competition imposes another form of restraint, narrowing the range of "practical" options that managers can afford to consider. Even in nonunion environments there is an informal negotiation with workers that further qualifies management's control, and in a union setting where workers' capacity to mobilize is more developed and protected, this negotiated outcome means that employees may accept certain management goals, but these are marbled with compromises that concede a degree of independent power to workers.[6]

These complexities are not easily untangled, but recognition of the problematic nature of "empowerment" is the starting point for examining lean production, both as it affects workers, and as it is affected by them.

Since the terms of this debate take their meaning from the historical context in which their definition is contested, the first step in this examination is to define that history—to specify, first, what lean production is or is claimed to be, and second, to situate these claims in their relationship to preceding and coexisting forms of work organization.

After Japan

Lean production joins Total Quality Management and a host of managerial nostrums derived from Japanese practice. An all-encompassing model that combines diverse elements of Japanese production management (''just-in-time,'' ''work teams,'' etc.), lean production is distinguished by its minimalist approach to factory management. Inventories in a ''lean'' plant are taken on a just-in-time basis to minimize handling and expose defective parts before they accumulate in the warehouse; stockpiles of in-process work are also sharply reduced so that defects are immediately exposed at their source, before they fill the plant's repair bays with defective products; ''indirect'' labor (supervision, inspection, maintenance) is pared and specialized job classifications are reduced or eliminated, replaced by teams of cross-trained production workers who rotate jobs and take on responsibilities for quality control, repair, housekeeping, and preventive maintenance.

Lean-flexible production is more efficient, it is argued, because workers can commit themselves to continuously improving productivity and quality, building the product right the first time rather than passing defective work down the line. ''Building in quality'' will reduce costs, not increase them, because there is less need for specialized repair, inspection, and maintenance personnel, and less need for the factory space and tools these ''non-value added'' workers use. ''Lean production is 'lean','' say the MIT researchers, ''because it uses less of everything compared with mass production—half the human effort in the factory, half the manufacturing space, half the investment in tools, half the engineering hours to develop a new product in half the time.''[7]

According to Womack, Jones, and Roos, what makes these results especially noteworthy is that the lean-flexible production system, as it maximizes productivity and quality, also humanizes the process. The Japanese model, says the IMVP, is inherently good for workers. Under lean production, the ''freedom to control one's work'' supposedly replaces the ''mind numbing stress'' of mass production. Armed with ''the skills they need to control their environment,'' workers in a lean production plant have the opportunity ''to think actively, indeed *proactively*,'' to solve workplace problems. This ''creative tension,'' as they call it, makes work in a lean production factory not only more challenging, but more ''humanly fulfilling.''[8]

The IMVP is not alone in such claims. Turn to any business publication from the mid-1980s onwards, and you'll find a consultant or an academic (sometimes one and the same) making a pitch for the beneficial effects of worker empowerment. ''You do not get love without empowerment,'' says Selwyn Becker, professor of ''Psychology and Total Quality Management'' at the University of Chicago. With ''fully empowered, self-contained cross-functional teams,'' a company will not only produce quality improvements of 200 to 600 percent, by Becker's generous accounting, but also ''a highly motivated team of people who *love* the challenge of coming to work to solve problems.''[9]

Ohno and Taylor

For the advocates of lean production, the exemplar is Toyota, whose Taiichi Ohno pioneered the ''lean'' model in the years immediately following World War II. In the impoverished and chaotic conditions of Japan's postwar economy, necessity was Ohno's guide. Since consumer demand was low, and since the company's bankers would only finance production for orders already placed with dealers, Ohno had to schedule production in small batches, relying on cross-trained workers who performed direct labor tasks when the lines were up, and did maintenance or housekeeping when the lines were down. Universal machine tools and quick-change dies maximized the flexibility and uptime of expensive capital equipment. Just-in-time delivery of parts minimized inventory costs, and subcontracting to low-wage suppliers cut labor costs and reduced capital commitments. Over the subsequent decades, Toyota refined and modified these features of low-volume, flexible manufacturing, even as the company's output mushroomed from a mere 23,000 automobiles in 1955 to a staggering 3.3 million in 1980. Nissan and other Japanese competitors followed suit to lesser degrees, until the ''Japanese model'' became the standard against which all others measured their performance. In 1955, Japanese auto production had been less than 1 percent of American output; in 1980, just twenty-five years later, Japanese production surpassed the United States.[10]

MIT's International Motor Vehicle Program spent five years and five million dollars—contributed by the major auto companies and governments of Europe, the United States, and Japan—measuring the performance of this Toyota Production System across three continents and ninety assembly plants. Their conclusion: Japan's home-based auto plants in 1989 required a weighted average of only seventeen labor hours per car, compared to twenty-five hours in North American plants of the Big Three and thirty-six hours in the plants of Europe's volume producers (Fiat, Peugeot, Renault, and VW). Equally striking, these results apparently required no sacrifice in quality. Indeed, the same Japanese companies that led the world in productivity also produced, according to MIT, cars with 50 percent fewer defects than their American and European competitors. Since the MIT findings indicated that Japanese managed factories in North America produced roughly the same high level of quality as in Japan, and with productivity performance second only to Japan's home-based plants, these results did not seem to depend on the unique characteristics of Japanese culture, but on organizational principles that American automakers could also adopt.[11]

These principles, according to MIT, encompass not only the factory, but the entire process of engineering and marketing an automobile, from initial design to distributing the final product. The unique achievement of Taiichi Ohno and Toyota was in "putting all the pieces together to create a complete system of lean production, extending from product planning through all the steps of manufacturing and supply system coordination on to the customer." This "complete system" included a new approach to pre-production planning. Instead of the organization that prevailed in the Big Three, with separate and sequential steps from design to product engineering to manufacturing, each functionally segregated from the other, Toyota pioneered the use of cross-functional product teams so that ease of manufacture would be a simultaneous concern with styling and product engineering. "Flexibility" became the byword of this inter-dependent model, with cross-functional teams of white-collar engineers and product designers in pre-production planning matched in the factory by cross-functional groups of blue-collar workers.[12]

There is no equivocation in the MIT study concerning the importance of these shop-floor teams and the wider responsibilities they collectively shoulder under lean production. It is, in their words, "the dynamic work team that emerges as the heart of the lean factory." Lean production "transfers the maximum number of tasks and responsibilities to those workers actually adding value to the car on the line," permitting these empowered workers to continuously improve the work process and even stop the assembly line whenever serious defects demand their attention.[13]

This apparently stands Frederick Taylor on his head. As the preeminent business consultant of the early twentieth century, Taylor argued that most people strived to avoid work, and the more empowered the workers, the less diligently they applied themselves. Craft methods that relied on workers who owned their own tools and set their own work pace were therefore deemed obsolete and unprofitable—and for that reason had already been eliminated in older branches of capitalist industry, such as weaving and shoe making. But craft methods still prevailed at the turn of the century in many sectors of metalworking, where skilled workers cast, machined, and assembled the components for new and complex metal machines. Low-volume production of specialized equipment (pumps, engines, machine tools) and of expensive consumer goods with continual design changes (the early automobile) initially favored the use of skilled workers who could flexibly apply their craft knowledge to new product designs. Small-scale workshops that specialized in these machine-building crafts also couldn't afford expensive machinery to replace craft labor, and there was less incentive to do so as long as volumes remained low and product design was experimental. But a larger market beckoned, and Frederick Taylor advocated a new kind of "Scientific Management" that would standardize work procedures, reduce unit costs, and disempower craft labor. His chief antagonists were skilled foundry men, blacksmiths, machinists, boilermakers, and fitters, many of them organized in craft unions to defend their collective control of the workshop against encroachment by managers and unskilled workers.[14]

A key aim, therefore, of Tayloristic management as it strived to increase production and standardize procedures was to eliminate the craft norms that empowered skilled workers. "All possible brain work should be removed from the shop," said Taylor in 1903, "and centered in the planning or laying out department," where engineers would simplify and subdivide the work into unskilled tasks. Once management had stabilized the product design and blueprinted the work process, the company could replace skilled craftsmen with workers "of smaller caliber and attainments," as Taylor put it, and issue them detailed, standardized work instructions from which there could be no deviation. Thus, as Harry Braverman observed in his analysis of Taylorized work, management separated conception from execution and used "this monopoly over knowledge to control each step of the labor process and its mode of execution." These principles are sometimes dismissed today as authoritarian and "traditional," but in the opening decades of the twentieth century they conveyed management's claim to a thoroughly modern perspective in which the customary and habitual practice of craft workers gave way to "objective" analysis. This was *Scientific* Management, no less, and it hardly mattered to advocates of the new approach that it rested on the *unscientific* claim that a fair day's work always equaled the maximum physiological capacity of the worker.[15]

Fordism and Mass Production

Management knew best. "The average worker wants a job in which he does not have to think," said Henry Ford, who applied Taylor's principles to the mechanized assembly line and coordinated the production process in one continuous flow, from blast furnace to final assembly. Mechanization and standardization were the bywords of Ford's system, and as the Model T captured more than half of North American auto sales in the early 1920s, "Fordism" became the standard of mass production, emulated by industrial corporations around the world. No other country, however, could match America's extreme application of Ford's principles. No other country, for that matter, had the resources or motivation to do so, for it was only in the United States that all the ingredients of mass production lay close at hand. Compared to Europe's smaller markets dominated by elite tastes, the U.S. was a huge "democratic" market growing by mass immigration and continental expansion, and therefore promising and requiring economies of scale that would keep specialized machines and narrowly trained workers fully utilized. Compared to Europe's slower development, America's pell-mell growth in the late nineteenth and early twentieth centuries generated a surplus of job-hungry immigrants and rural migrants willing to work long hours (at least until returning home or moving to the next job) that would maximize wages for family support or repatriation. At the same time, America's perennial shortage of skilled workers (compared to Europe) made alternative craft methods even costlier compared to mechanized mass production. And to protect the new system there was a dominant ideology of private enterprise that frequently made government the handmaiden of corporate expansion and union busting.[16]

With success, the new system demonstrated its malleability, both as it varied from one national economy to the next, shaped in each case by unique social and political pressures, and as it varied over time. At least four transformations shaped this Fordist regime as it became predominant. First was the growth of advertising and the promotion of a conformist, consumer-focused culture to insure a mass market for mass production. Second was the growth of state intervention as governments sought to stabilize the system with social programs and public spending that "primed the pump'' of mass consumption and secured some degree of popular support during economic downturns.

Third was the growth of a new kind of union movement. Fordism, as it destroyed many of the remaining bastions of craft production in metalworking, destroyed the basis of craft unionism as well, but in doing so, helped prepare the ground for a more encompassing form of industrial unionism. Instead of a workforce characterized by the extremes of skilled craft labor on the one hand and unskilled pick-and-shovel labor on the other, the mechanization and standardization of work created a relatively more homogeneous mass of machine-tenders, assemblers, and semi-skilled operatives. For a brief time in the closing years of World War I and the social turmoil that followed, left-wing movements in Europe and North America based themselves in this new industrial working class, raising demands for ''workers control of production'' and the overthrow of capitalist management. Thereafter, reformist trends predominated. In the United States, this movement emerged in the 1930s in the form of all-grades unions organized by industry (auto, rubber, steel) rather than by company (as with Japan's enterprise unions) or by craft amalgamation (as with Britain's engineering and general workers unions) or by economy-wide sectors (as with Germany's metalworkers union, incorporating auto, steel, machine building, and other industries in a single organization).[17]

This kind of industrial unionism, marked in the auto industry by the rise of the UAW after the 1937 sitdown strikes, aimed to regulate rather than overthrow the new regime of mass production. Previously, foremen had exercised unilateral control, favoring friends with easier jobs while punishing the rest with grunt work or pink slips when layoffs occurred; at its worst in the Depression years, the system tolerated the foreman who sold jobs and coerced favors from desperate workers. Now, the UAW forced management to standardize personnel policies and restrain the foreman's favoritism. Taylor's minute division of labor was codified in a negotiated system of job classifications, each defined by a detailed specification of tasks, with wage rates pegged to particular jobs rather than (as in Japan) the individuals holding them or (as in Britain's auto plants) the piecework group. Union workers accrued additional job rights as they ''invested'' their labor in the company: transfers, promotions, shift preferences, layoffs, and recalls would be determined, at least in part, by the objective standard of seniority. As it evolved over the next several decades in a context of global war and cold war, this ''job control'' unionism left management in command of strategic decisions and day-to-day operations, as codified in the contract's ''management rights'' clause; challenges to management practice were channeled through an increasingly legalistic grievance and arbitration procedure. Occasional strikes ratcheted wages and benefits upwards, and pattern bargaining made these wage rules the universal standard in Big Three plants.[18]

Finally, as the U.S. became globally predominant in the post-World War II economy, Fordism grew increasingly *un*lean and top heavy. Apparently guaranteed markets combined with low energy prices persuaded Big Three managers that they could afford to dismantle their concentrated production centers in Dearborn, Detroit, and Flint where "just-in-time" delivery was first developed, and decentralize to suburbs, rural areas, and far-flung locations where markets were growing and unions were weak. Corporate bureaucracies grew apace, with an ever-expanding corps of marketing specialists, personnel managers, and financial "bean counters" crowding out the engineers and former mechanics who once led the industry. Buffered, high-volume, and relatively rigid production systems became characteristic and apparently permanent features of the American economy in the 1950s and 1960s, and it was in this context that Braverman discerned a fundamental continuity of Tayloristic management, seeking always the same monopoly of knowledge and control evident in early Fordism, and deskilling even the new forms of service and clerical work.

Post-Fordism?

With hindsight, it is evident how this temporary predominance of U.S. capitalism masked the growing inefficiencies of mature, bureaucratic Fordism. It took the severe recessions of 1974 and 1979 to underline the arrival of a new set of circumstances, marked by rising energy prices and the reappearance of European and Asian competitors. Both these downturns were far deeper than any previous recession of the post–World War II era, and, more telling, both occurred in a context of fundamental shifts in technology and world trade. In short order, new product innovations, new technologies, and new competitors fragmented mature markets and undermined the established oligopolies that once regulated American business. Corporate managers accustomed to easy success lost low-end sales to foreign and domestic competitors who expanded from these beachheads into the heart of once secure markets. Some long-established companies disappeared altogether as the contracting economies of the early 1980s winnowed the weak and infirm; other companies and whole manufacturing sectors pulled up stakes and moved to low-wage economies, leaving behind shuttered workplaces and foreclosed futures. The labor movement also spiraled downward as old factories closed and nonunion competitors grabbed market share. In the auto industry, Japanese firms opened eleven assembly "transplants" in North America between 1979 and 1989—seven of them nonunion—while the Big Three closed dozens of factories and cut its net roster of assembly plants by nine, from sixty-three to fifty-four. By 1990, 39 percent of total auto industry employment was nonunion; outside the Big Three, as independent suppliers closed older facilities and repelled UAW organizing drives at newer plants, the nonunion sector grew from 41 to 76 percent of employment.[19]

In the midst of this downward spiral, Michael Piore and Charles Sabel postulated that the world economy had arrived at a second industrial divide, no less significant than the Fordist revolution seventy years previous. Unlike Braverman and other Marxists who argued that Taylorism and deskilling were an inevitable feature of capitalist management, Piore and Sabel emphasized the political and contingent forces that promoted mass production and suppressed viable craft alternatives in the late nineteenth and early twentieth centuries. From their perspective, the economic crises of the 1970s and 1980s not only made the presumed superiority of mass production less compelling, it also revealed a potential for new forms of work organization which they called "flexible specialization." Mass production no longer fit the changed circumstances of the world economy, they argued, given the fragmentation of mass markets into niches, the accelerating turnover of consumer taste, the consequent need to continually develop new products, and the arrival of programmable technologies that could be flexibly deployed for batch production at substantially lower break-even points. Where mass production emphasized economies of scale and functional specialization, Piore and Sabel saw flexible specialization promising economies of scope, functional flexibility, and multi-skilling for workers who could reengineer their own jobs. By their account, these possibilities marked the potential end of Fordism.[20]

Writing a decade after Piore and Sabel, Martin Kenney and Richard Florida went a step further in their 1993 book, *Beyond Mass Production*, claiming that this post-Fordist potential had already been realized in the Japanese model of factory management. Unlike the MIT study, Kenney and Florida included a critical note in their assessment of how this new system has been transferred to North America, calling attention to the intense workplace, long hours, and higher injury rates in some of the Japanese transplants. In their estimate, however, most of these "transitional" problems stemmed from sources outside the system, particularly in the failure of American managers to properly implement the Japanese model. Kenney and Florida acknowledged that this model relied on a unique system of peer pressure and intense socialization to company norms, but they concluded that "hegemonic" management control is more than compensated by the system's "unleashing of workers' creative capabilities." For Kenney and Florida, "innovation-mediated production," in which the factory becomes a "laboratory" and workers in "self-managing" teams "design their own jobs," is superior to and distinct from the Fordist regime of top-down regimented work. Yet, when describing the positive side of "innovation-mediated production" they rely almost exclusively on interviews with managers from nonunion transplants, principally Toyota (Kentucky), Honda, Subaru-Isuzu, Nissan, and Nippondenso. Naturally, these executives are eager to portray the "self-initiative and voluntaristic behavior" of their quality-conscious workers—to do otherwise would contradict the media image they promote in ads featuring enthusiastic worker "associates." Significantly, Kenny and Florida cite no matching chorus of workers to verify these management claims about an empowered workforce. Given this overwhelming reliance on self-interested accounts of the "post-Fordist" workplace, Kenney and Florida—like many other promoters of the Japanese model—seem to be describing an *ideal type* rather than an actual production system.[21]

Other observers detect a Fordist foundation to the "epoch-making new model" that Kenney and Florida claim to have discovered. From this alternative perspective, lean production, rather than marking the end of Fordism, extends it by modifying certain features and retaining essential elements of the Fordist regime: jobs are still subdivided into narrowly defined tasks (though workers sometimes rotate through a few tasks within their immediate area); work is still regimented by the assembly line and by strict adherence to standardized procedures (though workers are expected to suggest refinements and solve minor problems); mass production at high volumes still characterizes the system's output (though at somewhat lower levels and shorter runs per model than the peak years of the past); and management retains fundamental control of the overall production process. In contrast to Kenney and Florida, some MIT researchers take note of the Japanese model's continuities with Taylorism. "Many of Ford's principles in their purest forms are still valid and form the very basis of what we now know as the Toyota Production System," observes John Krafcik, the IMVP's lead analyst. Lean production, in his words, is "original Fordism with a Japanese flavor."[22]

Taking the Cure

Like an anxious patient confronting a long-term illness, harried management seeks a remedy to restore profitability. One miracle cure follows another, each promising more than it can deliver. The macro elixirs of supply-side economics and free trade are supplemented at the micro level by a proliferation of enterprise-based concoctions, most of them claiming inspiration from the patented Japanese formula. "Benchmarking," "reengineering," "synchronous manufacturing," "results driven quality," "total quality leadership," and "high performance systems" are among the popular variants. Consultants and university business schools promote favored remedies with a proprietary zeal that exaggerates their curative power and understates their generic ingredients. MIT's book promotes lean production without mention of Total Quality Management; the University of Southern California's Center for Effective Organizations returns the favor by reporting on TQM without a single reference to lean production; and Lehigh University's Iacocca Institute advocates "Agile Manufacturing" as the next "paradigm shift," superseding both lean production and TQM. "It's a great time to be in the guru business," as business author Richard Pascale told a 1993 conference of the American Management Association. "You folks are great consumers."[23]

Even when interest in these new approaches has all the earmarks of a management fad, the core ideas can still represent a genuine break with past practice. Before "Scientific Management" was christened as such by Louis Brandeis in 1911, it too was a movement fragmented by the contending claims of rival consultants. Frederick Halsey's Premium plan, Henry Gantt's Task and Bonus method, Harrington Emmerson's Efficiency System, and Frank Gilbreth's Micromotion Study all competed with Frederick Taylor's system of Functional Foremen. Less prominent men peddled their own versions of the new approach, which, for all the variation, promoted the same basic idea that control of the shop should move upward into the expanding ranks of "scientific" managers and engineers. Even the handful of reformers who called for a "humanized" Taylorism still put their faith in the new management elite—specifically, those few managers who sought to win the consent and participation of workers rather than their forcible submission. Then as now, corporate leaders were "great consumers," particularly for a top-down management system that legitimated their growing power. "Scientific management as a movement is cursed with fakirs," observed the U.S. Commission on Industrial Relations in 1912. "The great rewards which a few leaders in the movement have secured for their services have brought into the field a crowd of industrial 'patent medicine men.' " Employers, the commissioners concluded, "have thus far proved credulous."[24]

Credulity, however, is not long sustained in the absence of performance. Scientific Management, particularly in the mechanized and vertically integrated form it took as Fordism, became the dominant model of work organization because it demonstrated the potentials of a new social organization of capitalist production. There was no doubting the spectacular productivity performance of Fordist methods, though it took the emergence of a new labor movement and years of adversarial bargaining to realize, at least in part, the claim that mass production created mutually beneficial outcomes for workers and managers.

Today's proponents of lean-flexible production promise something more—performance that not only surpasses mass production, but *requires* "win-win" outcomes for all concerned. There can be no other result according to the MIT study. "Lean production is unlikely to prove more oppressive than mass production," as Womack, Jones, and Roos describe it, because "simply put, lean production is *fragile.*" This fragility stems in part from the lack of "just-in-case" buffers, of both parts and support workers, that protect mass production from disruption. But an additional source of fragility, according to MIT, is the extraordinary commitment the system requires from its workers. In a truly lean-flexible plant, as the MIT researchers put it, "it is essential that every worker try very hard." Asked to perform the same direct-labor tasks that characterize mass production, the worker in a lean plant must also continuously improve the process, rotate through jobs, and do such indirect tasks as inspection, repair, and minor maintenance. Workers will only take on such additional responsibilities if management meets its reciprocal obligation to provide job security and decent working conditions. If management fails in this regard, say the MIT researchers, workers will simply go through the motions, and "lean production will revert to mass production."[25]

It is this claim that lies at the heart of any debate concerning the impact of lean production on workers. If, as the advocates of these new systems argue, there is a self-correcting "hidden hand" that obligates management to empower rather than exploit workers—on pain of losing the performance edge that lean-flexible production promises—then unions are superfluous. But what if there is no such inherent equilibrium that brings the interests of workers and managers into automatic alignment? Fear of unemployment or the peer pressure of company-dominated teams might actually push people beyond the effort norms that individual workers would otherwise choose. To what degree can these kinds of pressures make lean production systems sufficiently robust that management can drive people to the limits of their endurance, favoring a privileged core of workers and drawing replacements for the system's burned-out victims from the ranks of the unemployed?

It is a question which even Japanese workers now ask. "It would not be exaggerating to claim that the level of workers' exhaustion . . . [has] almost reached a critical point," says the Confederation of Japanese Automobile Workers' Unions, reporting on their 1992 survey of six thousand members. "We must listen to the workers' voice very carefully: 'We feel all petered out. How much harder must we work?' " For a union confederation previously known as a reliable supporter of Japanese auto management, the JAW draws a surprisingly grim conclusion. "Under the pretext of sharing a common destiny, which is pleasing to the ear, companies do seem to have been too demanding of their workers."[26]

While these concerns trouble many trade unionists in North America and Europe, management is bedeviled by an altogether different question. For corporate leadership, it comes down to the proverbial bottom line: since the implementation of a lean-flexible production system requires a considerable up-front investment in training, time, and start-up costs, what are the prospects that this system will really pay off for the company?

Judging by MIT's assembly plant study, investment in lean production pays huge dividends in improved productivity and quality, representing an eight-hour advantage in labor-hours per car and a 50 percent reduction in defects compared to the Big Three's traditional mass production methods. It is not always clear, however, what this gap between average Japanese versus average Big Three performance represents. A look at specific cases reveals a sizable range among the Big Three's practitioners of mass production, with GM plants well below average and Ford plants well above—in fact, Ford's productivity and quality by the late 1980s compared favorably with Japan's lean production benchmark. How can this be so? In answering this question, Womack, Jones, and Roos abandon their usual reliance on massive quantification and turn instead to casual observation. Their early studies of Ford "found that the basic union-management contract had not been changed. . . . Workers continued to have narrow job assignments and no formal team structure was in place. Yet as we walked through plant after plant we observed that teamwork was alive and well. Workers were ignoring the technical details of the contract on a massive scale in order to cooperate and get the job done." For Womack and his fellow authors, this is a sufficient indicator that Ford was *already* a lean producer by the late 1980s—hence, its superior performance.[27]

While these anecdotal claims misrepresent the nature of shop-floor change at Ford and probably exaggerate the impact of worker participation on productivity, it is true that the Employee Involvement (EI) circles of the early 1980s had somewhat altered the tenor of work relations at Ford. This was not because EI changed the formal delegation of authority in the factory. As defined by the principles negotiated between the company and the union, EI circles met off-line during paid work time to discuss shop-related matters and suggest improvements that impacted morale or efficiency (and sometimes both); participation by hourly workers was voluntary, and EI circles had no authority to implement their suggestions. In some plants only a handful of workers volunteered, while in others as much as two-thirds of the workforce participated in projects to improve housekeeping, ergonomics, work environment, and quality. Participation tended to decline over time as the novelty wore off, and as the initial round of successful projects were followed by proposals that failed to win management approval or follow-through. By the late 1980s, EI circles had faded in many plants for a lack of volunteers, giving way to plant-wide committees and special "task force" projects that involved fewer people, but still gave formal support to the consultative principles and problem-solving features of worker participation.[28]

Even so, this falls well short of the *systematic* workplace transformation prescribed by advocates of lean production. Ford's labor force was *numerically* "leaner" after the massive layoffs and forced downsizing of 1979–1982, but in the late 1980s the company's assembly plants had few of the organizational attributes deemed to be "the heart" of lean production in the factory: there were no all-inclusive teams that required workers to assume responsibility for on-line operations; there was no system of task rotation; and there was no wholesale abandonment of job classifications. In all these regards, Ford's assembly operations differed little from GM or Chrysler before 1990—yet Ford's plants were more productive. This superior performance can be more plausibly explained by two factors which MIT acknowledges but relegates to secondary importance. First, the company's near bankruptcy in the early 1980s prevented Ford from matching GM's ill-considered spending on unreliable technology and unnecessary plant capacity; second, Ford marketed automobiles and trucks that sold well, that were relatively easy to build, and that kept plant capacities *fully utilized*. This final factor, operating at 100 percent capacity, is especially important, for even if the "indirect" labor of supervision, maintenance, housekeeping, inspection, and repair is substantially cut back, the irreducible minimum of such overhead is less of a burden on productivity when it is spread over the plant's maximum output. Research by Dan Luria of Michigan's Industrial Technology Institute suggests the importance of this axiom. In his study of twenty North American assembly plants in the late 1980s, including both Big Three and transplant operations, the level of capacity utilization accounted for 41 percent of the productivity variance between the plants, nearly double the 23 percent of variance associated with "modern" versus "traditional" forms of work organization.[29]

If capacity utilization is so important, then it follows that the "upstream" elements of the production process, particularly investment decisions and pre-production planning, deserve priority attention. Substantial improvement in plant performance can apparently be achieved with a hybrid strategy that emphasizes simultaneous design-production engineering, incremental automation, reinvestment to upgrade existing capacity, and the necessary adjustments to work organization required by these new technologies and engineering practices. It should be emphasized, however, that at Ford this approach did not include the full menu of shop-floor change prescribed by some advocates of lean production.

Thus "unbundled," lean production can be taken as a variable mixture of discrete elements, selectively recombined on a case-by-case basis. It is not clear, however, which elements of the "lean factory" would be the more important if unbundled; nor is it always clear what exactly constitutes each of the specific elements. Definitions of "leanness" vary over time and from one observer to the next, each emphasizing a different mixture of organizational measures: from the number of training hours and job classifications, to the amount of floor space devoted to repairs, to the number of workers trained in Statistical Process Control. Most advocates of lean-flexible production do at least agree on the primary role of work teams, but there is little elaboration or agreement on the details of team organization. Teams are frequently called "self-directed," yet the specific responsibilities and roles of team members are often left to the imagination. Do workers elect their team leaders, chair their team meetings, control their budgets, and define their own schedules for relief, training, job rotation, vacation, personal leave, and other matters? Or does management "empower" supervisors to make these decisions (or fuzzier still, do supervisors "facilitate" the "consensus process") and thereby control team dynamics? In most models of lean production, the unstated—and unproven—assumption is that these "details" can vary without significantly altering team dynamics or performance.[30]

Even if we set these "details" aside, the larger question remains: whether companies blessed with the good sense (or good fortune) to have marketable products and fully utilized factories can still win an additional edge with shop-floor innovations—lean or otherwise—that tap worker participation. The available evidence suggests that they often can. David Levine and Laura D'Andrea Tyson of the University of California at Berkeley reviewed twenty-nine studies that focused on the productivity outcomes of worker participation and found that fourteen indicated a positive impact, while two indicated negative effects and the remainder were inconclusive; however, the positive results were more decisive for on-line work teams with decision-making powers than they were for EI circles with a limited consultative role and no authority to make decisions. Their study did not address the issue of whether these positive effects were increased or diminished by the presence of a union, but two recent studies have taken up this crucial question. Maryellen Kelley and Bennett Harrison of Carnegie Mellon University, analyzing survey returns from 1,015 plant managers, found that while employee participation had a significantly more positive impact on productivity in unionized settings, the presence of the union *alone* corresponded to even higher productivity in multi-plant companies, superior to nonunion and unionized workplaces *with* employee involvement. Traditional union governance, they hypothesize, offers a form of "worker participation" that EI circles and labor-management committees simply duplicate in bureaucratized form. William Cooke of Wayne State University, in a study of 841 manufacturing firms in Michigan, also found that union firms were more productive than comparable workplaces where there was no union, and that worker participation had a far more positive impact in unionized settings. Among the several reasons he offers for the superior performance of unionized workplaces, Cooke draws attention to both the feedback role of unions in articulating workers' collective voice, and their protective role in safeguarding worker input against reprisal by authority-conscious managers.[31]

Ironically, however, there is evidence that while union environments enhance the productivity impacts of worker participation, it is generally not the union that initiates the move toward these new forms of work organization; in a survey of unionized firms, Cooke found that management had initiated the program in 85 percent of the locations surveyed. Moreover, team systems are not particularly widespread, even in the companies that have adopted them. Edward Lawler, Susan Mohrman, and Gerald Ledford of the University of Southern California, reporting on a 1990 survey of personnel managers and senior executives from over three hundred major corporations (union and nonunion), found that nearly half used self-managing work teams, but only one in ten reported that these teams covered more than 20 percent of their workforce. Even so, among those indicating any use of self-managing work teams, 60 percent said that this form of worker empowerment had a significantly favorable impact on plant performance.[32]

A growing number of companies will likely "take the cure" and adopt some variant of the lean production model—Lawler, Mohrman, and Ledford report that 60 percent of the companies they surveyed planned to increase the use of so-called "self-managing" work teams in the near future. The federal government is also pushing worker empowerment as the centerpiece of its program to "reinvent" the public sector, with the Defense Department playing an especially prominent role. The Pentagon has adopted the current innovations in management strategy with a crusading zeal, embracing, in succession, TQM, lean production, and agile manufacturing. This all-encompassing endorsement not only means that the military services, particularly the navy and air force, are planning to reorganize their support operations around "self-managing" work teams, but that aerospace companies and other private sector suppliers are encouraged to do the same. The Pentagon will give lean-agile production an additional boost with lavish research funding for university programs that support these new management strategies—five million dollars in defense subsidies, for example, will go to Lehigh University's Iacocca Institute, matched by another five million to MIT's "Lean Aircraft Initiative."[33]

Auto Motives

When Frederick Taylor's contemporaries cited best-case examples of mass production, they pointed to the Ford Motor Company, where Scientific Management and extreme mechanization came together as Fordism. Today, when defense contractors search the contemporary landscape for examples of lean-flexible production, they cite NUMMI, the GM-Toyota joint venture in Fremont, California, or Saturn, the new GM division located in Spring Hill, Tennessee. At the 1992 national quality seminar for aerospace and defense contractors, executives from these auto plants were featured speakers on an agenda that promised to impart "the essential tools of lean manufacturing."[34]

The auto industry is also the focus of this book. In manifold ways, automaking serves as a bellwether and laboratory for lean-flexible systems that are now finding applications in a wide range of manufacturing and service industries. Many of these new approaches to work organization found their first application in the auto industry, and the accumulation of case histories therefore offers the best opportunity for investigating the impact of lean production on workers. The presence of both a well-organized union sector and a growing nonunion transplant sector provides the opportunity to compare radically different environments and contrasting systems in the North American market, and the international reach of automaking provides a comparative context unmatched by any other industrial setting.

In Part 1, the overall implications of lean production are debated from three different perspectives. In the lead-off essay, Mike Parker and Jane Slaughter define lean production as a system of "management by stress" that purposefully pushes operations to the breaking point. By constantly "stressing" the system, management can identify weak points, redeploy resources, and eliminate excess buffers of workers, tools, and time. Parker and Slaughter argue that management control over *individual* workers is substantially increased when a production system is made so fragile that it immediately exposes and magnifies any deviation from the standardized process, leaving workers with less authority and more accountability. In their estimation, a limited degree of worker participation in designing the job merely refines Frederick Taylor's approach by pressuring workers to continually transfer their knowledge to management. As Parker and Slaughter see it, an independent union can alter this dynamic only by fighting for the very buffers that lean production seeks to remove. Ironically, in the absence of such buffers, the system's vulnerability to disruption may enhance the *collective* power of workers who use concerted action to advance their bargaining agenda.

John Paul MacDuffie also argues that lean production has much in common with the technical organization of mass production, but he sees a considerably greater role for worker empowerment in the system. In a lean-flexible factory, workers rotate through a variety of work stations and develop a broader contextual understanding of the overall production process. In addition to this enhanced cognitive role, lean production also develops social networks among team members which Taylorism ignored or suppressed. Yet as MacDuffie argues, this emphasis on teamwork is focused on promoting a personal identification with the enterprise and the overall production process, rather than the sectional interests of a particular team. To win over workers, management in a lean production environment therefore becomes more of a competitor with the union, seeking the loyalty and commitment of workers in ways that challenge the union's traditional claims of class or occupational solidarity. Indeed, unions which make industry-wide pattern bargaining a priority will inevitably collide with the local imperatives of such an enterprise-focused system. On the other hand, MacDuffie sees unions playing a positive role if they refocus their mission on the strategic-level decisions that guide each enterprise, and on correcting the kinds of mismanagement—speedup, favoritism, and domineering managers—that can poison the fragile structures of commitment and trust.

Adrienne Eaton's survey of managers and union representatives in a large sample of midwestern manufacturing firms has implications for both of the preceding essays. While all of the factories in her survey used some form of employee involvement, up to and including shop-floor teams, in most cases workers and their unions played little role in designing and implementing these new approaches. More often, management defined the limits of worker empowerment. This might indicate that these systems will operate along the lines suggested by Parker and Slaughter, but it might also mean that management will promote the kind of cognitive and social roles that, in MacDuffie's view, serve the long-term interests of both workers and managers. It could be argued that the absence of union participation is a failing that compromises a true test of lean-flexible production, but Eaton cautions against the tautological potential of such an argument—the claim that "lean-flexible production depends on worker empowerment, therefore any contradictory examples cannot be truly lean." Unlike Parker and Slaughter, Eaton concludes that lean-flexible production systems are not inherently exploitative. But unlike MacDuffie, she does not believe that unions should define their mission solely in terms of enterprise goals. Labor's power, she concludes, is never inherent in a production system; power has to be taken, and independent unions therefore "must have sources of power separate from those provided in the employer's social system."

In Part 2, John Price and Hideo Totsuka give ample evidence that Japanese history, rather than some immutable and ahistoric "culture," has defined, and continues to redefine, the social organization of lean production in its home economy. Price takes up the question of whether lean production represents a post-Fordist departure from the previous regime of mass production by examining the system's formative years in Japan, from 1946 to roughly 1970. He finds a paradox: lean production does represent a breach in the Fordist division of labor between conception and execution, but it does not otherwise depart from the "American model" of routinized jobs, short job cycles, and task standardization. Based on his review of the parallel histories of Suzuki and Toyota, Price rejects the claim of Florida and Kenny that Japan's production system represents an accommodation of the working-class demands of the immediate postwar period; instead, Price finds an "accord" dominated by management, who defeated the militant unions of 1946–1950 and imposed a system that dispensed with contract bargaining, downgraded union-management councils to consultative bodies, pegged pay to the supervisor's evaluation of performance, and replaced or co-opted independent unions.

Totsuka emphasizes that the resulting system was not without variation in its particulars, as he found in his study of the enterprise unions at Japan's two biggest auto companies. Totsuka calls these firms "A" and "B" in his presentation of the results, which strongly suggest that he is describing Nissan and Toyota, respectively. At Toyota, the extensive interviewing which Totsuka and his colleagues conducted in 1984 and 1985 revealed the same enterprise union that Price describes in his historical study: dominated by foremen who conceded unilateral control to their management superiors and only played a consultative role on shop-floor matters. Toyota's social organization of production also included the paternalistic controls of the company town and company housing, as well as quality circles dominated by foremen; moreover, a sizable portion of workers' pay was pegged to the same foreman's assessment of individual and group performance. At Nissan, however, Totsuka and his colleagues found something different. Here, the union was also dominated by foremen, but for many years the leadership of the Nissan union had organized these front-line supervisors to a dual allegiance, encompassing both the company and the union. With a far larger leadership cadre than Toyota's union, the Nissan union engaged in plant-level bargaining, focusing primarily on changes in manning levels, overtime, production schedules, and transfers. Totsuka concludes that the Japanese model is not a monolithic social system, but accommodates a range of historically determined labor-relations systems. Even though Nissan management ousted the union's leadership in 1985–1986 and eliminated the union's veto power and shop-floor bargaining, Totsuka does not see an inevitable convergence towards the Toyota model. That model, as he stresses, is the historical outcome of unique circumstances—including the dominance of greenfield plants in a company town and a growing industry—that are not available to Nissan or, for that matter, Toyota, given the recent troubles of the Japanese economy.

In Part 3, the measurable outcomes of lean production are debated from three angles. Karel Williams and his colleagues take the radical step of rejecting the term altogether, arguing that MIT's methods for measuring assembly-plant productivity cannot precisely or plausibly correct for the many differences between individual plants and vehicles. Instead of the IMVP's plant-by-plant comparisons, Williams et al. propose a sectoral analysis of companies and national auto industries that measures value added and total hours. Based on these measures, the authors find that while Toyota and Japan do perform at higher levels of productivity by the late 1970s, the gap is overstated by MIT, and the ''average'' Japanese auto companies (i.e., all besides Toyota) operate at roughly the same levels as Ford and Chrysler. All these average companies lag behind Toyota for structural reasons (trade patterns, market fluctuations, debt) that are beyond the control of company management and cannot be redressed by lean production.

Candace Howes focuses on a specific range of structural advantages enjoyed by Japanese transplants in North America, and contends that Japan's automakers have not exported, and probably will not export, the core of their production system to the United States. Rather, branch-plant operations to assemble the car and manufacture commodity parts are transferred to North America to insure access to the market and to secure cheap labor—cheap because the assembly plants employ younger workers with lower medical and pension costs than the Big Three's older workers, and cheap because the parts plants employ nonunion workers at low wages. Japanese auto companies, according to Howes, cannot transfer the design-intensive core of their production system—engines, drive trains, suspensions, and a sizable number of finished cars—without jeopardizing the system of rewards that sustains worker and supplier loyalty in Japan.

Transplant investment, therefore, does not represent the positive development which many see in the transfer of the lean production system, since it negatively impacts domestic makers of machine tools and other engineering firms that depend on a fully integrated auto industry in the United States. Like Williams et al., Howes' analysis indicates that North American automakers cannot solve their problems by adopting lean production, but must address structural issues with the appropriate trade and industrial policies.

John Paul MacDuffie and Frits K. Pil respond to these critics by describing the ongoing adjustments to MIT's international comparison of assembly plant performance. Acknowledging the advantage of broader productivity measures that include capital and energy as well as labor, they point out the difficulties of securing comparable data across national boundaries. Moreover, recent studies comparing Japanese and American automakers indicate that capital productivity varies much less than labor productivity; explaining the latter is therefore the more compelling research question. In order to make productivity comparisons that are consistent across a variety of plants, the International Assembly Plant Study (IAPS), now in its second round, is refining a set of "Standard Activities" that exclude stamping, seat assembly, wire harnesses, and other operations that are not always found in assembly plants. Further adjustments are made to eliminate differences in capacity utilization, absenteeism, and product characteristics—the latter including the number of options and the "manufacturability" of the design. Responding to the criticism of Williams et al. that these adjustments are *inevitably* too numerous and crude to permit useful comparison, MacDuffie and Pil argue that such an a priori conclusion is self-defeating. Where certain adjustments are less precise— specifically, "manufacturability" is only partly captured by comparing the number of welds or the age of the design—the task is to find more sophisticated proxies: for example, the IAPS is now considering a measure that identifies how early the assembly plant's blue- and white-collar personnel interact with product designers, on the assumption that early interaction correlates with enhanced design-for-manufacture. Any basis for comparing production systems requires adjustment, MacDuffie and Pil remind their critics, including the national and sectoral figures used by Williams and his colleagues. The difference is that the IAPS figures are useful indicators for plant managers and workers considering the plant-level factors that improve performance.

In Part 4, six case studies focus on the shop-floor dynamics of lean production in a cross-section of North American plants. Laurie Graham's work as a participant-observer at Subaru-Isuzu's Indiana plant provides a rare perspective on lean production in a nonunion setting; Graham found a contested terrain in which teams served both as mechanisms of management control and as havens of worker solidarity in opposition to the intensification of labor. Paul Adler's study of NUMMI, the GM-Toyota joint venture in Fremont, California, concludes that the production system at this UAW organized plant is a form of "democratic Taylorism"; the workplace is intense and the technical organization still exhibits the tightly scripted, repetitive tasks associated with "despotic" Taylorism, but workers are committed to continually improving the work process because of reciprocal management obligations and job security provisions contained in the collective bargaining agreement. James Rinehart, Chris Huxley, and David Robertson report a different outcome at the GM-Suzuki joint venture (CAMI) in Ingersoll, Ontario, where the Canadian Auto Workers (CAW) negotiated a unique opportunity to survey the plant population on four occasions over two years; workers gave a consistently positive appraisal of the social solidarity that developed in their work teams, but contrary assessments of work intensity and management's unilateral actions grew throughout the survey. These negative appraisals found expression in the 1992 strike over issues of team organization and team-leader selection. I found similar disputes in the survey research conducted by the UAW local at Mazda's Michigan assembly plant; distinguishing between "worker centered" and "supervisor centered" teams, I describe the negotiated change in the team-leader selection process, and the consequent modification of team dynamics.

The two remaining case studies in Part 4 shift the focus to Mexico. Harley Shaiken challenges the popular perception that low-wage Mexican production cannot match high-tech, lean production operations in the U.S. and Canada by examining Ford's state-of-the-art assembly plant in Hermosillo. Shaiken reviews the superior quality and productivity performance of this Mexican "transplant," and examines the unique features of a lean production system in a low-wage, low-skill economy. While acknowledging the unstable features of the Mexican environment, including the bitter strikes and mass firings at Hermosillo, Shaiken stresses that lean production in Mexico has so far been more robust than fragile, giving American management ample motivation to move south and exploit the prevailing low wages.

Susan Helper, however, draws a different conclusion from her analysis of Maquiladora plants producing auto parts for export. The U.S. transplants that locate inside Mexico's northern border are, as Shaiken observes, drawn by low wages and by the proven capacity of Mexican workers to produce high-quality parts. But Helper draws attention to the hidden costs of Mexican production, which place limits on its appeal to rational management. Long-distance transportation and communication both create obstacles to just-in-time delivery and simultaneous engineering that are difficult, but not impossible, to overcome. More troubling is the high turnover rate caused by low wages; since lean production's emphasis on "continuous improvement" depends on a sustained training program that deepens employee understanding of the work process, high turnover is counterproductive. As a result, the plants which Helper examined tended to channel their improvement efforts through managers and engineers, with little input from production workers. The result is a "robust" system, but with no sustained capacity to generate improvements by front-line workers; in this regard, high-wage operations in the U.S. and Canada can be competitive if they enlist genuine worker input.

In Part 5, Christian Berggren and Ulrich Jürgens present two European models for high-wage, participatory work organization. Berggren's focus is the Volvo plant at Uddevalla, Sweden, where management and labor took the radical step of eliminating the assembly line and reorganizing production around worker-centered teams that assembled finished cars from the ground up. When Volvo closed the plant in 1993, many observers concluded that this noble experiment had proven to be uneconomical, but Berggren draws attention to the plant's high learning curve and its superior flexibility and performance in building a variety of cars tailored to customer tastes. Uddevalla was closed, he argues, despite its superior performance because of factors beyond the plant's control—particularly, a precipitous collapse in sales after 1989, and management's failure to develop new products. Volvo had to close excess capacity, and internal union and company politics favored the larger production complex at Gothenberg; Uddevalla, in Berggren's estimate, still stands as a viable alternative to the "revived" Fordism of lean production.

Ulrich Jürgens contrasts the "German model" of production organization with both the Swedish and the Japanese alternatives. A key difference, as Jürgens indicates, is the unusually high skill base in German industry, which in practice means that nearly three-quarters of the production workforce has completed a trade apprenticeship. Matched with unusually high levels of automation, these skilled workers have built up-scale vehicles of high quality in relatively small batches and remained competitive on world markets. Lean production had little appeal until the early 1990s, when recession, declining sales, and growing Japanese competition forced a reexamination of Germany's high-cost production system. Yet even in this crisis atmosphere, the German model imposes a unique dynamic on the lean production debate: in contrast to the North American setting, where worker participation is imposed in nonunion settings or bargained company-by-company in unionized sectors, in Germany federal law mandates a system of "co-determination" that requires every auto company to negotiate these changes with elected work councils. While management may be able to evade or dilute co-determination by relocating production to east Germany and beyond, the system still imposes a more deliberate, negotiated pace in the core plants of the German auto industry.

Part 6 returns to North America and focuses on the training issues that accompany the lean production debate. James Jacobs analyzes the training system at MACI, a nonunion parts supplier and joint venture of Toyota Loom and Nippondenso located in Jackson, Michigan. Jacobs found that training was, in fact, central to the plant's lean production system, but the nature of that training differed in significant ways from the promised scenario of empowerment and multi-skilling. Much of the training effort was focused on skilled trades and engineers, while the training for production workers was limited to memorization of standardized, company-specific procedures for problem-solving. This training agenda was consistent with the operation of a branch plant in which the key production decisions were made in Japan, and worker input was restricted to narrowly focused suggestions for amending management's unilateral agenda.

Gary Saganski describes a very different training agenda at Rouge Steel, an automotive steel supplier in Dearborn, Michigan. Part of the difference lies in the targeted workforce, a group of one thousand skilled workers preparing for new forms of team organization. Another key difference was the presence of a union and a corresponding emphasis on a "worker-centered" approach to learning. In this case, rather than delivering a packaged training format with standardized "lab" and textbook exercises, the Rouge training project built upon the workers' already existing framework of knowledge and tailored a learning process that incorporated "real-life" plant issues. A unique feature of the program was the use of peer instructors who could shape the curriculum and encourage workers with varied aptitudes to proceed at their own pace.

Part 7 concludes the debate with two contrasting views of the public policy issues surrounding lean production and worker empowerment. William Green draws the more sobering conclusions from his review of the legal terrain in which labor operates. Legislation that eliminates the current distinction between mandatory and permissible subjects of bargaining might help labor negotiate for a wider role in the employer's strategic-level decisions, and card-check certification and other reforms that protect organizing efforts could also help the labor movement regain the initiative. But the Clinton administration is not likely to push for co-determination rights, and even Canada's stronger labor laws have not enabled the CAW to organize nonunion transplants. In the meantime, many federal judges and a sizable number of liberal reformers are persuaded that "empowered" workers may no longer require the protection of the National Labor Relations Act—many advocate repeal of the NLRA's prohibition of company-dominated labor organizations in nonunion settings, arguing that work teams are necessary to enhance productivity and competitiveness and shouldn't be hobbled by lingering uncertainty about federal labor law. Even if a weakened labor movement could fend off these "reform" proposals, says Green, it may not make much difference given the multinational reach of American corporations. Ultimately, the fate of the labor movement may therefore lie in the direction of international alliances with unions and workers in other countries.

Irving Bluestone is more hopeful that labor law reform can counter anti-union trends and enhance the prospects for a joint-action agenda between management and labor. Restoring a "level playing field" in the labor-relations arena requires substantial changes in the content and administration of the law, including a ban on permanent replacement of strikers, and, to improve the prospects for organizing in the face of determined (and often illegal) management opposition, such reforms as card-check certification, first-contract arbitration, stricter time limits, and tougher penalties for unfair labor practices. Bluestone stresses that even with these protections, unions have to meet the new challenge of organizing in circumstances where management offers the appearance, though rarely the substance, of worker empowerment in a "union-free" environment. Unions can succeed, says Bluestone, when they demonstrate that without a collective voice, workers are seen rather than heard when it comes to genuine participation in decision-making. True economic democracy also requires that public policy act as a catalyst, first by promoting genuine empowerment in the public sector, and then by protecting and extending the joint-action process in the private economy.

Competition and Solidarity

The contributors to this volume present a range of opinion concerning lean production and the potential for worker empowerment: from Parker and Slaughter, who argue that real empowerment is negated by lean production, to MacDuffie, who contends that empowerment is a necessary condition of lean production, to Eaton, who maintains that in any production system empowerment is something workers have to take for themselves.

Underlying these alternative perspectives is a related and fundamental question: to what degree should worker empowerment be defined, and perhaps limited, by the dictates of global competition, and to what degree should worker empowerment be an end-value in itself, a beachhead of worker solidarity, self-actualization, and economic democracy in the otherwise autocratic realm of corporate management?

Some argue that competition and solidarity are not incompatible, that strong unions and worker-centered teams are the best means for enhancing economic performance and competitive success. But on either side of this middle ground there is still an irreducible difference in the opposing perspectives that define ''competition'' and ''solidarity.'' The former dominates the perspective of capital, increasingly mobile and focused on global markets; the latter springs from the concerted activity of labor, locally-situated and focused on concerns of work and family. Competition defines labor as a factor of production, as a cost or an asset; solidarity defines labor as humanity, the collective activity of workers seeking a better life. Competition is maximized in a free-market environment unrestrained by public regulation and union work rules; solidarity is maximized in an environment where public policy protects collective action and promotes social justice.

Workers who press the claims of solidarity don't thereby reject the claims of competition. In an economic system where daily life is presented as the struggle of competing individuals and companies, most workers adopt a corresponding ''common sense'' that accepts pervasive competition. The competitive struggle is also the binding force that sometimes brings workers into an ''enterprise solidarity'' with management. ''Worker solidarity,'' in contrast, is expressed in workers' concerted efforts to distribute the rewards of that struggle more equitably, and to remove human exploitation from the competitive equation.

The essays in this collection tend to favor the claims of solidarity over the dictates of competition, though a practical concern for the latter is evident throughout. The predominant assumption is that without countervailing intervention by unions and public policy, the ''free market'' will favor outcomes that are deformed and precarious: deformed, to the degree that unrestrained market forces reward those companies that pay workers less and squeeze them for more, thereby undermining the values of equity and justice that constitute democratic life; and precarious to the degree that this downward race to the lowest common denominator in acceptable wages and working conditions has no finish line—economies that currently lure private investment with ''business first'' incentives will inevitably face new competitors that offer still lower standards.

Competition, in short, has two faces. Its positive profile is celebrated for the efficiencies it forces on any enterprise, and this dimension of global competition puts a growing premium on ''empowered'' workers who can solve problems and continuously improve the system. Evidence even suggests that unionized settings, by insuring a more genuinely empowered workforce, are more productive and therefore provide a competitive edge over coerced labor in nonunion workplaces. However, competition has another, less celebrated face. Profit, not mere efficiency, is the ultimate goal in our corporate economy, and competitive pressures combined with the lure of short-term profitability can make a disempowered workforce attractive to management: unionized settings may be more *productive*, but weak-union environments can still be more *profitable* if the savings from lower wages and intensified labor compensate for the higher costs of turnover and the inefficiencies of an intimidated workforce. Under these circumstances, unrestrained competition turns ''empowerment'' into its opposite: by cutting personnel to the bare minimum and forcing intensified labor on the surviving workforce; by defining every second of ''recovery time'' within the job cycle as ''idleness'' and ''waste'' that needs to be eliminated; and by socializing hard-pressed team members to ''self-manage'' their peers by putting pressure on medically restricted workers, absentees, and those who are just plain slower or weaker.

Public policy can discourage this kind of ''mean-lean'' production with a variety of prescriptions for genuine empowerment—from ''co-determination'' laws that require worker participation in decision-making, to laws that protect worker rights and restrain the aggressive union busting that has flourished in recent years. Inevitably, conservative and media opinion will describe any such intervention as a violation of our private enterprise system. In fact, the historical record is full of cases where unrestrained competition proved so dysfunctional that public intervention was necessary to protect minimum standards of compensation and work safety. Competition can inspire innovation, but it can also drive individual companies to protect their short-term profitability by postponing the risk and expense of developing *radically* new products or processes. America's Big Three automakers pursued such a short-term profit strategy in response to the Japanese challenge, shunning new technology and cutting corners to produce such disasters as the Ford Pinto and Chevrolet Vega—among the more infamous of the compact models that secured Detroit's reputation in the 1970s for shoddy engineering and poor quality. The disastrous consequences of this short-term profit strategy are still with us, measured in plant closings, ''downsized'' communities, and dislocated families.[35]

Public policy can counter the tendency to produce ''on the cheap'' by enforcing standards and providing seed capital for initiatives individual corporations would otherwise postpone. Such ''non-market'' interventions by government have spawned important innovations in modern industrial technology, from interchangeable manufacturing to computers to programmable machine tools. In the auto industry, public regulation has forced important technological changes where "the market" moved slowly or not at all: more fuel efficient engines, catalytic converters, and airbags among them. Public initiative is playing a similar role in nudging, or forcing, the industry to offer vehicles powered by alternative energy sources— electricity, natural gas, even hydrogen—that might slow the steady strangulation of our planet by gasoline-powered engines. Likewise, just as public policy already defines minimum standards for wages and workplace safety, so can it also define a higher standard of worker participation in decision-making.[36]

Worker solidarity, however, cannot be legislated. No law ever organized a union in the absence of worker support, and the most eloquent statement of public policy remains a dead letter if workers don't develop the capacity to mobilize on their own behalf. Even with good laws, workers will have to organize the solidarity and collective voice that pressures management to do the right thing, and many unions have found that such a mobilization requires a significant change in their traditional bargaining strategies and internal practices. In effect they are turning to a strategy of bottom-up organizing that is the mirror image of the worker empowerment prescribed for a high-performance workplace, except that while the latter builds a better product, the former builds a stronger solidarity.

Unions are discovering in a painful process of trial and error that it is no longer enough to simply service the members and represent them at the negotiating table as if they were passive clients and bargaining was a technical (if somewhat acrimonious) process of top-down administration. This "service model" unionism has delivered important benefits to members, but it can also be too top-heavy and too far removed from the technological and social changes now occurring in the workplace. Oftentimes, management goes directly to workers and tells them that their job security depends on their commitment to some variant of lean production, with participative structures that may circumvent or deny the union's role. In too many cases, companies have drawn the line by also demanding massive concessions in wages and work rules, and then bargaining to impasse and unilaterally imposing their terms. It is in response to these management initiatives that a growing number of unions have adopted an "organizing model" that widens their base of shop-floor participation, designating one union activist for every twenty or so members to act as a "coordinator" (or "mobilizer," or just plain old "steward") for their work group. With this shop-floor network, elected union leaders communicate with members through direct one-on-one contact, and members personally convey their needs and insights through the same face-to-face network. This two-way communication can tap worker initiative and generate membership activism.[37]

It remains to be seen whether such an organizing model of unionism can overcome the fatalism and mistrust which prevails in many union halls concerning the factory of the future. But there is little doubt that if unions are to win the kinds of participative structures that truly empower workers, it will only happen when the campaign for such a workplace is based on the solidarity of empowered union members.

Notes

1. "The gaijin shusa," *Forbes* (13 April 1991): 129; "Read All About it: It's the Machine that Ate Detroit," *Automotive News* (7 January 1991): 12.

2. United Automobile Workers, *Constitution of the International Union*, Preamble (June 1989), 4; United Automobile Workers, *Resolutions of the Constitutional Convention* (June 1989), 44–45; William Green, letter to author, 20 December 1993, reprinted in *UAW Solidarity*, March 1994, 5; GM chairman Robert Stempel quoted in *Detroit Free Press*, 24 February 1992.

3. On overtime bargaining in Germany, see Wolfgang Streeck, *Industrial Relations in West Germany: A Case Study of the Car Industry* (New York: St. Martin's Press, 1984), 106–136.

4. For a model of collective action that focuses on mobilization of resources, see Charles Tilly, *From Mobilization to Revolution* (New York: Random House, 1978).

5. See Rick Fantasia, *Cultures of Solidarity: Consciousness, Action, and Contemporary American Workers* (Berkeley: University of California, 1988).

6. Richard Wellins, William Byham, and Jeanne Wilson, *Empowered Teams: Creating Self-Directed Work Groups that Improve Quality, Productivity, and Participation* (San Francisco: Jossey-Bass, 1991), specifically recommend that management promote a process that encourages workers to take management's goals as their own. In their words, foremen should "coach others to internalize and self-manage much of the 'control' that was previously imposed by supervisors and managers" (129).

7. James Womack, Daniel Jones, and Daniel Roos, *The Machine that Changed the World* (New York: Rawson Associates, 1990), 13.

8. Ibid., 13–14, 99–102.

9. Selwyn Becker, "TQM Does Work: Ten Reasons Why Misguided Attempts Fail," *Management Review* (May 1993): 32–33.

10. See Michael Cusumano, *The Japanese Automobile Industry: Technology and Management at Nissan and Toyota* (Cambridge: Harvard University Press, 1985); and Michael Cusumano, "Manufacturing Innovation: Lessons from the Japanese Auto Industry," *Sloan Management Review* (fall 1988): 29–39. Production figures are taken from Cusumano, *The Japanese Automobile Industry*, 392–393, and *Automotive News, 1990 Market Data Book*, 3.

11. Womack, Jones, and Roos, *The Machine that Changed the World*, 85–90.

12. Ibid., 277.

13. Ibid., 99.

14. On the history of craft production and worker resistance to Tayloristic management, see David Montgomery, *Workers' Control in America: Case Studies in the History of Work, Technology, and Labor Struggles* (New York: Cambridge University Press, 1979); Dan

Clawson, *Bureaucracy and the Labor Process: The Transformation of U.S. Industry, 1860–1920* (New York: Monthly Review Press, 1980); Daniel Nelson, *Managers and Workers: Origins of the New Factory System in the U.S., 1880–1920* (Madison: University of Wisconsin, 1975); and Milton Nadworny, *Scientific Management and the Unions, 1900–1932: An Historical Analysis* (Cambridge: Harvard University Press, 1955). On the auto industry, see Steve Babson, *Building the Union: Skilled Workers and Anglo-Gaelic Immigrants in the Rise of the UAW* (New Brunswick: Rutgers University Press, 1991), and David Gartman, *Auto Slavery: The Labor Process in the American Automobile Industry, 1897–1950* (New Brunswick: Rutgers University Press, 1986).

15. Frederick Taylor, *Shop Management* (New York: Harper, 1947), 98–99, 105; Harry Braverman, *Labor and Monopoly Capital: The Degradation of Work in the Twentieth Century* (New York: Monthly Review Press, 1974), 119, 85–123.

16. On Ford's production system and the genesis of Fordism, see David Hounshell, *From the American System to Mass Production, 1800–1932: The Development of Manufacturing Technology in the United States* (Baltimore: Johns Hopkins University Press, 1984), 217–301; Stephen Meyer, *The Five Dollar Day: Labor Management and Social Control at the Ford Motor Company, 1908–1921* (Albany: State University of New York Press, 1981); Stephen Meyer, "The Persistence of Fordism: Workers and Technology in the American Automobile Industry, 1900–1960," in *On the Line: Essays in the History of Auto Work*, ed. Nelson Lichtenstein and Stephen Meyer (Urbana: University of Illinois Press, 1989), 73–99. For a comparative history of Fordism that focuses on international variations in mass production and the unique features of American practice, see Steven Tolliday and Jonathan Zeitlin, eds., *The Automobile Industry and Its Workers: Between Fordism and Flexibility* (New York: St. Martin's Press, 1987), and Jean-Pierre Bardou and others, eds., *The Automobile Revolution: The Impact of an Industry* (Chapel Hill: University of North Carolina Press, 1982). See also Michael Piore and Charles Sabel, *The Second Industrial Divide: Possibilities for Prosperity* (New York: Basic Books, 1984), 40–43, 133–164; Alfred Chandler, *The Visible Hand: The Managerial Revolution in American Business* (Cambridge: Harvard University Press, 1977), 498–500.

17. On the "social landscape" of the factory and the contrasting "careers at work" of craftsmen, semi-skilled workers, the unskilled, and rural migrants, see Charles Sabel, *Work and Politics: The Division of Labor in Industry* (Cambridge: Cambridge University Press, 1982). For an overview of the World War I era movements of left-wing workers, see Charles Maier, *Recasting Bourgeois Europe: Stabilization in France, Germany, and Italy in the Decade after World War I* (Princeton: Princeton University Press, 1975).

18. On the foreman's pre-union role in the 1920s and 1930s, see Nelson Lichtenstein, " 'The Man in the Middle': A Social History of Automobile Industry Foremen," in *On the Line*, Lichtenstein and Meyer, 153–189, and Sanford Jacoby, *Employing Bureaucracy: Managers, Unions, and the Transformation of Work in American Industry, 1900–1945* (New York: Columbia University Press, 1985), 185–199, 232–237. For contrasting perspectives and case histories of job control unionism, see Harry Katz, *Shifting Gears: Changing Labor Relations in the U.S. Automobile Industry* (Cambridge: MIT Press, 1987), 13–47; Nelson Lichtenstein, *Labor's War at Home: The CIO in World War II* (New York: Cambridge University Press, 1982); Steve Jeffreys, *Management and Managed: Fifty Years of Crisis at Chrysler* (New York: Cambridge University Press, 1986); Piore and Sabel, *The Second Industrial Divide*, 111–131; Steve Fraser, "Dress Rehearsal for the New Deal: Shop-Floor Insurgents, Political Elites, and Industrial Democracy in the Amalgamated Clothing Workers," in *Working Class America: Essays on Labor, Community, and American Society*, Michael Frisch and Daniel Walkowitz eds. (Urbana: University of Illinois, 1983). For a comparative study, see Steven Tolliday and Jonathan Zeitlin, "Shop-Floor Bargaining, Contract Unionism and Job

34

Control: An Anglo-American Comparison," in *The Automobile Industry*, Tolliday and Zeitlin, 99–120.

19. On Japanese transplant investment, see Martin Kenney and Richard Florida, "How Japanese Industry Is Rebuilding the Rust Belt," *Technology Review* (Feb.-Mar. 1991): 25–33. Unionized transplants were limited to joint-venture operations: NUMMI (GM-Toyota, in California), Diamond Star (Chrysler-Mitsubishi, in Illinois), CAMI (GM-Suzuki, in Ontario) and Mazda (of which Ford owns 25 percent, in Michigan); nonunion transplants were owned by Honda (two plants in Ohio, one in Ontario), Nissan (Tennessee), Toyota (Kentucky and Ontario), and Subaru-Isuzu (Indiana). Big Three plant numbers are compiled from Harbour & Associates, *The Harbour Report, A Decade Later: Competitive Assessment of the North American Automotive Industry, 1979–1989* (Troy, MI: Harbour & Associates, 1990), 105–128; union density figures from Stephen Herzenberg, "Towards a Cooperative Commonwealth? Labor and Restructuring in the U.S. and Canadian Auto Industries" (Ph.D. diss., MIT, 1991), 230.

20. Piore and Sabel, *The Second Industrial Divide*; Sabel, *Work and Politics*, 194–231. For a review of the literature in this debate, see Stephen Wood, "The Transformation of Work?" in Stephen Wood, ed., *The Transformation of Work? Skill, Flexibility, and the Labour Process* (London: Unwin Hyman, 1989), 1–43.

21. Martin Kenney and Richard Florida, *Beyond Mass Production: The Japanese System and its Transfer to the U.S.* (New York: Oxford University Press, 1993), 9–10, 25, 108, 117, 299–300. Kenney and Florida describe the shop-floor attributes of the Japanese model in the same general terms as MIT: teams, workers designing their own jobs, rotation of tasks, QC meetings, cross-training, continuous improvement, and so on. Descriptions of this system in Japan (pp. 63–70) are drawn from secondary sources and interviews with Japanese management. Evidence that this model has been successfully transferred to the North American transplants of Toyota (Kentucky), Honda, Subaru-Isuzu, Nissan, and Nippondenso is presented in chapters 4 and 5 (pp. 102–111 and 131–139), citing interviews with management forty-six times and interviews with workers only four times. In the more mixed reviews of problems at NUMMI and especially Mazda in chapter 4, interviews with management are cited only twice while interviews with workers are cited fourteen times. Chapter 9, which focuses primarily on the problems at these two transplants, also relies heavily on worker and union interviews, especially with the president of UAW Local 3000 at Mazda (cited nine times). Kenney and Florida say that American managers subvert the Japanese model at Mazda and elsewhere, citing Mazda workers (who can't credibly serve as experts on *Japanese* practice) and Japanese managers (who may welcome the opportunity to scapegoat their American partners). It apparently doesn't occur to Kenney and Florida that NUMMI and Mazda workers may be talking about a harsh reality that workers at Honda, Toyota, and other nonunion transplants would also describe if they weren't afraid of management reprisal. Kenney and Florida do note in passing that a former worker at a nonunion transplant indicated workers were afraid to "speak out against the company for fear of being branded 'difficult' or 'troublemakers' " (275) but this isolated observation didn't deter them in their near exclusive reliance on management accounts of the nonunion transplant workplace.

22. John Krafcik, "Triumph of the Lean Production System," *Sloan Management Review* (fall 1988): 42.

23. Eugene Sprow, "Benchmarking: It's Time to Stop Tinkering with Manufacturing and Start Clocking Yourself against the Best," *Manufacturing Engineering* (Sept. 1993): 56–69; Gary Vasilash, "Reengineering: Your Job May Depend on It," *Production* 105 (June 1993): 9–16; Edward Lawler, Susan Mohrman, and Gerald Ledford, *Employee Involvement and Total Quality Management: Practices and Results in Fortune 1000 Companies* (San Francisco: Jossey-Bass Publishers, 1992); John Sheridan, "Agile Manufacturing: Stepping beyond

Lean Production," *Industry Week* (19 Apr. 1993): 31–32; Pascale quoted in Oren Harari, "The Eleventh Reason Why TQM Doesn't Work," *Management Review* (May 1993): 35. See also Fred Bleakley, "Many Companies Try Management Fads, Only to See them Flop," *Wall Street Journal* (6 July 1993): A1; and Andrzej Huczynski, "Explaining the Succession of Management Fads," *The International Journal of Human Resource Management* 4 (May 1993): 443–463.

24. U.S. Commission on Industrial Relations quoted in Alfred Chandler, "Mass Production and the Beginnings of Scientific Management," HBS Case Services, 9–377–223 (Cambridge: Harvard Business School Case Study, 1977), 23. Chandler reviews the genesis of scientific management and its relation to rival systems. See also Nadworny, *Scientific Management and the Unions*. On liberal variants of Scientific Management associated with the Taylor Society, see Jacoby, *Employing Bureaucracy*.

25. Womack, Jones, and Roos, *The Machine that Changed the World,* 102–103.

26. Confederation of Japanese Automobile Workers' Unions, "Japanese Automobile Industry in the Future: Toward Coexistence with the World, Consumers, and Employees," Printed document (Tokyo: Confederation of Japan Automobile Workers' Unions, 1992), 11, 22.

27. Womack, Jones, and Roos, *The Machine that Changed the World*, 99–100, 238. At no point do the authors go beyond the two sentences quoted from page 100 to substantiate their claim that Ford was already a "lean" producer in the late 1980s. They also assert (pp. 99–100) that the UAW's "job-control" contract with Ford hadn't changed since it was first negotiated in *1938*. It is well known that the UAW did not organize Ford until 1941, and the first agreement was a pocket-sized pamphlet of twenty-four pages—hardly the same as the four-volume, 1,241-page contract of the 1990s.

28. On the factors that limit the long-term viability of quality circles, see Edward Lawler III and Susan Mohrman, "Quality Circles after the Fad," *Harvard Business Review* 85 (January-February 1985): 65–71. On EI and "Quality of Work Life" (QWL) circles, see Katz, *Shifting Gears*, 73–131, and Mike Parker, *Inside the Circle: A Union Guide to QWL* (Boston: South End, 1985).

29. Dan Luria, "The Future of Ford in the U.S. Car and Light Truck Market, 1990–1995," Industrial Technology Institute (2 Feb. 1990). Labor hours per car varied from nineteen to sixty in the plants Luria studied. His comparison corrected for differences in model size and complexity. On the high capacity utilization at Ford in the late 1980s, see David Versical, "Squeezing Turnips at Ford," *Automotive News* (21 November 1988): 1.

30. IMVP researcher John Krafcik developed an early index of factory leanness based on four measurable elements: (1) the degree of "teamwork" in the plant, (2) the amount of floor space devoted to repairs, (3) unscheduled absenteeism, and (4) the use of visual controls to regulate work flow. The last two of these are supposed to serve as proxies for, respectively, "worker participation" and "worker span of control," but these are crude associations at best, and almost certainly reflect such additional factors (in the case of absenteeism) as the amount of overtime, the presence or absence of Employee Assistance Programs, and the psychological impact of severe downsizing. See Krafcik, "Triumph of the Lean Production System," 47–49, 52. Womack, Jones, and Roos dropped half of Krafcik's measures and expended the list to six measurable "Work Force" elements of lean production in the factory: (1) the percentage of workers in teams, (2) the amount of job rotation (0 = none, 4 = frequent), (3) suggestions per employee, (4) number of job classes, (5) training hours for new production workers, and (6) absenteeism. Ford's assembly plants could not have been ranked as particularly lean by these criteria in the late 1980s, except perhaps for number 3, and number 5 for *incumbent* workers only. See Womack, Jones, and Roos, *The Machine that Changed the World*, 92. Krafcik and John Paul MacDuffie subsequently developed a "Human Resource

Management'' index of lean production which offered yet another overlapping mixture of variables: (1) teams, (2) rotation, (3) degree to which production workers inspect their own work and (4) do statistical process control, (5) the percentage of workers in employee involvement groups, and (6) the number of production-related suggestions received and implemented. See John Paul MacDuffie and John Krafcik, ''Integrating Technology and Human Resources for High-Performance Manufacturing: Evidence from the International Auto Industry,'' in *Transforming Organizations*, ed. Thomas Kochan and Michael Useem (New York: Oxford University Press, 1992), 209–226.

31. David Levine and Laura D'Andrea Tyson, ''Participation, Productivity, and the Firm's Environment,'' in *Paying for Productivity*, ed. Alan Blinder (Washington, DC: The Brookings Institute, 1990), 183–235; Maryellen Kelley and Bennett Harrison, ''Unions, Technology, and Labor-Management Cooperation,'' in *Unions and Economic Competitiveness*, ed. Lawrence Mishel and Paula Voos (Armonk, NY: M. E. Sharpe, 1992), 247–286; William Cooke, ''Employee Participation Programs, Group-Based Incentives, and Company Performance: A Union-Nonunion Comparison,'' *Industrial and Labor Relations Review*, 47, no. 4 (summer 1994): 594–609.

32. William Cooke, *Labor-Management Cooperation: New Partnership or Going in Circles?* (Kalamazoo, MI: W. E. Upjohn Institute, 1990), 66–67; Lawler, Mohrman, and Ledford, *Employee Involvement and Total Quality Management*, 27–28, 57–61.

33. Lawler, Mohrman, and Ledford, *Employee Involvement and Total Quality Management*, 116–117; Breck Henderson, ''Navy Orders Full Speed Ahead on Total Quality Program,'' *Aviation Week and Space Technology* (9 December 1991): 60–61; William Scott, ''USAF Using TQM to Exploit Scaled Back Forces,'' *Aviation Week and Space Technology* (15 February 1993): 60–61; John Morrocco, ''USAF Aim: Lean Production,'' *Aviation Week and Space Technology* (24 May 1993): 23–24; Sheridan, ''Agile Manufacturing,'' 30–46.

34. 2nd Annual Seminar for Aerospace and Defense, ''TQM: America's Advantage,'' advertisement in *Aviation Week & Space Technology* (9 December 1991): 60.

35. On the Big Three's short-term profit strategy and its consequent disastrous record of poorly engineered cars, see Robert Sobel, *Car Wars: Why Japan Is Building the All-American Car* (New York: McGraw-Hill, 1984); Emma Rothschild, *Paradise Lost: The Decline of the Auto-Industrial Age* (New York: Vintage, 1973); Brock Yates, *The Decline and Fall of the American Automobile Industry* (New York: Vintage Books, 1984); and Mark Dowie, ''Pinto Madness,'' *Mother Jones* (Sept.-Oct. 1977): 18–32.

36. On interchangeable manufacturing, see Merritt Roe Smith, *Harpers Ferry Armory and the New Technology: The Challenge of Change* (Ithaca, NY: Cornell University Press, 1977); on computers, see Harry Wolforst, *Breakthrough to the Computer Age* (New York: Scribners, 1982); on programmable machine tools, see David Noble, *Forces of Production: A Social History of Industrial Automation* (New York: Alfred Knopf, 1984). In the absence of a stronger tradition of public enterprise, the government initiatives indicated here all centered on the military.

37. On the ''union empowering model'' of worker participation see Andy Banks and Jack Metzgar, ''Participating in Management: Union Organizing on a New Terrain,'' *Labor Research Review*, no. 14 (fall 1989): 1–55. Other issues of *Labor Research Review* focus on a wide range of case histories concerning the organizing model of unionism, including numbers 7, 10, 15, 16, and 17.

PART 1 | OVERVIEW

2

Unions and Management by Stress

MIKE PARKER and JANE SLAUGHTER

The vision of work that MIT's International Motor Vehicle Program describes is one without independent unions. In *The Machine that Changed the World*, Womack, Jones, and Roos refer to unions fewer than half a dozen times, and these few include mistaken historical references and the prediction that the UAW will be unlikely to organize transplants not connected to the Big Three. In part, this lack of attention to unions reflects the incredible shoddiness of the book. It also reflects the authors' approach, which defines superiority in terms of productivity figures and speedy development times. But the main reason the authors can disregard unions is that in their view of lean production, there is really no need for them. The system's dependence on worker commitment, they claim, makes lean production incompatible with exploitation; it is self-correcting. We argue, in contrast, that lean production is designed to obligate workers to intensified labor in a system we call "management by stress." In the harsh environment of a "lean" factory, an independent union is all the more vital to the well-being of its workforce.[1]

"Win-Win"

MIT's enthusiasm for the Japanese model seems to know no bounds. "We think it is in everybody's interest to introduce lean production everywhere as soon as possible," say Womack, Jones, and Roos, "ideally within this decade."[2]

"It is in everybody's interest." It is win-win for all concerned. Management gets high productivity and high quality. Workers get dignity, respect, skilled jobs, authority, good working conditions. And best of all, these results do not depend simply on the good intentions of management. Lean production, they tell us, has at its center dynamic work teams based on skilled, involved workers. For the plant to be competitive, this is the way that work *must* be organized. If managers are good managers—that is, if they understand the system's requirements—then workers will have their needs met. It is lean production which both requires and produces worker dignity—not the union.

Indeed, an array of lean production propagandists trumpets the production system as one which solves "the labor problem," ends inherent class struggle, and replaces the adversary relationship with mutual-interest problem-solving. Even many friends of labor, including several authors in this volume, have adopted some version of this model, if not all its implications: that lean production requires worker empowerment, skills, and direct, honest communication between workers and managers. They, however, argue that there is a role for unions: to give workers more voice in those cases where management hasn't learned the new system properly or makes mistakes, and to participate in management to help realize the potential of the system. If we accept this happy model of lean production, the debate over unions turns on how cost effective it is to have an organized institution like a union around to intervene in a family dispute. Predictably, unions come off poorly in this kind of assessment. After all, isn't the first principle of lean production to get rid of all indirect labor—anything that does not add value? Doesn't a union fit into that category?[3]

The implications go well beyond academic debate and are enormous. For workers to receive the blessings of this model, unions are asked to give up hard-won contractual rights and accepted practice. The same argument is being carried into the legal sphere. In the United States, at least, the assumption that workers and management have opposing interests is the basis of labor law and the legal rights of unions. If mutual gainsharing is now the assumption, why not modify labor law to eliminate one of the last pro-union elements that the National Labor Relations Board (NLRB) still upholds? We refer to the illegality of management-dominated "employee committees'' in nonunion shops. Sanctioning what used to be known as company unions has been a primary concern of the Commission on the Future of Worker-Management Relations appointed by President Clinton in 1993. Non-adversarialism, as defined by lean production, is to be the officially sanctioned new world order in industrial relations.

We do not propose rejecting the benevolent lean production model simply because the role of unions is dealt with in footnotes. Nor are we saying that it is impossible to conceive of a production system that is truly based on worker participation, skill, and self-management. We propose rejecting the mutual-interest, worker-centered image of lean production because this image is a myth grafted on to a fundamentally oppressive production system.

Here is a small sample of that reality. In April of 1993, a supervisor at NUMMI issued a series of edicts at a group meeting, including this: ''From now on there will be no bathroom break when there is only one Team Leader off the line because if he is on the line giving bathroom breaks, who will answer the cord pulls? I will have to and lately I have been busy running. . . . Breaktime and lunchtime . . . are to be used to refresh yourself and to go to the restroom, so don't wait until the line is running because . . . if only one team leader is free you won't go unless you have a doctor's verification to do so or in extreme emergencies.'' This decree reveals much about the relationship between supervisors and workers at NUMMI, and the reality of dignity or worker control in the plant.[4]

We argue that ''lean production'' is not driven to advance the interests of workers. Just the opposite: the success of the system is based on its ability to more efficiently *force* employees to do precision work, at the expense of workers' long-term interests, health, and safety. Under lean production, independent unions can resist and can win important improvements for worker—but only at the expense of the system's self-regulating mechanisms. Thus, independent unions are, at the same time, a greater problem for management and more necessary for workers.

Management by Stress

The term ''lean production'' is important because it conveys a particular image of what the system is and how it works. Naturally, defenders wish to define it with a name that implies its excellence. In America, being ''lean'' is good—who wants to be associated with the implied alternative, the ''fat'' or ''bloated'' production system?

We think a more accurate term for lean production is "management by stress." We call it that in order to identify its central operating dynamic and to challenge from the beginning the terms used to promote the system. Indeed, the ideology of lean production is carefully crafted to win support by using words that trigger strong positive responses: "lean," "teams," "teamwork," "job rotation," "empowerment," "multi-skilling," "job security." In fact, none of these concepts, if understood by their common sense meanings, are central to the lean production system. Yet management uses these terms to describe features that *are* essential to the system.[5]

The essence of the system is not that it turns over control to workers, but that it increases *management* power by using a different form of work-force control. The system does not rely on an army of supervisors to monitor the performance of each worker. Nor does it rely simply on "consent," or on convincing workers that their human fulfillment and reaching management's goals are one and the same. While these are part of the system, the key is that the system itself is designed so that any deviation in the process—any failure by a worker or any other part of the system—is immediately exposed and magnified. This disciplines the whole system and allows management to focus its attention on the weak spots.

Therefore, under management by stress, the buffers or reserves that would traditionally shield production from minor glitches are intentionally removed. If a chain is slack it may be difficult to identify a weak or broken link. But stressing the chain instantly reveals the bad link. Likewise, a production system can run with a relatively small number of managers if it is kept under stress at all times so that problems become immediately apparent. The removal of buffers means that a stoppage in one area will quickly bring large parts of the system to a halt, and immediately make the problem apparent to upper management. This in turn creates added pressure from above for rapid correction.

Thus it is vital for management to continuously remove any slack that develops—especially slack that workers create for themselves. Stress becomes a vital management tool both for monitoring and for forcing all personnel to keep up. It is management by controlling stress throughout the system.

One way to maintain the stress is by continually pushing past the point of comfort. Thus the term "lean" is not accurate. The principle of the system is always to push for something less than lean—anorexia, perhaps—in order to "constantly improve." Like an anorectic, the system is never satisfied with itself, no matter how lean it gets. It is always striving for a better (production) figure, no matter what the cost to other parts of the body. The principle is that if the system is continually squeezed, only the strong will survive and productivity will increase.

Does management really think this way? Consider the advice of consultant Masaaki Imai as he draws on the originator of the Toyota Production System, Taiichi Ohno, to explain "how top management can deliberately make sure that kaizen [continuous improvement] is occurring": "For example, let's suppose that a start-up department has the requirement to make one hundred cars per day. Mr. Ohno would give the department the resources to make ninety percent of what was required. Specifically, they received ninety percent of the manpower required, ninety percent of the space, ninety percent of the equipment, etc. . . . As time went on, the department team would find problems or obstacles that would be resolved or overcome through kaizen activities. . . . As soon as a no-overtime equilibrium was met, Mr. Ohno would again remove ten percent of the resources."[6]

Consider also the logic behind the "killer software" developed by Cypress Semiconductor Corporation. If a supply delivery is late arriving at Cypress, but no one has explained the cause of the delay to senior management, the software will automatically shut down all the computer systems in the purchasing department. To get the systems back into operation, the guilty party must contact the supplier, get a delivery date, and report to the chief financial officer. The idea is to magnify the minor problem so that it causes a major disruption. The theory is that employees will then be more alert to avoiding even minor problems. As Cypress CEO T. J. Rodgers says, "It draws everyone's attention." Cypress also has software that automatically shuts down its inventory system if parts sit for more than ten days. In this case, management began with a limit of two hundred days, gradually working down to the maximum stress level. *Business Week* reports that Rodgers has received requests for details from fifty other companies.[7]

The bottom line is that management reduces resources and staffing, while demanding increased output through appeals to pride, institutional loyalty—and fear of job loss. Authority and real power move upward, while accountability is forced to lower levels. "Employee involvement," in practice, means the worker gets to figure out how to survive the new parameters. Thus the bathroom break incident at NUMMI is no anomaly. Bathroom breaks are at issue in many sections of the plant and management has issued a written warning about abuses. This is not the result of supervisors who fail to grasp the principles of a good system. Rather, the system necessarily pushes supervisors in this direction: work standards are constantly *kaizened* upward so that team members work fifty-seven out of sixty seconds; buffers are eliminated so that workers cannot pace themselves and create a break; relief personnel are reduced or eliminated and absent workers are not replaced; responsibility for handling these disruptions is forced downward; the supervisor is therefore pressured to fill out more papers and take on more tasks; he protects himself by holding out the team leader for production breakdowns, which means team members cannot get bathroom relief when they need it. The result that management desires is for workers to pressure each other to reduce absenteeism and bathroom breaks.

Misleading Terms

Let's return to the real meaning of some of the terms mentioned earlier. The system is sometimes referred to as "bufferless production." But in practice, all production systems, including lean production, require buffers to deal with the inevitable glitches that bedevil a complex manufacturing process. Lean production does remove or sharply curtail those buffers that add significant cost—a stock of work-in-progress, backup machinery, extra workers, or spare time—but it replaces these with an alternative. The real buffer in "bufferless" production is the workers, who are expected to put out extra effort over and above their normal job to maintain production *despite* the unavoidable glitches. If overtime is required and workers have to forego personal plans, that's the job. Using workers as the shock absorbers of the system costs management little, but it may be very costly to the workers involved. In addition, many of the perceived advantages of just-in-time are achieved not by eliminating buffers, but by shifting or hiding them. Often, for example, parts inventories are not really eliminated; the responsibility for maintaining an inventory of parts is simply transferred (i.e., forced) onto the supplier.

Although the term "team concept" is widespread and the word "teams" is written into many union contracts, the system is not built around groups functioning as teams in any reasonable sense of the word. At Mazda's plant in Flat Rock, Michigan, for example, most teams do not meet as such. Rather, weekly "unit" meetings combining several teams are chaired by the supervisor, who communicates information or admonitions to workers. At NUMMI, many teams do not meet for months at a stretch, and others meet infrequently or only for a few minutes to hear a supervisor's exhortations. By offering a free meal, supervisors try to bribe workers to meet at lunch time. At CAMI, few teams meet regularly and monthly safety meetings by area are only held because the union has insisted on this practice.[8]

What about teamwork? Mazda's training manual provides the following illustration of how a team should deal with an imbalance in the percentage of time in each cycle that team members must actually perform work, as indicated in figure 2.1. The common sense notion of teamwork, and the egalitarian impulse, would suggest the arrangement illustrated in figure 2.2. But Mazda says no, priority must be given to the ''accumulation'' and then elimination of idle time (or waste), as pictured in figure 2.3. Notice that relaxation time or free time on the job is defined as waste. Notice also that it is not enough to eliminate one person from the team—the remaining team members in 2.3 still should not share the work equally, because equality and sharing are not the aim. The team members must continue to concentrate the idle time in only one job. Why? Because it is easier for

FIG. 2.1
Line Cycle Time

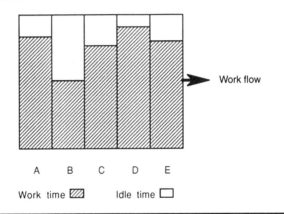

A   B   C   D   E

Work time ▨   Idle time ☐

FIG. 2.2

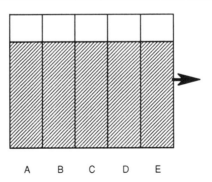

A   B   C   D   E

FIG. 2.3

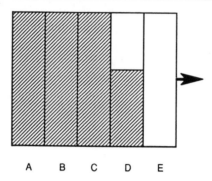

A   B   C   D   E

management either to add work to that one job, or to find ways to eliminate it. This approach is not unique to Mazda. Toyota's training manuals prescribe the same approach eliminating "waste" in the work cycle.[9]

Teams do have a role in lean production. When the team is made the responsible unit for getting the assigned work done, a powerful peer pressure is set up; if one person is absent, the system forces the other team members to take up the slack, with the likely consequence that their frustration will focus on the absent team member.

The system does not require much job rotation. At NUMMI and Mazda, during model launch and whenever there are quality problems, management has tried to place strict limits on rotation or to temporarily eliminate it. In most cases a minimum amount of job rotation is all that management requires: (a) just enough worker training so that management can flexibly rebalance jobs and reassign workers, and (b) just enough rotation to make it difficult for individual workers to develop "secret" job knowledge. More rotation than this adds variance to the system, and makes it harder to identify the causes of errors. Indeed, unions in management-by-stress plants have had to fight to keep and expand rotation and make it a worker right rather than a management option—particularly where members want to rotate during the work day. (Here, as with many of workers' coping responses to the management-by-stress system, rotation is a two-edged sword. Many workers like rotation because their backs might be able to take two hours of installing seats, but not eight. But the use of rotation to "solve" the problem of jobs that are just too hard also relieves the pressure on management to find a different solution—such as mechanical aids or hiring more workers.)

Whether the system produces a more skilled workforce depends on how skill is defined. MIT's approach of simply adding up the number of minutes spent in classrooms tells us little about the nature of the training or the skills imparted. Management-by-stress plants do increase the training time that is focused on increasing identification with company goals and procedures. Training in problem-solving and communication skills is mixed in with this, though these classes tend to be cut back once production is under way. At the same time, training for production workers in technical and job skills is limited: engineers have already broken the jobs down into tiny, simple steps that are as easy as possible, so that workers are as interchangeable as possible. The system seeks to remove job discretion from the individual and place it in the machinery ("autonomation"). Because of the emphasis on "doing it right the first time," there are also fewer jobs in repair and metal finishing, jobs that in traditional plants require exceptional skill. For the skilled trades, the system seeks to contract out those portions of the work that require the most skill: major construction and complex or lengthy repairs. The in-plant skilled trades jobs are reduced as much as possible to predictable, standardized preventive maintenance tasks.

The job security of the core workforce depends on maintaining a considerable number of temporary workers within the plant and extensive outsourcing to absorb most of the impact of a downturn. While the core workforce does not have to fear cyclical layoff, they do have to worry about a permanent plant closing, a threat NUMMI management consciously promotes. Individuals also have good reason to fear that they will not be able to survive the intensified workplace.[10]

The system does not repudiate Taylorism, if Taylorism is understood to mean that workers are required to carry out precisely defined steps exactly as management instructs. Nor does the fact that management seeks to "harness workers' knowledge" make it different from Taylorism. Taylor himself insisted that scientific management demanded "the deliberate gathering in on the part of management's side of all the great mass of traditional knowledge, which in the past has been in the heads of workmen, and in the physical skill and knack of the workmen, which [they have] acquired through years of experience." The difference between management by stress and traditional Taylorism lies in the methods used to gather workers' knowledge. Today, workers are expected to willingly turn over their job-knowledge and even to seek out new ways to speed themselves up. Under lean production, this is labeled "responsibility" and "creativity." If knowledge is not given willingly, the system has ways of collecting it, through rotation, peer pressure, and working supervisors.[11]

System Fragility

Management by stress works only to the extent that workers actually are vulnerable to the pressures established by the system. Workers who refuse to speed up to compensate for absent team members *and can defend themselves* are not vulnerable.

Womack, Jones, and Roos correctly point out that the system is fragile. But the system also has many weapons to handle the resistance of *individual* workers. The stop-cord/andon system (pull cords that stop the line, and flashing lights on the "andon" board indicating the work station) immediately identifies who stopped the line—who is not keeping up. Group leaders and team leaders can be mobilized against anyone who disrupts production and challenges authority. At the same time, the system strips workers of the means to defend themselves individually by getting rid of those work rules and areas of worker discretion they might use or invoke as rights. In a system where management has all the authority, in the name of flexibility, supervisor favoritism in job assignments, response to injury, and leniency for special needs is a potent weapon.

This is where the union becomes so important. Management by stress is vulnerable to concerted action, and workers must depend on their collective power to have any dignity at all under the system. That is why we have so much to learn from the struggles in unionized transplants, where the very existence of an independent union tends to generate action around certain issues. It is crucial to understand that these issues which unions take up are not a consequence of management incompetence in managing a fundamentally good system—a claim that, unfortunately, many transplant workers believe. The issues are generated because the system only works by maintaining the stress that creates such issues.

In the North American transplants where independent unions have mobilized their members and taken the available opportunities to act, they have managed to modify the management-by-stress system, humanize working conditions somewhat, and in so doing strengthen the union's independence. Every such victory proves that the system is not all powerful. Among the contractual changes or practices that unions have won in one or more of the transplants are the following:

- Restrictions on unilateral changes in job descriptions.
- Establishment of a category of replacement workers for absentees.
- The right of team members to elect team leaders.
- Establishment of posting and seniority for job openings to counter the authoritarian flexibility of management.

- Discretion in taking vacation or personal time off, to give members more control over their lives (and also, incidentally, providing members with a tool to punish bad supervisors).
- Upgrading of temporaries to secure jobs with full rights.
- Offices for union officials separate from management's, and union representatives' right to meet separately with members.
- Preservation of an objective and relatively flat wage structure, as opposed to a wage system based on supervisor evaluations, as in Japan.[12]

In addition, unions have encouraged and trained team leaders to see their job primarily as defending and assisting team members rather than supervising. To build their independent base, unions have also used working stewards ("union coordinators") for two-way communication between officials and members, and for mobilization to support contract negotiations and protest unfair policies.

We need to be clear that these union gains challenge, and in some cases defeat, essential controls in the management-by-stress system. For this reason, "lean" management finds an independent union an indigestible obstacle to making the system function. Either the union must be a tamed "enterprise union," as in Japan, which sees its role as a junior partner of management, or management wants no union at all. It is telling in this regard that despite the success of NUMMI and the cooperation of the UAW there, Toyota is fighting the union's organizing efforts at its plant in Kentucky.

Social Costs

Ultimately, unions and their supporters have to go beyond challenging management by stress in the plant or office to challenging it as social policy.

The much praised plant-level productivity figures and cost savings of management by stress are achieved by shifting the costs to others. Job security and high wages are promised to a few at the top of the pyramid, which is maintained by those at the bottom: low-wage suppliers, temporary workers, part-timers without benefits, and full-timers without job security. But does such a system improve the productivity of society as a whole? Certainly, companies can get higher plant productivity through elaborate screening of job applicants and intensified work that consumes people's energies and pushes aside those too burned out to continue. But is it really good social policy to encourage a system that pushes people to their limits when we are faced with an epidemic of repetitive strain injuries?

Analysts keep saying with some surprise that the U.S. economy isn't creating enough jobs for a growing workforce. Is it any wonder, when "lean" companies hire as few people as possible and then meet expansion with overtime, ten-hour days, and temporary workers?

Labor's vision and struggle for a workplace of dignity, skill, and worker participation are both righteous and vitally necessary for the whole society. But these can only be built on a base of solidarity and union strength—not on illusions about lean production and enterprise unionism.

Notes

1. James Womack, Daniel Jones, and Daniel Roos, *The Machine That Changed the World* (New York: Rawson Associates, 1990), 252–253. The most significant mistake made by these authors is the repeated assertion that the union-management relationship from the beginning centered around "job control" contracts.

2. Ibid., 256.

3. Some argue that the union role is to look after the pieces that management misses. W. Edwards Deming, when asked to provide an example of the appropriate role of unions, told of a case where the union secured a space for a shrine desired by the workers.

4. Group Leader *Agenda* for Group Meeting at NUMMI, dated 1 April 1993. Management has also distributed a plant-wide leaflet warning about bathroom break abuses.

5. For additional background on the concept of management by stress, see Mike Parker and Jane Slaughter, *Choosing Sides: Unions and the Team Concept* (Boston: South End Press, 1988), and Mike Parker and Jane Slaughter, "Managing by Stress: The Dark Side of Team Concept," *ILR Report* 26, no. 1 (fall 1988): 19–23.

6. Masaaki Imai, *Kaizen Communique* (Winter 1988/89).

7. Richard Brandt, "Here Comes Attack of the Killer Software," *Business Week* (9 December 1991): 70; T. J. Rodgers, "No Excuses Management," *Harvard Business Review* (July–Aug. 1990).

8. Information comes from interviews by the authors with plant workers and union officers.

9. Production Engineering Department, IE Section, Mazda Manufacturing (USA) Corp., *Kaizen Simulation* (Flat Rock, MI: Mazda Manufacturing Corp., n. d.). On Toyota, see Terje Gronning, *Human Values and "Competitiveness": On the Social Organization of Production at Toyota Motor Corporation and New United Motor Manufacturing, Inc.* (Ph.D. diss., Ritsumeikan University, 1992), 132.

10. For a survey of Mazda workers concerning (among other things) fears about injury, see Steve Babson, "Lean or Mean: The MIT Model and Lean Production at Mazda," *Labor Studies Journal* 18, no. 2 (summer 1993): 3–24. On NUMMI see Caroline Lund, "GM-Toyota Plant Backs Down on 10-Hour Day," *Labor Notes* 173 (Aug. 1993), 3, 14. On CAMI

see CAW-Canada Research Group on CAMI, *The CAMI Report: Lean Production in a Unionized Auto Plant* (Willowdale, Ont.: CAW-Canada Research Dept., 1993).

11. Frederick Winslow Taylor, "Testimony," in *Scientific Management* (Westport, CT: Greenwood Press, 1974), 40.

12. CAW, *The CAMI Report*; Mike Parker and Jane Slaughter, "Surviving Lean Production: Two Auto Worker Locals in the United States," paper presented to the "Lean Production Conference: Labour's Response to the New Managerial Agenda," sponsored by York University, Port Elgin, Ontario, 30 September–3 October 1993.

3

Workers' Roles in Lean Production: The Implications for Worker Representation

JOHN PAUL MACDUFFIE

The writings on lean production, particularly those of the International Motor Vehicle Program (IMVP) at MIT that introduced the term, emphasize the performance advantages of this new production paradigm over mass production throughout all aspects of the automotive industry, from product development to manufacturing to supplier relations. Within manufacturing, many researchers have emphasized the distinctive differences between mass and lean production in the organization of work and the management of people. They attribute the performance advantages of lean production, in part, to a production logic that makes the contributions of production workers central to a process of improvement based on ongoing problem-solving activities.[1]

Others emphasize the ways in which the distinctive roles for workers under lean production lead to exploitative treatment based on ''management by stress''—an intensified workpace, exacerbated by the elimination of buffers and combined with management pressure. There is also divided opinion among researchers about the implications of lean production for unions, with supporters seeing a potentially broader role for worker representation and critics seeing a weakening of the collective and countervailing power of unions as one factor that increases the potential exploitation of workers.[2]

Evidence that lean production offers improved economic performance in relation to mass production tells us little about these important questions because this outcome could arise as much from exploitation of workers as from the enlargement of worker contributions. Worker roles under lean production can only be understood through exploration of the complex dynamics that integrate worker contributions into the overall production system. Furthermore, how we think about worker representation under lean production depends heavily on how we understand worker roles. Different worker roles could imply different worker interests to be represented, or they could imply that the same worker interests must be represented in different ways. In either case, the analysis of workers' roles is the appropriate starting point before exploring issues of worker representation.

Workers' Roles in Lean Production

I will describe three primary roles for workers in lean production systems, drawing on observations from my fieldwork in connection with the International Assembly Plant Study: physical labor ("doing" work), cognitive input ("thinking" work), and member of a social entity ("team" work).

First and foremost is the provision of manual effort to assemble a vehicle. While auto manufacturing is extremely capital-intensive in its welding and painting processes, the final assembly process remains highly labor-intensive. Most production work at an auto assembly plant continues to require difficult and demanding physical labor, a fact that is sometimes neglected in the rosier accounts of lean production. The fact that lean production shares with mass production the use of a moving assembly line and a narrow division of labor means that the *physical* experience of "doing" work is not dramatically different in these two settings.[3]

A second role is cognitive—the involvement of workers in "thinking" as well as "doing." The cliche that workers know their jobs better than anyone else is undoubtedly true under any production system. What's different about lean production is its goal of developing a broader contextual knowledge in the workforce about the production system, so that a worker's deep, often tacit knowledge of one specific task becomes linked to an understanding of how the overall system works, and how one's piece of it relates to other upstream and downstream tasks. Also different is the deliberate organization of work to encourage worker ideas to be surfaced, specified, and legitimized as an input to making changes in the production process—the process known as *kaizen.*

For management to want access to worker knowledge about the production process is not new. Frederick Taylor wanted such access, but without having to deal with the worker. Taylorism legitimized management's role in ferreting out information about how work was done, but in the process, delegitimized the worker's role. In one memorable quote, Taylor states that "Any improvement which [the workman] makes upon the orders given to him is fatal to success."[4]

In some respects, the organization of work under lean production resembles Taylorism. Worker ideas are not the dominant influence on the organization of work in a lean factory; engineers still establish the initial specification of the work process for each new model. *Kaizen* suggestions from workers are subject to careful documentation and comparison with the current process before adoption, and must be approved by engineers or managers; after a suggestion is adopted, the work is again standardized for all workers (including across shifts) who perform it, until the next change in specifications is proposed.[5]

But the fact remains that workers are encouraged, even expected, to contribute their ideas about improving their jobs; their suggestions are seen as valid and significant by managers and engineers, and are often adopted; and work organization and training policies are directed towards improving worker abilities to contribute to this cognitive process, rather than the reverse. Not only are the numbers of problem-solving suggestions per employee high in lean production plants, but the implementation rate is often extremely high as well, a telling indicator of the legitimacy afforded those ideas. If one believes, as I do, that the fundamental, core principle of Taylorism is the separation of conception and execution—of "thinking" work from "doing" work—the priority given to "thinking" by workers stands Taylorism on its head.[6]

Third is a social role—workers' involvement in "team" work. From management's viewpoint under mass production, the fact that labor was viewed as a commodity and that workers were seen as interchangeable and easily replaceable parts simplified its task with respect to the social organization of production. A random assortment of interchangeable parts does not add up to a social group. Mass production managers, whose job was to make sure that nothing would disrupt daily production, showed some concern about individual morale, due to the potential impact of high turnover or absenteeism on production consistency, but rarely worried about group morale.[7]

Under lean production, the social entity is too important to be ignored by management. Just as it legitimizes workers' cognitive inputs to improving the production process, lean production also legitimizes the informal social network in a company as an important source of coordination and commitment. Goals and incentives are formulated and work is organized to support the central influence of social interaction on the operation of the production system. The term "team" is difficult to define precisely in a lean production plant because it refers not only to the work team, the formal structural unit, but also to a notion of "team work" that embodies the goal of a cooperative relationship among work teams, among departments, among functional specialties, and among organizational levels.

The most important social relationship under lean production is with the company. Employees are encouraged to identify themselves with the company, rather than their team or department, because appealing to overarching company-level goals (including satisfying the customer through superior quality) provides a rationale and motivation for setting aside normal inter-group differences. At the same time, identification with company goals around performance, competitiveness and survival pulls workers towards identifying their interests as overlapping with managers at *their* company, and away from identifying with workers at other companies in the industry. (In lean production plants in Japan, this pull towards identification with the company is consistent with the enterprise model of unionism, but outside Japan, it conflicts with industrial unions, which want workers to identify their interests at the industry or class level, as will be discussed further below.)[8]

The social relationship *within* the work team is also extremely important for lean production to be effective. The peer relationships among team members, and the quasi-coach, quasi-staff support provided by the team leader, replace the traditional foreman whose rule was authoritarian in style and rule-based. In its place is the interdependence that accompanies a multi-skilling strategy and a "no buffer" philosophy that eliminates utility workers, so that absenteeism for one worker affects the workload of his or her teammates. The peer controls that emerge in such a situation can easily turn poisonous if there is not some degree of group cohesion, some process of close-to-the-source dispute resolution, personal influence that is based on expertise rather than seniority, and incentives that align team member interests with each other and with other teams in the plant.

To summarize, while traditional mass production managers tend not to think about the workforce as a social entity, lean production makes a deliberate and explicit effort to organize the informal social network in the production system to align employee interests as closely as possible with company goals.

With these three worker roles in mind—physical labor, cognitive input, and member of an explicitly-organized social entity—I turn now to the implications for worker representation.

Implications for Worker Representation

Contrasting worker representation under mass and lean production is more complex than comparing worker roles, for most of the benefits that lean production offers to individual workers pose challenges for unions. While there may be opportunities under lean production for unions to boost their influence and effectiveness in representing their members, each opportunity is accompanied by risks. In this section, I will outline three challenges for unions under lean production, and then explore the risks and benefits of each.

Central to this analysis is the idea that the "logic" of lean production assumes (and works to create) more overlap between managerial and worker interests than mass production, while important areas of conflict remain. Thus, all of the challenges posed to unions by lean production require coming to terms with the enlarged domain of shared interests, while continuing to address the issues involving conflicting interests. In this sense, unions face a situation similar to the period in the late nineteenth and early twentieth centuries, when mass production was supplanting craft production. Industrial unions had to find different ways of protecting workers under mass production that were consistent with preserving the economic gains of the new system. So must today's unions find ways under lean production to promote worker interests not shared with management (as discussed below) that are consistent with the system's fundamental logic—a logic from which shared benefits are derived.

The three challenges are as follows:

1. Lean production dismantles "job control" mechanisms used by unions historically to protect against abuses of management discretion over the allocation of labor.
2. Lean production gives management more incentive to pay attention to worker skill and motivation, and to encourage identification with company goals.
3. Lean production pulls towards an enterprise model of unionism.

Lean Production's Impact on "Job Control." Under the "job control" unionism model that dominated the U.S. auto industry for many years, wages were explicitly tied to jobs and not to worker characteristics; indeed, this approach required that all workers doing the same job receive exactly the same pay, regardless of any individual difference in how the job was performed. Collective bargaining contracts specified an elaborate job classification system, with much attention paid to the exact requirements of each job, and the seniority rights that guided promotions, transfers, and layoffs. Job security was emphasized, in the sense that workers were seen as "owning" a job earned through seniority. Disagreements between labor and management about the application of this system were directed through a grievance process that was also highly formalized.[9]

Under lean production, wages are detached from specific jobs. Job classifications for production workers are reduced to two or three (often from over one hundred), and workers in these broad classifications are paid the same basic wage for learning a number of different skills and jobs. Thus a worker's job no longer has a fixed definition; it has fluid boundaries and can change over time. Furthermore, the movement of workers across jobs can no longer be pre-specified via promotion, transfer, and "bumping" rules based on seniority rights. Finally, rather than "job security" based on "owning" a job, lean production typically provides employment security assurances that assume movement across jobs within the firm.

Workers are organized into teams, within which skills can be learned and jobs can be rotated. Workers may move across teams as well, in response to continual efforts to find process improvements that increase productivity and quality, and to adjust labor inputs to changes in volume. Many grievances may also be resolved at the team level with the assistance of a team leader—typically an hourly worker whose responsibilities overlap with those of management. When bonus plans are in place, management can potentially reward individuals for their contribution to production system improvements, further differentiating pay outcomes based on individual characteristics.

These features of work organization under lean production, all of which boost the cognitive role (the "thinking" work) of workers, render many of the work rules associated with "job control" ineffective. Indeed, this reflects a broader trend across industries in which management seeks more flexibility to deploy workers in different ways depending on market and/or production conditions. This change is threatening to unions, to the extent that they have drawn much of their power and influence at the plant level from the "job control" approach.[10]

However, the "job control" model is only one way for a union to exert influence, one that is relatively unique to the United States. In the face of pressures to grant more shop-floor flexibility to management by relinquishing the mechanisms of job control, unions can (and are) asking for more influence over issues at the strategic level, ranging from competitive decisions about production levels and product changeovers, to investments in new technologies, involvement in hiring and training, and promotion decisions. Unions can also insure that the competitive situation facing a plant is well understood by the workforce, and in turn, that plant management understands the concerns of the workforce, particularly during periods of uncertainty.

In the auto industry, the NUMMI case shows the importance of both a sustained commitment to a "no layoff" policy and extensive information sharing with the union to the ongoing effectiveness of that joint venture plant. A more extensive union involvement is found at Saturn, where the union is directly involved in governance structures and has a major influence on managerial decision-making. In both cases, human resource and labor issues have a higher level of influence within corporate decision-making due to the expanded role of the union. Accomplishing this influence, however, requires new skills from union leaders, who must learn to manage change and wield influence in new ways based on their ability to locate and process information, educate and mobilize members, and communicate rank-and-file interests when they join with management in the decision-making process.[11]

Lean Production as a "Fragile" System. The second challenge for unions is that lean production provides incentives for management to respond to workforce needs and actively boost worker motivation and skill. These incentives arise because lean production is a "fragile" system with respect to the role of workers, while mass production is "robust."[12]

Mass production attempts to protect the production process from potential variations in the quantity and quality of worker effort by relying on narrowly defined jobs that can be filled by interchangeable, low-skilled workers, inventory buffers that minimize the disruption caused by production errors or poor-quality parts, and an automation strategy aimed at minimizing worker discretion—all in the service of high-volume production to achieve economies of scale. It is "robust" because it can tolerate high turnover and absenteeism among demotivated and unskilled workers without a serious impact on its normal operating procedures and customary performance levels.

In contrast, lean production relies heavily on the contributions of a skilled and motivated workforce, as argued above, to make workable such production features as just-in-time inventory systems, small lot production, quick die changes, worker self-inspection of quality, and a flexible product mix. Rather than using buffers (e.g., incoming parts inventories, work-in-process inventories, repair areas) to protect the production process from disruptions, lean production deliberately eliminates buffers to make problems visible, but then relies on "thinking work" from workers to minimize the disruptive consequences. In a way, workers thus provide the capability to deal with uncertain or changeable conditions that is provided by buffers under mass production. Lean production is "fragile" because its vulnerability increases if workers withhold their attentiveness at spotting problems and their skill at solving them. There is also an incentive for management to maintain a healthy relationship with the union, since with low buffers in the supply chain as well as in the assembly plant, even brief work stoppages can rapidly shut down production at multiple sites.

The risks for unions arise from the way a "fragile" system blurs the line between managerial and worker interests. First, as management exerts more effort to boost worker morale and skill, it becomes more of a competitor with the union for influence over workers and for worker loyalty. Second, if management provides voluntarily some of the things that unions have always struggled to obtain for workers, in order to keep the production system operating smoothly, then the rationale for having a union may be weakened in workers' eyes. Third, if management succeeds in having workers identify primarily with company goals, union efforts to achieve consistent organized action across the whole industry may be threatened. Finally, the more management involves workers (and unions) in strategic decision-making, the more constrained workers (and unions) will feel about taking actions that potentially affect a plant's competitiveness.

Unions have traditionally opposed participation programs initiated by management for these reasons. Furthermore, unions have found that management commitment to participation is often short-lived—lasting only until the first sign of economic difficulty. Ironically, this episodic enthusiasm (and disenchantment) with respect to worker participation has always limited the impact of such initiatives on unions. What is significant about lean production, therefore, is that management's reliance on "thinking work" and "team work" from the workforce provides a much stronger incentive to persist with participative efforts throughout the business cycle than when participation is viewed as an end in itself. This persistence potentially makes the risks outlined above more real.

What are the benefits for unions in the "fragile" nature of lean production? First, there are gains for their members from the cognitive and social roles for workers in the production system. There is considerable evidence that workers in lean production plants respond favorably to these expanded roles. Particularly noteworthy is that workers with prior experience in traditional mass production plants typically say they never want to go back to that setting.

Second is the enhanced power for the union in a tightly interdependent production system. As noted above, the low buffers of lean production mean that a union can readily inflict pain on a company through short, targeted work stoppages and other actions that fall short of a full strike, or use the threat of such action to boost their short-term bargaining power. Examples of unions using the ''tight coupling'' of a just-in-time (JIT) system to their advantage are already apparent.[13]

Third, even though management has incentives to attend to worker concerns, management and union agendas will differ, requiring an active union role in pursuing certain worker interests. Foremost is collective bargaining on distributive issues—nothing about lean production prevents unions from seeking fair wages and benefits that are carefully calibrated to industry patterns. Other issues relate to the physical role (the ''doing'' work) of workers in the production system—workpace, health and safety, ergonomics, use of overtime. While managers may pay some attention to these issues under lean production, unions can make them a much higher priority, an effective way to preserve worker loyalty and commitment to the union. Unions are likely to have greater leverage on these issues because lean production is more sensitive, in terms of economic performance, to a decline in worker morale than mass production.

Fourth, as noted above, unions can trade concessions on ''job control'' unionism for an enhanced role in influencing strategic decisions. In addition to engaging such strategic issues as capital investment, choice of technologies, outsourcing, and product planning, unions can influence how lean production concepts are interpreted at a given company, for example, the scope of supervisory roles or the process for selecting team leaders. Although many observers portray lean production in Japan as monolithic, there is in fact considerable variation in how this approach is implemented in different Japanese companies. We can expect similar variation in the U.S. and Europe as aspects of lean production are adapted to different national and company contexts, in part through the active influence of unions.

A final reality about the ''fragile'' nature of lean production is that not all companies, plants, or individual managers will be willing or able to accept the larger and more central role it gives to workers—particularly in companies making the transition from mass production. Not all companies using (or moving towards) lean production are equally competent with respect to understanding its principles or being able to implement them consistently over time. Either deliberately or inadvertently, managers schooled under mass production are likely to make decisions that violate the lean production logic in some important way. Then unions will be able to (and will need to) assert their primacy as representatives of worker interests.[14]

Unions should be attentive to certain "logic-violating" transgressions that may appear in plants using or moving towards lean production. One example is using *kaizen* for speedup, that is, a more intensified workpace over time, rather than efficiency gains through more effective organization of work tasks. Another is supervisor favoritism in the treatment of workers, in the absence of work rules governing the allocation of labor (such as transfers) and the boundaries of job duties. A third is a reluctance to implement worker suggestions because of management attitudes that do not tolerate a legitimized role for worker input. A fourth is a willingness to exploit norms of long work hours and frequent overtime. This is particularly relevant to Japan, where such norms have been strongly reinforced on a societal basis and have proven difficult to change, despite recent pressure from the government and unions.[15]

Lean Production's Pull Towards an Enterprise Model of Unionism. The third challenge for unions, the pull towards enterprise unionism, concerns union structure in relation to the production system. Union structure is typically viewed as related to the scope of the labor market and the product market, with craft unions representing skilled workers organized by occupation and geographical area, and industrial unions representing skilled and unskilled employees organized by firm on a national basis. But union structure is also influenced by the boundaries of knowledge in the division of labor of a production system.

In a craft system, the specific crafts are defined by the knowledge required to work effectively with certain materials and processes, for example, bricklayers with brick, and pipefitters with pipe. Jobs are broadly defined, integrate conception and execution, and require multiple skills. Innovation in work processes (and to some extent in products as well) occurs within the boundaries of the craft. Craft unions define themselves in terms of this knowledge boundary, and work to preserve the separateness of that knowledge (and the associated control over certain jobs) from that of other crafts.

Industrial unions define their jurisdiction on the basis of industry, but beyond that, also adhere to the boundaries associated with particular knowledge. Under mass production, skilled workers are organized on the basis of their craft knowledge, albeit within the industry. The much larger group of "unskilled" workers in industrial unions is also identified in terms of knowledge—what they *don't* know and don't have to know. With a narrow division of labor creating jobs with very low skill/training requirements, worker knowledge counts for little. Production jobs can be filled as easily by inexperienced workers as by experienced ones. With no defined knowledge base to justify the claim of "unskilled" workers to jobs, industrial unionism has relied on job classifications to establish "ownership" of a set of job responsibilities and a structure for workers to move across jobs on the basis of seniority. These "unskilled" classifications and associated work rules have become relatively standardized in the industry as a way to regulate job movement and settle disputes over who "owns" a job.[16]

The boundaries of knowledge under lean production are different from both craft production and mass production in ways that complicate worker representation and union structure. The core conceptual knowledge is the production system of a particular company. Jobs are narrowly defined, but workers move among jobs over time to develop both conceptual knowledge and multiple skills. Innovation is focused as much on the interstices between jobs as within jobs—that is, the inter-group problem-solving that works from the information that a tightly inter-dependent, low-buffer system provides. With this inter-dependence, much of the knowledge that workers develop spans traditional boundaries—between unskilled production and skilled crafts workers, between the craft domains themselves, and between workers, engineers, and managers.

This blurring of boundaries renders both craft and industrial union structures problematic. It weakens the ties of skilled trades workers to a well-defined domain of knowledge and, by boosting the firm-specific component of their knowledge, weakens their ties to an occupational group that spans firms. Furthermore, it turns "unskilled" workers into skilled workers, in part by legitimizing the knowledge such workers have always had, and in part by developing a mix of both firm-specific and general (e.g., problem-solving) skills. Thus, the logic of lean production may, in part, push towards an enterprise model of worker representation because firm-specific knowledge about the production system is the clearest boundary to organize around.[17]

This is just one of a number of forces for decentralization that pose major challenges for national unions. Harry Katz examines evidence of decentralization in collective bargaining in six countries (Sweden, Australia, Germany, Italy, the U.K., and the U.S.) and argues that these trends "are similar and can be best explained by changes in work organization at the local level: More local bargaining seems to be a natural product of the increase in worker and union participation in enterprise and shop floor decision making. It also appears that local bargaining is essential for the identification and implementation of new, more flexible forms of work organization." Similarly, Richard Locke, in his study of industrial relations in Italy, claims that the local variation in work organization and industrial relations practices resulting from union-management productivity coalitions at some plants and companies undermines national unions. What is striking in both accounts is how the dynamism of union activity at the local level poses challenges for unions at the national level.[18]

The changes cited by these researchers result from the confluence of several economic and technological forces, many of which are independent from lean production. But the fact that the boundaries of knowledge under lean production are so strongly associated with a single firm rather than a craft or industry provides an additional push in the direction of local variation and enterprise unionism. Thus, like these other trends, the diffusion of lean production raises worrisome issues for national unions. How will national unions be able to take wages and working conditions out of competition across an entire industry if there is high variation in work arrangements across companies and plants, and workers identify their interests strongly with a particular company? What safeguards will prevent management whipsawing local unions, pitting them against each other to gain new products or new technologies to stay competitive? What protections will exist for workers at financially weak companies if unions adopt the stance that collective bargaining should be based on the situation of each company and abandon industry-wide norms?

For national unions dealing with these issues, the main hope lies, I would argue, in recognizing the greater leverage afforded by the enlarged roles of workers under lean production. Since, under lean production, motivated and skilled workers are crucial to the competitive advantage of firms, unions have an opportunity to demand strong policies on employment security and training. By making labor more of a fixed cost while also boosting its value in a human capital sense, such policies will give companies an incentive to avoid competing on the basis of wages and working conditions.

Conclusion

This essay argues that the role of workers under lean production is substantially larger than under mass production. The dependence of lean production on workers for "thinking" work and "team" work, as well as "doing" work, has benefits for the self-development of workers as well as the economic performance of firms. This poses three challenges for unions. First, they will face pressures to abandon "job control" unionism, which conflicts with key principles of lean production. Union efforts to preserve a "job control" strategy will result in a "lose-lose" struggle with management that is certain to affect economic performance adversely, and hence threaten the employment security unions seek for their members. However, unions can (and do) seek greater influence on management's strategic decisions in return for allowing greater flexibility in work organization. Second, unions will find that managers have more incentive to be concerned about workforce skill and motivation under lean production. While this can benefit workers, it places management more directly in competition with unions for worker loyalty and identification and increases management willingness to maintain "voice" mechanisms that provide an alternative outlet for worker concerns. However, unions can strengthen the commitment of workers by supporting management initiatives that lead to mutual gains while also pushing hard for management to respond to issues (e.g., ergonomics, avoidance of speedup, limits on overtime) that will be higher priorities for workers than for managers. Third, unions under lean production will have to deal with changes in the boundaries of knowledge and with the blurring of boundaries across knowledge domains—both of which pull towards more local variation in industrial relations practices and an enterprise model of unionism, thus posing challenges for national unions.

There is a hypothesis in the making here, that those companies or plants utilizing lean production principles that respond most effectively to worker interests should demonstrate more consistent and higher economic performance over time. This hypothesis assumes that lean production plants which do *not* respond to worker interests will suffer deteriorating performance because of the "fragile" nature of the production system. It also assumes that unions are the form of worker representation best able to represent worker interests, but does not preclude the possibility that other forms of "voice" for workers in nonunion plants may have some of the same effect. The time dimension is important here, for no one doubts that lean production, like mass production, can show short-term performance gains through exploitative pressure on workers. At the same time, even if the hypothesis holds over the long term, it will not resolve questions about the implications for national unions. To answer those, we need to observe whether the dynamics of lean production described here hold over time, and whether it continues to spread in its current form or instead takes on hybrid forms, combining elements of mass and lean production, as it is adapted to different contexts.

The rise of lean production provokes uneasy reactions among union leaders and other supporters of labor for it seems to foretell the certain dismantling of union strategies and structures that have been dominant, and effective, for most of this century. In return, there is the uncertain promise of new benefits for workers if unions can shift their approach to take advantage of the greater centrality of worker roles. Yet lean production seems certain to continue diffusing, if only because of its performance advantages. Unions will be better able to represent their members effectively if they proactively grapple with the challenges and opportunities of lean production than if they try to block it or simply hope it goes away.

Notes

Thanks to Paul Adler, Peter Cappelli, Sue Helper, Chip Hunter, Harry Katz, Tom Kochan, Frits Pil, Saul Rubinstein, and participants at the Harman Program seminar at Harvard University for helpful comments on earlier drafts of this paper.

1. John Krafcik, "Triumph of the Lean Production System," *Sloan Management Review* 30, no. 1 (fall 1988): 41–52; James Womack, Daniel Jones, and Daniel Roos, *The Machine that Changed the World* (New York: Rawson Associates, 1990); John Paul MacDuffie, "Beyond Mass Production: Flexible Production Systems and Manufacturing Performance in the World Auto Industry" (Ph.D. diss., MIT, 1991); John Paul MacDuffie, "Human Resource Bundles and Manufacturing Performance: Flexible Production Systems in the World Auto Industry," unpublished paper; Robert Cole, *Strategies for Change: Small Group Activities in American, Swedish, and Japanese Industries* (Berkeley: University of California Press, 1989); Paul Adler, "The 'Learning Bureaucracy': New United Motor Manufacturing, Inc.," in *Research in Organizational Behavior*, ed. Barry Staw and Larry Cummings (Greenwich, CT: JAI Press, 1993); Paul Adler and Robert Cole, "Designed for Learning: A Tale of Two Auto Plants," *Sloan Management Review* (spring 1993): 85–94.

2. Mike Parker and Jane Slaughter, *Choosing Sides: Unions and the Team Concept* (Boston: South End Press, 1988); Joseph Fucini and Susan Fucini, *Working for the Japanese: Inside Mazda's American Auto Plant* (New York: Free Press, 1990); Steve Babson, "Lean or Mean: The MIT Model and Lean Production at Mazda," *Labor Studies Journal* 18, no. 2 (summer 1993): 3–24; Laurie Graham, "Inside a Japanese Transplant: A Critical Perspective," *Work and Occupations* 20, no. 2 (1992): 147–173; CAW-Canada Research Group, David Robertson, et al., *The CAMI Report: Lean Production in a Unionized Auto Plant* (Willowdale, ONT: Canadian Auto Workers, 1993).

3. For some observers, particularly Christian Berggren in *Alternatives to Lean Production: Work Organization in the Swedish Auto Industry* (Ithaca, NY: ILR Press, 1992), this fact supports the conclusion that lean production does not differ from mass production in any significant way. While I will argue that it is the cognitive and social roles for workers under mass and lean production that are most fundamentally different, the involvement of workers in revising task specifications, rearranging equipment layout, and contributing ideas for design changes often reduces the physical demands of a given assembly line job.

4. This quote is from 1906; the source is unknown, probably a speech. It is included in the educational videotape "Clockwork: Frederick Taylor and Scientific Management" (1982), produced by California Newsreel.

5. On the relationship between Taylorism and lean production, see Paul Adler, "Time and Motion Regained," *Harvard Business Review* (Jan.–Feb. 1993): 97–108.

6. Even if we leave aside plants in Japan (where suggestions per employee may exceed one hundred per year, due to a long history of promoting worker suggestions and the use of monthly quotas to boost suggestion levels), suggestion rates and implementation rates are much higher at lean production plants than at mass production plants. For example, 1993 data from the International Assembly Plant Study shows that lean production plants in the U.S. averaged 4 suggestions per employee per year, with a more than 60 percent implementation rate, compared with 0.4 suggestions per employee in more traditional U.S. plants, with a 25 percent implementation rate.

7. This critique of mass production was developed by socio-technical systems (STS) theory, which arose in response to Taylorism's separation of "thinking" work from "doing" work. STS emphasizes the importance of informal social interactions in work groups and the relationship between the technical and social systems at work. See Eric Trist and Kenneth

Bamforth, "Some Social and Psychological Consequences of the Longwall Method of Coal-Getting," *Human Relations* 4 (1951): 6–38; Fred Emery and Einar Thorsrud, *Democracy at Work* (Leiden, Netherlands: Martinus Nijhoff, 1976); William Pasmore, *Designing Effective Organizations: The Socio-Technical Systems Perspective* (New York: John Wiley, 1988).

8. Research on the factors affecting company and union commitment suggests that these may differ depending on whether workers attribute their favorable and unfavorable experiences with their jobs to the company, the union, or both. Thus the question of whether strong identification with the company weakens union commitment (or vice-versa) is ultimately an empirical question. See Peter Sherer and Motohiro Moroshima, "Roads and Road Blocks to Dual Commitment: Similar and Dissimilar Antecedents of Union and Company Commitment," *Journal of Labor Research* 10, no. 3 (1989): 311–30.

9. On "job control" unionism, see Harry Katz, *Shifting Gears: Changing Labor Relations in the U.S. Automobile Industry* (Cambridge: MIT Press, 1985); Michael J. Piore, "American Labor and the Industrial Crisis," *Challenge* 25 (Mar.–Apr. 1982): 5–11.

10. See Thomas Kochan, Harry Katz, and Robert McKersie, *The Transformation of American Industrial Relations* (New York: Basic Books, 1986). This change equally threatens traditional management roles. Expanding the cognitive role for workers eliminates the rationale for "management rights" (i.e. unilateral management authority over all conditions and methods of work) as much as it does for "job control."

11. Claire Brown and Michael Reich, "When Does Union-Management Cooperation Work? A Look at NUMMI and GM-Van Nuys," *California Management Review* 31, no. 4 (summer 1989): 26–44; Saul Rubinstein, Michael Bennett, and Thomas Kochan, "The Saturn Partnership: Co-Management and the Reinvention of the Local Union," in *Employee Representation: Alternatives and Future Directions*, ed. Bruce Kaufman and Morris Kleiner (Madison, WI: Industrial Relations Research Association, 1993); Ann Frost, "The Determinants of Local Union Capabilities: An Historical-Institutional Approach," working paper (Industrial Relations Section, MIT, 1994).

12. Haruo Shimada and John Paul MacDuffie, "Industrial Relations and 'Humanware': Japanese Investments in Automobile Manufacturing in the United States," working Paper (Sloan School of Management, MIT, 1987).

13. For example, in the summer of 1992 the brief strike at a GM components plant in Lordstown, Ohio shut down production at several assembly plants, including Saturn. Overuse of this tactic can be counterproductive, however, since management can easily revert to mass production practice and begin stockpiling inventories again.

14. Differences in management competency and motivation will be another source of variation as lean production diffuses. Mass production principles were also implemented erratically and incompletely, particularly in Europe, due to the persistence of craft principles. See Wayne Lewchuk, *American Technology and the British Car Industry* (Cambridge, UK: Cambridge University Press, 1988).

15. Japanese Auto Workers, "Japanese Automobile Industry in the Future: Towards Coexistence with the World, Consumers, and Employees," mimeo (1992).

16. Even where managers (and especially foremen) are aware of the important "working knowledge" of production workers, there is no legitimized way for them to recognize or validate this knowledge. The logic of mass production requires minimal modifications of the production process to achieve economies of scale, and vests the authority to decide what modifications are made in engineers and staff.

17. This is obviously not the causal direction historically. Japanese companies had already established enterprise unions before the innovations of lean production emerged and were refined into a full production system. See Michael Cusumano, *The Japanese Auto Industry: Technology and Management at Toyota and Nissan* (Cambridge: Harvard University

Press, 1985); Andrew Gordon, *The Evolution of Labor Relations in Japan: Heavy Industries, 1853–1955* (Cambridge: Harvard University Press, 1985). However, as lean production spreads into other countries, special collective bargaining arrangements are often made to accommodate the logic of the production system. The dynamic of the relationship between union and management thereafter is what demonstrates this pull towards enterprise unionism.

18. Harry Katz, "The Decentralization of Collective Bargaining: A Literature Review and Comparative Analysis," *Industrial and Labor Relations Review* 47 (Oct. 1993): 17, 3–22; Richard Locke, "The Demise of the National Union in Italy: Lessons for Comparative Industrial Relations Theory," *Industrial and Labor Relations Review* 45, no. 2 (1992): 229–249. On the economic forces that boost the influence of local unions, see also Harry Katz and John Paul MacDuffie, "Collective Bargaining in the U.S. Auto Assembly Sector," in *Contemporary Collective Bargaining in the Private Sector*, ed. Paula Voos (Madison, WI: Industrial Relations Research Association, 1994).

4

The Role of the Union
and Employee Involvement
in Lean Production

ADRIENNE EATON

Among the many debates regarding lean production, a central concern is whether this management strategy fundamentally empowers or exploits workers. The International Motor Vehicle Program at MIT emphasizes the system's empowering aspects. MacDuffie and others suggest that the logic of production under a lean system necessarily empowers workers by placing them at the center of factory operations. Lean production involves, among other things, continuous improvement in the manufacturing process with a special emphasis on elimination of ''wasted'' or unnecessary time and effort. Further, at least in theory, workers themselves are the key participants in the improvement process. This participation is seen to engage workers' cognitive abilities in new ways as they acquire or sharpen a new set of skills.[1]

Empowerment, in this formulation, results from both increased skills and the reliance on worker input and cooperation for the success of the system. In a traditional mass production environment, the firm's need for the skills and cooperation of highly skilled craft workers (the maintenance and tool making trades) places them in a strategically key position for any exercise of collective power. Theoretically, all production workers in a lean production system now occupy this strategic position. For this reason, the system is often described as "fragile." Since lack of full cooperation by workers can quickly cause the system to break down, that cooperation must be secured. Womack, Jones, and Roos suggest that worker cooperation is won through management guarantees of job security. Adler, on the other hand, suggests that the tensions inherent in lean production require a "robust governance process in which the voices of management and labor can be clearly heard and effectively harmonized on high-level policy issues as well as on work-team operating issues."[2]

The exploitation school sees quite different outcomes resulting from the same processes. In particular, continuous improvement, as well as tight buffers, are viewed as resulting primarily in speedup and the intensification of work effort. Empirically, this view is supported by worker reports of exhaustion and by high rates of repetitive motion injuries in some lean production facilities. Any increase in the exercise of cognitive skills on the part of the workforce is downplayed since it is viewed as being purely in the service of management goals.[3]

Thus, the question of whether or not lean production empowers or exploits workers is both an empirical and an interpretative one. It is important that we examine lean production systems as they actually function, not as they are designed or believed to function. At the same time, it is possible for two observers to see the same "reality" and define it quite differently. The continuous improvement process described above has been called "democratic Taylorism," though "participative Taylorism" strikes me as more accurate. The empowerment school emphasizes the democratic or participative part of the term, and sees it as a significant advance for workers over the failure of mass production to engage workers' minds. The exploitation school emphasizes the Taylorism part of the definition, and argues that while lean and mass production differ little in the essential nature of the work, lean production often involves significant reductions in negotiated protections for workers.[4]

The following empirical work is offered in an effort to shed some light on actual practices, however they may be interpreted. The study I will describe was conducted in 1990. It involved the survey of both management and labor representatives from approximately eighty bargaining units located in Wisconsin and surrounding states. These eighty units were first surveyed in 1987 as part of a study of union involvement in participative programs. As such, they all had some type of employee involvement (EI) program in place in 1987, skewing the sample towards workplaces apt to be "innovative." Of these eighty units, sixty-two union representatives and forty-nine management representatives responded with usable data.[5]

A number of caveats are necessary regarding this empirical work. First, I have not studied lean production as a fully integrated system. Indeed, since it appears there is no agreed upon definition of what is included in such a system, it is not clear how it would be possible to study it in a quantitative way. I have, however, examined five new production techniques, the first four of which are clearly associated with most definitions of lean production: just-in-time (JIT), Statistical Process Control (SPC), cell manufacturing, work teams, and Total Quality Management (TQM). Definitions of each appear in the Appendix to this essay. Given the salience of work teams in discussions of lean production, it should be noted that managers frequently claim their workforce is organized into teams even when there is no formalized and continuing role for such groups in the day-to-day operations of the plant. In this study, however, the term indicates the type of continuing team organization most often associated with lean production, one that is characterized by cross-training, job rotation, and collective responsibility for a set of tasks.

My second caveat is that the survey does not focus exclusively on the auto industry, the focal point of the lean production debate and the central concern of the studies in this volume. Of the roughly sixty-two labor respondents in the survey, eleven came from factories that could be defined as part of the auto industry. This group included one auto, one motorcycle, and one truck assembly plant. The other eight were non-Big Three supplier facilities; the results for this group may therefore represent conditions in what is sometimes referred to as the "second tier" of the auto industry, the unionized supplier segment.

Finally, conclusions regarding the impact of these techniques on empowerment rely on the crucial assumption that the participation of workers in decision-making leads to empowerment only when that participation is formalized. Indeed, this assumption appears consistent with Adler's notion that lean production requires mechanisms for worker, as well as management, voice. Adler himself indicates that in the case he studied, NUMMI, the union provided that voice. In the survey, formalized participation is operationalized in two ways: through unions and collective bargaining, and through formal EI programs. Thus, I explore the interrelations between new production techniques on the one hand and both formal EI programs and unions on the other, and the degree to which EI programs and unions have been involved in the implementation of these new production techniques.[6]

The Survey Results[7]

Use of the new production techniques by the sample was fairly high as reported by both sets of respondents. The technique most often used was

SPC, with roughly two-thirds of labor and close to four-fifths of management respondents reporting its use. Following close behind was JIT (61 and 52 percent) and TQM (48 and 56 percent). Approximately one-third of both respondents reported the use of cells and work teams. It should be pointed out that these rates may well be higher than those for bargaining units generally, since, as noted above, sample members are probably more ''innovative'' than the general population of bargaining units.[8]

Significantly, the auto portion of the sample reported greater use of new production techniques in all five categories. Indeed, all of the ''auto'' labor respondents reported the use of both SPC and JIT. (Slightly fewer than all of the ''auto'' managers reported the use of these same techniques.) This probably results, at least for the parts suppliers, from the requirement by original equipment manufacturers, the auto assemblers, that suppliers engage in these two practices.

These five techniques do not necessarily constitute an integrated production system. While there are strong intercorrelations between the use of SPC and JIT, other correlations are weak or inconsistent. For instance, while most users of cell or work teams also use JIT, most JIT users do not also use cells or work teams. Perhaps less surprising, TQM is only marginally related to either JIT or SPC, though its use is significantly correlated with the use of work teams.

The interrelationship between formal EI programs and these five techniques appears to be complex. This interrelationship can be examined in two alternative ways. The first examines the impact of new techniques on continued survival of formal EI; since all of the sample members had EI programs in 1987, the relevant question is how many of these programs survived the three-year period between the surveys. The second approach examines the use of formal EI to implement the new techniques.

Two alternative hypotheses can be tested concerning the use of new production techniques and the survival of EI. On the one hand, it may be that either for rational reasons or because of changing management fads, managers seeking increased productivity will move away from EI as they implement new techniques that actually reconfigure the production process. If that is the case, we might expect new production techniques to be associated with the declining use of formal EI programs. However, precisely the opposite would be expected if we view employee involvement as a crucial complement to these new techniques.

The data tend to bear out the latter hypothesis, at least for the labor respondents. JIT, SPC, TQM and teams were all positively and significantly associated with continued survival of formal EI for the labor data. (Only TQM had a significant association in the management data and that was positive and weak.) EI programs were not likely to be destroyed by the use of these new production techniques, but they were not frequently used to implement the new approaches. The worst offender in this regard was JIT. Seventy percent of the labor respondents (though only 17 percent of management) reported that the EI program had no role in implementing JIT. Approximately 30 to 40 percent of the respondents from both groups reported that the EI program played no role in implementing SPC, TQM, and cell manufacturing. Only in the case of work teams did a large number of respondents report that EI played an extensive role in implementation. Further, in many of the cases where EI played no role in implementing a new technique, it was reported that workers were not involved in the implementation at all. Again, this was particularly true for JIT.

With few exceptions, the role of EI in the auto segment of the sample differed little from the full sample. The only important differences concerned JIT and work teams. In the case of JIT, both sets of auto respondents reported that the EI program played a somewhat greater role in implementing new production techniques than it did in the full sample. On the other hand, the role of EI in implementing work teams was significantly smaller in the auto portion of the sample according to both sets of respondents. Thus, for the auto sample, there was little difference from technique to technique in the role of EI, and that role was small.

Likewise, unions were rarely involved in the implementation of these techniques. Again, JIT was the worst offender with over 80 percent of union and 64 percent of management respondents reporting no union role. An extensive union role was reported most frequently (35 to 40 percent) for work teams. Otherwise, an extensive union role was reported infrequently, at least by labor respondents. The other three programs lay somewhere between the two extremes, with cells the closest to work teams. The auto group was again quite similar to the full sample, though the auto labor respondents reported a slightly smaller role for the union in implementing both cells and work teams.[9]

Among those who reported that the union had played a role in the implementation of new production techniques, most indicated that the mechanism for the union's involvement was collective bargaining. In particular, respondents reported bargaining over wages rates and changes in job titles and descriptions accompanying the adoption of cells and work teams. In only a couple of cases was the union involved in the actual design of the cells or teams. The other specific roles mentioned for the union were more in the nature of "moral support." Thus, unlike Adler's description of NUMMI, unions were not providing worker voice in these particular "high-level policy issues."

Conclusions

What conclusions can we draw regarding the empowerment or exploitation of workers under lean production? Clearly, neither workers nor their representatives participated extensively in the implementation of the new production technologies in the majority of cases studied. If we assume that such participation is a good indicator of the overall empowerment of workers in the system, there is not much empowerment going on. It is still possible that the empowerment emphasized by MacDuffie and others—that is, the empowerment resulting from the work-related problem-solving process—exists in these workplaces. However, this remains a limited type of empowerment; most of these cases fall short of the high commitment, intrinsically-fulfilling workplaces advertised so often in the business and popular press.

There are clearly some exceptions to this overall finding. As mentioned above, a few respondents reported extensive union and worker involvement in the reorganization of work into teams or cells. The advocates of the empowerment school may well argue that the lack of involvement that is more common to this study represents improper implementation of lean production, or a violation of its production logic. Further, systems that violate that logic are unlikely to yield the potential results of a lean system. While there may be some merit to that argument, it also carries a danger of becoming tautological: lean production involves empowerment, therefore if there is no empowerment, it can't really be lean production.

My own conclusion, drawn from this as well as other empirical work, is that neither empowerment nor exploitation *necessarily* result from the lean production process. This is because unions function both as a part of the company's social system *and* as a separate social institution or system. Structures and systems, like lean production, may create power for individuals and groups within a company. But unions, as separate institutions, must have sources of power separate from those provided in the employer's social system. Like other social movements, labor's power must be taken; it cannot simply be given. It is this central fact that seems at times to be insufficiently understood by those in the empowerment school. Thus, while the lean production system, particularly its tight buffers, creates possibilities for the exercise of relative power, unions must also engage in active union-building.

Let's consider specific examples. To the extent the UAW local at Mazda has been able to modify lean production in a more worker-friendly direction than it was originally designed, it has been through the exercise of relative power: through organizing and using fairly traditional pressure tactics. Similarly, the UAW local at Saturn could be described as powerful, but I would suggest that its power derives as much from internal organizing efforts as it does from its structural position as a co-manager of the business. Indeed, the local has implemented several union-building processes, including a "Town Hall" (monthly union meetings held during the work day on both shifts); "Rap Sessions" (monthly meetings for each business team where union members ask the local president questions); and an annual "Member to Member Survey" for which team leaders conduct a forty-five minute interview with each union member on the concerns they would like the union to address.[10]

Finally, one of the findings from my earlier work on unions and EI is that the failure of unions to exert control over these programs is not merely or not even particularly a result of low relative bargaining power as traditionally defined. Rather, oppositional stances toward EI have tended to blind unions, first, to the necessity of organizing themselves to defend against the potential bad outcomes of EI, and second, to the opportunities for using EI to achieve union goals. My work indicates that the local unions with the most control over EI were those which had either singly or jointly initiated the program, had reached out to other unions and to educational institutions to improve their ability to deal with EI, and had the backing of a national union that made support for EI conditional on protections for workers and the union.[11]

These findings will likely also apply to union approaches to lean production. In short, it seems clear to me that empowerment does not necessarily result from the lean production system. Nor, however, does exploitation. Rather, it is incumbent on unions to organize themselves to defend workers' well-being within these systems. This may not mean, however, defending traditional limits on management discretion (e.g., rigid job classifications). It does mean working to eliminate what is exploitative in the system and to reinforce or defend what is potentially empowering in the system.

Appendix: Definitions of New Production Techniques

Just-in-time (JIT) is an inventory system in which reserves are kept to a minimum and suppliers deliver parts or components in small quantities as needed.

Statistical Process Control (SPC) is a quality control system using sampling techniques and statistical methods to measure product conformance with specified tolerances.

Cell Manufacturing involves a group of machines and workers that produce a finished product from raw materials or perform a series of operations on parts which have similar design or manufacturing sequences.

Work Teams are designated groups of workers usually characterized by reduced job classifications, team responsibility for a set of tasks, and the rotation of team members to different jobs within the team.

Total Quality Management (TQM) is a program of "built in" quality control where error-free performance is the standard. The goal is prevention of problems at their source. Machines and workers stop when defective work is produced and the cause of the defect is immediately addressed.

Notes

1. James Womack, Daniel Jones, and Daniel Roos, *The Machine that Changed the World* (New York: Rawson Associates, 1990); John Paul MacDuffie, "Beyond Mass Production: Organizational Flexibility and Manufacturing Performance in the World Auto Industry," unpublished paper (University of Pennsylvania, Wharton School, 1992).

2. Womack, Jones, and Roos, *Machine*, 103; Paul Adler, "Time-and-Motion Regained," *Harvard Business Review* (Jan.–Feb. 1993): 107.

3. Mike Parker and Jane Slaughter, *Choosing Sides: Unions and the Team Concept* (Boston: South End Press, 1988); Steve Babson, "Lean or Mean: The MIT Model and Lean Production at Mazda," *Labor Studies Journal* 18, no. 2 (summer 1993): 3–24.

4. On "democratic Taylorism," see Paul Adler, "The 'Learning Bureaucracy': New United Motor Manufacturing, Inc.," in *Research in Organizational Behavior* 15, ed. Barry Staw and Larry Cummings (Greenwich, CT: JAI Press, 1993): 111–194.

5. For details of the 1987 study see Adrienne E. Eaton, "The Extent and Determinants of Local Union Control of Participative Programs," *Industrial and Labor Relations Review* 43, no. 5 (July 1990): 604–620.

6. Adler, "Time-and-Motion," 106–108.

7. For a full presentation of the data, see Adrienne E. Eaton, "New Production Techniques, Employee Involvement, and the Union," unpublished paper (Rutgers University, Labor Education Center, 1993).

8. The difference between the labor and management responses represent real differences in perception rather than differences in the workplaces represented in the two samples. These perceptual differences are evidenced when matched pairs, that is, labor and management representatives from the same workplace, are reviewed.

9. Respondents were also asked the degree of union involvement in EI. The most common response (roughly 50 to 60 percent) was that the union had played "some role" in implementing EI. The mean for the sample was about the same as for the cells.

10. See Babson, "Lean or Mean"; Joseph Fucini and Suzy Fucini, *Working for the*

Japanese: Inside Mazda's American Auto Plant (New York: The Free Press, 1990); Saul Rubenstein, Michael Bennett, and Thomas Kochan, "The Saturn Partnership: Co-Management and the Reinvention of the Local Union," in *Employee Representation: Alternatives and Future Directions*, ed. Bruce Kaufman and Morris Kleiner (Madison, WI: Industrial Relations Research Association, 1993).

11. Eaton, "Local Union Control of Participative Programs." In the quantitative analyses, each of the factors identified (initiating the program, seeking educational resources, national union policy) were significant determinants of union control over EI, though a number of other factors were also important.

PART 2 | JAPAN

5

Lean Production at Suzuki and Toyota: A Historical Perspective

JOHN PRICE

In 1985, Dohse, Jürgens, and Malsch in Germany criticized emerging management theories that attributed Japan's success in automobile production to alternative forms of industrial organization, including worker participation in quality circles. They maintained that in Japan, worker "participation occurs in a controlled context in which the topics, goals, and forms of articulation are, for practical purposes, limited to company interests." Despite worker participation in intellectual activities, the authors asserted, autowork in Japan retained a Fordist bias for repetitive work routines dictated by mass, assembly-line production.[1]

This critical perspective was challenged by scholars such as Martin Kenney and Richard Florida: "We contend that the social organization of production in Japan has reached a level of development that is post-Fordist, and we refer to this new and unique social organization of production as 'post-Fordist' Japan. Post-Fordist production replaces the task fragmentation, functional specialization, mechanization, and assembly-line principles of Fordism with a social organization of production based on work teams, job rotation, learning by doing, flexible production and integrated production complexes."[2]

These perspectives bracket the continuing debate in comparative and international labor studies about whether Japanese "lean production" methods represent a form of "management by stress" that exploits workers, or a post-Fordist alternative that taps worker creativity. The debate has proved enduring because lean production has inspired a new production paradigm, both through example, that is, through the spread of successful Japanese automobile transplants in other countries, and through emulation, as non-Japanese automakers adopt many features of Toyotism. Furthermore, the new production model has inspired a resurgent quality movement in North America that bears remarkable similarity to the quality movement in Japan in the 1960s.[3]

Ironically, in Japan itself, automakers and unions are increasingly questioning these same production methods and objectives. In a startling 1992 statement, the Japan Automobile Workers Union (JAW) conceded that the automobile industry was hobbled by "triple sufferings: the employees are exhausted; the companies make only little profit; and the automobile industry is always bashed from abroad." The union's advisor and noted scholar, Shimada Haruo, echoed this refrain: "Workers have lost out due to long working hours, which are unimaginable for workers in advanced countries." Shimada also recognized that Japan's auto unions had somewhere gone amiss: "Trade unions cooperated in this desperate competition for a share. Working hard, they lost their vision about for whom and what growth should be achieved." While not explicitly blaming lean production or Toyotism, these statements are an indication of the serious reflection taking place in Japan about production issues. Are we in danger of adopting a system that has already proved outmoded in Japan?[4]

The present study focuses on the formative period of lean production as it evolved at Suzuki Motors and at Toyota in the 1946–1970 period. The research results from these two case studies uphold the contention of post-Fordist advocates that there was indeed a breach in the Fordist division of labor between conception and execution. On the other hand, the study also confirms that there was no fundamental break with other Fordist norms. This apparent contradiction constitutes what I term the paradox of Japan's production politics: Workers were involved to some degree in conceptual activities, were organized in teams, and rotated jobs; yet, despite these digressions from the American model, lean production as it evolved at Suzuki and Toyota retained a strong bias towards routinized jobs, short cycle times, and task standardization. An understanding of the historical determinants that shaped the production regimes in Japan's automobile industry can help penetrate this paradox, contribute to the current debate, and perhaps facilitate what Christian Berggren calls the amalgamation of "the contributions of lean production and of European human-centered manufacturing to create new syntheses."[5]

There are many differences between Suzuki Motors and Toyota, but for the purposes of this historical discussion I have concentrated on some crucial similarities between the two companies, including the establishment of enterprise unions, the development of a performance-based wage system, the emergence of a common drive towards mass production, and the elaboration of extensive employee involvement programs. These four elements were among the most significant ingredients in the emergence of an integrated production complex that eventually established a new benchmark in Fordist standards. That new benchmark has the following specific features: (a) a Taylorized division of labor based on interchangeabale parts, standardized jobs, and job routines; (b) mass, assembly-line production that can quickly accommodate changes in product lines; (c) an integrated but highly stratified production complex with a small core workforce (mainly male) enjoying the benefits of high wages and tacit job tenure; (d) managerial control over production matters contingent on support from a ''production-first'' union, a performance-based pay and promotion system, and a relative absence of job rules; (e) worker's participation in some conceptual activities via quality and productivity improvement programs; and (f) an ongoing but qualified commitment to automation. These standards share many of the features of conventional Fordism, including routinized jobs and relatively high wages. But other aspects break with the American model—for example, even though workers' have few regulatory rights on the job, the companies have made a relatively high commitment to job tenure.

Examination of the postwar history of Suzuki and Toyota indicates that, like the Fordist regimes in the United States and Canada, lean production is a hegemonic project, containing elements of overt coercion but also elements of compromise. Ideologically speaking, it evolved as a system in which consent to market values was strongly reproduced throughout the workplace.

The Suzuki Regime[6]

Suzuki began as a textile machine manufacturer in the 1920s. It thrived and, like many other industrial companies, switched to armaments manufacturing for the duration of World War II. At war's end it dismissed 2,900 regular employees, the majority of which were women, as well as 800 conscripted workers and 110 Korean prisoners of war. It proceeded to rehire a few hundred workers, nearly all men, to start up peacetime production.

Suzuki first concentrated on textile machinery, but by the early 1950s it had begun to focus on "mo-ped" and motorcycle production.

Workers at Suzuki unionized in 1946 as part of the nationwide labor offensive that accompanied the collapse of the imperial government and the enactment of laws protecting union organization. The labor movement, long suppressed by government and military action, flourished in the new environment as American New Dealers and their Japanese allies implemented democratic reforms and purged prominent war criminals from government and corporate leadership. Union densities shot upwards from 0 to over 50 percent between 1945 and 1949, with a corresponding jump in strike actions as Japanese workers pressed their demands for job security and democratization of management. At Suzuki, the union affiliated with the Shizuoka branch of the Japan Metalworkers Union and won a landmark first contract in August 1948. Under the new agreement Suzuki employees won a closed shop, a union veto over hiring and firing, 50 percent representation on the management council, and the right to automatically and indefinitely extend the contract upon expiration if a new collective agreement could not be concluded. These gains were not bestowed upon workers by a benevolent employer, but wrested from Suzuki through union struggle, including rotating strikes, mass negotiations, and the occupation of factories.[7]

But the political and social climate was already turning against militant trade unions, including the Metalworkers Union. As U.S. policy shifted towards a global preoccupation with containing Soviet and Chinese communism, the policy emphasis in Japan moved from reform to stabilization. In 1947, the U.S. occupation authorities had already reversed their initial prohibition of a national employers' federation, and in 1948 the Federation of Japanese Employers' Associations—Nikkeiren—called for a national campaign focused "On Securing Management Authority." Backed by the U.S. occupation forces and a newly elected conservative government, Nikkeiren coordinated a major counteroffensive against independent unions. Under the guise of anti-communism, employers sought to reassert their control within the workplace, deny workers their newly won rights, and divide the union movement. At Suzuki, the new era began with demands for wage concessions and layoffs, and quickly escalated into unilateral cancellation of the collective agreement. Workers fought back and went on strike to counter management's aggressive moves, but their efforts confronted the same repressive strategy that felled many other independent unions after 1949. With the police and occupation forces mobilized to intimidate union leaders and members, the company sponsored the formation of a second, "scab" union. Supporters of the first union had no legal recourse for countering unfair labor practices—indeed, the tribunals had specific instructions to promote the purging of "radical elements" from the unions. At Suzuki they succeeded. With the union leadership fired and with the establishment of a second union supported by the company, workers had little choice but to accept defeat and return to work.[8]

The new enterprise union granted the concessions Suzuki demanded, the collective agreement was annulled, wages and working conditions deteriorated, and management reimposed its control on the shop floor. The enterprise union's acceptance of this company agenda allowed management to intensify work, lengthen working hours, and generally take advantage of the situation. From 1950 on, the union hitched its wagon to Suzuki's success in the marketplace, acting, at best, as an occasional warning whistle to let managers know when the limits of exploitation were being reached. At worst, the union collaborated in establishing the new production norms and stifling any opposition. With no collective agreement in place at Suzuki until 1967, the enterprise union became an essential ingredient in the emergence of lean production at Suzuki.

Scientific Management and Mass Production at Suzuki

In February 1957, the aging founder of Suzuki, Suzuki Michio, retired and was replaced as president by his son-in-law, Suzuki Shunzo. The younger Suzuki represented the new breed of "rational" managers imbued with the desire to modernize production management. He had joined one of the first delegations to study American management methods organized by the Japan Productivity Center beginning in 1955, and his ascent to the presidency marked the onset of Scientific Management at Suzuki.

On March 1, the new president convoked a general meeting of all employees to announce his management orientation. At the top of his list of five points was the modernization of management methods and a clarification of responsibilities. He also stressed the necessity of improving morale, correctly distributing profits, clarifying the difference between business and personal matters, and insituting a system of rewards and punishments.[9]

At a meeting of departmental and section heads a year later, Suzuki summed up the progress he perceived since the beginning of his stewardship. Managerial reform had been necessary, he stated, because some people still clung to the mistaken belief that the company was a clan. This perception had to be corrected. "The company is a public institution in society," he told his front-line managers. Much progress had been made in instilling modern organizational methods and rationalizing production, but, he warned, further efforts would be needed: "If we don't adopt management methods suitable to the organization of mass production, we will lose to the competition."[10]

As part of this reorientation towards mass production, Suzuki Shunzo made concrete changes in the organizational structure of his corporation. First, he created an executive board to run the day-to-day affairs of the company. The executive board reported only to the board of directors and was composed of the president and senior managing directors. Suzuki next proposed a planning department that reported directly to the executive board and served as the nerve center of the company, responsible for overseeing the managerial revolution. Subcommittees for design and production were created within the planning department, subsequently joined by a third committee to plan for the introduction of quality control. To round out the management structure, department heads joined managing directors in a planning conference that also reported to the executive board. This was mainly a consultative forum that met irregularly to discuss Suzuki's overall plans and any issues related to their implementation. In 1958, the small personnel committee was expanded into a full-scale section to oversee human resource management.[11]

These structural reforms marked a first step in the application of Scientific Management at Suzuki. As the company moved into mass, assembly-line production in 1958, the Taylorist principles installed at the top of the corporate hierarchy began to affect the shop floor. In terms of product development, the new management put its main emphasis on motorcycle production, while also taking the initial steps to develop the production of small vehicles. The inauguration of the first assembly line at Suzuki's motorcyle plant in August 1958 marked the eclipse of craft-based production methods and the dawn of fully Taylorized operations. Chroniclers of Suzuki's history unabashedly reported that under the new assembly-line methods,

> the skills and types of jobs were restricted to a limited number of occupations such as pilot vehicle production, pattern makers, custom tool and equipment fabricators, as well as welding, fitting, and press operations. In many cases, operations such as assembly and machine processing required substantial amounts of labor but not skills and so standardized work operations were implemented.
>
> Work operations were minutely analyzed using work factors, and the time, workers, and routines for the labor process and operations were standardized.
>
> For example, in order to assemble a designated part in a few seconds while the line flowed by, workers on the motorcycle assembly line were subject to a severe mode of production that did not allow

even the slightest of margins. This sort of thing is standard everywhere in the automobile industry but it underscored the necessity of reforming our system of labor management.[12]

In order to install assembly-line production, Suzuki created a job analysis committee in 1957 that undertook the work of delineating the standards for specific jobs. Part of the committee's task was to also assign job descriptions (*shokumu kijutsu sho*) for every employee. But according to the company history, constant expansion created such confusion that, although standard operation routines were successfully insitutionalized, job descriptions were not.[13]

By 1960, Suzuki was producing 150,000 motorcycles a year, compared to less than 6,000 four-wheel vehicles. However, Suzuki had clearly identified automobile production for strategic expansion. In 1959, a typhoon had destroyed some of the main plant facilities and construction of a new plant for vehicle production began immediately. But even this new facility was not enough to accommodate the anticipated expansion of vehicle production, and in early 1961, Suzuki broke ground for a new factory and began to actively recruit new employees. The number of workers jumped to over 2,000 by 1962, compared to just 880 in 1957.[14]

From a Status- to a Performance-Based Wage System

Expanded markets, mass production, and the influx of new employees underlined the haphazard labor relations practices of the past. The company characterized its labor relations up to this time as an individual, status-based system (*mibun seido*). Permanent Suzuki employees (*shain*) had been broadly classified into two categories: office, technical and managerial personnel constituted the white-collar staff (*shokuin*), while production workers were classified as simple laborers (*koin*). Staff members were paid on a monthly basis while laborers were still on a daily wage system. According to Suzuki, "prior to the introduction of the performance-based system, the wage structure included a base-wage determined by length of service, a bonus system based on output, and a series of special allowances."[15]

Production workers faced substantial discrimination in salaries, promotions, transfers and employment opportunities. According to the company history, "These differences in rank even among permanent employees were a problem in terms of unifying the company's thinking and ran counter to building a system of united cooperation. It was an issue which called for rapid reform.''[16]

The first step Suzuki took in abolishing divisions between white- and blue-collar workers was to put all employees on a monthly salary beginning in 1959. The following year, the company took the more substantial step of introducing a uniform, performance-based, incremental salary system. All employees were classified into office, technical and production streams and then ranked on a scale in grades one through twenty. Eight incremental steps were later attached to each grade. An employee's starting rank was fixed according to education level and sex, and promotion up the ladder was thereafter based mainly on yearly performance evaluations by one's supervisor. While the installation of this uniform wage grid nominally ended the age-old distinction between office and plant workers, it did nothing to end gender-based wage discrimination—starting wages for female employees continued to be pegged at lower rates than males with equivalent education levels.[17]

The new wage package was based on two major components, the base wage and the merit supplement. On the surface it would appear that the performance evaluation would only affect the latter component, the merit supplement. In fact, the base wage within each grade varied according to ability, age, length of service, and performance evaluation, while the merit supplement was based exclusively on the performance evaluation. Thus, after the reforms of 1960, annual wage increases negotiated between the union and Suzuki management were neither across-the-board nor percentage increases. Only a small percentage of the increase was automatic and much of the pay raise depended on performance evaluations. In negotiations, the union pushed for maximization of the ''base-up,'' in other words maximizing the basic raise for all, while the company insisted on maximizing its discretionary control over assignment of wage increases.[18]

With the introduction of this performance system, the previous productivity-based wage supplement was gradually phased out. One part of the supplement, a production allowance, was folded into the grades. The second component of the wage supplement, a group-based productivity allowance, was altered to a company-wide system. In other words, workers received a small productivity allowance based on the performance of the company as a whole. Even this wage supplement was eliminated a few years later.[19]

The transformation of the wage system at Suzuki from one based on length of service and status to a uniform performance-based system (also called a merit or incentive system in North American industrial relations parlance) was not an isolated event—many large plants in Japan had instituted a similar system in the 1950s, making performance-based pay the central component of Japan's wage system. Yet, industrial relations specialists in both Japan and North America often describe the wage system in Japanese industry as a "seniority-based" system. In doing so, they ignore the fact that when an employee's career development, wages, and bonuses are largely dependent on favorable evaluations by the supervisor, this dependence has a more fundamental impact on workplace culture than the residual elements of seniority pay. Management naturally views digression from its standards and values in a negative light, and the fact that management can punish nonconformity through negative performance evaluations and consequent lower wages therefore creates a powerful weapon against a labor-oriented workplace culture. It does not take much imagination to realize that worker participation in management—for example, in non-remunerated quality circle activities after shift—may have less to do with some cultural disposition to loyally serve one's company than it does to scoring well on the next performance evaluation.

To the degree this performance-based wage system made workers dependent on the supervisor's evaluation, it also undermined employee support for unions. Whatever general wage increase the union negotiated, its transmission to the individual worker was now directly mediated by the performance evaluation. Thus the strong link between one's paycheck and the union-negotiated pay raise (as is found in the North American automobile industry, for example) was broken.

The organizational revolution that accompanied the assembly line and mass production methods at Suzuki brought modern management structures, standardized job routines, and the performance-based incremental wage standard. None of these developments were unique to Suzuki. Central planning departments and routinized jobs were legion in the U.S. automobile industry, and even the performance-based wage system was not unknown. Having said this, however, two Japan-specific features should be noted: first, job descriptions and classifications were never institutionalized at Suzuki, in contrast to the usual practice in North America; second, Suzuki's performance-based wage structure, while not unusual in large factories in Japan, had been spurned by organized labor in the United States and Canada. As we shall see, the performance-based remuneration system and the absence of job control unionism in Japan's factories would be two crucial factors that permitted managers to constantly change the production system and shape employee involvement.[20]

Production Management and Employee Involvement

At the same time as Suzuki moved from batch to mass production and transformed its labor relations system, it also began to implement a quality improvement program. The embryo of the program was a suggestion system introduced by the planning department and personnel section in 1958. This program faltered early on, however, and the number of suggestions actually declined from 236 in 1958 to 124 in 1959. Rectification of the suggestion system only occurred later as part of the quality movement that gripped the company in the 1960–64 period.[21]

As mentioned previously, a quality control committee had been established within the planning department in 1957. At the time, this committee limited its activities to traditional methods of quality assurance through inspection, sampling, and statistical verification. With expansion in the late 1950s, Suzuki attempted to develop a more systematic training program for its new recruits and also for its supervisory personnel. As part of this program, Suzuki sponsored in-house courses in 1960–1961 on statistical quality control sponsored by the Japan Union of Scientists and Engineers (JUSE). In April 1960 a quality control section was established within the manufacturing division, and that November, Suzuki dedicated the month to quality improvement. To this point, however, quality improvement measures remained piecemeal and technically oriented towards enforcing standardization in engineering, operations, and inspection.[22]

In this same period, however, Suzuki Shunzo became a convert to Japan's quality movement, and in January 1962, he issued a "Presidential Circular Concerning the Promotion of Total Quality Control." The circular emphasized the importance of quality control and the necessity for all employees to thoroughly embrace the ideology of quality. As part of the new program, regulations concerning the supervision of work rules and the implementation of job standards were established and propagated throughout the company. A two-year education program was designed around an in-house journal (*Our Quality Control*) and a slide show, both of which were used in meetings that included every employee. The company also carried out three company-wide quality audits in this period.[23]

The 1962 circular marked the transformation of statistical quality control from a technical engineering method of sampling into a pervasive employee involvement program with significant ideological dimensions. The quality control committee under the planning division was upgraded at this time to full departmental status. As part of its quality plan, it called for the adoption of a company motto that would communicate the principles of the new program and serve as a means of initiating the ever-enlarging number of new hires to the "Suzuki way." The motto, adopted on March 16, 1962, included three parts: "1) Taking a consumer viewpoint, make products with value; 2) Through united co-operation, build a fresh company; 3) Work for improvement of the self, let's always progress with determination."[24]

In the explanatory note accompanying the motto, management articulated its concept of employee involvement:

> The "scientific approach" to management and "democratization" constitute the [company's] foundation. . . . Employees must go all out in accomplishing their work and at the same time, by correctly discerning the organization's horizontal relationships and through united co-operation, work to build a company [workplace] that has fresh appeal and that continues to develop. . . .
>
> The human potential is limitless but the development of that potential is completely dependent on one's own effort and responsibility. The realization of one's maximum potential as an employee, as a human being, must wait for self-improvement through endless effort and study. . . .
>
> However, it is the responsibility of the manager concerned to evoke [in each employee] the consciousness and desire appropriate for members of an organization. We must emphasize that crack human resources are built through effort and leadership.[25]

Thus, apparently innocuous slogans in fact contained strong messages that both reflected and shaped the workplace culture at Suzuki. Democratization, a powerful demand of the labor and popular movements in the early postwar period, had now been appropriated by management. Workers who were hitherto viewed as little more than beasts of burden were now acknowledged as members of the firm, a status formerly accorded only white-collar workers. But this nominal status was not without strings. Workers were assigned the responsibility of maximizing their potential and desire, and supervisors were accorded the role of making sure this happened. In this context, the performance-based wage system represented a powerful tool in management's arsenal of incentives.

The year 1963 was a watershed year for the quality movement at Suzuki. Supervisory personnel were all given fifteen hours of training in quality methods, while production workers and employees in other departments received ten hours. By the end of the year, 1,384 employees had attended quality seminars. According to Suzuki, it was at this point that the quality movement reached critical mass—workers began to spontaneously form quality circles after work hours to improve production methods. A closer reading of the documentation reveals, however, that quality circles were neither spontaneous nor worker-led. In fact, it was lead hands (*hancho*) and foremen who began to meet after hours. These meetings were fully supported by upper management and then used as a nucleus for forming broader groups.

Any thoughts of non-participation among the faint-hearted evaporated when, in November 1963, Suzuki Shunzo announced that the company would compete for the coveted Deming Prize for quality control. To win the Deming Prize, the company had to go through a grueling audit of its entire operations to ensure they conformed to the highest standards of quality control. As the Suzuki history put it, "over the next year, the whole company exerted itself until blood literally stained the floors." Despite these efforts, however, the auditors reserved judgment on Suzuki's quality performance, recommending Suzuki continue its efforts and be reassessed the following year. The company declined the offer, and although management attempted to put the best light on this setback, the quality movement ran into problems at this time.[26]

According to the company, "beginning about 1965, activities in the circles became formalistic. Upon investigation it was learned that the main reason was that we had relied too much on the autonomous nature of the groups—group supervisors or leaders were not paying enough attention to the work." Koguri Tadao, a manager in the main plant production section, put it more bluntly: "When looking for the reasons for stagnation of the circle movement, examination revealed that the major problems were that everything was being left up to the workers themselves, the guidance and concern of the control supervisors had deteriorated considerably, and the circle movement was not being viewed in the right way."[27]

The solution Suzuki seized upon was to introduce a formal evaluation system for quality circle meetings. Each circle was required to submit a written report at the beginning of each month that recorded the number of suggestions, frequency of circle meetings, attendance rate, monetary savings, rank of suggestions, amendments to operation standards, reports given at conferences, reports published, and violations of production standard. Each category was assigned a point value and the results tallied and used in awarding yearly prizes. But this report was kept on file and was also used in the regular performance evaluations, since the names of all members of the groups were submitted with the form. Furthermore, personal self-evaluation forms could be submitted along with the circle report. Formalizing the reporting mechanism not only created a competitive environment between groups but integrated quality circle participation into the performance-based wage and promotion system.[28]

Suzuki points to the evaluation system as the key in reforming its quality program. According to the company, employees became more conscious of quality and worked to uphold production standards without direct supervision. The number of quality circles also expanded from 125 in 1966 to 282 by the end of 1969. That year, Inoguchi Tadayoshi, a lead hand and quality circle leader from Suzuki, mounted the podium at the fifth annual national quality awards ceremony to receive the FQC (Quality Control for

Foremen) prize from J. M. Juran, a U.S. expert on quality with a large following in Japan. The bitter memory of failure in the Deming competition of 1964 was washed away in the public recognition of Suzuki's star employee.

Suzuki had transformed statistical quality control from a sampling method for inspectors to a shop-floor system of employee participation, but questions remain regarding the spontaneous nature of this circle movement. Foremen and lead hands played the dominant role as circle leaders, and, as described above, reports on employee participation in circles were integrated into the performance-based evaluation system. These were indications of a top-down incentive system that compelled employee participation. Commenting on similar evidence at Nissan and Toyota, Michael Cusamano, in his landmark study of Japan's leading automakers, concluded "that stereotypes of decision making in Japanese firms as being 'from the bottom,' that is with initiatives rising upward from the lower ranks of the company, rather than 'top down,' need review."[29]

To this point I have attempted to outline the sequential relationship from Suzuki's conversion to mass production (a reaction to growth and perceived potential for expansion), to the adoption of "Scientific" Management techniques, many of which were based on U.S. industrial engineering methods, to its subsequent adoption of the performance-based wage and promotion system that was prevalent in Japan at the time. These combined factors created the basis for the specific regime at Suzuki: a Taylorist regime, but one distinguished from similar regimes in the United States by the greater degree of management control in the workplace. This heightened control was due to the fact that the enterprise union exercised minimal influence over job rules, and management was able to use the wage system as an instrument to shape employee activities. But these rather despotic features of lean production were accompanied to some degree by improvements in job security, a shortening of the work week, and relatively high wage increases in the 1960s, particularly for male employees. Thus coercion and consent both played their roles in defining a hegemonic regime in which market values became even more solidly embedded than in the conventional Fordist plants of the United States or Canada.[30]

Of course the specific production regime at Suzuki contained other elements besides those discussed above. It developed a stratified production complex with an extensive subcontracting and supplier system, sophisticated inventory control, engineering value analysis, and flexible production techniques that included production leveling. These were all integral to the system of lean production that evolved at Suzuki. But the regime that developed at Suzuki was only one variant of lean production. The prototype regime evolved first at Toyota, from whom Suzuki learned much, particularly through its network of subcontractors. To better understand the evolution of this type of intensified Fordist regime and, in particular, to grasp the specific conditions requisite for its development, it is necessary to examine the Toyota example.[31]

Lean Production at Toyota

Of all the automobile producers in Japan, Toyota has become the most famous for its version of the lean, flexible Fordist regime. Ogawa Eiji, a professor of economics at Nagoya University who studied the Toyota system in the 1970s, emphasized the following features: (1) supermarket-style demand-pull processing; (2) small-lot production and transport; (3) automated quality checking; (4) education regarding constant waste reduction; (5) conservative automation measures; (6) the *kanban* system of production and inventory control; (7) visual control systems (andon); and (8) autonomous management.[32]

Ogawa calls the system "a simple management mechanism" based on "visual management and voluntary participation by workers." Ogawa's own critique of the system, however, highlights some important contradictions in this evaluation. "In terms of self-management," Ogawa observes, "management authority is delegated extensively to supervisors and foremen, but not line workers." Furthermore, those who could not adjust to this system did not remain a part of it. Concretely, this meant that at Toyota, according to Ogawa, "workers having value gaps, ill health, and weak minds became dropouts."[33]

This analytical observation by a production economist is not only confirmed by popular accounts, such as Kamata Satoshi's *Automobile Factory of Despair*, but also by recent academic works and to some extent even by the autoworkers union. These accounts indicate that employees of Toyota and other automakers were put under severe stress through the process of constant rationalization, expanding job tasks, routinization of standard work movements, and long work hours. This led in a number of cases to high accident rates, elevated dropout rates among temporary employees and, in a number of cases, suicide. These are not inconsistent with Ogawa's observations and oblige us to seriously question the claims made on behalf of autonomous workers' participation, with its implicit message that "what was good for Toyota was good for Toyota workers."[34]

History of the Toyota System

From an historical perspective, the relationship between Toyota's labor relations and its production management exhibits many of the same features evident in the history of Suzuki and other automakers. The transformation of an adversarial union into an enterprise labor organization, the introduction of the performance-based wage system, and the top-down development of the quality movement bear similarities which cannot be dismissed as coincidence. Indeed, they constitute essential elements in the operation of lean production.[35]

In the immediate postwar period, Toyota, like many other companies, attempted to switch from military to civilian production. Unlike Suzuki, Toyota had already begun producing four-wheel vehicles in the prewar and wartime period. On 25 September 1945, the American occupation authorities authorized production of trucks for civilian use and Toyota restarted operations, building eighty-two trucks that month—well below wartime production levels which went as high as two thousand units per month.[36]

Workers at Toyota founded their union on 19 January 1946, just as workers at Nissan and Isuzu Motors were also forming unions. Instead of creating an industrial federation, however, the unions affiliated directly with the militant National Congress of Industrial Unions (NCIU). As Communist Party influence grew within the NCIU, the Toyota union decided to withdraw from the militant federation, and it encouraged the Nissan union to do the same. In April 1947, the two unions sponsored the creation of the JAW (Japan Automobile Workers Union or Zen Nihon Jidosha Sangyo Rodo Kumiai, Zenji for short). Despite their disaffiliation from the NCIU, the Toyota and Nissan unions remained relatively independent of management, and both actively fought company attempts to cut salaries and lay off employees during the 1949 employers' offensive. At Toyota, the union compromised by allowing a 10 percent cut in wages in return for a written guarantee that Toyota would not resort to layoffs. As events transpired, Toyota would renege on this agreement.[37]

In January 1950, the Bank of Japan informed Toyota that it would not continue to finance the company unless it took drastic measures to avert bankruptcy, including the creation of an independent sales corporation to handle Toyota marketing, restriction of production to quotas assigned by the sales division, acceptance of a four hundred million yen limit for restructuring, and layoffs of redundant employees. Toyota agreed to these terms and raised the issue of a new sales company with the union at meetings of the management council in early 1950. The union agreed to the separation as long as the company certified the union at the new sales organization and agreed to the same contract as existed at Toyota's main production facilities. By the spring, Toyota was failing to pay its workers their full salaries and it was becoming evident that the company was contemplating layoffs despite ironclad written assurances to the contrary. On 7 April, the union informed Toyota management that it would begin job actions to protest these developments. In response, negotiations within the management council were terminated, collective bargaining began, and on 22 April, Toyota proposed an adjustment package that called for plant closures and the voluntary retirement of 1,600 employees. The union rejected this proposal and in early May applied to the courts for an order prohibiting layoffs, basing its case on a clause in the collective agreement that obliged the company to obtain union approval before laying off any worker.[38]

Toyota contested this, asserting that the perpetual duration clause was void. In the meantime, the confrontation escalated as Toyota employees carried out job-site actions to protest the layoffs. Only 304 trucks came off the line in May, compared to 619 the previous month. Toyota president Toyoda Kiichiro responded with the largely symbolic gesture of resigning his post, thereby taking responsibility for the crisis, but the company pressed ahead with its forced recruitment of early retirees and by 7 June it had garnered 1,760 employees. The union had lost the battle to maintain jobs, and on 10 June it accepted the company's adjustment program (including the closure of two facilities, bringing the tally of job cuts to 2,146). Thereafter, the union shifted its bargaining agenda to focus on winning rehiring rights for those laid off, and preventing the company from punishing the remaining workers by deducting pay for on-the-job protest actions. This 1950 setback and the ensuing divisions within the union created the conditions for the eventual transformation of the Toyota union.

In 1953, both the Nissan and Toyota unions underwent fundamental changes following their defeat in a struggle to win a reformed wage system. That year, the autoworkers' union federation demanded a guaranteed base rate with incremental increases to be based solely on age. Of the two unions, the Nissan unit was the stronger and the company conspired with the employer federation, Nikkeiren, to break the original union and create a new enterprise union. At Toyota, the company also took a hard line, refusing any wage increases and docking workers' pay when they took part in on-the-job protests. Unlike the situation at Nissan, however, Toyota was able to transform the union from the inside. During the 1953 confrontation Hayashida Senkyo, head of the engineering department at the main assembly plant, played a key role in helping to turn the union around and to make sure there would be no repeat of the 1950 struggle.[39]

The company-directed plan to housebreak its union had begun much earlier, however. According to Toyota's official history:

General affairs director Yamamoto Masao and the auditing section chief Yamamoto Yoshiaki devoted single-minded efforts to the transformation of labor relations. In April 1951, their efforts bore fruit with the establishment of a group based mainly among graduates of the technical training school (the predecessor of the Toyota Industrial Training Institute). Through the labor strife that had occurred, these people had come to realize that they were the ones who could make the company better. Realizing that everything depended on people, and painfully aware of the necessity to develop a meeting of the minds through direct contact with employees, Yamamoto and others were out meeting every night with groups they had formed around [the employees'] workplace, educational affiliations, or place of origin. On holidays they would participate in softball tournaments.[40]

This management-inspired caucus conspired to overcome independent unionism, and it was in this process that Toyota's celebrated "humanism" was born. The company history describes its subsequent diffusion: "The idea of having this type of people at the center of things, having their hot blood pulse through the management structure, and having their knowledge reflected in management later spread to our suppliers, sales offices, and regional companies. Moreover, efforts continued to spread the concept of human relations into politics, government, and business." In other words, Toyota understood early on the political and ideological importance of developing people with "correct" ideas, and has worked at it assiduously ever since.[41]

The defeats at Nissan and Toyota in 1953 led to the demise of the autoworkers' union federation in 1954. The Toyota union rejected any further industrial affiliations and, at its 1955 convention, adopted the slogan, "The two wheels of progress are stability in workers' livelihood and the development of the industry and enterprise." A few months later, Toyota union representatives joined an overseas study mission to the United States sponsored by the Japan Productivity Center. This, according to Toyota, "was another indication of the rebirth of the union."[42]

The 1949–1953 transition from adversarial to enterprise unionism at Toyota had several important repercussions. First, the new union abandoned the demands for minimum wage guarantees and an age-based incremental system. In its place, the union accepted a performance- and productivity-based wage system that, as in the case of Suzuki, gave management significant power to set individual wage rates. At Toyota, union influence at the shop-floor level also declined, giving management a clear field to develop the intensified Fordist methods that have become synonymous with the Toyota production system.[43]

Making the Link: The Rise of Toyotism

The rise of Toyota production methods coincided with the decline of adversarialism. Ohno Taiichi, the Toyota engineer credited as the leader in the development of the Toyota production system, provides further evidence for linking enterprise unionism with intensified Fordism. In his treatise on production, Ohno describes the process of deskilling that took place at Toyota in the late 1940s and early 1950s:

> It is never easy to break the machine-shop tradition in which operators are fixed to jobs, for example, lathe operators to lathe work and welders to welding work. It worked in Japan only because we were willing to do it. The Toyota production system began when I challenged the old system.
>
> With the outbreak of the Korean War in June 1950, Japanese industry recovered its vigor. Riding this wave of growth, the automobile industry also expanded. At Toyota, it was a busy and hectic year, beginning in April with a three-month labor dispute over manpower reduction, followed by President Toyoda Kiichiro's assuming responsibility for the strike and resigning. After this, the Korean War broke out.
>
> Although there were special wartime demands, we were far from mass production. We were still producing small quantities of many models.
>
> At this time, I was manager of the machine shop at the Koromo plant. As an experiment, I arranged the various machines in the sequence of machining processes. This was a radical change from the conventional system in which a large quantity of the same part was machined in one process and then forwarded to the next process.
>
> In 1947, we arranged machines in parallel lines or in an L-shape and tried having one worker operate three or four machines along the processing route. We encountered strong resistance among the production workers, however, even though there was no increase in work or hours. Our craftsmen did not like the new arrangements requiring them to function as multi-skilled operators.[44]

In his study of Toyota, Cusumano interviewed Ohno and confirmed this version of events. Through deskilling and technical innovation (the appropriation of craft workers' knowledge, and assigning it to machines), one worker was operating up to seventeen machines at Toyota, although the average was between five and ten in the 1950s. More important, Ohno recognized how union opposition to his schemes could have blocked his experiments. "Had I faced the Japan National Railways union or an American union," he told Cusumano, "I might have been murdered." Ohno's dramatic speculation regarding his own fate only serves to emphasize the significance he attached to the absence of an independent union. It seems reasonable to conclude that the classic Taylorist division of work into conception and execution, with engineers doing the conceiving and machinists executing the orders, was part and parcel of Toyota's emerging system.[45]

Even innovations such as flexible manufacturing, just-in-time inventory, and *kanban* (the use of visual aids to signal upstream suppliers to replenish parts) were not so much deviations from Taylorism as they were ways of implementing Taylorist work methods when production volumes were relatively low. Toyota's small and erratic sales volume would not support the overhead costs of specialized machines and narrowly defined job classifications, but even as workers were flexibly assigned to a variety of tasks, each one of those tasks bore the mark of Taylorist methods. Ohno had actually begun the process of standardizing work methods at Toyota during World War II, when ''skilled workers were being transferred from the production plant to the battlefield and more and more machines were gradually being operated by inexperienced men and women. This naturally increased the need for standard work methods.'' According to Ohno, the standard work sheet detailed cycle time, work sequence, and standard inventory, and this has changed little in the past forty years. ''I have always said that it should take only three days to train new workers in proper work procedures''—a tenet Ohno shared with his kindred spirit, Henry Ford. As Cusumano points out, the standard work methods employed by Ohno were developed with classical Taylorist techniques, including time-and-motion studies.[46]

Finally, a word should be said about the fundamental anti-labor bias of the Toyota system. According to Ohno, the Toyota production system views ''economy in terms of manpower reduction and cost reduction. The relationship between these two elements is clearer if we consider a manpower reduction policy as a means of realizing cost reduction, the most critical condition for a business's survival and growth.'' Ohno traces this propensity to reduce the workforce to Toyota's experience with the 1950 layoffs and labor dispute. ''Immediately after its settlement, the Korean War broke out and brought special demands. We met these demands with just enough people and still increased production. This experience was valuable and, since then, we have been producing the same quantity as other companies but with twenty to thirty percent fewer workers.'' Automation, in this context, must be labor-saving in the sense of reducing the labor force: ''But if it is simply used to allow someone to take it easy, it is too costly.'' This philosophy was the basis for the lean look of Japan's automakers and the extensive subcontracting system which became hallmarks of the newest stage of Fordism.[47]

Toyota's Quality Program

When Nissan won the coveted Deming Prize for quality control in 1960, Toyota was inspired to begin its own formal quality program. Prior to this, Toyota managers had studied quality theory and implemented a suggestion program as early as 1951. Managers such as Ohno, however, resisted traditional quality programs, which emphasized the establishment of extensive sampling and inspection departments. Keeping staffing levels to an absolute minimum was essential, and quality assurance was therefore integrated into line responsibilities.[48]

Toyota began to promote quality circles in 1961, but as with Suzuki's program, the circles initially tended to languish. In the 1968–1971 period, however, a major overhaul occurred as the suggestion program and circle activities were merged. Cusumano describes the change: "Like QC attendance, the practice [of making suggestions] stopped being voluntary after 1960; managers set quotas, kept records of who submitted suggestions and used these data when determining bonuses. Staff superiors also gave out awards for suggestions and criticized workers who failed to contribute their share." Workers at Toyota, as at Suzuki, were obliged to conform to performance standards that were not of their own making. Whereas only 169 circles were functioning in 1967, by 1971 the new ground rules had boosted the number to nearly 2500. By the 1980s, 65 percent of circle activity was directed at quality, control procedures, costs, and efficiency, while 35 percent focused on safety and equipment maintenance. Workers did become involved in conceptual activities and received instruction in the use of Pareto diagrams, cause-and-effect diagrams, check sheets, histograms, dispersion and control charts, and graphs. These were standard tools promoted in most of Japan's quality programs. But we should not exaggerate the significance of worker participation programs under lean production. At Toyota, for example, managers and specialists retained explicit control over the right to introduce major reforms to the system. Given this and the control mechanisms that existed outside the division of labor, worker participation in conceptual activities was limited to fine-tuning the production process, based on the management-defined system and values at Toyota.[49]

Commentary

Stephen Meyers has correctly pointed out that Fordism is in a state of constant revision: "The classic Fordist paradigm existed for less than the decade after the mid-1910s; a more flexible Sloanist variation quickly superseded it in the mid-1920s.'' In a sense, the Toyota system was, and is, another stage in the evolution of the Fordist regime. The specificity of this variation is its advanced flexibility, its intensity, and its institutionalization of the appropriation of workers' knowledge. If Ohno Taiichi put less emphasis on automation in the Toyota system it is because he had the opportunity to flexibly deploy labor unencumbered by the web of work rules that obliged managers in the U.S. to turn to automation as a panacea for low productivity. In Japan, extended managerial control over workers and the labor process, buttressed by enterprise unionism, a manipulative wage system, and motivational education campaigns, allowed Toyota and Suzuki to develop highly efficient production systems.[50]

But these systems hardly disposed with Fordist methods of exploitation. Work remained dictated by the standard work sheet with detailed instructions on cycle times, work movements, and job standards. The time-and-motion expert and industrial engineer remained an integral part of the production complex. What is different, however, is that workers were obliged to participate in the process instead of attempting to subvert, oppose, or passively accept it. The top-down nature of the quality movement at Suzuki and Toyota, with the dominant role played by foremen and lead hands, highlights the limits of worker autonomy in the Japanese automobile industry. Even so, the rise of the quality movement and the participation of workers in defining the labor process does pose certain problems for those who theorize that capitalist management pursues a single-minded approach to deskilling work. Clearly, Ford's advice to his workers to park their brains at the doorway was not the Toyota or Suzuki approach. Lean, flexible Fordism allows substantial input from workers, and a limited but real recomposition of the roles of conception and execution. Workers are allowed to use their brains, but employers assure that the values that guide brainwork are market-driven and conform to capitalist standards, while the performance-based wage system and enterprise unionism help assure that workers conform to management expectations. In this light, lean production represents a distinct, more efficient form of Fordism that, despite worker participation, remains as strongly anti-labor as Ohno Taiichi intended it to be.[51]

History Lessons

As documented here, the pattern of development of lean production at Suzuki and Toyota fundamentally contradicts Martin Kenney and Richard

Florida's latest interpretation of Japan's production history. In their 1993 publication *Beyond Mass Production*, Kenney and Florida develop their theory of the underlying dynamics of Japanese capitalism by

> exploring the origins, historical determinants, and evolution of innovation-mediated production in Japan. The basic contours of the argument are as follows. The rise of innovation-mediated production in Japan was tied in large measure to the specific constellation of political and economic forces acting on Japan in the immediate postwar years. During this crucial period, intense industrial unrest at the point of production, popular struggle, and class conflict unleashed a set of forces that altered the balance of class power or "class accord," produced a distinct pattern of capital-labor accommodation, and resulted in a dramatic restructuring of work and production organization.[52]

Key to this early period were the struggles for production control (1946–47) which, according to Kenney and Florida, "essentially, established the roots of the Japanese system of team-based work organization." The authors recognize that the early "laborist" period was superseded by a managerial offensive in 1949, but they contend that "many of the characteristics now interpreted as indicating capital's control of labor were initially labor demands. Like the postwar accords of the United States and Western European countries, only later were these demands integrated into the logic of capitalist accumulation." This postwar accommodation was reflected in the new system of industrial relations that "revolved around guaranteed long-term employment, a seniority-based wage system, and enterprise unionism for the core of the labor force."[53]

This rather agile attempt to reconstruct Japan's labor history finds little substantiation in fact. As indicated in the Suzuki and Toyota experience, labor's demands in the early postwar period included an egalitarian wage system based mainly on age or seniority; union security through perpetual extension clauses in union contracts (contracts automatically and indefinitely rolled over in the absence of a new contract); a labor veto over hiring and firing; and equal representation within management councils. Kenney and Florida contend such rights were later integrated into the capitalist order, but such an interpretation obscures the fundamental transformation that occurred in that process. The new wage system was based primarily on performance, not seniority or age; union contracts were either done away with, as at Suzuki, or generally so diluted that they played only a minimal role in regulating labor relations; unions lost any control over employment levels, and management councils were substantively downgraded to consultative bodies with few decision-making powers. In many cases, management-dominated enterprise unions replaced the independent unions of the earlier period. In all these ways, the postwar "accord" in Japan was quite unlike the accords in Europe and the United States. In the latter cases, the accords represented compromises worked out when labor was, relatively speaking, on the rise, whereas in Japan, for historical reasons, the postwar compromise was based on labor's defeat and decline.[54]

Furthermore, while Florida and Kenney contend that modern worker participation and team-based work organization emerged from the production-control period of 1946–1947, the authors provide no evidence to back up this claim and none emerges from the Suzuki or Toyota stories. In fact, the opposite appears to be the case. The quality circle movement seems to represent the major component of worker participation, and it only consolidated in the late 1960s. This was well after lean production as a system had been defined by engineers such as Ohno Taiichi who, in his own account, documented that many of his innovations were resisted by Toyota workers. It would seem reasonable to hypothesize that worker participation at Toyota or Suzuki was not based on incorporating workers' aspirations but on reproducing and refining the cost-reduction-at-any-price values of lean production. In the end, the historical conditions that gave rise to this system were not an accommodation between labor and management, but the general poverty of the Japanese population and the consequent low sales volume, which forced automakers to adapt mass production methods to small-scale production levels.

Theoretical Issues

Understanding the paradox of Japan's production politics requires a multi-dimensional understanding of employer control. Control of conceptual activities was a significant aspect of that control, as labor process theory correctly emphasizes. But worker participation in conceptual activities under lean production, no matter how limited, poses a challenge to those who would stress the primacy of employer control of the labor process. Burawoy and others have pointed out the limits of such a perspective and stressed the importance of taking a much more comprehensive approach to labor issues. This study confirms Burawoy's point. As significant as it may be, the labor process is only one component of the overall process of production and we must be prepared to look at other aspects, including national variations in the forms of valorization, in the relations of production, and in what Burawoy terms the relations in production. This allows us to begin to explore how social relations are reproduced through the mechanisms of both consent and coercion. In this historical study, emphasis has been placed on the wage structure and enterprise unions, but many other variables have shaped Japan's factory regimes. Issues such as gender, region, status, and culture, while not examined here, are also fundamental to understanding how capital in Japan was able to reproduce the social relations necessary for continued and accelerated accumulation under lean production.[55]

Notes

1. See Knuth Dohse, Ulrich Jürgens, and Thomas Malsch, "From 'Fordism' to 'Toyotism'? The Social Organization of the Labor Process in the Japanese Automobile Industry," *Politics and Society* 14, no. 2 (1985): 142.

2. Martin Kenney and Richard Florida, "Beyond Mass Production: Production and the Labor Process in Japan," *Politics and Society* 16, no. 1 (Mar. 1988): 122.

3. The debate about Toyotism was originally integrated with the debate about flexible specialization sparked by Michael Piore and Charles Sabel's work, *The Second Industrial Divide* (New York: Basic Books, 1984). For an early review of the literature and an introduction to the scope of the debate see Stephen Wood's essay, "The Transformation of Work," in *The Transformation of Work*, ed. Stephen Wood (London: Unwin Hyman, 1989), 1–43, and Martha MacDonald, "Post-Fordism and the Flexibility Debate," *Studies in Political Economy* 36 (autumn 1991), 177–201. The debate has increasingly focused on Toyotism as it evolved in Japan and internationally. The literature is rapidly expanding but some central works in English include the articles by Dohse, Jürgens, and Malsch, and Kenney and Florida cited in notes 1 and 2; James Womack, Daniel Jones, and Daniel Roos, *The Machine that Changed the World* (New York: Rawson Associates, 1990); Martin Kenney and Richard Florida, *Beyond Mass Production* (New York: Oxford University Press, 1993); Mike Parker and Jane Slaughter, *Choosing Sides: Unions and the Team Concept* (Boston: South End Press, 1988); Koji Morioka, ed., "Japanese Capitalism Today: Economic Structure and the Organization of Work," a dedicated edition of *The International Journal of Political Economy* 21, no. 3 (fall 1991); David Robertson, James Rinehart, and Chris Huxley, " 'Kaizen' and Canadian Auto Workers," *Studies in Political Economy* 39 (autumn 1992); Christian Berggren, *Alternatives to Lean Production* (Ithaca: ILR Press, 1992).

4. Confederation of Japan Automobile Workers' Unions, "Japanese Automobile Industry in the Future," policy statement (Tokyo, 1992), 1, 31–35. Shimada today is less inclined to see enterprise unions in a positive light. He still tends to see the issues from an organizational perspective (Japan's enterprise unions are unique) but he has at least recognized that they have problems that go beyond organizational issues. He postulates that they have become captive to an "industrial culture," "And, second, they are mentally restricted by the narrow scope of enterprise-level labor-management relations." See Shimada Haruo, "Japan's Industrial Culture and Labor-Management Relations," in *The Political Economy of Japan, Volume 3: Cultural and Social Dynamics*, ed. Shumpei Kumon and Henry Rosovsky (Palo Alto, CA: Stanford University Press, 1992), 267–291.

5. Berggren, *Alternatives to Lean Production*, 17.

6. This study is part of a larger research project on postwar industrial relations in Japan.

The main sources are primary materials in Japanese, supplemented with fieldwork and secondary works in both English and Japanese. All translations are mine. Unless otherwise indicated, management information about Suzuki is based on two corporate histories both commissioned by Suzuki. They are *40 Nen Shi* [40 Years in the Making] (Hamana Gun: Suzuki, 1960) and *50 Nen Shi* [50 Years in the Making] (Hamana Gun: Suzuki, 1970).

7. On the history of Japanese labor relations in this period see Andrew Gordon, *The Evolution of Labor Relations in Japan: Heavy Industry, 1853–1955* (Cambridge: Harvard University Press, 1985), 329–366. The history of the Suzuki local is contained in Shizouka Ken Rodo Undo Shi Hensan linkai, ed., *Shizuoka Ken Rodo Undo Shi* [A History of the Labor Movement in Shizuoka Prefecture], (Shizuoka: Shizuoka Ken Rodo Kumiai Hyogikai, 1984), 292–295. The entire 1948 collective agreement is reproduced in Shizuoka Ken Rodo Undo Shi Hensan linkai, ed., *Shizuoka Ken Rodo Undo Shi, Shiryo (Ka)* [Documents, Vol. I: The History of the Shizuoka Labor Movement], (Shizuoka: Shizuoka Ken Rodo Kumiai Hyogikai, 1981), 399–402.

8. Gordon, *The Evolution of Labor Relations in Japan*, 367–393. For a detailed study of the interaction between corporate and government elites see Howard Schonberger, *Aftermath of War* (Kent, OH: Kent University Press, 1989). This account of the Suzuki strike is based on the original union's history, Moto Zen Kinzoku Roso Suzuki-shiki Shokki Bukai hen, *Sogi Kiroku* [Chronicle of the Dispute], (Hamamatsu, 1951) as reproduced in Shizuoka Ken Rodo Kumia Hyogi Kai hen, *Shizuoka Ken Rodo Undo Shi, Shiry (Ka)* [A History of the Labor Movement in Shizuoka Prefecture, Documents, Vol. 2], (Shizuoka, 1981), 351–364.

9. Suzuki, *50 Nen Shi*, 54.

10. Ibid., 124.

11. Ibid., 54.

12. Ibid., 440–441.

13. Ibid., 443.

14. Suzuki Jidosha Kogyo Rodo Kumiai Shi Henshu linkai, ed., *Niju Go Nen Shi* [A 25 Year History], (Hamana Gun: Suzuki Jidosha Kogyo Rodo Kumiai, 1976), 250. This is the Suzuki union's own history.

15. Suzuki, *50 Nen Shi*, 443.

16. Ibid., 442.

17. Upon reflection, the union's leaders at the time considered that Suzuki was among the first in the region to abolish distinctions between pay systems for blue- and white-collar workers. The discriminatory wage policy that paid women less than men began around 1956 and continued after the 1959–1962 reforms. See Suzuki Kumiai, *Niju Go Nen Shi*, 245, 250.

18. It was not possible to obtain historical documentation on the evolution of the relative weight of the components of the wage system. According to officials at Suzuki, however, of the 8,500 yen average monthly increase negotiated for 1988, only 2,610 was automatic or part of the "base-up." Nearly 70 percent (5,890 yen) was based on performance evaluations or manageral discretion.

19. Ohnoda Itsuhiko, secretary of the Suzuki union at the time, recalled that Suzuki management also attempted at this time to introduce the Scanlon plan to calculate summer and winter bonus rates. The Scanlon plan was a profit-sharing scheme developed by a former steelworker, Joseph Scanlon, and endorsed by the United Steelworkers of America in the 1950s. While later discarded, Suzuki's attempt to introduce the plan is another indication that management was studying American management techniques.

20. On performance-based wages in North America, see Bernard Ingster, "Appraising Hourly Performance," Milton Rock, ed., *Handbook of Wage and Salary Administration* (New York: McGraw-Hill, 1972), 5–27.

21. Suzuki, *50 Nen Shi*, 447.

22. See Suzuki, *50 Nen Shi*, 332–335, for details on standardization.

23. Ibid., 326.

24. Ibid., 74–75.

25. Ibid.

26. Ibid., 78.

27. Ibid.; Koguri Tadao, "Providing Incentives to the QC Circle through an Evaluation System," Asian Productivity Organization, *Japan Quality Control Circles* (Tokyo: Asian Productivity Organization, 1972), 168.

28. The assessment form is contained in Tadao, "Providing Incentives to the QC Circle," 170.

29. Michael Cusumano, *The Japanese Automobile Industry* (Cambridge: Harvard University Press, 1985), 379.

30. Suzuki was rare among Japan's automakers in that it allowed women to work on the line. However, wage discrimination was explicit in lower starting rates and women did not advance up the wage scale as quickly as men.

31. Given the focus and limitations of this article, I have not concentrated on the other elements of Suzuki's production system. Suffice it to say that Suzuki developed many of the features of flexible production that have become hallmarks of the new regimes. For details see Suzuki, *50 Nen Shi*, 292–324. The peripheral workforce, a large proportion of which are women, was not the subject of this study. An English-language source is Norma Chalmers, *Industrial Relations in Japan: The Peripheral Workforce* (London: Rutledge, 1989).

32. Eiji Ogawa, *Modern Production Management: A Japanese Experience* (Tokyo: Asian Productivity Organization, 1984), 127–128. This is a translation of Ogawa's original work, *Gendai no Seisan Kanri* (Tokyo: Nihon Keizai Shimbun, 1982).

33. Ogawa, *Modern Production Management*, 130.

34. Kamata Satoshi, *Jidosha zetsubo Kojo: aru Kisetsu Ko no Nikki* [The Automobile Factory of Despair: Diary of a Seasonal Worker] (Tokyo: Gendai Shuppan Kai, 1973). Satoshi's account of life in an auto plant was translated and published in English as *Japan in the Passing Lane* (New York: Pantheon, 1982). Relevant academic works are cited throughout the notes and the union statements are cited in note 4.

35. For information on Toyota I have used the company's own history, Toyota Jidosha Kabushiki Kaisha, ed., *Sozo Kagiri Naku, Toyota Jidosha Goju Nen Shi* [Unlimited Creativity, 50 Years of Toyota Automobiles Ltd.], (Toyota City: Toyota, 1987), as well as other secondary sources including Yamamoto Kiyoshi, *Jidosha Sangyo no Roshi Kankei* [Labor Management Relations in the Automobile Industry] (Tokyo: Tokyo Daigaku Shuppan Kai, 1981); Totsuka Hideo and Hyodo Tsutomu Hen, *Roshi Kankei no Tenkan to Sentaku* [Transition and Choice in Industrial Relations] (Tokyo, Nihon Hyoron Sha, 1991), and Cusamano, *The Japanese Automobile Industry*.

36. Toyota, *Sozo Kagiri Naku*, 191.

37. Cusumano, *The Japanese Automobile Industry*, 144; Toyota, *Sozo Kagiri Naku*, 217.

38. Toyota, *Sozo Kagiri Naku*, 219. The banks also demanded that Suzuki lay off hundreds of employees in 1949. Further research into their role during the 1949 crisis is necessary to fully understand the pivotal position finance capital played in this period. The clause the union cited in court was common to many contracts in the 1946–49 period when the labor movement was on the rise.

39. Some details of the Nissan battle are contained in Michael Cusumano, *The Japanese Automobile Industry*, 137–185. See also Toyota, *Sozo Kagiri Naku*, 308.

40. Toyota, *Sozo Kagiri Naku*, 309.

41. Ibid., 309–310. Based on research by Nomura Masami, Totsuka and Hyodo include

a section on Toyota's "human touch" in their book *Roshi Kankei no Tenkan to Sentaku*, 166–173.

42. Toyota, *Sozo Kagiri Naku*, 309.

43. According to Nomura Masami, the Toyota union questioned the wage system in 1975 but nothing ever came of their concerns. See Totsuka and Hyodo, *Roshi Kankei no Tenkan to Sentaku*, 140–141.

44. Ohno Taiichi, *The Toyota Production System* (Cambridge, MA: Productivity Press, 1988), 10–11. This is a translation of Ohno's original Japanese book, *Toyota Seisan Hoshiki* (Tokyo: Daiyamondo, 1978).

45. Cusumano, *The Japanese Automobile Industry*, 272, 306. The historical insights Ohno affords us deserve further comment and research. It is clear that, despite the absence of craft unions in Japan, machinists at Toyota had embraced the principle of "one machine-one machinist" so highly valued and guarded by machinists' unions in Great Britain, the U.S., and Canada. Whether the union at Toyota failed to protect this tradition because it lacked a craft perspective or because adversarialism was declining is not clear.

46. Ohno, *The Toyota Production System*, 21–22; Cusumano, *The Japanese Automobile Industry*, 271–273.

47. Ohno, *The Toyota Production System*, 53, 68.

48. Totsuka and Hyodo, *Roshi Kankei no Tenkan to Sentaku*, 146.

49. Cusumano, *The Japanese Automobile Industry*, 336, 355, 357; Totsuka and Hyodo, *Roshi Kankei no Tenkan to Sentaku*, 146–147. Cusumano and Totsuka and Hyodo offer the same estimates of the proportion of circle activities devoted to particular issues, based on Toyota sources.

50. Stephen Meyer, "The Persistence of Fordism: Workers and Technology in the American Automobile Industry, 1900–1960," in *On the Line, Essays in the History of Auto Work*, ed. Nelson Lichtenstein and Stephen Meyer (Urbana: University of Illinois Press, 1989).

51. Harry Braverman, *Labor and Monopoly Capitalism* (New York: Monthly Review Press, 1974) presents a theory of management control that cannot easily accommodate the Japanese model.

52. Kennedy and Florida, *Beyond Mass Production*, 23–24.

53. Ibid., 28–29.

54. It would, however, be wrong to therefore interpret Japan's production politics as simply a return to the despotism of coercive capitalism. High wages and tacit job security for core workers did emerge in Japan and become part of the postwar order. These aspects provided the essential underpinnings for a hegemonic regime, that is, one that was based on consent as well as coercion.

55. Paul Thompson provides a summary of labor process theory and current debates in his book, *The Nature of Work* (London: Macmillan, 1989). See Michael Burawoy, *The Politics of Production* (London: Verso, 1985).

6

The Transformation of Japanese Industrial Relations: A Case Study of the Automobile Industry

HIDEO TOTSUKA

It is commonly held that labor relations in Japan's auto industry conforms to a single model of enterprise unionism. This essay presents an alternative to that popular perception, based on the findings of case studies I undertook with a group of researchers several years ago on Companies A and B, both of which are well known auto manufacturers in Japan.[1]

In the first section I will describe the research methodology which, in my view, conditions the significance and limitations of our work. In order to clarify our position, I will also outline the ways in which our approach is different from the conventional methods adopted in Japan. I will then summarize some of the results of our research, with particular emphasis on those findings which demonstrate that there is no uniform, fixed model of industrial relations in the Japanese auto industry. Discussion of the varied structures and procedures of enterprise unionism leads, in turn, to the related issue of how workers respond to the Japanese manufacturing system. Thus far, two opposing views have been expressed about this question, one asserting that their responses can and should be explained mainly by factors of economic and social coercion, and the other attaching importance to positive commitment on the workers' part. Although our own findings on this question are very limited, I will present some tentative conclusions.

In the final section, I will address the ongoing transformation of industrial relations in the Japanese auto industry. For several years now, there has been considerable discussion among top corporate executives and among trade union leaders concerning the need to reform the Japanese management system and, therefore, Japanese industrial relations. The direction this reform might take will become an important focus of investigation from now on; this essay will conclude with some initial speculations on the possibilities for the future.

Research Methodology

Since the auto industry established its position in the 1970s as one of the key industries in Japan, quite a few researchers have tried to investigate the realities of management and labor relations on the automobile assembly lines. However, most of the requests made to automakers and their enterprise unions for their cooperation in such research have been denied. The negative response seems to have been due, in part, to the fact that the very severe competition among automakers prompts them to be secretive. But the negative reaction seems to have also been motivated by political and social considerations. On the whole, company managers and union leaders have been reluctant to allow outside researchers—particularly those holding critical views of Japan's industrial relations system—to conduct case studies on their own shop floors. The conditions under which Japanese researchers must work are therefore quite different from those in western countries, where researchers can organize their fieldwork relatively more easily. Given the difficulty gaining access to the shop floors of the auto industry, Japanese researchers have had to rely on some unorthodox methodologies, including the following:

1. Participatory observation and reportage of life on the assembly line by actually getting employed and working as an assembly worker. The labor shortage which grew serious during the period of high economic growth gave ambitious intellectuals the opportunity to get employed on a temporary basis and make firsthand observations of how the assembly lines were run. Satoshi Kamata's renowned work was based on his own experience and observations as a *kikanko* (a worker employed for a certain period—six months in Kamata's case).[2]

2. Research based mainly on interviews with autoworkers living in the vicinity of an auto plant, or in a "company town." Researchers who use this methodology approach their interviewees at random or through various social networks, and gather information about the experience and opinions of individual workers.[3]

3. Research based mainly on collaboration with union activists working on the assembly line, and also of ex-managers who have already left the company. Activists collaborating in research projects of this sort do so by keeping written records of their shop-floor observations, and also by systematically collecting the pamphlets and leaflets circulated by management and the union.[4]

4. Research based mainly on examination of written documents submitted to court as evidence in cases involving militant workers. In the Japanese context, where formal grievance procedures are generally weak, this approach has sometimes proved effective.

I would say that, in contrast to these approaches, the methodology we used in our research project was rather more orthodox. We approached both the management and the union from the "front door," and, very fortunately, our request for access to the shop floor was granted, though in a limited way, by Companies A and B and their enterprise unions. At the same time, we also tried to identify the written as well as unwritten rules of industrial relations *actually at work* in the enterprise, at the company, plant, and shop-floor levels. We succeeded in organizing interviews with plant managers, foremen, team leaders, and also with branch union officers and shop stewards during their on-duty time. Although the research facilities offered to us were still limited—five days at Company A and only three days at Company B—we were the first team of outside researchers to conduct such interviews inside the plants of Japanese automakers. We took advantage of this rare opportunity as best we could, trying to gather the information necessary for clarifying the following points, among others:

1. The plant-level industrial-relations procedures which facilitates the so-called flexible and efficient utilization of labor power.
2. The ways in which managerial activities—in particular, those pertaining to production management and work organization—are carried out, and the method used to monitor work efficiency on the shop floor.
3. How enterprise unions in the auto industry are governed internally—in particular, what roles shop stewards and branch union officers perform within the union.

Procedures for Handling Production and Manning Problems

As many observers have pointed out, the current structure of industrial relations in Japan, particularly at big private corporations, is characterized by the predominance of labor-management consultation. As table 6.1 demonstrates, the consultative machinery that defines the collaborative relationship between labor and management was well established in large unionized firms by the 1970s. However, we should not forget that these consultative bodies came into existence as a historical product, and also that, as indicated in table 6.2, even today the scope and depth of consultation can vary significantly from one company to another, depending on various factors.[5]

When our research team conducted fieldwork in the mid-1980s, both Company A and Company B were pursuing much the same production system, now widely known as "lean production." Nonetheless, we found the structure of industrial relations at the two automakers to be considerably different from each other.

At Company A, the union exercised a significant degree of influence on management decisions about production and manning. The union and management not only held well-organized joint consultation sessions on a monthly basis at the enterprise level, but also at the plant level, and often at the departmental level as well. In these meetings the parties discussed such issues as the production schedule, the actual working hours (including overtime and holiday work), and the manning levels—that is, the question of how many workers were to be transferred to other shops on a temporary basis, and the question of how many were to be redeployed to other shops or other plants on a more permanent basis. The issue of greatest concern to the union was working hours, especially decisions on overtime. As a matter of fact, the union at Company A was not particularly successful in shortening the total working hours well below those at Company B; but it is quite noteworthy that this very consultation procedure was so fully respected by the management of Company A that managers were unable to enforce the work schedule of their own preference without first getting the consent of the union branch officers. I find this situation quite similar to what I found at British Leyland's Cowley Body Plant towards the end of the 1970s, what is called "mutuality."[6]

Company B also had a joint labor-management consultation process that was supposed to take up production and manning problems. But these matters were brought up only for explanation by management, not for mutual discussion. Unlike their counterparts in Company A, the managers of Company B felt free to order their workers to work overtime, often with very short notice of only two or three hours before the end of shift. Whenever production activities were falling behind the day's production schedule, they could issue orders for overtime without having any prior consultation with the union.

As table 6.3 demonstrates, the consultation mechanisms at work in

TABLE 6.1
Proportion of Establishments with Joint Consultation Body

Size of company / Union presence	Total			For companies with two or more establishments						For companies with only one establishment		
		With consultation body	Without consultation body		With consultation body	Both at company and establishment levels	Only at company level	Only at establishment level	Without consultation body		With consultation body	Without consultation body
1972 total	100.0	62.8	37.1	100.0	68.5	24.3	28.5	15.7	31.5	100.0	49.8	49.9
1977 total	100.0	70.8	29.2	100.0	75.8	47.5	25.3	3.0	24.2	100.0	53.2	46.8
5,000 or more	100.0	92.6	7.4	100.0	92.6	69.1	23.0	0.5	7.4	n.a.	n.a.	n.a.
1,000–4,999	100.0	85.7	14.3	100.0	86.0	64.3	18.9	2.8	14.0	100.0	62.9	37.1
300–999	100.0	73.0	27.0	100.0	73.1	40.7	29.2	3.2	26.9	100.0	72.2	27.8
100–299	100.0	54.7	45.3	100.0	58.2	25.6	28.0	4.6	41.9	100.0	50.8	49.2
With labor union	100.0	82.8	17.2	100.0	85.9	56.2	27.6	2.1	14.1	100.0	68.1	31.9
Without labor union	100.0	40.3	59.7	100.0	43.9	20.2	18.1	5.8	56.1	100.0	33.1	66.9
1984 total	100.0	72.0	28.0	100.0	74.4	51.5	20.6	2.3	25.6	100.0	65.1	34.9
5,000 or more	100.0	94.2	5.8	100.0	94.2	79.3	13.9	1.0	5.8	100.0	100.0	—
1,000–4,999	100.0	83.6	16.4	100.0	83.5	67.1	15.7	0.7	16.5	100.0	88.4	11.6
300–999	100.0	74.4	25.6	100.0	74.5	44.0	26.2	4.3	25.5	100.0	73.7	26.3
100–299	100.0	57.6	42.4	100.0	52.3	24.7	24.7	2.9	47.7	100.0	63.0	37.0
With labor union	100.0	87.9	12.1	100.0	87.9	62.0	24.2	1.7	12.1	100.0	88.1	11.9
Without labor union	100.0	40.7	59.3	100.0	40.5	25.2	11.5	3.8	59.5	100.0	41.1	58.9

Source: Policy Planning and Research Department, Minister's Secretariat, Ministry of Labor, ed., 1985.
Note: The figures do not include "unknown."

TABLE 6.2

Scope and Depth of Consultation, 1989

		Subject matter taken up									
		Taken up		Explanation only		Opinion listened to		Discussion		Mutually agreed	
	Subject matter	a	b	a	b	a	b	a	b	a	b
Matters relating to management	Basic management strategy	56.5	48.2	79.0	74.3	8.5	8.4	10.9	13.8	1.6	3.5
	Basic production and sales plan	59.5	53.9	73.2	50.6	11.6	14.6	13.4	30.7	1.9	4.0
	Reorganization of company structure	59.6	48.0	60.8	62.9	13.4	11.8	19.7	18.6	6.1	6.8
	Introduction of new technology	55.8	49.3	46.5	22.2	15.9	24.7	34.1	45.6	3.4	7.5
Matters relating to personnel management	Standard of hiring and deployment	50.9	44.7	47.4	29.9	18.2	27.9	27.4	33.7	7.0	8.4
	Transfer and work on loan	58.3	45.1	30.5	24.6	16.4	21.1	37.7	34.9	15.4	19.4
	Layoff, redundancy, and dismissal	61.9	51.2	9.2	14.3	5.9	14.8	58.7	48.1	26.2	22.8
Matters relating to working conditions	Change in work shift, etc.	79.2	74.5	7.5	18.6	7.8	20.0	64.3	44.1	20.4	17.3
	Worktime, holiday, and vacation	85.8	89.8	7.0	12.9	3.9	20.0	61.6	46.4	27.5	20.7
	Health and safety on the shopfloor	85.6	84.2	11.4	11.7	17.5	18.5	61.4	62.8	9.7	7.0
	Retirement system	69.9	67.0	9.4	20.9	3.4	14.0	55.4	33.8	31.8	31.2
	Wages, bonuses	69.9	65.1	7.6	35.2	2.1	9.5	57.7	41.8	32.6	13.5
	Retirement allowance, pension	65.7	61.4	10.3	30.2	2.1	12.7	54.2	40.0	33.3	17.2
Other matters	Education and training plan	63.3	66.6	47.8	28.4	19.2	18.0	25.6	45.9	7.3	7.7
	Welfare facilities	81.5	80.1	16.1	12.2	17.4	26.4	57.0	55.3	9.5	6.1
	Cultural and sports activities	72.8	73.7	20.5	8.8	19.9	26.1	50.8	57.6	8.9	7.5

Source: Ministry of Labor, *Survey on Communication between Management and Workers,* 1989.

Note: a = companies with union recognition, b = companies without union recognition. All numbers expressed in percentages.

TABLE 6.3
Scope and Depth of Consultation at Companies A and B, 1973 and 1983

Subject matter	Company A		Company B	
	1973	1983	1973	1983
Rationalization of production and office work	Consultation at level A	Consultation at levels A, B & C	Report & explanation at levels A & B	Prior report & explanation at level A
Production schedule	Consultation at levels A, B & C	Consultation at levels A, B & C	Report & explanation at levels A & B	Prior report & explanation at levels A, B & C
Equipment planning	Consultation at levels A, B & C	Consultation at levels A, B & C	Report & explanation at levels A & B	Prior report & explanation at levels A & C
Introduction of new machinery and new technology	Consultation at levels A, B & C	Consultation at levels A, B & C	—	Prior report & explanation at level A; & ex post facto report at levels A & C
Measurement of productivity	Consultation at levels A, B & C	Consultation at levels A, B & C	—	—
Standard for personnel change	Consultation at levels A, B & C	Consultation at levels A, B & C	Mutual agreement at level A	Prior report & explanation at level A

Source: Federation of Japanese Auto-Workers' Unions, *Survey on the Welfare Facilities and Related Matters*, 1975 and 1985, as quoted by Hiroshi Ueda, "Formation of Flexibility and Industrial Relations in Autoparts Makers," in *Kikan Keizai Kenkyu* (Osaka City University, 1993).
Note: Level A = company level; level B = plant level; level C = shop level.

Companies A and B were different both in terms of scope and depth. It should be mentioned that at Company B the "measurement of productivity"—that is, the formula for measuring productivity gains—was not regarded as a subject for consultation, report, or explanation. In other words, the formula for calculating the production bonus at Company B was unilaterally determined and put into effect by management.

These findings indicate that there is no single labor relations procedure in the Japanese auto industry; rather, there is a spectrum of procedures by which management implements their lean and flexible production system. Where in that spectrum would the two procedures at companies A and B fall? Much more needs to be clarified before that question can be definitively answered, but it appears that these two systems may represent the extreme cases, with a majority of the industry's other firms falling somewhere between the two.[7]

Contrasting Types of Enterprise Unions

It is well known that the enterprise union is the basic institution of trade unionism in Japan, particularly in big companies in the private sector. It should be kept in mind, however, that there are other types of union organization, such as general unions and occupational unions. Moreover, the predominance of enterprise unions in Japan does not necessarily mean that there is only one enterprise union in each big company. In quite a few enterprises we find militant unions which, despite having been reduced to minority status, still remain active. In Company A, one such left-leaning minority union still survives; Company B, in contrast, has never had such a minority union of militant workers.[8]

The structure and governance of the major enterprise unions at Companies A and B has been described elsewhere by one of the members of our research team. What I want to emphasize here is as follows: although the two enterprise unions are similar to each other in terms of their formal structure, the way in which each is governed is significantly different on at least the following two counts.[9]

First, the breadth, capabilities, and resources of union leadership at Company A were considerably greater than at Company B. There were several indications of this quantitative difference. The total number of branch officers and shop stewards in a typical plant of Company A was much larger—some three or four times so—than in a comparable plant of Company B. Generally speaking, branch union officers at Company A also had more years of experience as union officers than their counterparts at Company B. Moreover, union officers at Company A were given greater facilities for union activity during on-duty hours.

The second and more important difference concerns the role of supervisors. The union at Company A had been intensively organizing shop-floor supervisors such as general foremen (*kakaricho*) and foremen (*kumicho*). These shop-floor supervisors had formed societies of their own, such as the General Foremen's Society (Kakaricho-kai) and the Foremen's Society (Kumicho-kai), which explicitly encouraged their members to work for both the company and the union. They emphasized, for instance, that ''We love our company, and so do we our union,'' and that ''All the general foremen should have the spirit to work as permanent shop stewards.'' These same mottoes were frequently emphasized by the union during our research. However, we could not find similar supervisors' societies in Company B.

These findings indicate that in Japan we have contrasting types of enterprise unionism which are distinguished by something other than political ideology (indeed, the union leaders at Companies A and B were regarded by many as uniformly right-leaning). What makes these unions different is the role of supervisors. What I call a Type 1 enterprise union is one in which supervisors do not occupy any important union leadership positions. I presume that the union at Company C, on which we have collected a limited amount of information, may be classified under this heading. The union at Company C cannot exert significant influence on management through the consultative process because, having very few workers of the supervisory class as officers, the union can gather only a limited amount of information. This perhaps explains why an enterprise union of this type seems to place greater importance on the collective bargaining machinery than on the consultation machinery.

An enterprise union of what I call Type 2 is one in which supervisors serve in important union leadership positions, as was the case at both Companies A and B. But Type 2 unions can be further differentiated into sub-types, depending on whether these supervisors identify themselves as primarily allied with management, or with the union. In fact, the pivotal question in the history of Japan's labor movement turns on this issue of how the supervisors ally themselves within the firm. In this context, the real nature of enterprise unionism depends very much on the social character of the supervisory class and its relationship with the union. To discuss enterprise unions without examining the behavior of shop-floor supervisors and the social relations surrounding them is to commit a cardinal error of over-generalization.

Different Approaches to Industrial Engineering

Corporate managers who attach importance to the principles of "scientific management" have made the work study method of industrial engineering a commonplace in factories around the world, including Japan. What is noteworthy in Japan, however, is that this "scientific" approach has been modified as it applies to the shop floor. Roughly speaking, blue-collar workers do their own work study and make proposals for improvement on the basis of their own job analysis. In other words, work study in Japan is not usually regarded as a job to be performed exclusively by a group of qualified specialists, or industrial engineers.

Our case study of Companies A and B confirmed this, but it also revealed some important differences in their approaches to industrial engineering. First, the term *kaizen*, or continuous improvement, seemed to have different connotations in the two firms. In Company A, the *kaizen* of machinery and equipment was considered more important than the *kaizen* of job sequences or work organization, while in Company B the latter was given more emphasis. In other words, *kaizen* efforts at Company A were usually understood to require large sums of investment expenditure, while these efforts at Company B were thought to require a large amount of "wisdom or input" by shop-floor workers, but not much hard cash.

Second, in the case of Company B, managers claimed that they could not tell us the exact number of industrial engineers because most of the supervisors and team leaders had learned the basics of work study and the company therefore had no need for such a group of specialists. They further emphasized that groups of indirect workers (called "*kaizen* teams") were the principal source of advice on *kaizen*. At Company A, in contrast, individual engineers deployed throughout the plants were expected to take the lead in *kaizen* efforts focused primarily on machinery and equipment.

Third, there were also different reward systems for workers' *kaizen* efforts. In Company B, a production bonus based on each work group's performance improvement represented approximately 40 percent of the average total monthly wage earnings for a worker. A special feature of this bonus system was a concept of "basic time" that measured efficiency in each section of the plant and, once fixed, was not to be adjusted even if the operation was subsequently improved by *kaizen*. It is worth mentioning that this measurement of "basic time" did not include any allowance for personal time. As this kind of productivity monitoring was also applied to shop-floor supervisors, it created a harsh inter-sectional competition for higher efficiency that increased the pressure on subordinates for additional *kaizen* efforts. The union at Company B had no say in this process.

By contrast, Company A had no such production bonus scheme. The basic concept for monitoring work efficiency was "standard time," calculated by a work-factor method and fixed through "consultation" between the industrial engineering department and the supervisors on the shop floor. Although the union had no direct say in this process, junior supervisors—all of them union members and some of them branch officers—sometimes resisted excessive reductions in the standard time. The union insisted that the standard time should be calculated based on a formula which would multiply the net work time by certain factors of allowance, for instance, by a factor of 15 percent for general operations, and a factor of 25 percent for painting operations.

Acquiescence and Positive Commitment

The process of organizing workers' acquiescence and positive commitment at Company A was substantially different from the process at work in Company B. In the case of Company A, management had until the mid-1980s tried to organize workers' commitment mainly through close consultation with the union. A well-organized consultation scheme at the company was working effectively enough to ensure a willing commitment of the enterprise union to the company's production schedule. The union's prominent role in this consensus-building process depended on elected shop stewards whose main responsibility was to monitor production and manning problems and represent rank-and-file workers in the consultation meetings. Any contravention of shop-floor custom and practice could be checked by these shop stewards. As a corollary of this extensive participation in the consultation process, the union at Company A also accepted the responsibility for securing the membership's cooperation in achieving targeted production levels. This, in turn, was one reason why the union at Company A was so sensitive to potential "troublemakers" who might disrupt the production schedule.

As I have mentioned earlier, an amicable labor-management consultation scheme was not unique to Company A. However, the consultation process at Company A merits attention for at least two reasons. First, the union was unusually eager to have a say in the formulation of management strategies. It is evident from its history that the union has been especially anxious about job security since its establishment in the early 1950s as a pro-management, second union. It held fast to a view that labor-management consultation must be the vehicle for guaranteeing both the company's prosperity and the workers' job security. Second, the company appreciated such a union position and relied to a significant extent on the union's cooperation in attaining higher productivity. The management of Company A, one might say, followed a kind of "management by consent" strategy.[10]

In contrast, management at Company B relied on a policy of paternalistic social control, implemented in the context of a company town, to encourage loyalty and hard work among its employees. For this purpose, Company B promoted a wide range of "human relations" activities. For instance, various in-house groups were organized for employees of different strata (superintendents, foremen and team leaders, etc.) and for employees of different educational backgrounds (college, high school, and graduates of the company-run training school). All these in-house groups were expected to foster a "family-like atmosphere" by frequently sponsoring sporting, cultural, and other recreational activities. In addition to these group-sponsored events, various other shop-floor recreational activities were organized and sponsored by management. All the employees are encouraged to participate in these sporting and cultural competitions held at the company, plant, and department levels.

Management at Company B spends significantly more time and energy on these activities than is the case at Company A. It should be emphasized that these human relations activities are very extensive, covering even the employees' private lives. For instance, the Housing Section of the company's Human Resource Department is in charge of company dormitories for single workers, taking good "care" of the residents in various ways. Every new recruit fresh from a high school is assigned to the care of a "shop floor senior," or "big brother," who is a model employee several years senior to the freshman and working in the same shop. The "shop senior," as a dormitory roommate of his "junior," is supposed to pay brotherly attention to all matters of the freshman's everyday life, both on duty and off.

A paternalistic personnel-management system of this sort seems to induce workers to make a positive commitment to corporate prosperity. In addition to the system for evaluating individual workers' performance as a basis for determining their annual wage increases, several other devices are used to encourage employees to keep working for the company until their retirement. As figure 6.1 demonstrates, the proportion of male workers who want to stay at Company B is significantly higher for age groups of thirty years and older. This is mainly because workers usually begin to purchase their own houses in their thirties with low-interest housing loans provided by the company. Falling into debt at a time when their company-specific "skills" begin to lose pecuniary value outside the firm, many of them elect to stay with the company until their retirement age, when they can expect

FIG. 6.1
How Workers View Company B

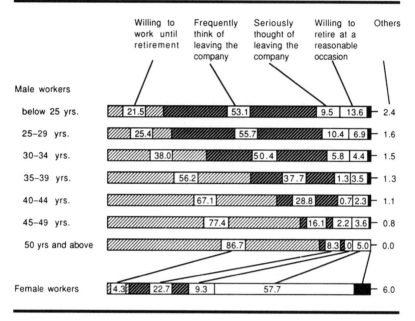

Source: Trade Union Survey on Workers' Consciousness at Company B, 1990.
Note: All numbers expressed as percentages. Totals do not equal 100 because of rounding.

to get lump-sum retirement payments. In this connection, it is worth noting that the company's promotion policy rewards all loyal employees, including the less competent, with elevation up to the rank of junior foreman or team leader by the time of their retirement. Needless to say, the post of foreman carries with it a prestigious social status in the company town.[11]

Worker Commitment through Small Group Activities

Since the early 1970s, "workers' participation in management" has been a fashionable topic of discussion when debate turns to the Japanese system of industrial relations. In dealing with this issue, however, we must ask what kinds of participation schemes have actually developed over time.

As described above, labor-management consultation was the main channel for workers' participation at Company A. Nikkeiren (the Federation of Japanese Employers' Association) has taken the position that "direct participation" by individual employees should be the basic form of workers' involvement, with "indirect participation" through employees' representatives performing a secondary role. But at Company A, the union contested this formulation by insisting that worker participation should be implemented primarily through union channels.[12]

In the case of Company B, management succeeded in carrying out what it called *"sagyo kaizen"* (work improvement) primarily on the basis of small group activities, in particular, the activities undertaken by Quality Control circles. Systematic promotion of small group activities was aimed not only at achieving higher productivity, but also at instilling in the employees a conviction that their participation in the high-volume production of quality cars would offer them a chance to contribute to the well-being of society and the nation. Workers' response to such small group activities was by no means uniform, and in fact some workers responded negatively to the work improvement campaign on the grounds that it would inevitably lead to more intensified work. On the whole, however, more workers reacted positively in the belief that by using their own initiative, they would be able to make the work organization and environment more favorable for themselves. Needless to say, it would be wrong to assume that workers would voluntarily participate in such activities without being stimulated by strong leadership, or without being properly rewarded by management. As a matter of fact, the eagerness with which a worker participated in small group activities constituted an important factor in his performance evaluation scores. While this is true, we should not overlook the fact that workers participated partly because they saw some positive meaning in these activities. One remarkable case study has found that QC circles were not totally driven by an emphasis on greater "efficiency," but were also concerned with issues that defined the "quality of working life." A competent line supervisor, the case study pointed out, was motivated by a genuine enthusiasm for small group activities and had to possess the skills of a tough bargainer to convince higher echelons of management to accept the proposals of his QC circles. It seems likely, then, that the social character and orientation of small group activities is significantly affected by the quality of their leadership.[13]

Small group activities in Japan have, in most cases, functioned as a kind of channel for absorbing workers' opinions and directing them into actions that support corporate objectives. The process by which small group activities took on these features coincided with the process by which unions suffered a decline in their shop-floor influence.

Concluding Remarks: Any Signal for the Future?

Our fieldwork established that the system of industrial relations at Company A, as described above, came to a halt in 1985–1986 when management launched a frontal assault on the union president. At the time, top managers of Company A decided the existing "consultation" machinery was too rigid and too troublesome a hindrance to their campaign for increased productivity. In the end, they not only ousted the union president, who had held his position for more than twenty years, they also demoted those supervisors who were thought to be more loyal to the union than to the company. For its part, the union was too weak to organize an effective resistance. Consequently, industrial relations at Company A are now in the process of transformation.

In which direction? Some researchers predict that Company A and other automakers will inevitably move closer to the type of industrial relations practiced at Company B, Japan's industry leader with a significant competitive edge over its rivals. However, I cannot accept this convergence scenario for two reasons. First, the industrial relations system at Company B is based upon unique geographical and historical conditions, including the fact that the company's cluster of plants were built in greenfield locations far from the other, established industrial centers of Japan. Moreover, ever since the company successfully eliminated militant trade unionism from its plants in the early postwar years, it has been operating virtually free from any strong union influence. Japan's rapid and sustained economic growth in the postwar decades also guaranteed a high degree of prosperity and promotional opportunities for its workers. As the situation stands today in Japan, none of these conditions are likely to favor other companies in the years ahead, including Company A.

Second, the production system at Company B has its own contradictions and weaknesses. The successful elimination of parts "buffers" from its production process has made the system vulnerable to worker resistance. Figure 6.2 also demonstrates that workers' attitudes at Company B have been changing significantly despite its ostensibly amicable industrial relations. It is very clear from these survey results that the management of Company B was already facing serious problems of recruiting and retaining new workers.

This raises the wider question, now being debated in Japan, of the overall quality of working life in the Japanese auto industry. Figure 6.3 summarizes the very interesting findings of a survey conducted by the Japan Automobile Workers Union (JAW), a federation of enterprise unions in the Japanese automobile industry. According to the survey, autoworkers

FIG. 6.2
Workers' Preference for Work or Leisure as Surveyed at Company B, 1985 and 1990

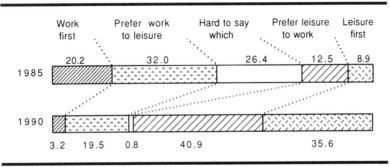

Source: Trade Union Survey on Workers' Consciousness at Company B, 1990.
Note: Numbers are expressed as percentages.

FIG. 6.3
Autoworkers' Evaluation of Their Industry (1)

"Do you want to persuade your child to work in the auto industry?"

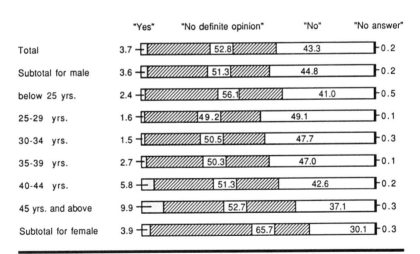

Source: Federation of Japanese Auto-Workers' Unions, Questionnaire Survey on Autoworkers' Motivation, Rodochosa [Labor Survey], September 1990.
Note: Numbers are expressed as percentages. Totals do not equal 100 because of rounding.

TABLE 6.4
Autoworkers' Evaluation of Their Industry (2)

Respondents choosing a specific reason as percentage of the total number of respondents of each group.

Reasons why autoworkers are reluctant to persuade their children to work in the auto industry	Total	Subtotal for male workers	Subtotal for female workers	Male workers of different age group					
				Below 25 yrs.	25–29 yrs.	30–34 yrs.	35–39 yrs.	40–44 yrs.	45 yrs. and above
Not paid too well despite hard work	50.2	49.9	53.4	49.7	55.7	54.9	51.0	39.7	42.0
Work itself is too boring	9.5	9.5	9.9	20.1	10.0	7.8	8.0	7.7	7.4
Anxiety about the industry's and the company's future	30.1	30.3	27.1	25.4	34.2	38.4	31.7	23.4	18.8
Too much holiday work and overtime	41.7	42.4	32.5	35.7	41.9	41.0	45.7	45.9	41.8
Too much work load and too intensive work schedule	35.3	36.5	20.5	28.1	31.4	29.6	39.7	46.6	47.7

Night shift work and shift rotation	23.6	24.0	19.2	32.9	15.9	16.1	20.0	34.5	38.0
Too frequent transfers and dispatches	9.0	8.7	13.7	7.3	7.7	7.1	8.7	9.9	13.3
Small prospects for promotion	13.0	12.6	17.8	16.1	13.9	11.2	11.7	11.2	13.8
Workers being treated not so warm-heartedly	33.4	33.9	26.4	18.3	28.0	33.3	35.6	44.1	43.2
Doubt about management strategy	18.6	18.8	17.1	17.8	20.1	20.9	18.0	16.5	17.3
Working just for earning a living	11.5	11.6	11.0	12.8	10.3	9.7	11.5	13.7	13.5
Without any particular reason	10.8	10.6	13.4	13.3	11.6	9.8	8.1	10.8	12.1

Source: Federation of Japanese Auto-Workers' Unions, Questionnaire Survey on Autoworkers' Motivation, *Rodochosa* [Labor Survey], September 1990.
Note: Repondents who answered "No" to the question "Do you want to persuade your child to work in the auto industry?" were asked to choose three out of a total of eighteen alternative reasons.

hold their industry in low regard. To the question, "Do you want to persuade your child to work in the auto industry?" fewer than 4 percent of the respondents answered in the affirmative. Why? The answer is immediately clear from table 6.4, which lists the reasons given by respondents who answered the above question in the negative. Asked to select three out of a total of eighteen alternative reasons, they chose as their top answer "Not paid too well despite hard work." This was followed in descending order by "Too much holiday work and overtime," and "Too much work load and too intensive [a] work schedule."

Based in part on these survey results, the JAW published its new policy guidelines in February 1992. The English version of the document is entitled "Japanese Auto Industry in the Future," with the subtitle "Toward Coexistence with the World, Consumers and Employees." However, the original Japanese version carried a more sensational subtitle: "Farewell to the Triple Suffering." In the JAW's own view, the first suffering is workers' exhaustion, the second is the auto companies' low profits, and the third is "Japan bashing" by foreign countries. The document asserts that if Japanese automakers try to sustain their current production policies, the industry will collapse from within due to labor shortages and low profitability. The JAW also proposes various corrective measures, including a new approach to measuring the value of labor, longer cycle times for model changes, relaxation of the excessively stringent quality control standards currently in use, and implementation of stricter controls on overtime.[14]

Of course, we should not take the wording of a policy document of this sort at face value. What implications do these measures really have? Which of the proposed measures are likely to be implemented, and in what ways? How are the individual companies responding to the proposal? Can we assume that Japanese enterprise unions are strong or competent enough to put into effect such a restructuring of the industry and such a reform of industrial relations? These are matters which remain to be investigated and ascertained.

Based on the foregoing discussion, I would like to conclude with several tentative statements. First, Japanese industrial relations are far from uniform or fixed, and should not be represented as a single or stable model. Second, the case of Company A, where the union existed somewhat independently of management, exercising a significant degree of influence even under a "lean production" system, should not be dismissed as entirely anomalous. To what extent and by what method can a union possibly circumscribe the workings of lean production? We need to discuss this question on the basis of empirical facts. Our research experience suggests that the issues in need of careful scrutiny include the following: overtime scheduling, transfer of workers, appointment of team leaders, the use of temporary workers, outsourcing, and training.

Third, various factors contributed to the defeat of the union at Company A, the most important being the fact that the union, including its president, was so accustomed to thinking and acting in the narrow framework of enterprise unionism. Without a strong link to other enterprise unions—that is to say, without a strong industrial base—the union's influence, however significant it might have once appeared, was fragile.

Fourth and last, the so-called lean production system adopted in Japan has disclosed its own contradiction. The system as developed and put into effect by Company B has certainly achieved a marvelous success in terms of efficiency, but precisely because of that success the system has collided headlong with the ecology of human beings. With the collapse of Japan's speculation-fueled "bubble economy" in the beginning of the 1990s, the question of how to restructure and reform the lean production system has become one of the top priorities for both labor and management.

Notes

1. Our main fieldwork was conducted in 1984 and 1985, with some supplementary work in 1987. The final report entitled *Transformation of and Choices for Industrial Relations* [Roshikankei no Tenkan to Sentaku], edited by Hideo Totsuka and Tsutomu Hyodo, was published in 1991 by Nihon Hyoronsha.

2. Satoshi Kamata, *Japan in the Passing Lane* (New York: Pantheon, 1982). The original Japanese edition is titled *Jidosha Zetsubo Kojo* (The Automobile Factory of Despair), and published in 1973 by Tokumashoten (Tokyo).

3. Hikari Nohara and E. Fujita, eds., *The Automobile Industry and Workers: The Structure of Labor Management and Workers* [Jidosha Sangyo to Rodosha: Rodosha Kanri no Kozo to Rodosha] (Horitsu Bunkasha, 1988); Y. Koyama, ed., *A Gigantic Corporate System and Workers* [Kyodai Kigyo Taisei to Rodosha] (Ochanomizu Shobo, 1985).

4. K. Yamamoto, *Labor-Capital Relations in the Japanese Automobile Industry* [Jidosha Sangyo no Roshi Kankei] (University of Tokyo Press, 1981).

5. In the turbulent years after the end of World War II, Japanese corporate executives were reluctant to establish formal labor-management councils within their companies because they feared that the then militant labor movement would turn this machinery into an arena for hard bargaining and undermine managerial prerogatives. It was during the period of high economic growth after the militant labor movements were crushed that the labor-management consultation machinery began to strike roots firmly in Japan. In other words, the establishment of the consultation machinery in earnest was preceded by a radical switch in the orientation of enterprise unions from the "class-struggle line" to the "labor-management cooperation line."

6. Hideo Totsuka, "A Case Study on the Transition from Piecework to Measured Day

Work in BLMC," *Annals of the Institute of Social Science* (University of Tokyo), no. 22 (1981).

7. If we extended our discussion into the steel industry, we could presume that the consultation procedures of the type at Company A were not exceptional. In the early 1960s, when top managers of the steel industry wanted to replace union leadership that adhered to the "class-struggle line" or "shop-floor struggle line" with one upholding the moderate or "collaborative line," they conceded to the union a consultation scheme for joint labor-management handling of workshop production matters. Since then, most of the enterprise unions in the steel industry have developed well-organized consultation schemes. See M. Nitta, *Workers' Participation in Japan* [Nihon no Rodosha Sanka] (University of Tokyo Press, 1988). The real picture of the scope and depth of labor-management consultation in Japan has to be described on an industry-by-industry basis.

8. Incidentally, a minority union's bargaining rights are guaranteed by Japanese labor law. The concept of a "bargaining unit" as a legal concept does not exist in Japan.

9. For a detailed description of the enterprise unions at Companies A and B, see Hiro-kuni Tabata, "Changes in Plant-Level Trade Union Organizations: A Case Study of the Automobile Industry" (University of Tokyo Institute of Social Science (ISS) Occasional Paper in Labor Problems and Social Policy, No. 3, 1989).

10. It should be remembered that the Japan Productivity Center—a driving force behind the movement for increased productivity during Japan's high economic growth period—began its existence in 1955 by advocating a "three-point principle": prevention of unemployment through the transfer of redundant workers and other means; joint labor-management research and consultation about measures for the promotion of productivity increase; and fair distribution of the fruits of productivity gains among management, workers, and customers. During the period of high economic growth, quite a few companies and unions came to accept this "three-point principle."

11. Obviously, the performance evaluation system (*satei*) is the key device for stimulating competition among employees, but front line supervisors often carefully keep the wage differentials among their subordinates within reasonable bounds, especially among loyal employees, so as not to disturb the "harmony of the shop floor."

12. Nikkeiren, *All Employees' Participation in Management* (1976).

13. H. Kobayashi, "Structure and the Norm of Assembly Line Workplace Community" [Line Shokubashakai no Kozo to Kihan], in *The Current Workplace Structure and Workers' Life at Automobile Enterprises* [Genka ni okeru Jidosha Kigyo no Shokubakozo to Rodosha Seikatsu] (Faculty of Education, Hokkaido University, 1987).

14. Confederation of Japan Automobile Workers' Unions, *Japanese Automobile Industry in the Future: Toward Coexistence with the World, Consumers and Employees* (Feb. 1992).

PART 3

MEASURABLE OUTCOMES

7

Beyond Management: Problems of the Average Car Company

KAREL WILLIAMS, COLIN HASLAM, SUKHDEV JOHAL, JOHN WILLIAMS, and ANDY ADCROFT

> Slowly we are learning
> We at least know this much
> That we have to unlearn
> Much that we were taught
> And are growing chary
> Of emphatic dogmas
> W. H. Auden, *Heavy Date*

This essay represents a critical reaction to what we have been taught by MIT about "lean production." In *The Machine that Changed the World*, lean production was dogmatically recommended as the one best way to manufacture cars and everything else: "lean production is a superior way for humans to make things," declared Womack, Jones, and Roos, so "it is in everyone's interest to introduce lean production everywhere as soon as possible." We reject this extravagant claim, but not because lean production's allegedly superior performance is based on intensification of labor and displacement of independent unionism. The end result of such moderate criticism would likely be a position we call "lean production (with regret)"; those who take this position accept lean production as an economically efficient new system, but regret its high social costs in terms of intensification and extension of management prerogative.[1]

Our own position is more radical. We have elsewhere dissected some of the pretensions and confusions of *The Machine that Changed the World*, and our historical work on Henry Ford's production of the Model T shows the extent to which the idea of mass production and lean production as successive eras rests on misleading stereotypes. Building on these foundations, our analysis presents the case for rejecting the concept of "lean production'' altogether. On the specifics of measurement, we dispute the size of the performance gap, challenge the preoccupation with physical productivity, and reconceptualize the problem by presenting a range of alternative measurements. In interpreting the causes of, and remedies for, uncompetitiveness, we challenge the lean production assumption that management is a privileged social actor that can always deliver cost reductions and, more positively, we argue that American owned car companies have structural handicaps which are beyond management.[2]

This essay, which argues a ''(without) lean production'' position, is organized into two main sections that deal separately with the intellectual problems of measuring the gap and identifying the causes of performance difference. The first section shows how and why the gap cannot be precisely measured using orthodox productivity measurement techniques, and presents a multi-dimensional alternative analysis where the best-to-worst gaps are generally smaller than the 2:1 ratio claimed by MIT. It also argues that best-to-worst comparisons are fundamentally misleading because they obscure the point that most American and Japanese car assemblers are average performers that share common problems about cost recovery. The second section begins by demonstrating that orthodox productivity measurement techniques do not identify the causes of performance differences, which are often beyond management control. It then argues that the option of taking labor out is often not available, and that American-owned assemblers suffer under the handicap of structural costs arising from the distribution of employment, social charges, and exposure to cyclicality. Readers who are persuaded by these arguments can draw their own conclusions; we do not aim to replace one emphatic dogma with another. A third short concluding section does, however, present our own understanding of the implications of the problem shift which we propose in the preceding sections; if the problems of the average (American) car company are beyond management, political intervention and regulation cannot be ruled out.

Measuring the Gap

The Machine that Changed the World, like the various *Harbour Reports* and the *Andersen Benchmarking Project Report*, all encourage us to think about performance gaps in a stereotyped and one-dimensional way. The comparisons, league tables, and quadrant diagrams encourage a basic dichotomy between good and bad sectors, companies, and above all, plants. The good and the bad are distinguished by one supposedly invariable characteristic: the good need a low labor input to assemble a vehicle or complete a given task, whereas the bad need a high labor input for the same operation or task. This position is associated with claims about a large performance gap between Japanese and Western firms dramatized by best-to-worst comparisons such as John Krafcik's notorious 2:1 comparison between GM-Framingham and Toyota-Takaoka. And it is garnished with the rhetoric of excellence; the phrase "world class" is used no less than seventy-nine times in the twenty-page Andersen report. What we want to do is to question this whole way of thinking about performance differences.[3]

The business school academics and consultants who promote these measures have borrowed the techniques of comparative physical productivity analysis first used in applied economics in the late 1940s. A "performance gap" is defined by differences in physical productivity at line and plant level which are measured using comparative ratios of (labor) input to physical output, as in vehicles per employee or hours to assemble. The comparison is usually made in the form of net ratios that correct for differences in output characteristics and in the amount of work undertaken; this complication cannot be ignored when there are, for example, large differences both in the span of process operations undertaken by different assemblers and in the size and complexity of the vehicles produced. The process of correction involves moving from gross to net by corrections that take the form of cumulative subtraction. Step by step, the calculation removes the non-matching differences between the cases that are being compared and, on the bottom line, isolates the residual net difference in efficiency. The common-sense case for adjusting gross ratios is overwhelming, but the question remains whether it is possible to construct valid like-for-like comparisons by correcting for the many differences in internal organization and external conditions.

Our position is that these cumulative correction techniques have never, and will never, produce a precise bottom line. This argument can be briefly summarized by presenting four strong reasons to doubt these techniques.[4]

The calculation quickly cumulates uncertainty because the individual adjustments at each step are not precise and independent. The process of adjustment only works if each step adds a precise adjustment, but many of the adjustments are necessarily imprecise either because they take an observable difference, or because they involve imputed relations of variation that are beyond the realm of the observable. It is, for example, not possible to make a precise allowance for differences in product type and complexity; this variable can only be roughly proxied by taking a related variable such as weight or number of welds. Nor is it easy to disentangle and separately allow for conceptually distinct variables like hours worked and capacity utilization, which are variably intertwined in different advanced economies.

The individual adjustments, which are typically made for less than five or six differences, correct for an arbitrary sample of the infinite number of differences that separate individual cases. If, for example, we correct for product type, hours worked, capacity utilization, and span of operations, why not also consider manfacturability, option content, and model run? Those who have done such calculations know the list of corrections must be short; if the list is extended, overlapping imprecise corrections generate wildly implausible bottom lines. But, logically, the list of variables to be controlled stretches out beyond five or six towards infinity.

Step-by-step correction makes the individual plant or company cases more alike at the expense of creating an increasingly implausible and bizarre counterfactual world. Suppose, for example, that we want to correct for GM's capacity utilization, which has averaged no better than 60 percent in most recent years. In that case, we are obliged to assume counterfactually that GM can take a 70 percent share of the American car market or find large new export markets in Japan or Europe.

The bottom line is ambiguous because it typically corrects for supply-side differences but ignores the effects of variable market demand pressure, which is a powerful pull-through influence on factory flow and labor utilization. Market pressure cannot be safely ignored because there is no simple positive relation between productive excellence and the ability to sell product. For assemblers, the relation is mediated by product design, distribution, and market maturity, while many component manufacturers face a derived demand that depends on the success of one or two assemblers.

If these general problems arise whenever net productivity ratios are compared, their effects are compounded in management discourse by the recent tendency to make comparisons across short spans of the productive process and an increasingly cavalier attitude to the business of adjustment. In recent management literature, the focus has been on comparisons of line productivity and final assembly factory productivity. The discussion of the early 1980s "productivity miracle" at British Leyland shows that almost anything can be proved by selective citing of line productivity figures, which may well not represent the company as a whole. Comparisons of vehicles per employee for major plants or companies are more interesting. Even then, bottom-line comparisons of individual assembly plants are not necessarily representative of company differences, and assembler company differences are a poor guide to sectoral differences because final assembly typically accounts for only 15 percent of the value of the vehicle.[5]

The other worrying tendency is the literature's increasingly cavalier attitude to the essential step-by-step adjustment for difference. In this respect, the recent degeneration of the method can be traced on a slide downwards from Krafcik's IMVP papers of the late 1980s, though the Harbour report to the Andersen benchmarking report. As we argued elsewhere, Krafcik's IMVP research papers are considerably more rigorous and interesting than the partial and misleading summary of that work in *The Machine that Changed the World*; the research papers make a serious but (necessarily) unsuccessful attempt to correct for differences using a methodology where the basis for correction is always disclosed and justified. By way of contrast, the plant league tables in the *Harbour Report* are the result of arbitrary decisions. In the case of Big Three plants, Harbour makes no adjustment to the gross scheduled output per employee, while unjustified adjustments to transplants nearly double Toyota Georgetown's productivity. In the Andersen benchmarking study, the individual component plants are not identified and it is simply not clear how much adjustment has been applied, and for what reasons, to individual plants and lines.[6]

The new combination of increasing assertiveness and diminishing care reflects a slippage. In the applied economics texts by Laszlo Rostas and others in the late 1940s, the productivity gap was the object of the discourse and everything depended on getting high quality measures. But this is not necessarily so in management texts, where measurement serves an illustrative rhetorical function in persuading the non-numerate; thus, in the Andersen report, the bottom line is only input for the "executive summary" claim that "world class plants" have 2:1 productivity superiority and 100:1 quality superiority. This kind of claim is part of the growing business of selling representations of difference to the unsuccessful in league table, bar chart, and quadrant diagram form. Consultants, who are judged by the amount of new business or sales revenue each report generates, are unlikely to spend much time worrying about the intellectual deficiencies of their methods.

Against this background of defective method and confused understanding, we can clarify the extent, variability, and multi-dimensional nature of the performance gap by using three different comparative measures to register some relatively simple points. First, at a sectoral level the gap between the American and Japanese industries is best illustrated in terms of sectoral hours to build: this series shows us that the hours gap between the two national industries is (and for over twenty years has been) considerably less than 2:1. Second, the considerable variation in plant and company performance can be approached by considering value added per employee on a company basis; this series gives us an instructive league table of companies showing the limits to best-to-worst comparisons when most Japanese and American assemblers cluster around an average and change positions over a decade. Finally, the complex and multi-dimensional char-

TABLE 7.1
Motor Sector Build Hours per Vehicle

	France	Germany	Japan	USA
1970	267	278	254	189
1971	257	270	224	162
1972	241	268	217	169
1973	238	266	203	167
1974	248	308	200	182
1975	292	379	176	174
1976	254	246	173	163
1977	251	258	158	165
1978	253	278	146	170
1979	241	294	147	179
1980	252	318	139	202
1981	260	271	138	204
1982	243	267	140	204
1983	225	262	139	163
1984	237	266	141	165
1985	220	258	139	155
1986	197	266	133	154
1987	175	255	132	173
1988	162	256	132	174

Source: Compiled from *Automotive News Market Databook, Labor Statistics Yearbook, Industrial Statistics Yearbook.*

acter of any performance gap can be explored further by introducing cash flow per vehicle produced as a third performance measure; this series shows the limits of Japanolatry because, on this measure, average car companies in Japan as well as America have real problems.

In our view, the physical gap between the Japanese and American industries is best illustrated by calculating sectoral hours to build, and table 7.1 presents the results of a calculation of build hours per vehicle for the French, German, Japanese, and American motor sectors. Sectoral hours to build are calculated by multiplying the number of employees in the national motor sector by average hours worked. Bosch and Lehndorff's studies provide realistic estimates of hours worked per year in several different national industries and act as a cross-check. The "health warning" for this calculation is that vehicle output always includes heavy trucks as well as passenger cars; but the importance of this difficulty should not be overestimated, since trucks over three tons accounted for only 2.5 percent of Japanese vehicle output in 1988 and, in the same year, trucks over six tons accounted for just 3 percent of American vehicle output.[7]

The table 7.1 series is interesting because it shows that it is possible to find a major national motor sector that currently does take twice as many hours as the Japanese to build a vehicle; in the latter half of the 1980s, the Germans took around 260 hours to build a vehicle against just over 130 hours in Japan. But the physical gap between the Japanese and the American motor sectors is much smaller, especially in years like 1985 and 1986 when demand was brisk in America and the American sector could build a vehicle in just over 150 hours; between 1983 and 1989, the American industry took between 12 and 32 percent more hours than the Japanese. Because the hours gap is so much narrower than the proponents of lean production suggest, relative wage levels and structural differences are of considerable importance in determining the balance of competitive advantage between Japanese- and American-based producers. We will return to this important theme in the second section of this essay.

Table 7.1 is also instructive because it provides a time series perspective on differences which the existing management literature constructs in snapshot form. The time series in table 7.1 is important because, like all our other time series, it shows substantial changes in relative position over the past twenty years. Management rhetoric about Japanese *kaizen*/continuous improvement is seriously misleading insofar as it implies or assumes that the Japanese sector has been opening up an increasing advantage over all the others. If we consider the four national sectors, it is possible to find one sector which is stuck on high hours—the Germans have managed no reduction on 255 hours over the past twenty years. The American industry illustrates the opposite case of a sector stuck on low hours, with no improvement on 160 hours over the past twenty years; cyclical fluctuations of demand are the main influence on build-hours variation, and the opening of Japanese transplant factories in America since 1983 has had no discernible effect. Stability in Germany and America is balanced by two cases of dramatic hours reduction: in the 1970s, the Japanese sector managed to halve its build hours from an initial level of 250 hours, and the French industry managed the same feat a decade later. Both industries have performed very strongly in recent years, with the Japanese sector building increasingly sophisticated cars in the same hours, and the French sector extracting further reductions in build hours; our work on Renault shows that Renault has achieved a 25 percent increase in vehicles per employee since 1988. The achievements of the French industry are real, but France is not Japan and it does not figure in the management literature.[8]

Any national sector is of course an average of companies and plants which perform at different levels. On the whole, company performance comparisons are more interesting than plant analysis because every company is a collection of plants which performs differently as differences in the salability of their product lines feeds through into variable capacity utilization. The Harbour tables of assembly plant productivity are little more than translations of capacity utilization into a different language; if we take Harbour's most recent productivity ranking of thirty-one Big Three car assembly plants, on our calculations, the top quartile have an average utilization of 87 percent and the bottom quartile an average utilization of 55 percent. If we are concerned with company-level differences in performance, the best single measure is value added per employee, which uniquely takes account of company-level differences in vertical integration. The adjustment is automatic because value added equals sales minus purchases of materials, components, and services; companies that buy-in more have a lower ratio of value added to sales. International comparisons of value added per employee require translation into a common currency, and we have chosen to translate into U.S. dollars. Variation in exchange rates will influence company ranking; but we argue that in the table 7.2 comparison between Japanese and American companies, the exchange rate is less a source of bias and more a fact of life for Japanese companies, which export components and finished cars to America and repatriate the proceeds. As long as cars are internationally traded, exchange rates are as relevant as factory efficiency in determining cash flow and profitability.

Here again we can begin by considering the snapshot for the most recent year. It is true that the difference between best and worst is substantial, but not 2:1; Toyota's value added per employee of $105,000 is 75 percent greater than the $60,000 at GM (U.S.). But it is doubtful whether this is a very interesting or illuminating observation because it tells us nothing about the broader distribution of performance, which shows a strong tendency towards clustering around the average, with Toyota as an outlier. Toyota is in a class of its own because it adds $20,000 more per employee than its closest rival; on a company workforce of around 100,000, this translates into a lump sum advantage of $2 billion in one year. As for the rest, all the other assemblers, Japanese as well as Ameircan, are clustered in the range $60,000 to $82,000 per employee, and the Japanese companies do not consistenly occupy the upper positions in this central range. The worst performer is GM (unsurprisingly), but the next-worst performance is turned in by Nissan, which only adds $5,000 more value added per employee than GM. From this point of view, we find it hard to see why "Japanese" transplants or manufacturing techniques should transform American performance. The Japanese have only one super company, Toyota; all their other assemblers do no better at adding value than their American counterparts.

As usual, the time series view does change the picture. It shows all the Japanese assemblers improving their position relative to the Americans during the 1980s; in 1983 the Japanese assemblers in table 7.2 occupied

TABLE 7.2
Company Value Added per Employee in $U.S.

	Honda	Nissan	Toyota	Chrysler	Ford US	GM US
1983	37,474	27,335	40,168	53,951	43,627	44,379
1984	42,863	27,794	44,211	43,386	49,813	44,368
1985	49,853	31,803	50,105	67,079	56,082	45,385
1986	78,872	44,902	67,359	69,938	60,747	42,708
1987	74,620	53,423	73,167	75,542	77,732	44,868
1988	82,683	62,176	89,002	65,312	86,474	53,737
1989	70,993	62,263	87,310	72,993	83,507	53,143
1990	68,370	60,525	96,340	68,080	76,145	55,212
1991	73,868	64,581	104,826	78,111	82,434	59,863

Source: Company report and accounts for each firm.

the bottom three positions, and only Toyota was within range of adding as much value as the American Big Three. Toyota has usually been the best of the Japanese companies; Honda's flash-in-the-pan performance of the mid-1980s owed much to the exchange rate effects of its early shift into American transplant production. Since 1989, Toyota has turned its Japanese lead into a world supremacy not seen since Henry Ford first opened his Highland Park plant. This lead can be attributed to the combined effects of Toyota's productive techniques and its strong domestic sales performance against companies like Nissan and Honda who, like the Americans, appear to be stuck on a value adding plateau. The two effects (techniques and market success) cannot be disentangled using a value-added measure, which shows marketplace ability to recover costs incurred in the factory. In this respect, the measure faithfully reflects the complexities and interconnections of the real world, and the implication is that where market space is limited it is not possible for all companies to be equally excellent. For the other Japanese assemblers, the problem is Toyota's dominance of the Japanese market, where it sells 43 percent of passenger cars. Their strategic response is not imitation of the techniques used by the super company, but a shift into export sales and transplant production—an attempt by the Japanese also-rans to fiind market space elsewhere. The Japanese also-rans must then suffer the effect of Yen appreciation, which depresses their value added in a way which is beyond management.

The argument so far suggests that it would be useful to shift the focus of analysis onto the average assembler companies, Japanese as well as American. In considering the average car company, a discussion of performance in terms of hours to build and the amount of added value is inadequate because for all companies the crucial issue is whether, at exist-

TABLE 7.3
Assembler Cash Flow per Vehicle Produced in $U.S.

	Honda	Nissan	Toyota	Chrysler	Ford US	GM US
1981	n/a	429	n/a	n/a	533	908
1982	n/a	430	n/a	334	1,357	1,034
1983	158	457	546	776	1,560	1,344
1984	390	415	600	1,467	630	1,133
1985	435	433	708	1,330	1,533	1,092
1986	470	526	909	1,324	1,785	1,161
1987	488	530	975	1,384	2,214	1,354
1988	546	780	1,160	1,146	2,321	1,683
1989	660	789	1,156	780	2,174	1,660
1990	739	769	1,334	710	1,752	634
1991	800	790	1,469	279	1,228	457

Source: Company report and accounts for each firm.
Note: Cash flow is defined as value added less labor's share.

ing costs and prices, they can recover their conversion costs in the marketplace and generate a surplus for product renewal that maintains or increases volume. Cash flow from existing operations is therefore the parameter which determines whether and how assemblers can stay in the business. To explore these issues, table 7.3 presents a simple analysis of cash flow, which is crudely calculated by subtracting labor costs from value added; to put all the assembler companies on a near equal footing, we caluclate cash flow per vehicle produced and express the results in U.S. dollars. The results are important because table 7.3 shows that, whatever the differences between assemblers, they do not translate into financial advantage in terms of cash flow. Furthermore, average car assemblers, Japanese as well as American, are mostly weak; the average assembler can recover its labor costs, which account for a normal 70 percent of value added, but cannot steadily generate a substantial cash surplus over and above labor costs. This problem is likely to have knock-on effects for the whole sector because component firms, which supply cash hungry assemblers, are unlikely to have fat margins on their OE (original equipment) contracts.

If we take the snapshot for the most recent year, a very interesting dispersion of performance needs some explanation. Only one Japanese assembler, Toyota, and one Big Three assembler, Ford, have strong cash flows, equaling $1,469 and $1,228 per vehicle, respectively, in 1991. The rest (Nissan, Honda, Chrysler, and GM) turn in much weaker performances with between $280 and $790 per vehicle. The immediate puzzle is why Toyota cannot turn its otherwise super performance into a cash gusher. Toyota does have a strong cash flow from the operations it undertakes in its own factories. This is a matter of simple arithmetic when labor's share of value added at Toyota (55 percent in 1991) is consistently below that of other car companies. But Toyota, like the other Japanese assemblers, is much less vertically integrated than its American Big Three counterparts; as table 7.6 in the next section demonstrates, Toyota's value added to sales ratio in recent years averages 14 to 15 percent against 20 percent in the case of Nissan and Honda and 31 to 37 percent in the case of the American Big Three. The problem is not that Toyota's vehicles don't generate cash, but that a large part of the cash is generated inside Toyota's supplier network, which does most of the work. It is hardly surprising that the upper tiers of this network are dedicated to supplying Toyota at prices which Toyota sets as it struggles against the consequences of vertical disintegration.

The time series again supplies a different, complementary perspective. The first interesting point is that the burden of vertical disintegration has been too much for Nissan; the Japanese home market boom of the late 1980s did no more than raise cash per vehicle to a cyclical peak of $790 in 1991, and the subsequent market downturn has damaged Nissan's cash flow and forced the company into operating losses. The news since then has been of Nissan's intention to postpone model replacement and rationalize componentry. In a broad historical perspective, there is an obvious analogy between Nissan in Japan and BMC/BLMC in Britain thirty years ago; like BMC, Nissan has high volume, substantial market share, and an unusually wide model range whose regular replacement is problematic because the company only generates the cash for new models in unusually favorable market circumstances. Nissan's only consolation is that some other major players are worse off; two of the American Big Three are even weaker. The problem of the American-owned assemblers is that their cash flow fluctuates dramatically according to cyclical movements in a saturated and mature American market. In a good year all three American companies can realize more than $1,250 on each vehicle and the strongest of them, Ford (U.S.), realized more than $2,250 at its peak in 1988; in a bad year, the two weaker American companies (Chrysler and GM) can only realize a surplus over labor costs of $500 or less per vehicle, and then have to borrow to cover the costs of model replacement. The regular alternation of cash on the upswing and debt on the downswing leaves all the American Big Three with a burden of short-term debt. Worst placed is GM; according to the company's 1991 report, GM's current debt was $95 billion, of which $51 billion was due within the year. If Nissan is weak it is not yet dynamically unstable like GM, and (like Ford and Chrysler) Nissan can only hope that GM will create market space for competitors' products by downsizing.[9]

Causes of Performance Difference

In *The Machine that Changed the World* differences in performance are confidently attributed to one active cause, differences in management practice. Lean production is a cluster of management practices and the Andersen report argues that these practices improve organization of the labor process in development, production, and distribution, and realize better materials flow inside and outside the assembly plant. Readers are assured that firms which adopt these practices will be rewarded with high performance; firms with poor performance have simply not made the right productive interventions. This position is broadly coherent with the more general a priori of the business school, where management figures as a purposive social actor whose rational decision-making or, more recently, "commitment to excellence," brings success. What we want to do is question this model of cause and effect.

We can begin by observing that orthodox productivity measurement techniques do not identify the cause of observed differences in productivity. The procedure of cumulative subtraction leaves a residual, the bottom line productivity gap which supposedly reflects the influence of an X variable whose presence/absence generates the difference. The X variable is identified by a process of addition which brings an external discourse to bear in a way that generates explanation or, more exactly, confirms what the discursively orthodox knew all along. In "Deconstructing Car Assembler Productivity," we showed that engineers and accountants identify X as production techniques and management accounting; economists identify X as quantity or quality of factor inputs; and business school professors identify X as management practices. These confident identifications cannot all be correct and they are all equally speculative. Attempts to vindicate particular identifications through empirical work on the covariation of different variables seldom vindicate the a priori identification of X. As we pointed out in our review of *The Machine that Changed the World*, Krafcik's results on the causes of productivity variation cannot be reconciled with the book's mono-causal assertive emphasis on lean production; Krafcik's research identified automation, manufacturability, and lean production as joint causes of high assembler productivity and there is no reason why "mass producers" should not automate or produce more manufacturable products.[10]

More fundamentally, we would question the whole model of management activity, the concept of the firm, and the assumptions about management competence which underlie texts like *The Machine that Changed the World*. It is doubtful whether management is a cost reducing activity be-

TABLE 7.4
Manufacturing and Sales Employment in Toyota and Nissan

	Toyota					Nissan			
	Motor Corp.		Motor Sales		Total employ-ment	Motor Corp.		Motor Sales		Total employ-ment
	No.	%	No.	%		No.	%	No.	%	
1985	61,665	77	18,236	23	79,901	58,925	54	49,575	46	108,500
1991	72,900	71	29,534	29	102,423	56,873	41	81,453	59	138,326

Source: Company corporate profiles.

cause much management is cost increasing; the general law of capitalist management is that "the number of suits expands to claim any surplus created in production." The American Big Three carry a burden of staff employment in head office and in divisional functions like financial control. And if the Japanese-owned firms do not employ these supernumaries in production, their extravagant system of home market distribution incurs large staff costs. Table 7.4 illustrates this point by presenting data on Toyota, which employes thirty thousand people in distribution, and Nissan, which has half Toyota's market share but employs no less than eighty-one thousand in distribution; the reason is simply that Nissan (unlike Toyota) owns a large part of its (unsuccessful) dealer network. Clearly, Nissan is a company that is sinking under the burden of unproductive white-collar employment, which is difficult to reduce without undermining an already weak home market performance.

Western business school analysts might argue that what the Americans and Europeans need is Japanese style production without the burden of unproductive Japanese distribution. But it is doubtful whether all or many Western firms can be redirected in this way because many of them are not unitary, controllable entities, and often management is not capable of defining and executing new strategies. Many firms are divided on functional or geographic lines into competing or semi-independent centers of power. Thus GM figures as the textbook example of a multi-divisional organization, but it does not have a single assembly division or central management group like Ford and Chrysler. When eight different organizations manage GM assembly plants, it is hardly surprising that GM's downsizing is always too little and too late. Furthermore, in most cases, managers are generally concerned with the routine business of incremental decision-making in firms moving along well-defined trajectories of possibilities. When that is not enough, management often does not innovate in the Schumpeterian sense, but behaves like turkeys voting for Christmas.

TABLE 7.5
Non-Auto Sector Purchases in Japan and America

	Major manufacturer sales revenue per vehicle	Motor sector value added per vehicle	Imputed non-auto sector purchases per vehicle	Non-auto purchases as percentage of selling price
	col. i	col. ii	col. iii	col. iv
United States	12,142	7,471	4,671	39%
Japan	12,559	7,367	5,192	41%

Source: Company report and accounts for each firm, industrial statistics yearbook.
Note: Col. iii is calculated by subtracting col. ii from col. i.

Thus, Mercedes Benz has discovered that it is a high-cost producer of luxury cars; the company is now considering whether to build a car smaller than the existing 190/C class and has already decided to open an American factory which will produce a four-wheel drive utility vehicle.[11]

Even if management controls its own firm in a purposive way, all management must face the fact that bought-in materials and components, whose costs are beyond internal management control, account for a substantial part of total costs. In any individual firm the bill for purchases is a major constraint on the possibility of cost recovery and on value added productivity because value added equals sales minus purchases. In a typical western manufacturing firm, bought-in materials and components account for more than half the value of sales; the components typically come from smaller suppliers and the materials from outside the industrial sector in which the manufacturer operates. If we consider the motor sectors of the industrially advanced countries, external costs are important because purchases from outside the auto sector account for a substantial proportion of the total cost of each car, and because the conversion costs in the lower tiers of the supplier network cannot be managed by assemblers and upper tier suppliers.

Car production is often discussed as though what happened inside the auto sector was the only influence on performance and competitiveness; in fact, the availability of cheap, high quality inputs from outside the auto sector is a crucial determinant of competitiveness. If this point has been lost in the management texts, it was apprreciated by new entrants like the Japanese in the 1960s and the Koreans in the 1980s. And its significance is underscored by table 7.5, which estimates the relative importance of non auto-sector purchases in America and Japan by subtracting the average value added per vehicle realized in a national sector from the sales revenue

TABLE 7.6
Value Added/Sales Ratios for Japanese and American Assemblers

	Honda	Nissan	Toyota	Chrysler	Ford US	GM US
1983	19%	17%	14%	30%	35%	37%
1987	21%	19%	13%	31%	36%	34%
1991	19%	20%	15%	28%	36%	38%

Source: Company report and accounts for each firm.

per vehicle realized by the two largest domestic manufacturers (GM and Ford in the United States, Toyota and Nissan in Japan). In both countries, purchases from outside the auto sector account for an estimated 40 percent of the sales revenue per vehicle.

If we now turn to consider costs within the car sector, the central point is that conversion costs in the lower tiers of the supplier network are always beyond the control of upper-tier management. The Japanese assemblers do, of course, organize their upper-tier suppliers into unitary *kieretsu* networks. But, as table 7.6 shows, these Japanese firms are substantially less vertically integrated than their Western counterparts; all these Japanese firms buy-in sub-assemblies, and the most vertically disintegrated assembler, Toyota, subcontracts the final assembly of nearly half its vehicles. Toyota's value added accounts for only 14 percent of the sales value of each car, against an average Western ratio of around 35 percent. Even if Toyota controls its first and second tier suppliers, it gains little extra leverage over costs than the average western firm, which undertakes many more processes in its own factories. And Toyota's choice of a vertically disintegrated structure is itself significant; if Toyota's manufacturing techniques are so wonderful, why don't they do it all in-house? Henry Ford at Highland Park chose vertical integration and brought work in-house because he could produce parts at half the cost of outside suppliers, even though Ford workers had the highest wages and the shortest working hours in the industry. Toyota lacks or cannot practice Henry's virtuoso technical ability, and chooses vertical disintegration instead; a vertically disintegrated structure allows Toyota to exploit a steep wage gradient into the supplier network, whose positive effects on costs partly compensate for the negative effects on cash.[12]

Because management does not control many costs, conversion efficiency and cost recovery are powerfully influenced by a set of structural variables which have different values in various national economies and car producing regions. On the supply or cost-incurring side, these variables include enduring conventions about wage levels and hours worked, national

145

TABLE 7.7
Hours Worked per Employee in Major Assembler Firms, 1990

	Honda	Nissan	Toyota	Ford Europe	GM Europe	VW
Hours worked	2,036	2,296	2,268	1,710	1,657	1,626

Source: Gerhard Bosch, "Working Time and Operating Hours in the Japanese Automobile Industry," (Gelsenkirchen: Institut Arbeit und Technik. 1992), and Stefan Lehndorff, "Operating Time and Working Time in the European Car Industry," (Gelsenkirchen: Institut Arbeit und Technik. 1992).

TABLE 7.8
Hourly Wage Costs in the Automotive Industry, 1991 in $U.S.

	Germany	Japan	US
Employer wage costs	26.80	20.40	21.10
Gross hourly earnings	15.59	15.70	15.41

Source: VDA communication.

systems for allocating social charges like retirement costs to firms, and a pattern of supply-side segmentation into differently sized firms with a definite wage gradient between large and small companies. On the cost recovery side, assemblers and their suppliers need a pricing structure and the market space to recover the costs incurred in production. In mature markets, where demand is cyclical, the pricing structure should allow a margin to cover the extra costs of capacity under-utilization in demand troughs. Under a particular national settlement, indigenous firms can exploit/must suffer the values of different structural variables which are embedded in institutional structures and enforced by social actors like trade unions. It is now often easier to shift production or try to find market space elsewhere so as to exploit a different national or regional settlement.

Supply-side structural variables have an obvious relevance to the competitiveness of national industries. This point can be illustrated by considering the structural burden on the German industry and the structural advantage of the Japanese. As tables 7.7 and 7.8 show, the German industry operates under the double disadvantage of short hours and a high mark-up for social costs. The German union I. G. Metall has obtained a standard thirty-five hour week for German workers whose Japanese counterparts worked a long day and a six-day week before the 1991 recession; as the Bosch and Lehndorff figures show, in 1990 the disparity in hours was such that a German firm like VW had to employ 1.5 workers to get the hours

TABLE 7.9

Wage Gradient and Employment Structure in the Japanese and American Motor Vehicle Manufacturing Sectors, 1988

	Japan		United States	
	Wage gradient	Share of Employment	Wage gradient	Share of employment
0–99	56.4	26.5	51.5	7.9
100–499	72.4	20.3	59.3	18.0
500–999	86.2	12.6	68.3	9.7
1000+	100.0	40.6	100.0	64.0

Source: Statistical Yearbook, Japan; Bureau of the Census, US.

that Toyota could get from one worker. The burden of extra employees is particularly punishing because German firms produce within a national settlement under which firms directly pay a large part of the costs of social security; as indicated by the statistical series of the Motor Manufacturers Association (VDA), the German industry pays a $15 hourly wage which is broadly comparable with wages paid by major assemblers in America or Japan, but a massive 72 percent social mark-up pushes German wage costs at least $5 an hour higher than its principal competitors.[13]

Table 7.9 on the auto sector's wage gradient illustrates another set of supply-side structural peculiarities, which in this case give Japanese-based firms an advantage over American- and European-based producers. The table shows that the Japanese motor sector has a large percentage of employment in small and medium firms with a steep wage gradient from top to bottom; in 1988, nearly 27 percent of total Japanese motor sector employment was in small establishments employing less than one hundred workers, and on average these establishments paid wages which were just 56 percent of those paid in large firms employing more than a thousand. No other major national industry operates with this double structural advantage; all the rest either have a shallower wage gradient and/or a smaller proportion of employment in small firms. Table 7.9 illustrates this by presenting comparative data on the American motor sector, which has a wage gradient just as steep as in Japan, but only 8 percent employment in firms with less than one hundred employees.

The demand-side variables influencing cost recovery are important and diverse. Not least of these is the question of relative prices; the Ludvigsen report demonstrates that retail prices for comparable or identical products are typically 25 percent higher in Europe than in America or Japan. The German industry's nightmare is competition from the Japanese, who can

TABLE 7.10
Car Registrations and Market Cyclicality

	Japan		United States	
	Car registrations	Annual change (%)	Car registrations	Annual change (%)
1970	2,379,128		8,388,204	
1971	2,402,757	1.0	9,729,109	16.0
1972	2,627,087	9.3	9,834,295	1.1
1973	2,933,590	11.7	11,350,995	15.4
1974	2,286,795	− 22.1	8,701,094	− 23.4
1975	2,737,595	19.7	8,261,840	− 5.1
1976	2,449,428	− 10.5	9,751,485	18.0
1977	2,500,095	2.1	10,826,234	11.0
1978	2,856,710	14.3	10,946,104	1.1
1979	3,036,873	6.3	10,356,695	− 5.4
1980	2,854,176	− 6.0	8,760,937	− 15.4
1981	2,866,695	0.4	8,443,919	− 3.6
1982	3,038,272	6.0	7,754,342	− 8.2
1983	3,135,610	3.2	8,924,186	15.1
1984	3,095,554	− 1.3	10,128,729	13.5
1985	3,104,074	0.3	10,888,608	7.5
1986	3,146,023	1.4	11,139,842	2.3
1987	3,274,800	4.1	10,165,660	− 8.8
1988	3,717,359	13.5	10,479,931	3.1
1989	4,403,745	18.5	9,852,617	− 6.0
1990	5,102,660	15.9	9,159,629	− 7.0

Source: Automotive News Market Databook, Corporate profiles.

live with substantially lower prices than the Germans need to recover costs. In the case of the Big Two Japanese assemblers (Toyota and Nissan) and the Big Three American assemblers, the relevant difference is in their home market bases. As table 7.10 shows, the American market is mature and shows a pattern of no sustained growth since the early 1970s combined with vicious cyclical fluctuations as volatile replacement demand is brought forward or postponed. By way of contrast, the Japanese market has doubled in size since the early 1970s and shows a pattern of sustained but unsteady volume growth with fewer, weaker downturns. These Japanese home market characteristics provide the demand-side basis for the techniques of productive intervention used by a firm like Toyota. If the basic objective is to improve flow so that less labor sticks to the product, that objective can only be attained when demand is brisk: flow cannot be sustained against market restriction. In Toyota's case, stability of demand is equally important because it allows production smoothing, which is the enabling condition for instruments like *kanban*. Finally, we would observe that Toyota's high performance after 1985 owes much to its 45 percent share of a two-million unit increase in home market demand between 1985 and 1990.[14]

After all the qualifications have been stated and all the complexities have been laid out, the fact remains that reducing motor sector labor hours is potentially a powerful instrument of cost reduction which can transform the cost recovery position of a company or national sector. Take the industry's most recent success story, the French: their reduction of sector build hours by some one hundred hours since the early 1980s removes around $2,000 from each product and safeguards the French position within the West European industry as producers of small cheap cars. But labor hours reduction is, as Tom Waits observed in a different context, "not for everyone" because it depends on initial conditions which are often not satisfied, and because the reduction is ultimately self-limiting.

Our work on Ford at Highland Park and on the more recent achievements of the Japanese and French, suggests that there are two crucial preconditions which must be met before hours reduction can be achieved. The first precondition is a large management prerogative over the labor process in factories where unions have little power; this condition is satisfied in all three cases and it is crucial for the Ford and Toyota style of productive intervention, which depends on endless recomposition of the labor process. The second initial condition is the market: both Ford (Highland Park) and the Japanese operated with increasing market shares of growing markets, and French firms like Renault have pulled the hours reduction trick with stable demand. The reduction in labor hours is ultimately self-limiting because all successful car firms sooner or later encounter market limits. Thus, Ford in the 1920s built the new Rouge factory, which was then the most perfect conversion apparatus the world had ever seen, but market limitations prevented Ford from exploiting the Rouge's full potential. The other limit on hours reduction is technical, because as long as car manufacture involves fabricating and assembling thousands of different parts into bodies, interiors, and major mechanicals there is an apparently irreducible minimum of well over 100 motor sector labor hours in any car. Ford at Highland Park around 1915 (like Toyota in the late 1980s) was never able to build a car with a negligible labor content; on our calculations, Ford took 123 internal hours to add value equal to 40 percent of the Model T selling price in 1915; more recently, if we exclude distribution employees, Toyota has taken 70 hours to add value equal to 15 percent of the value of a much more complex car. Henry Ford remains the master who established the possibilities and limits of hours reduction and a preoccupation with the imaginary system of lean production obscures that basic point.[15]

TABLE 7.11

Employer Labor Costs per Hour in the U.S. and Japanese Motor Sectors, 1980–91 in $U.S.

Year	Japan	United States
1980	7.40	12.67
1985	11.15	22.65
1990	18.03	20.22
1991	20.52	21.24

Source: VDA Frankfurt

As neither precondition is satisfied in the case of the American Big Three, the recommendation to reduce hours by appropriating lean production techniques is irrelevant and unattainable. Both the American and Japanese national industries have been highly competitive on motor sector hours to build since the mid-1970s when, as table 7.1 shows, the Japanese reached parity with the Americans at around 170 hours. Table 7.1 also shows that the Japanese sector has recently had a small advantage, which varied between 16 and 42 hours, according to market conditions, between 1983 and 1988. But the unionized Big Three, operating in a saturated and cyclical car market, are unlikely to be able to close that gap by management action; downsizing GM might help by removing a burden of unproductive excess capacity but that would not produce a significant hours improvement if a narrower range of GM cars captured a smaller market share. If hours are effectively fixed beyond management control, the gap between the American and Japanese industries can be reinterpreted as a cost gap determined by structural variables that are beyond management. In many ways, this is only restating the obvious: as 150 motor sector build hours (plus or minus 20) is around the irreducible minimum, the outcome of the contest between two national sectors operating around this level was always likely to depend on relative wages and other structural variables. And if we review the evidence, this is what we do find.

The structural sources of Japanese advantage do change over time. In the first decade after the Japanese had achieved parity, their relatively low wage levels were crucial. Table 7.11 presents the basic data on relative labor costs since 1980 in the two national sectors; the Japanese figures broadly represent cost per hour in the major assemblers rather than their lower wage suppliers. In the first decade after the Japanese industry had achieved parity with American build hours, they were absolutely unstoppable because their labor costs per hour in major assemblers were half or less those of the Americans; in small suppliers the ratio was even more favor-

TABLE 7.12
U.S. Motor Sector Structural Cost Handicaps per Vehicle against the
Japanese Motor Sector, 1988

1. Extra American wage cost arising from an industry structure which displaces less employment into small firms paying lower wages	**$543**
2. Extra social charges arising from American requirement for extra workers because each American worker supplies 2000 hours against 2300 hours in Japan	**$321**
3. Cyclicality burden arising because fall in demand from cyclical peak of 1986 raises sector build hours by 20 hours per vehicle	**$505**

Sources: Industrial Statistics Yearbook, Automotive News Market Databook, ILO, VDA, Japan Statistical Yearbook, U.S. Bureau of the Census.

able to the Japanese. Yen appreciation and rising real wages only slowly eroded the advantage of the low-wage competitors: as late as 1985, according to VDA figures, the Japanese hourly cost was $11 against $23 in the United States. Although wages in large Japanese assemblers have been close to American levels since 1990, the low wages paid by the sector's many smaller suppliers remain a potent source of advantage for the Japanese.

From an American perspective, we would now identify this as one of several major structural handicaps which have disadvantaged the American industry since the late 1980s. Table 7.12 presents the results of an illustrative calculation of the relative weight and importance of the three most important structural variables for one recent year. The calculation does not have an additive bottom line because that would be misleading when the relative importance of the variables shifts from year to year with changes in the market and capacity utilization, and when an exhaustive structural analysis of all the differences can never be made. But we cannot help observing that in an average year like 1988 the three structural variables in table 7.12 together account for nearly $1,400. In the same year, after allowing for wage gradient and the distribution of employment between differently sized firms in the two economies, we estimate that the American motor sector had an actual internal labor cost per vehicle which is some $1,500 higher than the Japanese sector's internal labor cost per vehicle. Thus, the three structural handicaps account for almost all of the observed difference in labor cost per vehicle.

This kind of comparison of national sectors is illuminating but incomplete when the American industry now includes many Japanese-owned transplants as well as American-owned factories: in 1991, transplant assembly plants produced 1,500,000 cars and by 1994 the transplant sector will have a capacity of 2,500,000 vehicles. The transplants are significant because they represent a form of internal competition that avoids many of the structural handicaps which afflict the Big Three's long established American plants. As new entrants with young workforces and no retirees, three transplants avoid many of the social costs which the Big Three must pay: according to Candace Howes, the hourly wage of $15 is roughly the same in the transplants and the Big Three, but employer labor costs per hour are $22.50 in Big Three plants against $17.50 in the transplants. As minor players with low market shares, the transplants are often able to avoid the worst effects of market downturn, which always hurts major players with large market shares. And because the transplants are branch assembly operations operating under a free trade regime, they can access cheap parts from the low wage supplier networks in Japan. The study of the (Ohio) Honda Accord by the University of Michigan Transportation Research Institute shows that 38 percent of the value of the car comes directly from Japan and most of the rest comes from transplant component suppliers whose propensity to import is high. Our own work on Bureau of Commerce data shows that in 1989 the Japanese transplant auto sector had an overall import to sales ratio of 48 percent. It is not necessary for the transplants to be super productive because their structural characteristics give them a large advantage over their American-owned competitors.[16]

Finally, we would observe that the American Big Three are challenged because they have fewer defensive and offensive options than their Japanese counterparts; for a variety of reasons, the Japanese are likely to find it easier to reduce break-even and increase volume so that they generate the cash to stay in the business. The Japanese can save costs by reducing their broad model ranges and lengthening their short model lives; the Americans, especially GM, which is too big, cannot take this option without risking market share, and Chrysler, which is too small, has the additional problem that every new model must be a winner. The Japanese can access cheap components from small Japanese suppliers while they slowly develop low-wage Asian alternatives; low-wage Mexico is half a continent away from the traditional Big Three plants in Michigan. Japanese companies together export half their output and can increase sales of components at the same time as they send higher value added cars to America and Europe; Big Three exports from American factories are negligible and will remain so when they have no distribution in Japan and GM or Ford exports to Europe would undermine their local manufacturing operations. Japanese companies operate in an environment where financial institutions have modest expectations of short-run profit and approach restructuring in a constructive way; whereas GM and Ford must rely on size to protect them from the financial engineers who buy and sell assets.

Living without Lean Production

In much productivity discourse there is a tension between the two roles of diagnosis and prescription; those who study productivity both measure the gap and act as agents of change. As management discourse increasingly appropriates productivity measurement, the tension has come to be increasingly resolved in favor of enthusiastic promotion of change because business school gurus and management consultants make their living by telling other people what to do. And in the world of "the executive summary," measurement itself functions as a rhetoric of change. Thus, in Andersen's benchmarking report, the first recommendation is "find out how far behind world class you are" and the second recommendation is "Use the resulting crisis to commit the firm to closing the gap."[17]

Western car companies are generally eager to use orthodox measures opportunistically in this way; the huge success of the lean production concept represents a case of academic supply meeting an insatiable industrial demand. Within these companies, the measures and the concepts serve to establish the necessity for change. They are often used in bad faith by management, which knows that Japan is not the answer. One French assembler tells us privately that its gap against Japanese best practice is 20 to 80 percent "depending on the measure and the year." The same firm organizes conferences where it publicly endorses the 2:1 ratio between itself and Japanese "best practice" because, we are told, that is an effective way of persuading managers and workers to accept the objective of competitiveness and the instrument of changes in organization and working practice.

Against this background, like Auden's poet living in "a low dishonest decade," all we can do is warn that it is better to live without the illusion of "lean production," which suits some car company managers but will not save struggling car companies. We have tried to establish this point by laying out a range of evidence and arguments that will allow readers to draw their own conclusions. In the first section of this paper we showed that productivity gap thinking misspecifies the extent and nature of the gap; and in the second section we argued that it grossly overestimates the capacity of management to deliver gap-closing performance improvements. On the basis of these arguments, we would make two recommendations which in effect are a proposal for a problem shift: (1) End the irrational preoccupation with hours per task which culminates in irrelevant advice to pursue hours reductions that are unattainable by most American car firms. By all means downsize GM, whose excess capacity does impose a substantial hours penalty, but do not imagine that this or anything else can remove real and persistent structural handicaps. (2) Reject the terms "lean," "excellent" and "world class" because they distract from the real problems of the average car company, whose profits are weak and cash flow unsteady. If you want Japanese examples, study Nissan, whose precarious mediocrity and multiple interconnected problems show us a world beyond management.

The problem shift has obvious implications for policy because it shows that many problems are beyond (company) management. Furthermore, insofar as competition is destorted by structural variables, public intervention to create a level field is entirely justifiable. Industries that seek redress against unmanageable structural disadvantage need not apologize for their existence and demands; trade unionists who see their national social settlement threatened by low-wage, nonunion competition should take the lead in pressing the case for regulation. This essay has concentrated on analysis rather than solutions, diagnosis rather than prescription, and at this point we prefer not to open the discussion about possible and necessary forms of intervention. This paper has served its purpose if it forces a problem shift and thereby establishes the case for action directed against real problems. As for *The Machine that Changed the World*, that can go back on the book shelf next to the other paperback self-help manuals offering multiple orgasms, higher self-esteem, and a million dollars for everybody who sets goals, thinks positive, and gets into training.

Notes

1. James Womack, Daniel Jones, and Daniel Roos, *The Machine that Changed the World* (New York: Rawson Associates, 1990), 225, 256.

2. See Karel Williams, Colin Haslam, John Williams, Tony Cutler, Andy Adcroft, and Sukhdev Johal, "Against Lean Production," *Economy and Society* (Aug. 1992): 321–54; and Karel Williams, Colin Haslam, and John Williams, "Ford versus 'Fordism': The Beginning of Mass Production?" *Work, Employment and Society* (Dec. 1992).

3. Andersen Consulting, *Benchmarking Project Report* (London: Andersen Consulting, 1992); Harbour and Associates, Inc., *The Harbour Report: Competitive Assessment of the North American Automotive Industry, 1989–1992* (Troy, MI: Harbour and Associates, 1992); John Krafcik, "A Methodology for Assembly Plant Performance Determination" (IMVP working paper, MIT, October 1988).

4. For a more complete discussion, see Karel Williams, Colin Haslam, John Williams,

and Sukhdev Johal, "Deconstructing Car Assembler Productivity," *International Journal of Production Economics*, unpublished, 1994.

5. See Karel Williams, Colin Haslam, and John Williams, *The Breakdown of Austin Rover* (Oxford: Berg Publishers Ltd, 1986).

6. Williams et al., "Against Lean Production."

7. Gerhard Bosch, "Working Time and Operating Hours in the Japanese Automobile Industry," (Gelsenkirchen: Institut Arbeit und Technik, 1992); and Stefan Lehndorff, "Operating Time and Working Time in the European Car Industry" (Gelsenkirchen: Institut Arbeit und Technik, 1992).

8. On Renault see Karel Williams, Colin Haslam, and Sukhdev Johal, "Machiavelli Not MIT: The Causes and Consequences of Volvo's Failure," a paper presented at the Arbetslivscentrum, March 1993.

9. General Motors, *1991 Reports and Accounts*, 39.

10. Williams et al., "Deconstructing Car Assembler Productivity"; Williams et al., "Against Lean Production."

11. On GM's management structure, see Harbour and Associates, *The Harbour Report*, 38; on Mercedes Benz, see *Financial Times* (6 April 1993).

12. On Ford Highland Park see Williams, Haslam, and Williams, "Ford versus 'Fordism.' "

13. Bosch, "Working Time and Operating Hours in the Japanese Automobile Industry"; Lehndorff, "Operating Time and Working Time in the European Car Industry"; Verband der Automobilindustrie (VDA), fax communication, Frankfurt, 1992.

14. Ludvigsen and Associates, *Report on European Car Prices* (London: Ludvigsen and Associates, 1992).

15. Williams et al., "Ford versus 'Fordism' "; Karel Williams, Colin Haslam, and John Williams, with Sukhdev Johal and Andy Adcroft, "The Myth of the Line," *Business History* (June 1993).

16. Candace Howes, cited in *US-Mexico Trade: Pulling Together or Pulling Apart?* (United States, Office for Technology Assessment, 1991); Sean McAlinden, David Andrea, Mike Flynn, and B. C. Smith, "The US-Japan Automotive Bilateral 1994 Trade Deficit," (Ann Arbor: Transportation Research Institute, University of Michigan, 1991); Karel Williams, Colin Haslam, John Williams, Andy Adcroft, and Sukhdev Johal, "Factories or Warehouses: Japanese Manufacturing Foreign Direct Investment in Britain and the United States" (University of East London Occasional Papers on Business, Economy and Society, No. 6, October 1992).

17. Andersen Consulting, *Benchmarking Project Report*, 5.

8

Are Japanese Transplants Restoring U.S. Competitiveness or Dumping Their Social Problems in the U.S. Market?

CANDACE HOWES

Popular perception, nurtured by decades of frustration with low quality vehicles, arrogant companies, and indifferent dealerships, and crystallized by MIT's findings in *The Machine that Changed the World*, holds that the U.S. auto industry is willfully uncompetitive. After years of colluding, seemingly with the intent of producing mediocre, environmentally abusive, and frequently life-threatening products, the Big Three are seen as hopelessly out of touch with the consumer. It has become axiomatic, therefore, that only strong and relentless competition will reform American car makers, and this competition must come from the same Japanese rivals who are said to have a vastly superior production system.

Yet, the prospect of unfettered Japanese competition inconveniently raises the issue of the U.S. trade deficit—half of it is with Japan, and over half of that is in autos. For that reason if for no other, the rush of Japanese firms to build assembly plants in the U.S. since 1982 has been heartily welcomed by free traders, who indulge the comforting belief that the appreciating yen was the primary incentive for Japanese firms to substitute U.S. production for imports. As the fashionable argument now goes, Japanese firms will transfer their superior production system to the U.S., provide the necessary competitive challenge to the Big Three, and in the process help reduce the bilateral trade deficit with Japan. U.S. firms will either adopt the Japanese model and become competitive, or they will be displaced by the superior competition. In that event, what does it matter whether the vehicles bear Japanese or American nameplates, as long as they are built with the most modern and efficient techniques, using U.S. labor and U.S.-made parts? Under the circumstances, it is argued that the best policy is to train our workforce and upgrade our infrastructure to lure Japanese investment.[1]

This essay focuses on the mistaken belief that Japanese firms intend to fully replicate their production system in the United States. I will argue that while Japanese firms do intend to compete with U.S. firms and win a very large share of the U.S. market, they do not intend to build a fully integrated Japanese production system in North America. Their strategy is rather to limit local production to final assembly and some commodity parts, the former to guarantee continued access to the U.S. market, the latter to exploit the advantages of a cheap labor force of young, nonunion workers. Other parts will not be produced in the U.S. because the lure of cheap labor is not sufficient to risk weakening the companies' organizational structure in Japan. Japan's U.S. production is analogous to the branch plant production practiced in developing countries, and the transplants' contribution to the U.S. economy is little better than that of imports.

The potential outcome of this production strategy is emphatically negative. Japanese firms will continue to import design- and engineering-intensive parts and machine tools. If U.S. assemblers lose additional market share, therefore, domestic demand for complex components and machine tools will stagnate. Whole stages of the production chain in auto manufacturing will be lost. The disemboweled U.S. industry will, like the industries of developing countries, be ultimately capable of assembling only knockdown kits from Japan, its machine-tool and parts supplier industries starved for want of a market. Hence, U.S. firms are forced to seek cost cutting measures that may jeopardize their prospects for restoring competitiveness in the long run—plant closings and massive workforce reductions, domestic and offshore outsourcing.

The presence of Japanese transplants in the U.S. has already changed the competitive calculus in the last few years, putting labor compensation back on the table. Because Japanese firms use younger workers in assembly plants, and younger, nonunion, low-wage workers in parts plants, they realize an average hourly compensation cost advantage of $7.50. Japanese firms have de facto broken pattern bargaining at the assembly level, putting U.S. firms in a stronger political position to seek wage and benefit concessions from hourly workers—in Mexico if not in the U.S. and Canada.

Unfettered competition will lead not to restored competitiveness, but to tremendous dislocation, declining wages, and a diminished production base. If the U.S. is serious about having a competitive auto industry, a sectoral policy must be designed that takes account of the real Japanese strategy in U.S. markets and its implications for U.S. competitiveness, and acknowledges the institutions necessary to restore competitiveness in U.S. firms.

In the sections which follow I explain, first, how the structure of the Japanese auto industry provides no incentive for Japanese firms to transfer their system to the U.S. except insofar as it gives them access to the U.S. market and to low-wage labor for commodity parts production. Second, I analyze the evidence which has been offered to date that a transfer has taken place, and that the high levels of productivity achieved by the transplants is possible only because they are transferring the whole system. I will also show that transplant claims of high local content are exaggerated. Finally, I will show that while transplants may be paying UAW-level wages in assembly plants, their overall labor compensation costs are far below those of U.S. firms because of benefit cost savings associated with the use of a young workforce, and because they source parts in the U.S. from very low-wage, nonunion plants.

But the Japanese Will Make a Better Car Here, Won't They?

Researchers who argue that Japanese firms have an economic incentive to build a fully integrated design-to-final assembly production system in the U.S. base this conclusion on an economic model that does not accurately represent Japanese firm strategies. In the orthodox economic model, firms base location decisions on the local costs of production and transportation. The model assumes that technical relations can be replicated at the plant level, that is, a Japanese firm will use the same number of labor hours to produce the same car, whether it is assembled in a U.S. plant or a Japanese plant. Therefore, given labor costs in the U.S. and after subtracting the cost of transporting a built-up car from Japan, if the cost of producing in the U.S. for the U.S. market is lower, the Japanese firm will do so. While that may be so, researchers who have looked at this question have failed to understand the true determinants of cost and competitiveness, assuming that only assembly labor and transportation costs at a single point in time are the relevant variables.

These researchers have failed to consider two essential factors which determine the behavior of Japanese firms. First, Japanese companies export partly because there is a national commitment to restrict imports while seeking self-sufficiency in manufactured goods. Japan has pursued policies at the national level to foster an overall trade surplus and a much larger surplus in manufactured goods. Since more than half of Japan's trade surplus has been its bilateral surplus with the U.S., and over half of that is a trade surplus in automotive products, if Japanese firms supplied the U.S. market from fully integrated production capabilities in the U.S., Japan's bilateral trade surplus with the U.S. would be greatly reduced. So, high-content transplant production would violate a national mission.[2]

Second, effective organization of production at the firm level depends on the firm's ability to maintain a steady flow of exports. Exporting per se is not what the Japanese system requires, but rather a steadily growing market that has been most easily achieved through exports. There is a symbiotic relationship between the need to export and the ability to export. In order to construct the highly effective organizations celebrated by MIT and others, Japanese firms had to export from the start; but it is, in turn, these effective organizations that now make them successful exporters.

Japanese production organization has proven effective because it does not rely exclusively on market incentives. Where competitive market forces may be destructive (for example, in suppressing innovation), they have been contained, while cooperation is encouraged. This is apparent in the industrial relations system of large firms, in the relationship between assemblers and first-tier suppliers, and in the relationship of large firms to their banks and stockholders. Many of the exchanges that would be mediated by the market in a Western firm are defined by negotiation and mutual agreement in large Japanese firms. For historically specific reasons, Japanese companies entered into relations with workers, suppliers, and financiers that entail a greater sharing of power than is characteristic in Western firms. The result is an incentive structure better suited to the needs of contemporary markets.[3]

For example, the permanent employment system in large firms, which was initiated in the 1950s to retain scarce skilled labor, is part of an incentive system which now draws a high level of commitment from employees. The technological and commercial dynamism of the system—new products are brought to market in half the time required of Western firms—is frequently credited to the scope and sophistication of this permanently employed workforce. The majority of the workers in a top-tier firm face a labor market only for entry level positions: once the worker joins the firm there is virtually no lateral mobility outside the company. Workers expect to spend their lifetime (until age fifty-five or sixty) in a single enterprise, and are rewarded for their loyalty through promotion and through group and individual performance-based productivity bonuses. Promotion is based on performance criteria which include some measure of the worker's ability to handle a broad range of tasks and work collectively in groups. Broadly defined tasks and job rotation, in turn, relieve the traditional boredom of the assembly line while raising the employees' awareness of firm objectives. Dore, Aoki, and Abegglen and Stalk all suggest that this incentive system successfully encourages employees to view their interests in common with the company.[4]

First-tier suppliers are part of the "team" as well, contributing to the design of the product from the early stages. Unlike Detroit-based firms, which have traditionally organized relations with suppliers through a competitive bidding process, Japanese firms have maintained long-term, frequently exclusive relations with suppliers. Because suppliers and assemblers often hold stakes in the equity of one another's firm, they are uniquely conscious of their common fortune. Consequently, Japanese assemblers have been able to exploit the design and engineering capabilities of their suppliers, while relying on a just-in-time system of inventory and parts delivery that ensures quality and efficiency without costly inspection.[5]

However, the mutually reinforcing incentives in this system of job security and shared prosperity depends on two things: first, export growth that ensures more shared benefits than shared losses; and second, cost flexibility built into the system through the use of contingent workers and lower-tier suppliers.

Robert Cole estimates that only about one-third of Japanese employees in all industries enjoy the benefits of lifetime employment; in the auto industry, this figure would incorporate those working in assembly plants or first-tier suppliers. For the approximately 500,000 people employed in Japan's auto parts industry, job security declines in each successive tier of the supplier chain. For the 40 percent of parts workers employed by third- and fourth-tier suppliers, there is no permanent employment and wages are about 67 percent of the level paid by assemblers and first-tier suppliers. An army of third- and fourth-tier suppliers that is never involved in planning, that does not have exclusive relations with any assembler, and that wins contracts through a cost-based bidding process provides cost flexibility for a system that is otherwise characterized by high fixed costs. This too is a crucial part of the Japanese system.[6]

It would substantially weaken that system if a large proportion of parts manufacturing was moved to the U.S., first because it would reduce the rewards available to suppliers and workers, and second because it would make collaboration in design and production difficult. It is a different matter, however, if such outsourcing is limited to commodity parts with little design content. Furthermore, such U.S. sourcing allows Japanese firms to exploit low-skilled cheap labor in the U.S. which may be unavailable or socially unacceptable in Japan.

A look at the planned distribution of Toyota production and employment between its U.S. and Japanese facilities confirms that U.S. transplants are branch operations. Toyota employs sixty-five thousand people in Japan designing, manufacturing, and assembling 3.6 million vehicles a year. Among its assembly plants are Takaoka, which produces the Corolla (the same vehicle assembled at the GM-Toyota joint venture in California—NUMMI) and Tsutsumi, which assembles the Camry (also assembled at the Toyota plant in Kentucky). In the U.S., Toyota ultimately plans to directly employ approximately ninety-three hundred people when it reaches full production of 740,000 cars in the mid-1990s. Therefore, each Toyota employee in Japan produces 55 cars annually. Each Toyota employee in the U.S. will produce 80 cars annually. The difference in cars per worker is not a measure of productivity differences: Japanese assembly workers in the Takaoka plant in Japan and American assembly workers in the NUMMI plant in California both require roughly the same number of hours in direct assembly of a car. Rather, it is clear evidence of the difference in levels of integration between U.S. and Japanese operations. For each vehicle produced in Japan, there must be substantially more labor involved in "system" work—design, engineering, high technology parts fabrication, research and development—than in the United States. The apparent difference in productivity really reflects the difference in the role of Japanese and U.S. production in the Toyota production system. The U.S. operations are branch assembly plants. While U.S. production is a marginal part of the "Toyota production system," employing less than 10 percent of the company's worldwide workforce, U.S. sales, which account for 25 percent of Toyota's worldwide total, certainly are not marginal.[7]

Toyota can fully realize the strength of its production system—the close relationship between assemblers and suppliers, the team approach to design, the troubleshooting role played by production workers—through its operations in Japan. Since it produces the same vehicles in Japan it can eliminate any of the problems in the production process there, allowing it to transfer a "debugged" assembly line to the U.S. and use production workers in fairly traditional ways (as it does at NUMMI). Since the assembly process is among the most mechanized and hence immutable parts of the production process (particularly body making and painting), there is less room for worker input than is the case in the design process or batch production. If the Japanese assembly workers make necessary changes during the start-up process in the sister plant in Japan, then the work of American production workers can be correspondingly standardized. Likewise, if the synergy with suppliers can take place in Japan and if most of the parts are designed there, there is little need for these relations in the United States.

To ensure that the integrity of their organizations are maintained, including the capacity to collaborate with parts makers and reward workers and suppliers with expanding opportunities, Japanese firms are likely to source most of their design-intensive parts in Japan. In the U.S., transplants will buy only low value-added, standardized parts from nonunion transplant suppliers paying low hourly rates.

Evidence

Three kinds of evidence have been put forth to suggest that Japanese firms really are setting up fully integrated systems in North America using collaborative labor relations, cooperative relations with suppliers, and just-in-time sourcing. First, researchers cite levels of productivity in transplants comparable to those in Japanese plants as evidence that Japanese management practices are being successfully adopted. Second, the large numbers of Japanese transplant suppliers and the extent of domestic sourcing claimed by Japanese manufacturers is cited as proof that Japanese firms are setting up concentrated networks of local suppliers to provide parts just-in-time. Third, researchers cite the high wage rates and extensive training at transplant assemblers as evidence that Japanese firms are treating their American workforce as collaborators and fixed assets, rather than disposable factors of production. As I will show, each of these pieces of "evidence" is not what it appears to be and in fact supports the earlier hypothesis, namely, that Japanese firms are transferring only final assembly and commodity parts production to the U.S., and only to secure access to the market and to sources of cheap labor.

Productivity

Some have argued that Japanese transplants have achieved levels of labor productivity superior to U.S. firms and in some cases comparable to Japanese plants. They suggest that to the degree transplants have achieved Japanese levels of productivity, this is so because they have adopted Japanese management practices, including collaborative labor relations, just-in-time sourcing techniques, and cooperative relations with suppliers. They further imply that transplants must adopt all these techniques and establish complete supply chains in the U.S. in order to achieve levels of productivity comparable to their Japanese firms. However, others have suggested that the design of the vehicle is the most important source of productivity differences. If that is the case, then whether transplants localize parts production in the U.S. may not be crucial to their success in the U.S. market.

Two significant engineering studies have been done on relative levels of labor productivity at the plant level. The first, comparing labor hours in Ford and Mazda assembly, transmission, and engine plants, found that there were 15 percent fewer total hours in a Japanese subcompact car than in a similar U.S.-built car, and about 32 percent fewer Japanese hours at the assembly level. This study attributed more than half of the labor hours differential to line balancing, automation, and the superior design-for-manufacturability of the Japanese vehicle.[8]

More recent work by Krafcik and MacDuffie extends the research to measure productivity differences between U.S. Big Three plants, transplants, and Japanese plants. They found that at the assembly level the average domestic Japanese plant required 33 percent fewer hours to assemble an automobile than the average Big Three plant. However, the average Japanese transplant required only 13 percent fewer hours to assemble a vehicle than the average U.S. plant, and 30 percent more hours than the average Japanese plant. In accounting for these differences, Krafcik and MacDuffie quantified three variables—automation, "management practices," and design-for-manufacturability—and found the first two far more important than the third. In their analysis, automation levels were measured by the number of automated operations in each plant, while "manufacturability" was measured by the age of the product design. Three indices—factory practice, work organization, and human resource management—were aggregated into the management practices index. The first of these, factory practice, measured a set of techniques indicative of just-in-time production (what they refer to as a "lean" factory), or "buffered" production. The second index, work organization, measured the degree of teamwork, the amount of employee involvement, the number of job classifications, and the frequency of job rotation, and combined these measures with an assessment of the degree to which production workers were responsible for inspection of their work and for the configuring or programming of flexible automation. The third index, human resource management, was meant to capture the effects of screening policies, performance incentives, and continuous training, all of which are said to contribute to the development of a flexible work force.[9]

While Krafcik and MacDuffie have done an impressive job of trying to quantify the effects of management practices, I would argue that they have failed to present a convincing case that Japanese management practices are being used extensively in U.S. transplants, or that these practices explain their good results. The proxies they use to measure the effects of management practices are very weak. For example, so many factors are grouped together in the single "management practices" index that it is impossible to distinguish between the effects of a Japanese-style industrial relations system, collaborative relations, and just-in-time sourcing from suppliers, and effective screening of new hires. Furthermore, their measure of design-for-manufacturability—the age of the product design—is grossly flawed because it assumes that all companies will have the same design practices at a given point in time. Hence, a three-year-old Toyota design will be just as manufacturable as a three year old GM design. Since this variable cannot possibly capture what it is intended to capture, the effects of design are likely picked up in the management practices variable.

So the evidence is ambiguous. One study suggests that design-for-manufacturability is the most important factor explaining differences in productivity, the other that differences in "management practices" broadly defined as "lean production"—just-in-time inventories, flexible and intensive use of labor—account for the productivity differences. But the conclusions of the latter study are questionable due to the imprecision inherent in quantifying "lean production," and the results could probably be reinterpreted to support the conclusion that design was the most important variable.

Therefore, it seems that we can at best conclude from this research that something other than automation explains differences in labor productivity and that more work will have to be done before credible weight can be assigned to labor and supplier-relations practices versus design practices. However, if design practices are the critical factor, then we have already established that the benefits of good product and process design can be captured in branch plants without localizing the whole production chain. Hence, there is no clear evidence, based on productivity measures, that Japanese firms are establishing or need to establish Japanese production systems in their transplants. Indeed, these facts could suggest that Japanese firms are not successfully transferring the system to the U.S., in part because they are not trying to.

Local Content

Florida, Kenney, and Mair concluded from a survey of seventy-three transplant suppliers that "the Japanese supplier system is being successfully transferred to America. . . . The great bulk of deliveries conform to "just-in-time" inventory requirements. . . . Engineers from assembly plants help suppliers overcome quality and production problems. . . . [The] survey also indicates that assemblers and suppliers interact quite frequently and commonly engage in joint problem solving. More than two-thirds said they participate closely with assemblers in the development of new products."[10]

Moreover, most transplants are currently claiming domestic content for their models in the range of 50 to 75 percent compared to Big Three models, which in 1988 ranged from 86 to over 99 percent. Researchers have interpreted these claims as evidence that Japanese firms are setting up concentrated networks of local suppliers to collaborate on design and just-in-time delivery of parts. Local content should measure the extent to which assemblers are purchasing those parts and services in the U.S. that could otherwise be imported. But the measure of domestic content cited by transplants (which is called CAFE content and is calculated for the U.S. Department of Transportation) is based on the *factory wholesale price,* which includes transportation to the dealer, cost of selling (e.g., advertising and dealer prep), and profits, all costs which would be incurred regardless of whether the vehicle was imported or built in the United States. If local content is based on the *cost of production,* which excludes transportation, selling costs, and profits, the contribution of transplants to the U.S. economy appears considerably smaller than is implied by their proclaimed content levels.[11]

One further twist makes local content appear greater than it is. Many of the parts that are sourced domestically are sourced from transplant suppliers who themselves import components for assembly into parts. In June of 1991, preliminary results from a U.S. Customs Service investigation were leaked indicating that "American made engines for the Honda Civic contained just 15 percent by value of North American parts. The biggest item of local content added at the Anna [Ohio] engine plant was depreciation of the factory's equipment. And most of that machinery had been imported from Japan."[12]

Using a methodology developed by Flynn, McAlinden, and Andrea to estimate real content, figure 8.1 illustrates the calculation of real content for a vehicle with a factory wholesale price of $11,000. Sixteen percent of the cost ($1,800) is in marketing, manufacturer's profits, and transportation, all costs which would be incurred regardless of whether the vehicle was imported or assembled in the U.S., and all involving services or operations that cannot be imported, hence are "non-tradeable." The "tradeable" costs of $9,200 include design, capital costs, management salaries, production labor, materials, and parts costs. Twenty-five percent of those

FIG. 8.1
Official CAFE Content Versus Real Domestic Content of a Transplant Vehicle

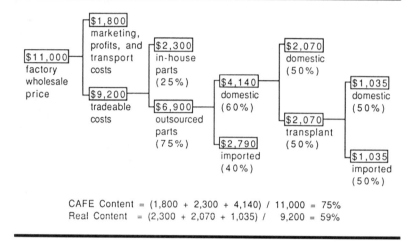

CAFE Content = (1,800 + 2,300 + 4,140) / 11,000 = 75%
Real Content = (2,300 + 2,070 + 1,035) / 9,200 = 59%

costs are incurred in-house, and 75 percent or $6,900 are the costs of sourcing parts and materials from outside suppliers, both foreign and domestic. In this scenario, 60 percent (by value) of parts and materials come from domestic sources, the remainder are imported. Of the $4,140 in domestic sourcing, half is from transplant parts suppliers who themselves import much of the content of their product, estimated at one-quarter to one-half the value of transplant parts. If the latter estimate is adopted, the transplant assembler with a 75 percent CAFE content has a real domestic content of only 59 percent, 16 points below the CAFE content. Alternatively, if the transplant parts manufacturers import only one-quarter the value of their product, the assembler's real domestic content will be 64 percent.[13]

McAlinden et al. found that Honda imported 48 percent of its parts in 1989, similar to the above scenario. While Honda was at the time claiming just under 75 percent U.S. content, its "real" local content was 62 percent. All other transplants for which data was then available imported 60 percent or more of purchased parts and materials. Their "real" local content was probably in the range of 48 percent while reporting CAFE content of 60 percent and above. Therefore, as of 1988, it is probable that the real content of U.S. transplants averaged about 50 percent.[14]

Most transplants claim they intend to reach content levels of 75 percent within a few years, and many researchers have assumed that projection in their calculations of the effect of transplants on employment and the trade deficit. But, in order to achieve CAFE content levels of 75 percent, transplants must produce drive trains in the United States. Only Honda has plans for local manufacture of engines and transmissions, including casting and machining of engine blocks, cylinder heads, and transmission cases. Toyota plans some casting. Other manufacturers plan engine assembly at most, an operation that represents only a fraction of the value of the drive train. Only Honda's claim that it will achieve 75 percent CAFE content (59 to 64 percent real content) is credible, since it alone is nearly at that point already. Those transplant assemblers that plan only engine assembly in the U.S. are unlikely to purchase more than 50 percent of parts in the U.S. and are unlikely to achieve real content levels in excess of 55 percent. Those with no plans for engine assembly will achieve content levels below 50 percent. Based on the stated plans of transplants for drive train sourcing, I estimate that on average, transplants will purchase only 50 percent of components and materials in the United States. By the time all 3.2 million units of planned North American capacity are in place, the average transplant will have a real content level of between 48 and 53 percent, as indicated in table 8.1.

Complex, engineering-intensive, and difficult-to-manufacture components such as engine, transmission, suspension, steering, and electronic controls are the real heart of the vehicle. Their development must take place as the car itself is being designed, and the earlier suppliers are involved in this design process the lower the overall development and manufacturing costs and the shorter the lead-time necessary for product development. Having suppliers of these complex parts or system components close by and intimately involved in the design process gives firms—Japanese firms—an enormous competitive advantage in terms of cost, lead-time, and quality. That is why these components are not being built in-house by the transplant assemblers, nor sourced from outside suppliers in the United States. They are being designed and largely manufactured in Japan in collaborative relationships between the assembly firms and the suppliers. The transplants are performing only assembly and stamping at their eleven assembly plants.[15]

As is typical of Japanese manufacturers, all other parts are outsourced, but most are being sourced to Japanese suppliers in Japan. Only hardware (door handles, locks, seat adjusters, mirrors, etc.), soft trim, plastic trim, glass, batteries, mufflers, tailpipes, tires, wheels, brake parts, seats, and windshield wipers are being bought in the U.S. from U.S. suppliers. What these parts all have in common is that they are relatively easy to manufacture, require little engineering, and are generic in nature—the same part can fit on several models without changing the basic identity of the vehicle. Those parts that are being sourced in the U.S. are being purchased almost exclusively from Japanese suppliers which have established branch plants

TABLE 8.1
Transplant Content
(in percentages)

Transplant firm	Planned CAFE content	Probable CAFE content	Probable real content	Drive train sourcing
CAMI	75%	62%	48%	drivetrain imported
Diamond Star	75	69	53	engine assembly in U.S.
Ford-Nissan	80	75	53	engine assembly from Nissan U.S.
Honda U.S.	75	75	59	engine and transmission manufacture in U.S.
Honda Canada	50–60 CVA	75	59	engine from Honda U.S.
Hyundai	60 CVA; 50 NAC	62	48	drivetrain imported
Mazda	75	69	53	half engines imported; half from Ford
Nissan	75	68.5	50.5	car engine assembly in U.S.; truck engine imported
NUMMI	75	62	48	drivetrain imported
Subaru-Isuzu	50–60	62	48	engine imported
Toyota	75	69	53	engine assembly and some casting in U.S.

Source: Compiled and estimated by author based on reports in *Ward's Automotive Reports, Automotive News, Ward's Auto World, Detroit Free Press, Detroit News,* and *New York Times* (1984–1992).
Note: CVA = Canadian value added; NAC = North American content (U.S. and Canadian combined).

in the U.S. (and in some cases formed joint ventures with U.S. firms). Only the simple, standardized parts—trim, glass, seats, wheels, and tires—are coming from U.S. suppliers.[16]

Susan Helper concludes from a survey of 453 auto parts firms in the U.S., most of which sold something to Japanese transplants, that they expected the relationship to be temporary, lasting until a Japanese supplier relocated to the U.S. They were allowed to sell only single components, not systems; they were not given substantial technical assistance by the customer, nor did the customer accept design modifications from the supplier. Says Helper, "these conclusions are not surprising given the nature of the relationships between Japanese automakers and their suppliers. Much of the success of the Japanese industry has been based on automakers' long-term commitment to their suppliers. Now that political and economic pressures have caused the automakers to start producing in the United States, they must walk a tightrope between alienating their new hosts in North America, and abandoning their traditional suppliers, particularly small suppliers, and employees, who cannot easily follow the assemblers to the United States."[17]

Japanese investment in the U.S. auto industry does not fit the profile of foreign direct investment as described by Graham and Krugman, Reich, Lawrence, and Florida, Kenney and Mair. In fact, the investment practices of Japanese automakers differs little from imports. Japanese firms have circumvented the restrictions of the Voluntary Restraint Agreement without really abandoning integrated production in Japan. The Japanese production system remains in Japan while something very close to the end product is exported to the United States. Furthermore, it appears that when Japanese firms come to the U.S. they have not had to sacrifice the factor-cost advantages associated with the dualistic structure of their home economy. They are not engaged in the transfer of technology to the U.S.; rather, they are dumping some of the social problems of their dualist production structure—low wages and employment insecurity—in the United States.[18]

Japan's Labor Cost Advantage in the U.S.

Real differences in factor costs follow from the different structures prevailing in Big Three and Japanese production operations in the United States. Big Three assemblers have an older workforce and source a higher proportion of parts from in-house facilities and from unionized parts suppliers. In contrast, Japanese firms, most of them operating in greenfield sites, employ a younger workforce and outsource a larger proportion of their parts, both from Japan and from low-wage, nonunion, Japanese-parent parts suppliers in the United States. There is little wage differential between the Big Three and their Japanese competitors at the assembly level, but there is a very large benefit cost differential. At the supplier level, there is a huge differential both in wage rates and benefit costs.

The Big Three companies are assembly-centered firms with varying degrees of vertical integration. General Motors produces about 50 percent of its parts in-house, Ford 40 percent, and Chrysler about 30 percent. The

TABLE 8.2
Hourly Earnings and Compensation Rates in the Auto Industry, 1986

Sector	Average hourly earnings	Index	Total compensation	Index
Big Three Assembler & Parts	$15.00	100	$22.50	100
Transplant Assembler	$15.00	100	$17.50	77
Parts:				
Total	$12.69	85	$16.88	75
Independents	$10.40	69	$13.00	58
Transplants	$8.00	53	$10.00	44

Source: Estimated by author from BLS sources and Richard Florida, "Wage Data for Transplants," computer printout (Department of Planning, Carnegie Mellon University, 1988). See note 19.

remainder of their parts are sourced from outside suppliers located largely in the United States. All in-house parts employees are covered under Big Three contracts and compensated at the same rate as assembly workers. Only 36 percent of the workforce of independent (non-Big Three) suppliers were still unionized in 1985, and the unionization rate is undoubtedly lower now. As indicated in table 8.2, the average compensation for workers in the parts sector (including workers in the Big Three) was about $16.88 in 1986, or 75 percent of compensation in the assembly sector; average compensation in the independents was about $13.00, or 58 percent of compensation in the assembly sector (and 77 percent of the average for the parts sector). Big Three firms operate approximately sixty assembly plants in the U.S. and Canada, many of which are thirty or more years old, and there are about two hundred in-house parts plants. The workforce in these Big Three plants, now comprised largely of workers with at least ten years seniority, averages forty-five to fifty years of age.[19]

Japanese firms now operate eleven North American assembly plants, and with the exception of the NUMMI plant, which is a retrofitted postwar GM plant, all of these are less than ten years old. Workers in transplant assembly operations are paid wages comparable to those in Big Three assembly plants—not surprising since five of the plants are organized (four by the UAW and one by the Canadian Auto Workers) and the rest are trying to avoid unionization. The average age of the workforce in these plants is twenty-five to thirty years old. The location policies and hiring practices of some transplants seem to be designed to avoid employing minorities, women, older workers, and people with union experience. Plants have been located in rural areas, far from traditional manufacturing centers, far from concentrations of minorities, where wage levels are well below those of established midwestern auto communities. Transplants have hired African-Americans in proportions substantially below their population ratios. In 1988, Honda was ordered to pay $6 million to 377 blacks and women for discriminatory hiring practices at its Marysville, Ohio plant. Honda was also charged by the EEOC with age discrimination and forced to hire with back pay and seniority 85 workers aged forty and over who unsuccessfully applied for jobs in 1984 and 1985.[20]

U.S.-sourced parts for Japanese assembly operations are either manufactured within the assembly plant or sourced from outside suppliers, the vast majority of these being U.S. subsidiaries of Japanese parts manufacturers. These "transplant suppliers" are almost exclusively nonunion and compensation rates, as indicated in table 8.2, are about 44 percent of those in Big Three parts plants and 59 percent of compensation rates for the parts industry as a whole. The three hundred Japanese parts firms are located largely in the upper southern United States and Ontario, around the transplant assemblers. While the new concentration of automotive production in the upper south suggests that economies of agglomeration have determined location decisions, equally important is the fact that suppliers have located at sufficient distance from the assembly plants and from one another to avoid the concentration which has traditionally facilitated unionization in this country. In an industry where wage rates were taken out of the calculus of assembly plant location long ago, Japanese firms are successfully bringing compensation back into competition.

These structural differences account for the enormous labor cost differential between U.S. and Japanese firms. There are two sources of this labor-cost advantage: the first comes from the tremendous savings in fringe benefit costs associated with the employment of a youthful nonunion workforce; the second comes from the use of low-wage third- and fourth-tier suppliers.

The Pension Cost Advantage

The real advantage associated with locating new plants in greenfield sites is the opportunity it affords to use a young, nonunion laborforce. Consider the fringe benefit cost differences. In 1987, the Big Three had defined benefit plans that guaranteed each employee a monthly income of $1,500 after thirty years of employment. The companies must contribute to the fund whatever amount is necessary both to meet the current obligations and guarantee that the fund will be adequately financed to cover future obligations. As the domestic industry has declined, an ever smaller base of workers has funded, through their hourly compensation, a pension fund that must support an ever larger pool of retirees. The companies did not anticipate in the 1970s that they would be supporting a retiree population as large as their active workforce by the mid-1980s. As a consequence, the cost of supporting these funds as a portion of active hourly labor costs has escalated over the last ten years. In 1987, the Big Three paid between $2,300 and $6,600 into the pension fund for each hourly worker, the equivalent of $1.10–$3.17 per hour, assuming 2080 paid hours per year.[21]

Even if a transplant pays UAW-level assembly base wages, there is a tremendous savings in benefit costs, especially for pension and medical insurance. Take the example of Toyota, where employees are covered by a defined contribution pension plan. Under the terms of the plan, the company will match contributions of the employee up to 4 percent of wages. Even if the employee chooses to contribute the full 4 percent of his or her wages, the maximum company contribution per employee will be $1,269 a year or 61 cents per hour, roughly 19 to 55 percent of the hourly pension cost of the Big Three. But the cost of the plan is driven by the savings behavior of employees and according to Teresa Ghilarducci, young workers are not inclined to save under the plans. Hence, the cost to the company is probably considerably lower than 61 cents per hour. Unlike the case for defined benefit plans, costs for companies with defined contribution plans are unlikely to escalate unexpectedly. Costs rise only with wage rate increases, improvements in the negotiated benefits, or changes in the savings behavior of employees, all predictable and controllable events.[22]

Mazda, Diamond Star (DSA), Nissan, and Honda all have defined benefit plans, as indicated in table 8.3. Mazda and DSA are both union plants and they probably negotiated defined benefit plans because the UAW pressured them to adopt plans comparable to the Big Three. Honda and Nissan, being the first transplants in the U.S., probably adopted defined benefit plans to avoid any obvious differences between compensation packages in their nonunion plants and those in union plants. Though the benefits to the workers will be comparable to those in Big Three plants, the cost of funding the plans is much lower because there are no current obligations to a large pool of retirees. It will be a very long time before these plants see active/retiree ratios comparable to those of the Big Three. All workers now legally vest (have the right to a pension) after five years of service, but the level of the benefit and the cost of funding provisions increases with years of service.

NUMMI, Toyota, and Subaru-Isuzu (SIA) have implemented defined contribution plans, though NUMMI switched to a defined benefit plan beginning in 1989. Since Toyota and SIA are latecomers, perhaps they real-

TABLE 8.3
U.S. Motor Vehicle Assemblers' Pension Plans, 1987

Firm	Date	Type	Benefit formula
Chrysler	1950	DB	32% of preretirement earnings for a thirty-year
Ford	1950	DB	veteran; no deduction for Social Security
GM	1950	DB	
Honda	1982	DB	2.5% of career average salary for every year of service
Nissan	1983	DB	max. 50% of salary (including Social Security) for 30 years of service
NUMMI	1985	DC	(DB beginning in 1989); maximum 3% of salary contributed to match employee's contribution
Mazda	1987	DB	.9375 of career average salary plus .9375 of salary above $\frac{1}{2}$ SS max earnings base. Approximately 1.5% of career average for every year of service
Toyota	1986	DC	limit 3% of earnings contributed to match employee's contribution
DSA	1989	DB	NA
SIA	1990	DC	NA

Source: Compiled by Teresa Ghilarducci, "Changing Pension Norms," from IRS Form 5500, 1987, for each company.
Note: NA: not available; DB: defined benefit; DC: defined contribution.

ized the threat of unionization was fairly minimal, especially after witnessing the repeated failure of drives at Honda and Nissan.

Participant/worker ratios differ greatly between companies, especially between transplants and Big Three firms. Participants include all retirees or their survivors, those eligible to receive a pension in the future but no longer working for the company, and current workers. Because of accounting methods which attribute all pension costs, both present and future funding, to the current cost of labor, a large pool of retirees (reflected in high participant-worker ratios) implies high pension costs per hour of labor. While hourly pension costs for Honda, NUMMI, and Toyota in 1987 were 50 cents or less, Big Three costs ranged from nearly $1 to almost $3, as indicated in table 8.4. The large difference between GM, on the one hand, and Ford and Chrysler, on the other, is in part due to the proportionately smaller pool of GM retirees. It may also reflect changes in investment return assumptions, which reduce the current liability for the company. NUMMI is an interesting footnote. Although the average age in the plant is probably comparable to the age in a GM plant (since most of the workers were drawn from the previous workforce employed by Chevrolet), hourly

TABLE 8.4
Pension Cost per Hour, 1987

Firm	Hourly cost per worker	Hourly cost per participant	Ratio: participant/worker
Chrysler	$2.90	$1.55	1.80
Ford	$2.63	$1.45	1.81
GM	$0.95	$0.58	1.62
Nissan	NA	NA	NA
Honda	$0.50	$0.50	1.00
Toyota	$0.43	$0.43	1.00
NUMMI	$0.39	$0.39	1.00
Mazda	NA	NA	NA

Source: Based on Teresa Ghilarducci, "Changing Pension Norms," table 3, and IRS Form 5500, 1987, for each company.
Note: NA: not available. Participants include all those eligible to receive a pension now or in the future: workers, retirees, survivor spouses, and those eligible in the future but not currently employed.

pension costs are low because GM absorbed the accrued pension liabilities when it entered into the joint venture with Toyota. For the purposes of estimating pension cost to NUMMI, these workers are only twenty-five to thirty years old.

Health Care Costs

The costs of funding a large number of retirees from the hourly labor of an ever-shrinking base of active workers is even more staggering in the case of medical insurance. Of course, one could not have predicted how large this factor would be back in 1982, when Japanese firms began to build plants in the United States. Pension funds are just that: funds which, in the best of cases, are pre-financed. But medical insurance is costed on a pay-as-you-go basis, and the savings associated with a young labor force are spectacular. Even if the transplants have exactly the same medical benefits as a typical Big Three firm, for a workforce with an average age of twenty-five, the cost will be half that of a workforce with an average age of forty-five. In 1989, seven years after Honda began production in the U.S., the average Honda worker was thirty years old; in contrast, Ford's production workers in 1989 averaged forty-eight years.

In 1988, the cost of medical benefits at the Big Three averaged $3 to $4 an hour. Each firm was spending almost $6,000 to $8,000 per year per active employee, or $520 to $660 per month to cover health insurance for both an older active work force and a large population of retirees. A pretty good individual insurance policy for a healthy person now costs about $300 a month. Suppose transplants are spending $300 a month ($3,600 per year) on insurance for healthy young workers and a negligible retired population. Their hourly health insurance costs would be approximately $1.75 per hour for a 2080 hour year. Since there are insurance discounts for large institutions, the actual cost would probably be lower.[23]

Supplier-Related Cost Advantages

Transplant assemblers enjoy an hourly labor cost advantage of between $2.50 and $5.50 an hour over the Big Three, due to the pension and medical benefit cost advantages of building greenfield plants and using a younger labor force. Further savings come from their parts sourcing strategy.

Sixty-five to 80 percent of the cost of a vehicle is in purchased materials, including semifinished materials—steel, aluminum, iron, fabrics, plastic—and component parts. For transplants the purchased materials share is closer to 85 percent. At this point, transplants enjoy lower purchased materials costs for several reasons. First, about 50 percent of their purchased components are still imported from Japan, where all the cost advantages of the Japanese system, including the use of tertiary suppliers, hold. Second, those components purchased in the U.S. come almost exclusively from Japanese suppliers operating in new greenfield plants themselves. Greenfield suppliers enjoy similar cost advantages to greenfield assemblers—a young workforce and lower benefit costs. As noted earlier, transplant suppliers have labor costs which are 44 percent of labor costs in Big Three parts plants and 75 percent of labor costs in the average independent parts supplier (table 8.2).

Suppose, hypothetically, that Big Three firms sourced 50 percent of their parts in-house (paying assembler level compensation rates of $22.50 in 1986), 40 percent of their parts from independents (paying $13.00 an hour), and 10 percent from overseas (where we will assume the same rate—$7.50 per hour—as parts sourced from Japan). As indicated in table 8.5, the weighted average labor costs for all hours of production labor embodied in the vehicle would be $17.20. Suppose that transplant assemblers sourced 15 percent of parts in-house at a cost of $17.50 an hour ($15 an hour in wages and $2.50 an hour in benefit costs), and 85 percent were outsourced, half to transplant parts suppliers (where average compensation rates are

TABLE 8.5

Average Hourly Labor Costs for All Production Hours in a Vehicle, 1986

	In-house assembly & parts	Outside domestic	Outside imports	Total weighted average	Index
Big Three Vehicle					
Hourly Compensation	$22.50	$13.00	$7.50	$17.20	100
(weight, %)	50%	40%	10%	100%	
Transplant Vehicle					
Hourly Compensation	$17.50	$10	$7.50	$10.06	58
(weight, %)	15%	42.5%	42.5%	100%	

Source: Compiled by author, based on data from BLS, *Employment and Earnings,* March 1989, and Richard Florida, "Wage Data for Transplants," computer printout (Department of Planning, Carnegie Mellon University, 1988).

$10 per hour), and half from Japan (where average hourly compensation costs for the industry were $7.50 in 1986). The weighted average hourly compensation rate for the transplants would be $10.06, 58 percent of the rate paid by the Big Three. This is a crude estimate, but the labor cost differential is of such an order of magnitude that any fine tuning would not significantly close the gap. Japanese firms retain a very large labor cost advantage due to the kind of investment they undertake in the U.S. market. In fact, since Japanese autoworkers' compensation rates in Japan rose to 76 percent of U.S. rates by 1988, Japanese firms actually widened the gap through transplant investment.[24]

Conclusion

Japanese firms retain an enormous labor cost advantage even when they come to the United States. The evidence most often cited to support the argument that Japanese firms are building fully integrated production systems in the U.S.—their high rates of productivity, high levels of local content, and high wage rates—have been shown to be either untrue or misinterpreted. Rather, the evidence seems to support the argument that Japanese firms are building branch assembly plants in the U.S. to secure access to the market and to sources of cheap labor.

Japanese firms cannot be counted on to restore competitiveness in U.S. auto production. On the contrary, it is more likely that they will participate in a hollowing out of the industry as they drive traditional manufacturers from the market and source their design- and engineering-intensive components, as well as machine tools, from Japan. The upstream linkages in the auto industry are critical to the overall health of U.S. manufacturing since the auto industry currently consumes 20 percent of all semiconductors and 50 percent of all machine tools. Furthermore, the process of displacement could idle some 360,000 workers and lead to a net job loss of 200,000 by the time Japanese assembly capacity is fully in place.

An alternative approach to restoring competitiveness is required, one that marshals trade and industrial policies to create a market for U.S. motor vehicles, protects them from excessive competition over the next decade, and provides micro-level institutions that assist and require U.S. firms to adopt production and organizational techniques that will make them sufficiently competitive by world standards.

Notes

1. The most prominent advocates of this position include Martin Kenney and Richard Florida, *Beyond Mass Production: The Japanese System and Its Transfer to the U.S.* (New York: Oxford University Press, 1993); James Womack, Daniel Jones, and Daniel Roos, *The Machine that Changed the World* (New York: Rawson Associates, 1990); and Robert Reich, *The Work of Nations* (New York: Basic Books, 1991).

2. See Edward Lincoln, *Japan's Unequal Trade* (Washington, DC: The Brookings Institution, 1990).

3. See Ronald Dore, *Flexible Rigidities* (Stanford: Stanford University Press, 1986); James Abegglen and George Stalk, Jr., *Kaisha: The Japanese Corporation* (New York: Basic Books, 1985); and Masahiko Aoki, "Toward an Economic Model of the Japanese Firm," *Journal of Economic Literature* 28 (March 1990): 1–27.

4. See note 3, and Kim Clark and Takahiro Fujimoto, *Product Development Performance: Strategy, Organization and Management in the World Auto Industry* (Boston: Harvard Business School Press, 1991).

5. See Michael Cusumano, *The Japanese Automobile Industry* (Cambridge: Harvard University Press, 1985); Banri Asanuma, "Manufacturer-Supplier Relationships in Japan and the Concept of Relation Specific Skill," *Journal of the Japanese and International Economics* 3, (March 1988): 1–30; Banri Asanuma, "Japanese Manufacturer-Supplier Relationships in International Perspective: The Automobile Case" (working paper no. 8 Faculty of Economies, Kyoto University, September 1988); Susan Helper, "Supplier Relations and Investment in Automation: Results of Survey Research in the U.S. Auto Industry" (Department of Economics, Case Western Reserve University, July 1990); Akira Takeishi, "A Study of Supplier Relationships in American and Japanese Automotive Industries" (master's thesis, MIT, 1990); Aoki, "The Japanese Firm."

6. Estimate of wage ratio compiled by author from Robert Cole and Taizo Yakushiji, *The American and Japanese Auto Industries in Transition* (Ann Arbor: University of Michi-

gan, Center for Japanese Studies, 1984), 160. On employment in Japanese parts making, see Japan Automobile Manufacturers Association, *The Motor Industry of Japan* (Washington, DC: JAMA, 1987), 18. See also Robert Cole, *Work, Mobility and Participation: A Comparative Study of American and Japanese Industry* (Berkeley: University of California Press, 1979), and Candace Howes, "Total Factor Productivity in the U.S. and Japanese Auto Industries, 1960–1985: A Firm Level Comparison" (Ph.D. diss., University of California, Berkeley, 1991), 9–10.

7. Toyota Motor Corporation, Public Affairs Department, *The Automobile Industry: Japan and Toyota, 1987 Edition* (Toyota Motor Corporation, 1987); John Krafcik, "Trends in International Automotive Assembly Practice" (International Motor Vehicle Project, Massachusetts Institute of Technology, September 1987).

8. "Telesis," private study for the UAW and Ford on the relative productivity of a U.S. and Japanese plant, 1984.

9. John Krafcik and John Paul MacDuffie, "Explaining High Performance Manufacturing: The International Automotive Assembly Plant Study" (paper delivered at International Policy Forum, International Motor Vehicle Project, Massachusetts Institute of Technology, Acapulco, Mexico, May 1989). The Telesis study (note 8) compared two plants, one in Japan and one in the U.S., producing a similar subcompact vehicle. The Krafcik/MacDuffie study was based on a sample of fifty-two plants, including eight Japanese plants, three transplants, and ten U.S. plants. The latter study did compare products standardized by size, options, levels of vertical integration, worker relief periods and absenteeism. In other words, they were measuring the hours worked on a similar product in fifty-two plants.

10. Richard Florida, Martin Kenney, and Andrew Mair, "The Transplant Phenomenon: Japanese Auto Manufacturers in the United States," *Economic Development Commentary* 12, no. 4 (winter 1988): 3–9. As the authors indicate in table 4 (p. 9), of the 229 transplant suppliers they identified in the United States, 61 percent are Japanese owned, 25 percent are U.S.-Japan joint ventures, and 14 percent are "other," a category that includes suppliers of unknown ownership and Japanese joint ventures with other foreign corporations.

11. Under the Environmental Protection and Conservation Act of 1975, all motor vehicle producers which sell vehicles in the United States are mandated to achieve minimum levels of fuel efficiency measured separately for domestic and import fleets. As required under the Corporate Average Fuel Economy (CAFE) regulations which implement the law, each firm reports the domestic content of its vehicles to the Department of Transportation for the purpose of assigning vehicles to the import or domestic fleet. This measure of domestic content is referred to as CAFE content. A range is given for the domestic content of the Big Three because separate computations are made for each model. The Big Three sold roughly 500,000 "captive import" vehicles in 1988, which reduced their total fleet-wide domestic content slightly. However, to correct the impression that Honda—unquestionably the most American of the transplants—is somehow more "American" than Chrysler, a generous fleet-wide estimate of the domestic content of Honda's U.S. sales in 1989 would be 43 percent as compared to Chrysler's 86 percent.

12. The summary of the Customs Service finding is from *Business Week* (18 November 1991): 106. See also Michael Flynn, Sean P. McAlinden, and David J. Andrea, "The U.S.-Japan Bilateral 1993 Automotive Trade Deficit," Office for the Study of Automotive Transportation, University of Michigan Transportation Research Institute, Report No. 89–18 (Ann Arbor: UMTRI, May 1989), 34: "Under CAFE rules, purchases of production parts and components that have received final processing in the United States, regardless of the percentage of their value that originates abroad, are treated as domestic content."

13. See Flynn, McAlinden, and Andrea, "U.S.-Japan Bilateral 1993 Deficit." The authors refer to this measure as the domestic content of the "tradeable portion" of the factory

wholesale price. They note that the "CAFE calculation of domestic content includes some items, such as marketing expenses and manufacturing profit that will be one-hundred percent domestic" (34). The model's prediction that real domestic content will be in the range of sixteen points below CAFE content is consistent with my findings based on *actual* measures of the share of foreign parts coming into transplant foreign trade zones. Since the actual measures could not account for the indirect import content in transplant parts, the real content of transplant assemblers may diverge even more than the predicted sixteen points from the CAFE content of 75 percent. Candace Howes, "Transplants and Job Loss: The UAW Response to the GAO" (Detroit: UAW Research Department, 10 May 1988).

14. Sean McAlinden, David Andrea, Michael S. Flynn, and Brett C. Smith, "The U.S. Japan Automotive Bilateral 1994 Trade Deficit," Office for the Study of Automotive Transportation, University of Michigan Transportation Research Institute, Report No. 91–20 (Ann Arbor: UMTRI, May 1991); Howes, "Transplants and Job Loss"; original source, Foreign Trade Zone Board Annual Report to Congress, and unpublished FIZB data.

15. These complex components are the ones every emerging auto-producing country wants to build because they embody the most sophisticated product and production technologies. Until the NAFTA agreement, Mexico, for example, required domestic production of engines and transmissions as a condition of sale in the local market.

16. This conclusion is confirmed by data from McAlinden, et al., "The U.S. Japan 1994 Trade Deficit."

17. Susan Helper, "Selling to Japanese Assembly Plants: Results of Survey Research" (Department of Operations Management, Boston University, February 1990), 1–3. Sixteen of the 453 respondents were Japanese owned companies.

18. Edward Graham and Paul Krugman, *Foreign Direct Investment in the United States*, 2d ed. (Washington, DC: Institute for International Economics, 1991); Robert Reich, "Who Is *Us?*" *Harvard Business Review* (Jan.–Feb. 1990): 53–64; Robert Reich, "An Outward-Looking Economic Nationalism," *The American Prospect*, no. 1 (spring 1990): 104–113; Robert Lawrence, "Foreign-Affiliated Automakers in the United States: An Appraisal Study Done for the Automobile Importers of America" (Washington, DC, January 1990); Florida, Kenney, and Mair, "The Transplant Phenomenon."

19. The measure of unionization in independent suppliers comes from Stephen Herzenberg, "The Internationalization of the Auto Parts Industry: 1958–1987 and Beyond" (U.S. Department of Labor, Office of International Economic Affairs, Bureau of International Labor Affairs, January 1989), table 48. Average hourly earnings in table 8.2 come from an unpublished 1985 Bureau of Labor Statistics study of independent parts suppliers and published BLS data (*Employment and Earnings*) for average hourly earnings in SIC 3711 (automotive assembly) and SIC 3714 (automotive parts and accessories) in 1986. The BLS study showed average hourly earnings at independent parts suppliers to be 82 percent of earnings in SIC 3714, which includes Big Three automotive parts production. Average hourly earnings in SIC 3714 were $12.69; 82 percent of $12.69 is $10.40; assuming a roll-up (negotiated and statutory benefits) of 33 percent in total parts, and 25 percent in independent parts, total hourly labor costs in the independent parts sector would be $13.00, and in SIC 3714, $16.88. Average hourly earnings in SIC 3711 (assembly) were $15.00. The roll-up in Big Three plants is 50 percent, so average hourly compensation is $22.50. Transplant assembler wages are comparable to those in the Big Three (Kathy Jackson, "Transplant Wages Will Rise to Match and Gain at Big 3," *Automotive News* [2 July 1990]: 2), but the cost of benefits is only $2 to $3 per hour. Earnings and compensation for transplant parts come from a survey done by Florida, Kenney, and Mair, "The Transplant Phenomenon," who found that "total wages and benefits per worker per year" average $21,268, which they divided by 40 hours times 52 weeks (2,080 hours per year) to equal $10 per hour. If the plants are working overtime, then 2,080 hours is

probably too low. According to the International Metalworkers Federation—Japan Council (*Wages and Working Conditions, Annual Survey* [Tokyo: IMF-JC, 1985]), the typical automobile worker in Japan works 2,300 yours per year. The UAW contract at Mazda U.S. permits mandatory overtime of 2 hours per day plus two out of three Saturdays. Ten-hour days with two out of three Saturdays for 52 weeks a year is 3010 hours per year. So total compensation could range from $10 per hour (40 hour weeks) down to $7 per hour (58 hour weeks). The Survey shows that the average starting wage at transplant suppliers was $7.21 in 1988, reaching $8.01 after one year, and that total wages and benefits were $21,268 ($10.22 per hour). So benefit costs were $2 to $3 an hour.

20. Jackson, "Transplant Wages Will Rise"; U.S. Internal Revenue Service, IRS Form 5500, 1987, for all auto firms; Robert Cole and Donald Deskins, Jr., "Racial Factors in Site Location and Employment Patterns of Japanese Auto Firms in America," *California Management Review*, no. 31 (fall 1988): 9–22; Martin Tolchin and Susan Tolchin, *Buying into America: How Foreign Money Is Changing the Face of Our Nation* (New York: Basic Books, 1988). UAW organized transplants are NUMMI, Diamond Star, Mazda, and Ford-Nissan; the CAW has organized CAMI. Robert Cole, who published the initial study alleging possible discriminatory practices, believes the situation is now improving. "You're seeing substantial change in minority hiring at the transplants," Cole told *Automotive News* (4 April 1990). "It's largely because of all the negative public attention they received."

21. IRS Form 5500, 1987, for each firm. It is important to note that the hourly labor cost of pensions (and other benefits also paid to retirees) is partly an accounting artifact. If a large part of the hourly cost of pensions is attributed to the cost of supporting retiree pensions, there is no obvious reason (except where increased costs result from bargaining increased benefits for retirees) why this should be part of hourly labor costs, rather than part of the overhead costs of operating the firm.

22. Teresa Ghilarducci, "Changing Pension Norms: The Case of Japanese Auto Transplants and U.S. Auto Firms" (Department of Economics, University of Notre Dame, April 1991). According to Jackson ("Transplant Wages Will Rise"), the top wage rate (including cost of living adjustment) for Toyota production and maintenance workers in 1989 was $14.23 and $16.28. The average of the production and maintenance wage was $15.25. Four percent of $15.25 is 61 cents; for employees who work 2080 hours a year and contribute 4 percent of their wages, the company will contribute $1,269 per year. The defined contribution plan is not only less expensive for the employer, but of less value to the employee. If a Toyota employee contributed $1,269 annually to his or her retirement fund, matched by a contribution from the company, after thirty years the fund would be worth about $120,000, which would, at a 7 percent annual rate, pay out $703 a month.

23. I estimated hourly health costs from the fraction of total company health care expense in the U.S. which is attributed to hourly workers, divided by estimated hours. Company health care expenses come from Bernstein Research, *The Shape of the Worldwide Automobile Industry* (New York: Bernstein Research, 1990); the fraction due to hourly workers is estimated from the share of hourly workers in the total labor force. These estimates of the comparative cost of health care for Big Three and transplant firms are confirmed by a Chrysler Corporation memo, "Internal Memorandum Comparing Chrysler and NUMMI Health Care costs," (1990). The study indicated hourly health care costs for NUMMI at $1.70 and for Chrysler at $4.20.

24. Japanese wages as a percentage of American in 1988 taken from U.S. Department of Labor, Bureau of Labor Statistics, Office of Productivity and Technology, "Hourly Compensation Costs for Production Workers: Motor Vehicles and Equipment Manufacturing (US SIC 371) 19 Countries, 1975–1988" (unpublished data, March 1989).

9

The International Assembly Plant Study: Philosophical and Methodological Issues

JOHN PAUL MACDUFFIE and FRITS K. PIL

The International Assembly Plant Study was the central research project in MIT's International Motor Vehicle Program (IMVP), and was featured prominently in the IMVP's summary book, *The Machine that Changed the World*. Its findings of large performance differentials across and within the U.S., Europe, and Japan, and its conclusion that the best-performing plants achieved their competitive advantage by following a lean production (as opposed to a mass production) approach have been highly visible and influential, both in the general business press and in the auto industry. Academic scrutiny has also been abundant and varied, ranging from insightful to uninformed. This essay is intended to provide more information about the goals and scope of the International Assembly Plant Study, and to describe the philosophical and methodological approach to performance measurement we have taken. In doing so, we also respond to critiques of the study raised in a number of settings, including the 1993 Lean Production and Labor conference in Detroit.[1]

The International Assembly Plant Study (IAPS) started on a small scale but grew over time to become an international project of tremendous scope. It began in 1986 when John Krafcik at MIT undertook a careful comparison of productivity differences among four plants—NUMMI (the

GM-Toyota joint venture), GM-Fremont (the closed plant that became the facility for NUMMI), GM-Framingham, and Toyota-Takaoka—using a methodology to correct for differences in plant characteristics. Eighteen months later, Krafcik's master's thesis at MIT reported performance differentials for a sample of thirty-eight plants and investigated some early hypotheses about the determinants of performance. From 1988 to 1990, John Paul MacDuffie joined Krafcik in expanding the sample to seventy plants from twenty-four companies and sixteen countries, and in developing a longer survey to collect more detailed data on such factors as level and type of technology, product mix complexity, manufacturing policies, work organization, and human resource policies. The much-publicized results on assembly plant performance are based on analyses of 1989–1990 data from this large sample.[2]

A second round of data is being gathered in 1993–1994 by MacDuffie, now at Wharton, and Frits Pil. These new data, from a sample that will be larger than the first round, will permit us to capture the dynamic aspects of change over time in both performance and production system characteristics. In this round, we have also had the opportunity to expand greatly the set of topics and issues researched, as well as to gather more in-depth data on issues studied in the last round. Some observers have failed to recognize the evolution of the IAPS over the past eight years, and persist in using the early stages of the research (back to 1986) as their reference point for the entire project.

The IAPS has a narrow but deep focus—it examines only assembly plants, but collects data on all aspects of plant operations, ranging from measures of technology and product complexity to measures of manufacturing policies and human resource practices; in the new round, this list expands to include supplier relations, design factors, and accounting systems. In this paper, we will primarily emphasize how we assess performance. Most coverage of the IAPS focuses on only one of the performance measures we use—labor productivity, as measured by the standardized comparison of labor hours required per car—so the bulk of this essay will address the philosophical and methodological issues associated with this measure.

However, from the start the IAPS has emphasized the importance of using multiple performance indicators as a way of eliminating biases that might result from using just one such measure. For example, we believe it can be very misleading to examine labor hours without also considering the quality of vehicles that are built. Thus, we will explain briefly the other performance measures we are using. Finally, we will touch on our measurement strategy for the independent variables—technology, manufacturing policies and human resource practices, product complexity—that help explain performance. After describing the IAPS methodology in all of these areas, we will address various critiques of the study.[3]

Performance Measures

All of the IAPS performance measures are plant-level measures. In the first round, we had two key indicators of plant performance: labor productivity and customer-perceived vehicle quality. In the second round, we added two other performance measures: first-time-through capabilities of different departments in the plant, and various indicators of employee well-being and satisfaction. A measure of environmental performance may also be developed.

Labor productivity. We measure labor hours per vehicle, standardizing for vertical integration, product size, and option content, and some design factors, and adjusting for actual work time and absenteeism. The productivity methodology is described in greater detail below.

Quality. The importance of quality as a factor affecting the vehicle purchases of U.S. consumers became evident during the competitive struggles between U.S. and Japanese producers in the 1980s. Vehicle quality is the outcome of many factors, including the quality of components received from suppliers and the design of the product. However, the assembly plant has a tremendous impact on a customer's perception of quality and overall satisfaction, particularly in "fit and finish" (the alignment of body parts, the appearance of the paint job, the care taken with assembly tasks, and the effective performance of all components), areas in which Japanese competitors appear to have a distinct advantage over U.S. companies.

To assess the impact of the assembly plant on quality, we needed a measure that could differentiate those problems the plant could control from those that originated outside of the assembly plant's domain, such as certain design or supplier-related problems. With the generous support of J. D. Power and Associates, we were able to develop such a measure. Every fall, J. D. Power surveys new car owners based on a random sampling methodology of new car registrations in the United States. All customers are surveyed at the same time, and at the survey date they have all owned their cars for three months. They are asked very detailed questions about their early experience with their new cars, with over one hundred different problem categories from which to choose.[4]

We start with these data, aggregated across all vehicles built at a plant, and construct a "defects per one hundred vehicles" measure that includes only those problems that are under the direct control of the assembly plant—for example, problems related to body finish, paint finish, squeaks and rattles, water leaks, and some electrical problems. Other problems related to the transmission, engine, steering and handling, and some electrical components (e.g., difficulty tuning the radio) that are attributable to vehicle design or component suppliers are excluded from our measure.

There is a subset of plants that do not sell vehicles in the United States. For these, we use correlation mapping with internal corporate data and non-U.S. market data to derive a measure of quality that is analogous to our J. D. Power-based measure.

First-time-through capabilities. In addition to the customer-based measure of quality, we want to know about a plant's ability to build high-quality products without extensive rework before a vehicle is shipped to the final customer. For that purpose, we now collect information on first-time-through capabilities for the body, paint, and assembly areas of a plant. First-time-through capability refers to the percentage of cars that are built right the first time around—cars that require no rework once the car leaves the main line.

Employee well-being and satisfaction. Here we emphasize plant-level measures that provide some indication about the attitudes and experiences of production employees. In the first round of IAPS, we measured labor turnover and absenteeism. In the second round, we added measures of injury rates, including the number of incidents and the severity in terms of days of work lost.

Environmental performance. A separate project at MIT seeks to evaluate the environmental performance of assembly plants in terms of energy usage, emissions from the paint plant, and the generation and processing of toxic wastes. Data from this project will be linked to our database when the environmental impact assessment is complete.

The Methodological Strategy for Measuring Productivity

The original elements of the productivity measure were developed by John Krafcik. To ensure comparability over time, we have retained Krafcik's methodology, with some fine-tuning. Krafcik's aim was to make an "apples to apples" comparison among assembly plants by adjusting for, or measuring the influence of, factors affecting productivity that vary across plants. The measurement strategy associated with this goal had several key components: (1) develop independent measures rather than asking for data from company records; (2) focus on labor productivity; (3) emphasize physical rather than financial measures of productivity; and (4) develop a productivity measure that adjusts for factors independent of firm choices about the plant's production system, for example, degree of vertical integration, product size, and complexity.[5]

Independent Measures of Productivity. While the use of independent measures of assembly plant productivity requires both the development of a methodology and the labor-intensive task of data collection, it is clearly the only way to achieve the desired goal of an "apples-to-apples" comparison. Companies develop their own extensive measures of plant productivity, but these are idiosyncratic. We have looked at data like these from many companies and found that there is no way to integrate them to permit systematic and accurate comparisons across companies. Even financial-based measures of performance, which would appear to be most directly comparable, vary greatly due to differences in internal accounting systems. This is the case even for companies located within the same country. Comparisons of financial data across companies are further complicated by the problems of interest-rate differentials, depreciation practices, and exchange-rate choices. Finally, companies are generally unwilling to release detailed plant-level financial data.

Publicly available information has different problems. For example, Harbour and Associates publishes a yearly report on assembly plant productivity that uses public information on the number of vehicles produced and the number of employees at a plant to develop a simple "hours per vehicle" measure. These data are available for all plants, can be obtained without company permission, and can be tracked over time. However, they in no way allow for true comparability across plants, since not even the most rudimentary adjustments for product differences or level of vertical integration are made.

Labor Productivity Focus. One common observation about many advanced manufacturing industries is that labor costs, as a percentage of total costs, have dropped dramatically over time, primarily due to automation. While this is generally true of auto assembly, particularly in the highly automated welding and painting departments, it is also true that final assembly of automobiles remains one of the most labor-intensive tasks of any advanced manufacturing setting. Furthermore, while direct labor costs do shrink as automation increases, it is less clear whether indirect (or overhead) labor costs decrease; some argue that they increase. Thus labor productivity, particularly if broadened as in the IAPS methodology to include direct, indirect, and salaried employees, is clearly a critical measure of assembly plant performance.[6]

While it would be advantageous to use a broader measure of productivity—for example, Total Factor Productivity, encompassing the full range of inputs to the production process (capital, materials, and energy as well as labor)—it is hard to get these data and impossible to ensure their comparability across countries. Furthermore, recent studies of company-level productivity differences in the automotive industry, comparing U.S. and Japanese companies, have found tremendous variation in labor productivity but nearly equivalent levels of capital productivity. Explaining the labor productivity variation becomes the intriguing research question. Finally, labor productivity is by far the most relevant productivity measure for a study that examines how human and technical capabilities are organized.[7]

Physical measures of labor productivity. As noted above, labor productivity is defined in this study as the hours of actual working effort required to build a vehicle at a given assembly plant. Thus it focuses on the physical conversion of labor inputs into outputs, and does not tell us directly about differences in the cost structure of plants. However, by focusing on effort rather than cost, the productivity measure is not affected by the problems with financial data noted above, nor by wage differentials or differences in national employment policies, which might influence a labor cost comparison.

For similar reasons, the "hours per vehicle" calculation is adjusted for absenteeism in order to exclude those people added to the payroll to cover for absent employees. This adjustment is warranted because absenteeism may be influenced by the type and availability of social benefits covering various absences as well as norms and customs specific to a particular region. Thus, only the number of working hours of people who actually build cars on a given day are included for the productivity calculation.[8]

Adjustments to Productivity. In order to develop a productivity measure that is consistent across plants and that captures the true differences in capabilities of the plants (rather than idiosyncratic differences resulting from factors outside of the plant's control), we make several adjustments. As described above, we extract absenteeism from our labor hours per vehicle figures. The other primary adjustments to the productivity calculation are for vertical integration and product differences. Both of these factors are largely independent of choices made about the plant's production system.

To adjust for differing levels of vertical integration at plants, the productivity methodology considers only a set of "standard activities" that are common to virtually every plant in the world. Some plants make their own body stampings, while many more receive stampings from a supplier plant. Therefore, stamping is not included as a standard activity. Many subassemblies, typically shipped to the assembly plant in completed form (e.g., seats, wire harnesses, fuel pumps) are also excluded from the standard activities. We further exclude activities related to the production of knock-down kits and other components intended for use at other plants.

Adjustments for product differences include size, option content, and product manufacturability. Since a large vehicle requires significantly more effort to assemble than a small vehicle, adjustments are made to a standard vehicle size. Likewise, installing options requires time. Some options are extremely time intensive (e.g., air bags, sunroofs, etc.), and plants that produce vehicles with high labor-intensive option content suffer a productivity handicap. Therefore, we adjust to a standard option content.

The design of a product can certainly affect how efficiently a car can be built. We adjust for the manufacturability of the design in the welding and paint departments. We do not make adjustments to productivity based on the impact of design in the assembly area (other than product size and option content corrections), because we have yet to find a good measure for this. The measure reported in *The Machine that Changed the World* was based on corporate reputations for manufacturability, as perceived by a small sample of respondents—hardly valid as data about a particular product at a particular plant.[9]

Ideally, a product manufacturability measure would be based on careful "teardown" data using a consistent methodology. We are exploring the possibilities of gaining access to such data in the second round. An alternative we are also pursuing is to measure aspects of the interaction between the assembly plant and product engineers during the product development process. The assumption is that manufacturability will be better the earlier the assembly plant sees the blueprints for a new model, the earlier plant personnel (from engineers to production workers) are involved in design decisions about prototypes, the more suggestions about manufacturability are communicated from the plant to designers, and the more the plant is involved in the building of pilot vehicles.

In lieu of the ideal measure of manufacturability, we study the effect of design on productivity by using product design age as a proxy variable. The strengths and weaknesses of this measure are described below.

Measuring Factors that Affect Performance

In addition to developing performance measures and collecting the necessary data, we also investigate the influence on performance of factors affected by firm choices about the plant production system, such as the level and type of technology, product mix, manufacturing policies, work organization, and human resource policies.

These are treated as independent variables, rather than being used to adjust the productivity measure directly. We saw an advantage in minimizing the number of direct adjustments made to the productivity calculation, since once such an adjustment is made it cannot be investigated through multivariate analyses of the determinants of performance. For example, we collect detailed information on the automation in a plant. With respect to flexible automation, we look at the number of robots by controller type, axes of motion, location in production process, and primary function within that process. We could use this measure to adjust the productivity measure, so that "hours per vehicle" would reflect the same level of robotics. Instead, we find it far more valuable to examine the impact on productivity of the use of robotics at different plants, given the potential variation in the technology strategy underlying capital investment in robotics and the effectiveness with which new technologies are implemented.

The "design age" variable is another good example. Product design age is defined as the weighted average number of years since a major model introduction for each of the products built at a given plant. We do not use the variable to adjust the productivity measure for two reasons. First, there are competing hypotheses about the impact design age should have on productivity. One hypothesis depends on a "learning curve" argument—that the longer you build a particular design, the more you learn and the better your productivity. The alternative hypothesis argues that newer product designs are more likely to have been conceived with ease of assembly in mind than older products, and thus could be produced more efficiently. We wanted to discover which of these effects on productivity was dominant.

Second, we recognized that design age, by itself, would tell us little about manufacturability across companies. There is no reason to expect that two products from different companies, each with three-year-old designs, would be similar in manufacturability. However, looking across the sample, those companies that have a rapid product development cycle (of four years, as in Japan, versus six to eight years, as in Europe) will have, on average, younger designs. If one assumes that a rapid product development cycle requires a great deal of concurrent engineering, during which the design and manufacturing functions interact very intensively, then a younger design age may well be associated with more manufacturable designs.[10]

In addition to focusing on factors affected by firm choices about the plants' production system, the development of survey questions about independent variables (predictors of performance) followed two additional guidelines: (1) Only measure policies and practices that can potentially be implemented in any plant in the international sample; that is, avoid measuring things exclusively associated with one company or country. (2) Draw upon fieldwork observations to choose which policies and practices to measure, emphasizing those that help differentiate best among different models of production organization. Let us look at each of these guidelines in more detail.

Measure practices that are potentially universal. Our thinking with respect to the measurement of company policies and practices was twofold. First, we customized our questions as much as possible to the assembly plant context. This reduced the possibility of confusion, particularly with an international set of respondents, and increased the reliability of responses. Second, we avoided measuring policies and practices that were unique or idiosyncratic to a particular nation or company, and would therefore function as a dummy variable for that nation or country. For example, with respect to Japanese employment practices, we did measure the use of teams, quality circles, and job rotation, since these are commonly found in other countries as well as Japan. We did not ask questions about such practices as the *nenko* wage system, the *satei* personnel evaluation system, enterprise unions, or lifetime employment—features that are more specific to the Japanese context.

Differentiating among models of production organization. From our fieldwork, we were aware of important differences in the model of production organization used in different plants. We wanted to measure those policies and practices that captured this variation in the sample. For example, the level of inventory—both of parts and of work in process—was an important indicator of different philosophies regarding the role of buffers in the production system, so we included several questions related to inventory. The use of "on-line" work teams and "off-line" problem-solving groups was another important differentiating factor, revealing different views about the role of worker involvement in the production process. Conversely, we did not include questions where there would be little or no variation within the sample. For example, all of the plants in our sample had a moving assembly line, so it made no sense to investigate variation for this variable.

Critiques of the Study

Because of the high visibility of the IMVP project, and particularly of the findings about assembly plant performance differentials, the International Assembly Plant Study has garnered a lot of attention in recent years. Several critiques have emerged, each of which falls into one of the following categories: (1) misunderstandings about what was measured and what adjustments were made; (2) disagreements about whether the measurements and adjustments were adequate to achieve true comparability across plants; and (3) arguments that any effort to measure plant performance (or a plant's production system) are doomed to fail because such measurements can never be accurate. Earlier sections of this essay will serve, hopefully, to correct simple misunderstandings. Here, we first address disagreements about what is measured and the adjustments that are made.

Critique: By focusing on "hours per vehicle," the study essentially blames direct labor workers for poor plant performance, neglecting the role of management decisions at the corporate level that affect capital investment, what products are built in a plant, and what organizational policies are followed.

Answer: Our measure of "hours per vehicle" includes not only direct labor hours but also indirect and salaried labor hours, so it reflects the inefficiency (or efficiency) of all employees in a plant. The adjustments made in the productivity methodology provide for an "apples to apples" comparison for many factors determined at the corporate level, such as the level of vertical integration, product size, and option content. The independent variables we measure almost entirely reflect management decisions, from the level of capital investment to what manufacturing or human resource policies to follow. How direct labor employees are managed in the context of the overall production system is the important factor for plant performance, not necessarily the personal characteristics of those employees.

Critique: The study doesn't adjust adequately for capacity utilization. A plant that is operating under capacity will obviously perform more poorly than one at full capacity, while plants doing overtime to run over capacity will appear to have superior performance.

Answer: We adjust for capacity utilization in two ways. First, for plants in an over-capacity situation, we exclude all overtime hours from the calculation of hours worked. We also exclude any temporary workers that may be brought on to reach higher production levels. Thus, over-capacity production has no effect on the productivity calculation. Second, for under-capacity situations, we look to see whether the downturn in production is short-term or long-term. If it is short-term, we ask the plant to give us data from their last period of regular (i.e., steady state) production. If the plant has operated well under its rated capacity for a long time, we take its actual production level as its de facto capacity, under the assumption that the plant has had the opportunity to adjust labor inputs downward to match the lower production level. This assumption is plausible with respect to labor productivity, while it would not apply if we were studying capital productivity.

Critique: The study doesn't adjust adequately for the difference between mass market and luxury vehicles. Luxury vehicles are so complex, they must take much longer to assemble.

Answer: Luxury vehicles benefit from two adjustments to the productivity calculation. First, luxury vehicles are generally bigger, so the adjustment of the Product Size Factor reduces their hours relative to plants with smaller cars. Second, luxury vehicles have many more options than mass market vehicles. The Option Content adjustment we make focuses on twelve different options, many of which appear only in more expensive cars: for example, power windows, doors, seats, sun roofs, and anti-lock brakes. The combination of these two adjustments can reduce hours per car for a luxury plant by over 20 percent.

Critique: The study doesn't adjust adequately for design factors. Plants with well-designed products that are easy to assemble will have a significant performance advantage over those with poorly-designed products.

Answer: As noted above, we make adjustments related to design factors in the weld and paint areas as part of the productivity methodology, and also look at product design age, which is likely to be moderately correlated with manufacturability. Ideally, one would like to have detailed teardown data on all products in the world, evaluated for "ease/difficulty of assembly" with a consistent methodology. We do not have access to such data, and therefore cannot adjust adequately for the influence of design differences on productivity in final assembly. However, we believe that the appropriate response to this measurement problem is to look for indicators of interaction between manufacturing and product designers during the product development process. How many months before product launch are engineers, managers, and workers from an assembly plant given a chance to look at product blueprints? How many months before launch are they consulted on the design of process equipment? Are prototype and/or pilot vehicles built in the assembly plant which will actually produce them? The operative hypothesis here is that earlier and more intense involvement of personnel from the assembly plant in the design process will be associated with more manufacturable designs. We are gathering data of this kind in the second round of the assembly plant study.

Critique: Plants that have multiple body shops or assembly lines are able to handle a complex product mix more easily than plants that must mix platforms and models on a single line. This would make them appear more productive.

Answer: The measure of Model Mix Complexity we use adjusts for the number of body shops and assembly lines. For example, a plant making two different platforms on two assembly lines would have the same Model Mix Complexity as a plant making one platform on one assembly line (or three platforms on three assembly lines.) With this measure, we can examine the impact of true model mix complexity (i.e., multiple platforms and models on the same line) on productivity and quality.

Critique: The organizational practices measured by the study are simply proxy variables for particular countries. For example, plants that use teams are obviously Japanese plants, and so the ''teams'' variable functions as a dummy variable for Japan. What this variable picks up, therefore, has nothing to do with teams, and everything to do with unique aspects of Japan (e.g., low cost of capital, work ethic of Japanese workers, the multi-tier supplier system).

Answer: As noted above, we took great care to avoid measures that would simply vary at the national level. Work teams may be commonly used in Japan, but they have been found in U.S. and European assembly plants for more than a decade. The same holds true for every manufacturing and human resource practice we measure. We apply this policy as much to Europe and the U.S. as to Japan. For example, we do not measure the use of works councils (applicable only in Europe) or the number of three-step grievances (applicable only in the U.S.).

Critique: Plants will provide erroneous information in the survey to make their performance look good.

Answer: This risk exists for any study. However, we have several reasons for being confident that there is minimum risk plants would do this deliberately, and that we catch most or all problems resulting from misunderstandings, poor translations, and so forth.

First, we keep all plant names completely confidential, and do not write reports or prepare graphs that allow any company or plant to be identified. This is essential for us to receive data from the auto companies—data that is often viewed as highly sensitive or even proprietary. However, it also means that a plant will not gain any public relations benefit from misrepresenting their performance to us. More importantly, plants provide us with data because, in return, we visit each participating plant, no matter where it is located, and provide in-depth feedback. This includes meetings with managers and union representatives to provide a detailed analysis of how the plant compares to others in its region, and other regions of the world on a series of practices and philosophies. Gathering the data we require is extremely time-intensive, and the plants view it as an opportunity for learning. Providing phony data would weaken the usefulness of the feedback we provide them—both because their performance would be mischaracterized, and also because the regional averages that we give them for comparison purposes would be biased.

We do extensive follow-up research with plants to insure that the data are accurate, including three or four pages of questions after receipt of the survey, and extensive phone and fax exchanges. During our plant visits, we also do on-site data verification of a set of key responses. Lastly, we have a systematic method for analyzing responses for internal consistency within the plant, among plants of the same company, and for the same plant over time. This allows us to pinpoint questionable responses and ensure they are corrected.

The broadest critique of the assembly plant study is that it is simply impossible to ever achieve "apples to apples" comparisons across plants, so there is no point in trying. Our immediate reaction is that such a view is self-defeating. Naturally, nothing can be learned when one starts with an a priori conclusion that nothing can be learned.[11]

Furthermore, those who take such a stand do not oppose all measurement. Indeed, they offer other data, generally at a company or industry level, in order to refute claims made by the assembly plant study. They assume, for example, that performance at the plant level can be inferred with greater accuracy from publicly-available data at an industry level than from a careful plant-level comparison using independent measures. They argue that "vehicle units produced" is an appropriate measure of output, regardless of whether those units represent trucks, minivans, or cars. They assume that company or even national aggregated information is a more valid way to assess the effects of organizational philosophies, technological policies, and human resource practices on productivity than using precise plant-level data.

These assertions and assumptions are unjustifiable, we believe. There is tremendous variation in the manufacturing requirements for different cars, and even greater differences between cars and trucks. (Trucks are actually much simpler to build, controlling for size.) Using national-level data to draw conclusions about plant-level performance assumes homogeneity across plants in the same country. But we have found huge variation in both performance and in production system practices across companies in the same country or region, as well as across plants in the same company. These variations are among the most interesting phenomena in the entire study because they allow one to assess the impact of different plant-level practices and philosophies holding constant either national or company-level characteristics.

A second response is that the performance differentials identified across and within regions during the assembly plant study are very large. Recall these regional averages in the 1989—1990 data for labor hours per vehicle: Japanese plants in Japan, 16.8 hours; U.S. plants in North America, 24.9 hours; European-owned plants in Europe, 35.3 hours. Suppose that the assembly plant productivity calculations are off by 10 to 20 percent (we should note that we don't believe they are). Even if this hypothetical measurement error were to favor plants from some regions consistently and hurt plants from other regions, the performance gap across regions would still be large. The same point applies to performance differences within regions. The best Japanese plant in Japan, at 13.2 hours in 1989, was almost twice as productive as the worst Japanese plant, at 25.9 hours. These differentials would not disappear due to measurement error.

We are convinced that the issues addressed by the assembly plant study are too important to be dismissed as "impossible to study." Many valuable insights emerged from the first-round data and these have had a profound impact on the thinking of many managers, union officials, workers, and customers. These insights would not have had much impact, and would not be accorded much legitimacy, if they were contradicted by other similar (i.e., plant-level) data or, more significantly, by the personal experience of people actually working in the auto industry. Many of the plants identified in the study as inefficient by world standards have been able to identify a considerable waste of time, people, equipment, and materials in their operations. While there may be legitimate disagreements about the best ways to improve performance, we believe there has been convergence on the idea that choices about how to organize the production system are critical—more critical than heavy investments in high-tech equipment or better product designs or a better-educated workforce.

We hope that we will be able to continue the International Assembly Plant Study beyond the current round so that it can provide increasingly greater insights into the dynamics of changing production systems and performance improvement over time. We will continue to work to improve the methodologies we use while maintaining comparability with previous data. We look forward to continued valuable feedback and suggestions from all sources, but particularly from those willing to familiarize themselves with the philosophy, research strategy, and methodological choices that have characterized the International Assembly Plant Study throughout its eight-year history.

Notes

1. James Womack, Daniel Jones, and Daniel Roos, *The Machine that Changed the World* (New York: Rawson Associates, 1990).

2. John Krafcik, "Learning from NUMMI," working paper (IMVP, MIT, 1986); John Krafcik, "Comparative Analysis of Performance Indicators at World Auto Assembly Plants" (master's thesis, Sloan School of Management, MIT, 1988); John Krafcik and John Paul MacDuffie, "Explaining High Performance Manufacturing: The International Assembly Plant Study," working paper (IMVP, MIT, 1989); John Paul MacDuffie and John Krafcik, "Integrating Technology and Human Resources for High Performance Manufacturing: Evidence from the World Automobile Industry," in *Transforming Organizations*, ed. Thomas Kochan and Michael Useem (New York: Oxford University Press, 1992).

3. More extensive discussion of these variables can be found in other papers: for measures of technology, see John Krafcik, "A Comparative Analysis of Assembly Plant Automation," working paper (IMVP, MIT, 1989), and John Paul MacDuffie, "Beyond Mass Production: Flexible Production Systems and Manufacturing Performance in the World Auto Industry" (Ph.D. diss., Sloan School of Management, MIT, 1991). For measures of manufacturing policies and human resource practices, see John Paul MacDuffie, "Human Resource Bundles and Manufacturing Performance: Flexible Production Systems in the World Auto Industry," unpublished, 1994; for measures of product complexity, see John Paul MacDuffie, Kannan Sethuraman, and Marshall L. Fisher, "Product Variety and Manufacturing Performance: Evidence from the International Automotive Assembly Plant Study," unpublished, 1994.

4. The J. D. Power and Associates Initial Quality Survey sample usually includes between one hundred and four hundred cars produced in each plant that sells products in the United States. Results are strictly confidential.

5. See Krafcik, "Comparative Analysis of Performance Indicators," and John Krafcik, "A Methodology for Assembly Plant Performance Determination," working paper (IMVP, MIT, 1988).

6. Chris Ittner and John Paul MacDuffie, "Exploring the Sources of International Differences in Manufacturing Overhead," manuscript (Wharton School, University of Pennsylvania, 1994); Jeffrey Miller and Thomas Vollmann, "The Hidden Factory," *Harvard Business Review* 63 (Sept.-Oct. 1985): 142–150. A related point is that the assembly plant accounts for only a portion of the total value added in the production of an automobile, given the high cost of both design and components. This critique is not relevant to the assembly plant study per se, which has never claimed to measure performance beyond the plant level. However, we acknowledge that excellent productivity at the assembly plant level won't translate into company-level profitability unless other key pieces in the value chain are equally efficient, pricing is appropriate in relation to the company's cost structure, and customers want to buy the company's products.

7. On Total Factor Productivity, see Robert Hayes and Kim Clark, "Exploring the Sources of Productivity Differences at the Factory Level," in *The Uneasy Alliance: Managing the Productivity-Technology Dilemma*, ed. Kim Clark, Robert Hayes, and Christopher Lorenz (Boston: Harvard Business School Press, 1985). On capital productivity and other factors affecting plant performance, see Michael Cusumano, *The Japanese Automobile Industry: Technology and Management at Nissan and Toyota* (Cambridge: Harvard University Press, 1985), and Marvin Lieberman, Lawrence Lau, and Mark Williams, "Firm-Level Productivity and Management Influence: A Comparison of U.S. and Japanese Automobile Producers," *Management Science* 36 (Oct. 1990): 1193–1215.

8. Since daily working hours will vary based on union contract and national norms, the methodology also adjusts total labor input for a standardized work day.

9. Specifically, to compensate for manufacturability of the design in welding and paint departments, adjustments are made for the number of welds in the design, which affects direct and indirect headcount in the welding department (depending on how automated the weld

process is) and for the amount of joint sealer that must be applied in the paint department, which affects direct labor headcount for this still labor-intensive task. In other words, plants with more welds (spot and arc) or joint sealer than the sample average receive a credit, in the form of a reduction in their hours per vehicle, while plants with fewer welds or joint sealer have their hours per vehicle adjusted up.

10. Kim Clark and Takahiro Fujimoto, *Product Development Performance: Strategy, Organization and Management in the World Auto Industry* (Boston: Harvard Business School Press, 1991).

11. Karel Williams, Colin Haslam, John Williams, Tony Cutler, Andy Adcroft, and Sukhdev Johal, "Against Lean Production," *Economy and Society* (Aug. 1992): 321–354.

PART 4 | NORTH AMERICA

10

Subaru-Isuzu: Worker Response in a Nonunion Japanese Transplant

LAURIE GRAHAM

From July 1989 through January 1990 I worked as a hidden participant-observer in the trim and final department at Subaru-Isuzu Automotive (SIA), a nonunion Japanese auto transplant located near Lafayette, Indiana. From this vantage point I was able to observe management's efforts to control shop-floor operations in a lean production plant, and workers' attempts to resist and amend those management initiatives through individual and collective protest. My analysis is based on daily field notes and informal discussions with approximately 150 people, including job applicants, employment specialists in charge of the hiring process, co-workers, team mates, team leaders, and management personnel. Both management and workers were unaware that they were under observation.

The Setting

SIA assembles the Subaru Legacy and the Isuzu pickup and sports-utility vehicles using production methods found in most Japanese auto transplants, including work teams, task rotation, a flat management structure, and worker involvement in quality control.

I worked on Team 1, one of fourteen teams on the final car assembly line, matched by roughly the same number of teams on the neighboring truck assembly line. My team was one of four which reported to a single group leader, the lowest level salaried employee. There were thirteen hourly workers on Team 1, including a team leader selected by management. During the time I worked at SIA, the plant was moving from start-up operations towards full production, with a corresponding increase in line speed, work intensity, and repetitive strain injuries. Eventually, half of the members of Team 1 (seven of thirteen) were working with job-related hand or wrist injuries. During these same months, the total plant population doubled from five hundred to one thousand workers; by management's estimate about one-third of the workforce were women, and fewer than 10 percent were African-American.

Shop-Floor Control

The theoretical framework for my examination of this work environment is a concept of shop-floor control that takes as its premise the conflict between managers and workers over the terms and conditions of work. Conflict may be muted or overt, constructive or destructive, but in whatever form, conflict is inevitable in a hierarchical factory setting. Managers seeking to maximize organizational goals must accommodate, redefine, or suppress the alternative goals motivating individuals and groups in the workforce. In this sense the shop floor is a contested terrain, an arena in which managers and workers try to control the daily struggle over who does which jobs, under what conditions, and with what outcomes. This concept of shop-floor control is central to my conclusions concerning the American labor movement's response to the Japanese model.

Control of the shop floor can be considered in two dimensions: control over the technical aspects of work, and control over the social aspects of work. In traditional U.S. auto production, management has focused on controlling the technical aspects of work through such processes as deskilling and task fragmentation. Traditionally, workpace is controlled through the assembly line and through supervisors who personally direct the workforce.

The social aspect of production is expressed in a shop-floor culture that defines worker behavior toward the boss and other workers. In metal-

TABLE 10.1
Social and Technical Controls at Subaru-Isuzu

Social Aspects of Control
1. Pre-employment selection process
2. Orientation and training for all new workers
3. Team concept
4. Philosophy of kaizen (continuous improvement)
5. Culture of egalitarianism
Technical Aspects of Control
6. The computerized assembly line
7. Just-in-time production

working, the archetype of workplace culture is described by labor historian David Montgomery as the craft workers' ethos of brotherhood: a collective code in which the skilled worker was expected to assume a "manly posture" toward the boss, to control his or her own output through working a certain stint each day, and to enforce the quota by discouraging rate busters. To neutralize this workplace culture, American management has put special emphasis on technical means of control that minimize worker discretion and reduce opportunities for "soldering."[1]

The Japanese model is distinguished by its multi-dimensional approach to controlling both the technical and social aspects of production. Such a strategy creates a system consistent with Michael Burawoy's concept of hegemonic control. Japanese managers focus their efforts on manipulating the naturally occurring phenomenon of worker solidarity, turning it away from acts of resistance and harnessing it to company goals. This emphasis on shaping shop-floor culture distinguishes the Japanese model from the traditional management schemes found in the U.S. auto industry. Of course, Japanese management continues to rely on such mechanisms of technical control as the assembly line, but its preoccupation with the social arena is what sets the Japanese model apart from other management strategies.[2]

At Subaru-Isuzu this system of control has seven components, five of which focus primarily on the social aspects of control, and two of which focus primarily on the technical aspects. Although many of these components overlap both the social and technical realms, they are best understood by their primary function, as indicated in table 10.1. The social aspects of control are the first and most salient experience for workers at SIA, beginning with an extensive process of pre-employment screening and testing focused primarily on an applicant's behavior during the selection process, rather than on previous job experience or qualifications. The orientation and training classes which follow emphasize behavioral norms and company philosophy, with considerably less time devoted to technical training. Team concept is defined, both in training and in practice, primarily in terms of peer pressure and the internalization of team responsibilities. The philosophy of *kaizen* based on group expectations of continuous improvement by each individual is introduced. Finally, management promotes an egalitarian shop-floor culture through symbols and rituals that obscure the outward status distinctions between managers and workers. Together, these social aspects of control define the appropriate behaviors and corresponding attitudes management hopes to promote among SIA workers.

Worker Resistance

When successful, SIA's social and technical control mechanisms merge in a system that effectively regulates the pace and intensity of work. The predominant response of workers is compliance, but resistance also emerges in a variety of forms and circumstances, beginning with individual manipulation of the screening process during hiring, and proceeding to collective manipulation of company norms during work. During the hiring process, for example, many workers indicated in private that they had lied on questionnaires and pretended to be team players in order to get the job. Once on the shop floor, workers then manipulated Subaru-Isuzu's egalitarian rhetoric by using it against the company. A type of informal, collective negotiation emerged, ultimately grounded in the underlying threat of unionization. Workers quickly learned that only through collective resistance were they able to extract meaningful concessions from management.

Worker resistance to SIA's system of shop-floor management took both collective and individual forms. Collective resistance emerged in acts of minor sabotage when workers forced unscheduled stops in the assembly process; in group protest when workers refused to participate in company rituals; in acts of insubordination when they refused management requests; and in organized agitation when they confronted management at team and department meetings. Individual resistance took the form of solitary refusals to participate in company rituals, and in personalized complaints through anonymous letters to the company. Each of these collective and individual forms of resistance deserves elaboration.

Minor sabotage occurred when workers on one of the trim and final teams discovered how to stop the assembly line without management tracing their location. The specific technique (which can't be revealed without identifying the team and the individuals involved) is less important than the opportunity it created for exercising a modest degree of control over the pace of work. In practice, whenever one of the members of that team fell behind and the "coast was clear," the team would stop the line. This not only allowed their team members to catch up, it also gave the rest of us time away from the line. In addition, it provided entertainment as we watched management scramble around trying to find the source of the problem. At one morning team meeting, our team leader reported that the line had stopped for a total of twenty minutes the day before, and the company was unable to account for the time. Clearly, that team was taking a chance, but the workers who were aware of the sabotage and its source never reported it to management. Whether their solidarity sprang from motives that were primarily selfish, because of the appreciated breaks, or from a sense of loyalty to other workers, their collective silence protected this opportunity for resistance and indicated a corresponding lack of commitment to company goals.

Resistance also emerged in the form of overt, collective protest. For example, as a group, workers refused to participate in exercises and team meetings in response to the company's unilateral action ending a five-minute clean-up period at the end of the day. This passive resistance eventually escalated to direct confrontation with management. Once the clean-up period was gone, workers refused management's request to work "after the buzzer" (the end of the shift) in order to clean-up and put away their tools. The group leader for our area called a special meeting of Team 1 and Team 2 to enlist our help in cleaning up after the buzzer. At the meeting several workers from both teams directly confronted the group leader. In an especially telling remark, a worker from Team 1 told the supervisor that "this is the kind of bull shit that brings in a union." A second worker added that "this place is getting too Japanese around here, pretty soon you will be asking us to donate our Saturdays." A worker from Team 2 assured the group leader that he was "not a volunteer." As a group, they were adamant that they would not work after the buzzer. On the following day, the line continued moving until the buzzer sounded; as it happened, I was so far behind on my station, that by the time the line stopped, I did not hear the buzzer and I kept working. As two team mates walked by they called to me, "Laurie, don't do it." Alerted to the implications of my continued efforts, I put down my tools. As I was leaving I overheard our team leader ask another team member a question concerning work. The team member replied, "look, it's after 3:00, I don't know," and he walked away. From that day on, whenever the line ran up to quitting time, everyone on the team dropped whatever they were doing and immediately walked out, leaving the team leader to lock up the tools and clean our areas. At one team meeting our team leader complained that she had stayed almost an hour after work cleaning up and putting away our tools. One team member told her she "was crazy to do it and we weren't going to."

Another example of direct confrontation occurred when two workers from Team 1 refused to work unscheduled overtime. When the manager from the car side threatened them with discipline, two other team members threatened to leave in protest. Confronted by this show of solidarity, and by the fact that if the additional workers left it would shut down the line, management capitulated and let the first two workers leave, without discipline.

Finally, collective resistance emerged through organized agitation at team and department meetings. This occurred as workers attempted to stop the company from instituting a policy of shift rotation. Management handed down the policy and stated that it was "not up for discussion," we would all have to rotate when the second shift was added. Workers informally passed the word around the plant to "keep the pressure on by bringing it up at meetings." Eventually, management announced that the company had reconsidered the policy and there would be no shift rotation.

A second category of resistance was characterized by individual acts of defiance. One form that emerged was a silent protest by individual workers who purposefully delayed their arrival to avoid morning exercises, or who remained sitting while others participated. A second form of individual protest emerged in anonymous letters to the company. This was a weaker form of resistance because it utilized a formal procedure instituted by the company, and posed little risk to the worker. As part of its "fair treatment policy," the company distributed prestamped, self-addressed envelopes for people to write in anonymously with questions or comments. The comments were posted throughout the plant on special bulletin boards with both the worker's comment and the company's reply. Between October 26, when the first batch was posted, and January 5, 150 comments, questions, and gripes were aired. At first they were optimistic, containing questions concerning the future. For example, people asked if there would be a credit union, a car purchase program, a daycare facility, or a fitness gym. However, soon it became a sounding board for complaints and dissatisfaction. Concerns emerged over scheduling overtime without notification. Parents complained that scheduling meetings after work and long hours of overtime conflicted with their children's hours at daycare. Other workers expressed concern that favoritism existed in parking, lunch hours, bonus plans, scheduling of overtime, and the loaning out of company cars. Repeated complaints emerged that group leaders and team leaders were being chosen without any job postings. Trim and final associates wanted to know why maintenance associates were paid two dollars more per hour. There were repeated concerns that quality was being sacrificed in order to meet daily schedules. Workers questioned why seniority was used for such things as enrollment in the pension plan, but not for transfers and promotions. One worker wanted to know why security checks were unequally applied, as people with lunch boxes were searched when leaving through the front door, while those with briefcases could walk on by. Another worker quoted state law concerning overtime pay, stressing that it was illegal for the company to require us to clean our areas and put our tools away after the shift had ended. There were also the more predictable complaints concerning food, long lines in the cafeteria, uniforms, gloves, and plant temperature. Most of the complaints were merely gripes, but many revealed that the company was not totally successful in instituting a spirit of cooperation and a culture of egalitarianism.

Conclusion

Although Burawoy's concept of hegemonic control best describes SIA's efforts to secure managerial authority on the shop floor, Burawoy misses the resistance that is evident in workers' adaptations to the production system. He implies that all forms of cooperation in production are consensual, and he fails to acknowledge, as Clawson and Fantasia put it, "the degree of external coercion necessary to preserve capitalist control, and the limits to and problematic character of this control." At SIA, workers' adaptation to management control can best be understood as a process of negotiation, not consent. Through collective acts of protest and resistance, workers were able to exploit the company's fear of unionization and increase their bargaining leverage. Their success in forcing specific concessions (e.g., canceling mandatory shift rotation) is a measure of the company's failure to completely manipulate shop-floor culture and turn the social aspects of production into a mechanism of company control.[3]

While the Japanese model, with its unique emphasis on securing management control of the social aspects of work, produces new challenges for U.S. unions, the present case study also suggests that it opens up new opportunities. Because of its focus on culture, teamwork, and "pulling together," management creates an atmosphere that heightens the individual's consciousness of being connected to the work group. This can reinforce the individual's commitment to company goals, but at SIA it also meant that workers could redefine their team as a haven of solidarity when they opposed certain company policies. The gap between the rhetoric and the substance of lean production also strengthened their collective resistance, particularly when workers perceived that management had failed to deliver on its frequent promise that SIA would provide an egalitarian work environment with ample opportunities for worker participation. Evidence of unequal treatment or unilateral management action provoked righteous indignation that the company had failed to "live by its own rules." Workers, in short, could appropriate both the language and the structure of team-based production and use them to mobilize collective resistance.

It is worth keeping in mind, however, that their concerted activity fell short of organizing a sustained, independent challenge to management prerogatives. In short, workers did not automatically move to the next step of union organization. For the most part, their solidarity was restricted to the immediate team or group, and even when it occasionally expanded to a plant-wide definition of worker solidarity, their protest aimed no higher than the informal pressures they could apply on management to amend specific policies. Contesting management's efforts to control the social dimensions of work is the starting point for worker resistance to lean production, but a sustained challenge to the system requires the explicit formulation of an oppositional culture that transcends specific grievances and makes worker solidarity a matter of permanent organization.

Notes

1. David Montgomery, *Worker's Control in America: Studies in the History of Work, Technology, and Labor Struggles* (Cambridge: Cambridge University Press, 1979).

2. See Laurie Graham, "Inside a Japanese Transplant: A Critical Perspective," *Work and Occupations* 20, no. 2 (May 1993): 147–173, and Michael Burawoy, *Manufacturing Consent: Changes in the Labor Process under Monopoly Capitalism* (Chicago: University of Chicago Press, 1979).

3. See Paul Thompson, *The Nature of Work: An Introduction to Debates on the Labour Process*, 2 ed. (Atlantic Highlands, N.J.: Humanities Press International, 1989); Dan Clawson and Rick Fantasia, "Beyond Burawoy: The Dialectics of Conflict and Consent on the Shop Floor," *Theory and Society* 12 (Dec. 1983): 675.

11

"Democratic Taylorism": The Toyota Production System at NUMMI

PAUL ADLER

The human aspects of Japanese manufacturing, in particular those techniques embodied in the Toyota production system, are currently under intense debate. Do they represent a positive model for the future of the American workplace? Some observers applaud the approach's reliance on teamwork, workers' problem-solving and multi-skilling. Other observers denounce what they see as work intensification, management by stress, and ultra-Taylorism.

The present chapter contributes to this debate with a discussion of the New United Motors Manufacturing, Inc. (NUMMI) assembly plant in Fremont, California. NUMMI, a joint venture between General Motors and Toyota, has implemented the Toyota approach with but little dilution. The plant is unusual in that its workforce is composed primarily of workers who had been laid off when the GM-Fremont plant closed in 1982. Moreover, the UAW has retained bargaining rights and exercises considerable influence in the operation of the plant.[1]

The examination of this case begins with a summary of the plant's background, followed by a description of some of the key policies governing NUMMI's production system and its labor relations. After reviewing the data on NUMMI's exceptional productivity and quality performance, I then turn to workers' assessments of the quality of work life at NUMMI. Some puzzling paradoxes emerge from this characterization, which I attempt to resolve by suggesting that NUMMI's production system can be understood as an unusual but potentially important form of organization that I call "democratic Taylorism."

Background

NUMMI was formed in 1983 as a joint venture between General Motors and Toyota. For its part, Toyota hoped that setting up plants in the U.S. would alleviate some of the growing political pressure on Japanese automakers to reduce their sizable trade surplus. NUMMI was conceived as the first step in that strategy, designed to help Toyota learn about U.S. suppliers and labor. General Motors, on the other hand, wanted to learn about Japanese manufacturing systems, and they needed a small car to fill a gap in the low end of their product line. Toyota contributed $100 million, and took responsibility for setting up the plant's day-to-day operations and designing the plant's primary product, the Nova, a variant of the Corolla. (NUMMI later changed the name to Geo Prizm, and would also produce Corollas and Toyota compact pick-up trucks.) GM contributed the facility and was responsible for marketing the Nova/Prizm.

The decision was made to house the new company at the old GM-Fremont plant, which had been shut down in 1982. Politically, it was inconceivable that the plant reopen without UAW involvement. A Letter of Intent was therefore signed with the union in September 1983 stipulating that NUMMI would recognize the UAW as the bargaining agent for the venture's employees. The letter further indicated that the company would pay prevailing U.S. auto industry wages and benefits, and that a majority of the workforce would be hired from among the three thousand workers laid off from GM-Fremont; however, seniority would not be a factor in their recall to the successor operation. In return, the UAW agreed to support the implementation of a new production system and to negotiate a new contract. The collective bargaining agreement was subsequently signed in June 1985.

NUMMI began hiring in May 1984. Of fifty-three hundred applications sent to former GM-Fremont employees, thirty-two hundred were returned. Over the next twenty months, the company hired twenty-two hundred hourly team members, approximately 85 percent of them from the old GM-Fremont workforce, including the entire union hierarchy. Some 300 salaried employees were also hired. The applicants for hourly jobs—

team leaders and team members—were evaluated jointly by managers and union officials.

NUMMI's overall business strategy was to build its cars at the lowest cost and the highest quality. The following sections highlight management policies that contributed to that goal in two areas: the production system, and the labor relations system.

The Production System

NUMMI's production management was modeled directly on the Toyota system. The key elements were the following:

Kanban. NUMMI did not use a computerized scheduling system. Instead, signs—or *kanban*—were passed to the upstream department whenever inventory pallets or dollies needed to be replaced. If no *kanban* arrived, the upstream department stopped production to prevent the build up of inventory.

Production leveling. In Big Three plants, line speeds remain fixed even as production schedules are constantly changing. Factory managers make the necessary adjustments in output by adding and subtracting overtime and taking on and laying off shifts. By contrast, NUMMI leveled the schedule over several months, and made periodic adjustments to output levels by varying the line speed. The leveling policy also shaped the day's build schedule: different models were mixed evenly throughout, rather than batched.

Kaizen. NUMMI paid enormous attention to *kaizen*—the continuous improvement of all aspects of production. Accordingly, all NUMMI workers were trained in problem-solving techniques, and management regarded worker participation in the suggestion program as a key measure of the plant's performance.

Visual control. This policy emphasized the use of visual indicators to signal abnormal conditions as rapidly and automatically as possible. *Kanban* is one form of visual control, signaling the need to replenish an inventory pallet. Another key element of visual control at NUMMI was the "andon" board, which signaled quality problems on the line with flashing lights.

Jidoka. This meant assuring quality in the production process itself rather than relying on inspections at the end of the process to detect problems. Workers pulled a "line stop" cord when they encountered a quality problem, triggering the andon board signal that alerted the team leader and the group leader. Unless the problem could be resolved within sixty seconds, the line would stop. *Poka-yoke,* or error-proofing, was another element of *jidoka*: parts packaging, equipment designs, and tool setups were specified so as to make inadvertent error almost impossible.

Team concept. At NUMMI, team concept encompassed both the cooperative labor relations system described below and the organization of small teams of four to six workers. Workers in each team were cross-trained to perform several tasks and most workers rotated between work stations. (Rotation was not practiced in Toyota's Japanese plants, but it was written into NUMMI's collective bargaining agreement.)

Standardized work. This practice was, in the words of a NUMMI manager, "the intelligent interpretation and application of Taylor's time and motion studies." Each job was analyzed down to its constituent gestures, and the sequence of movements was refined and optimized for maximum performance. Every task was planned in great detail, and each worker was expected to perform that task in the prescribed manner.

The combination of these policies created an extraordinarily disciplined organization.

Labor Relations

NUMMI's labor relations policies reflected a commitment to what former NUMMI president and CEO Kan Higashi calls the "team concept": "The team concept is not just the small groups on the shop floor. It also applies to the plant as a whole. The bigger team is the workers, managers, engineers and staff all working together to constantly improve our product. This way, the workers see that the company isn't the property of management, but of everyone together. And the key to this team concept is trust and respect."[2]

This policy was reflected in NUMMI's dress code—at least in the production function, everyone from the senior manager down wore the same uniform—as well as in the absence of management cafeterias and reserved parking. More substantively, it was reflected in a range of opportunities for worker representatives not only to give voice to workers' concerns, but also to help shape the company's response to those concerns. Every week, month, and quarter various levels of the union leadership met with the corresponding levels of management, and the union was consulted in advance on major operating and strategic decisions.

Management saw NUMMI's no-layoff policy as part of its commitment to the team concept. The collective bargaining agreement of 1985 stated:

> New United Motor Manufacturing, Inc. recognizes that job security is essential to an employee's well being and acknowledges that it has a responsibility, with the cooperation of the Union, to provide stable employment to its workers. The Union's commitments in Article II of this Agreement are a significant step towards the realization of stable employment. Hence, the Company agrees that it will not lay off employees unless compelled to do so by severe economic conditions that threaten the long term viability of the Company. The Company will take affirmative measures before laying off any employees, including such measures as the reduction of salaries of its officers and management, assigning previously subcontracted work to bargaining unit employees capable of performing this work, seeking voluntary layoffs, and other cost saving measures.[3]

The no-layoff policy was not without some sacrifice for workers. Not only did the union have to agree to many changes in operating philosophy, but in exchange for NUMMI's commitment to avoid layoffs, the contract exempted NUMMI from contributing to GM's Supplemental Unemployment Benefits plan. SUB benefits assured GM workers that if they were laid off they would receive close to full pay. Without this SUB pay, laid-off workers would get unemployment insurance at levels that were substantially lower.

NUMMI's "team concept" was also reflected in its organizational structure. There was only one classification for Division 1 personnel, as opposed to over eighty in the GM-Fremont contract. The number of skilled trades classifications had also been reduced from eighteen to two—general maintenance and tool and die.

Team leaders were hourly employees who played a role somewhere between the old-style "utility man" (a multi-skilled worker able to fill in for a broad range of positions) and foreman. The team leader filled in for absent workers, trained new workers, assisted workers having difficulty in their jobs, recorded attendance, assigned work when the line stopped, assisted team members in minor maintenance and housekeeping, assessed new team members, led *kaizen* efforts, and organized social events outside the plant. In March 1988, in response to workers' concerns with favoritism in the selection of team leaders, management agreed to a joint union/management selection process based on explicit and primarily objective criteria.

TABLE 11.1
NUMMI Productivity Comparisons

	Framingham	GM-Fremont	NUMMI	Takaoka
Uncorrected productivity (hrs/unit)				
• hourly*	36.1	38.2	17.5	15.5
• salaried	4.6	4.9	3.3	2.5
• total	40.7	43.1	20.8	18.0
Corrected Productivity** (hrs/unit)				
• hourly*	26.2	24.2	16.3	15.5
• salaried	4.6	4.9	3.3	2.5
• total	30.8	29.1	19.6	18.0

*excluding stamping, molding, and seat assembly personnel
**corrected for number of welds, welding automation, product size, relief time, and option content
[Source: Krafcik, 1986]

Performance

The productivity of the NUMMI plant has been extensively analyzed by John Krafcik; some key indicators of NUMMI's performance are summarized in table 11.1. Labor productivity, both corrected and uncorrected for differences in product and technology, was much higher at NUMMI than at the old GM-Fremont plant and at the GM-Framingham plant. (Krafcik chose Framingham because it was a GM plant somewhat comparable in product and technology mix to NUMMI.) By 1986, NUMMI was almost as productive as its sister plant in Takaoka and more productive than any other GM plant. This performance is all the more impressive when it is recalled that the NUMMI workforce was on average some ten years older than Takaoka's, and younger workers are in general better equipped to deal with the pressures of assembly-line work.[4]

The comparisons with the Takaoka plant are particularly useful because one of the factors contributing to NUMMI's productivity and quality performance was the "producibility" ("manufacturability") of their vehicles' designs. Not only were the designs already in production—which meant that most of the producibility problems that the original designs may have had were already ironed out—but Toyota was renowned for its ability to assure a high level of producibility in its original designs. The fact that NUMMI's overall performance had reached a level so close to Takaoka's suggests that this performance level was not due exclusively to the products' producibility.

More recent data indicate that these extraordinary results persisted into 1992. The J. D. Power and Associates Initial Quality Study of the number of problems per one hundred vehicles experienced by customers within ninety days of purchase show that NUMMI progressed from 116 per 100 vehicles in 1989 (compared to an industry average of 148 for all cars sold in the U.S.) to 93 in 1991, and to 83 in 1992 (versus an industry average of 125 for all cars sold in the U.S., an average of 105 for Asian nameplates, 136 for U.S. nameplates, and 158 for Europeans.)[5]

The Quality of Work Life at NUMMI

The key question is whether these efficiency and quality outcomes were obtained at the expense of workers' well-being. Certainly, NUMMI's extraordinary productivity clearly had something to do with the intensity of work. Standard task times at GM-Fremont had been set to occupy the experienced worker for approximately forty-five seconds out of a hypothetical cycle time of sixty seconds. NUMMI, in contrast, aimed to occupy the worker sixty seconds out of sixty and in practice averaged about fifty-seven seconds out of sixty.

This work intensity was the direct result of the Toyota production system and the organization of work it specified: no buffer inventories, detailed work methods closely calibrated to the real work situation, level production, rapid response to any breakdowns, and error-proofing of the process. The work organization embedded in this system was almost the mirror image of the Volvo model, which has become for many, especially in the labor movement, the yardstick for quality of work life. The Volvo model is best known through the innovations introduced in the company's Swedish operations, first at the Kalmar plant and then in a more radical form at the Uddevalla plant, before both facilities were closed due to a collapse of Volvo's sales.[6]

NUMMI's operations contrasted most directly with Volvo in the degree of autonomy experienced by workers. A key feature of the Volvo model was the idea that the work team should be as independent as possible. Teams were therefore accorded considerable discretion in how they performed their work and how they scheduled their work time, with buffers of in-process inventory provided upstream and downstream to facilitate this autonomy. Teams were also given extensive management responsibilities in such domains as scheduling overtime and ordering supplies. At NUMMI, in contrast, the emphasis on standardized methods meant that workers had no autonomy whatsoever in how they performed their tasks. The *kanban* principle also meant that there were no buffers upstream or downstream, and therefore no discretion in how the teams scheduled their work. And NUMMI's team concept gave team members only a narrow range of managerial responsibilities.

What evidence do we have, then, of workers' reactions to NUMMI's intensely disciplined and regimented environment? There is no doubt that workers had complaints. Assembling automobiles at NUMMI was enormously demanding work physically, and some workers I have interviewed were angry at what they perceived to be management's reluctance to recognize work-related injuries. Some team leaders and some management personnel were seen as "playing favorites" or as simply incompetent, and some workers expressed frustration because they felt they had been unfairly overlooked for special projects or promotions.

But how did workers evaluate their overall experience at NUMMI? Taken individually, none of the available indicators are, in my opinion, compelling. But they all seem to point in a common, favorable direction:

- In numerous interviews conducted between 1987 and 1993, I have yet to find anyone who would rather work in the GM-Fremont system.

- NUMMI surveys workers' opinions every two years. "Overall work satisfaction" grew from 76 percent in 1987 to 90 percent in 1991. Satisfaction with job security grew even more dramatically. In 1987, only 70 percent of team members expressed satisfaction with this dimension of their work experience. At the time, sales of the Nova were very sluggish—capacity utilization rates fell to under 60 percent—and workers weren't sure they could trust management's commitment to the no-layoff clause in the collective bargaining agreement. But management lived up to that commitment by redeploying workers into training classes, maintenance tasks, and *kaizen* teams. By 1991, satisfaction with job security had reached 89 percent.

- Participation in the suggestion program grew from 26 percent in 1986 to 94 percent in 1992. By that year, workers were contributing an average of nearly six suggestions a year.

- Absenteeism rates held steady at an exceptionally low level of approximately 3 percent, and turnover remained very low at less that 6 percent.

Democratic Taylorism

Why, then, would workers respond positively to a production system characterized by such high levels of regimentation? I believe that at least part of the answer lies in the feeling among workers that this regimentation was not imposed from above, but came from the joint deliberations of company engineers and union workers seeking the best way to accomplish a difficult task.

GM-Fremont had some eighty industrial engineers who worked in a remote office environment developing work methods and standards from company handbooks. By contrast, at NUMMI there were no industrial engineers performing such duties. Team members and team leaders were taught how to analyze their own jobs using a stop watch and assessing alternative work procedures proposed by their colleagues. Each team would compare notes with the teams upstream and downstream to assure the best allocation of tasks and line balancing, and then compare the result with similar analyses performed on the opposing shift. The resulting methods had to be applied with great consistency, but workers were strongly encouraged to suggest improvements for efficiency, quality, or safety, and management typically responded to such suggestions very promptly. Standardized work was seen as a better way to do the job, as evidenced by the remarks of a UAW team leader during one of the interview sessions I conducted with NUMMI employees:

> The GM system relied on authority. People with rank, the managers, ruled regardless of their competence or the validity of what they were saying. It was basically a military hierarchy. At NUMMI rank doesn't mean a damn thing. Standardized work means we all work out the objectively best way to do the job, and everyone does it that way. I might make some minor adjustments because of my height, for example, but I follow the procedure as laid out because it makes sense. We're more like a special forces unit than the regular military hierarchy. Management's delegated responsibility to the people who do the work, and that gives workers a sense of pride in their jobs.

This does indeed sound like "the intelligent interpretation and application of Taylor's time and motion studies." I submit that NUMMI's standardized work process represents something we might call "democratic Taylorism," in contrast to the more traditional "despotic" form of Taylorism. The contrast can be described along a number of dimensions:

• At NUMMI, workers actively participated in defining work methods; traditional Taylorism assumed that the methods would be imposed by the Methods Department.

• NUMMI's standardized work process focused on work methods and assumed that better time standards would emerge from the discovery of better methods; traditional Taylorism focused on time standards, and assumed that failure to meet them was due not to inadequate methods but to insufficient effort by the worker.

• NUMMI taught the standardized work techniques in the same program as the *kaizen* process because NUMMI's Taylorism was devoted to collective learning in the plant; traditional Taylorism was designed to coerce work effort from a recalcitrant workforce, and the resulting methods and standards were rigidly fixed, prisoners of the balance of power on the shop floor.

• At NUMMI, the central role of workers in the standardized work process forced management to share power with workers; traditional Taylorism was often a means for asserting management's power over the shop floor.

Precedents for such a vision of "democratic Taylorism" can perhaps be found in the Amalgamated Clothing Workers under Sidney Hillman. This version of Taylor's doctrine of Scientific Management was advanced by Taylorites such as Morris L. Cooke, intellectuals such as J. R. Commons, and socialists such as the young Walter Lippmann. It was also perhaps what Lenin was gesturing towards when he suggested that the Soviets should learn Taylorism and apply it to their collective goals.[7]

This view suggests that we should see Taylorism as a kind of organizational technology, and like equipment technology, it can be designed and implemented so as to empower or to enslave. Management's traditional assumption is that employees are recalcitrant and irresponsible. As a result, managers design both equipment technologies and organizational technologies to ensure compliance, minimize employees' scope of discretion, and reduce the company's reliance on employees' skills. Management should then not be surprised when employees respond to such an environment with apathy and antagonism—a result which in turn comforts management in their initial assumption that employees are recalcitrant and irresponsible.[8]

The NUMMI example suggests that if management begins with the assumption that workers want to contribute to the goals of the organization, they can design organizational technologies that invite, capture, and diffuse suggested improvements to standard practices. In that way, an organization can maintain and elicit a high level of commitment on the part of the workforce—a result which in turn comforts this alternative initial assumption.

How does an organization create and sustain these initial conditions, so workers want to contribute? What are the conditions under which this democratic version of Taylorism is feasible? I would highlight three prerequisites.

First, there has to be a shift in management attitudes and behavior. The criteria used to select the initial group of sixteen GM managers at NUMMI tell us something about the prerequisite changes. A pool of candidates was created from GM personnel files, selecting individuals with the appropriate experience, education, work evaluations, and age, and these candidates were invited to interview sessions in Detroit. Eric Jacobson, quoting from two GM managers responsible for conducting these interviews, summarizes the key selection criteria: "honesty, humility, groupism [group orientation], sensitivity, listening ability, and communication ability."[9]

A second prerequisite would seem to be a commensurate set of changes in workers' attitudes and behavior. One of the managers I interviewed assessed the issue in the following terms:

> The production people bought into standardized work very easily. They understood the technique, because it had been done to them for years; and they liked the idea, because now they had a chance to do it for themselves. Their biggest problem was that many of them don't have a lot of education, so some of the math [for statistical quality control, for example] is a bit challenging and maybe threatening. So you have to work on that. A second challenge comes from the fact that you're changing things. At NUMMI, we want people to constantly improve their standardized work and a lot of people just aren't used to that much change. So you have to work with people so they come to see that change not just as a disturbance but as an opportunity to improve things. That's hard sometimes.

The third prerequisite condition for democratic Taylorism is more structural. George Nano, the head of the Bargaining Committee, expressed his views on the matter this way: "Standardized work gives workers the right to set up their own jobs and that means that management has to share power and cooperate with us. . . . The key to NUMMI's success is that management gave up some of its power, some of its traditional prerogatives. If managers want to motivate workers to contribute and learn, they have to give up some of their power. If management wants workers to trust them, we need to be fifty-fifty in making the decisions with them. Don't just make the decision and say 'trust me.' " If managers want the powerful apparatus of Taylorism to serve learning ends rather than coercive ends, they will need to reconcile themselves to some real loss of power.

Which leads to the question: why should managers relinquish power? And if managers have no incentive to relinquish power, is not democratic Taylorism a temporary epiphenomenon? There are indeed many structural and institutional forces that should make us less sanguine about the prospects for democratic Taylorism, such as the overall configuration of power in the U.S. today and the peculiarities of the inherited institutional framework (of labor law in particular). But NUMMI's successes incline me to modest optimism: the loss of management's *power over* workers seems to be more than compensated by the competitive benefits of the associated increase in the organization's *power to* accomplish joint goals.

Conclusion

This essay has attempted to tease out of the NUMMI case some elements of a new model of work organization. I have proposed calling the kind of work organization that we find in this combination of lean production with a strong union presence "democratic Taylorism." I do not believe that NUMMI lives up to this model every day in every way. Nor is this model the only useful way of describing NUMMI's overall characteristics. But if it helps account for NUMMI's combination of world-class productivity and quality and high worker morale and commitment, it is a model that deserves our attention.

Notes

1. For detailed assessments of NUMMI see Paul Adler, "The Learning Bureaucracy: New United Motors Manufacturing, Inc.," in *Research in Organizational Behavior* 15, ed. Barry Staw and Larry Cummings (Greenwich, CT: JAI Press, 1993): 111–194; Paul Adler, "Time-and-Motion Regained," *Harvard Business Review* (Jan.-Feb. 1993): 97–108; Paul Adler and Robert Cole, "Designed for Learning: A Tale of Two Auto Plants," *Sloan Management Review* 34, no. 3 (spring 1993): 85–94.

2. This and quotes that follow are, as indicated, from interviews I conducted with NUMMI employees between 1987 and 1993.

3. UAW-NUMMI, *Collective Bargaining Agreement* (1985), Article III, p. 4.

4. John Krafcik, "Learning from NUMMI," MIT International Motor Vehicle Program, 1986.

5. J. D. Power and Associates, *The J.D. Power Report* (June 1992). Revised data for earlier years provided by J. D. Power and Associates.

6. Christian Berggren, *Alternatives to Lean Production: Work Organization in the Swedish Auto Industry* (Ithaca, NY: ILR Press, 1992).

7. Steven Fraser, *Labor Will Rule: Sidney Hillman and the Rise of American Labor* (New York, Free Press, 1991), 187. For unsympathetic surveys of liberal-left interpretations of Taylorism, see Samuel Haber, *Efficiency and Uplift: Scientific Management in the Progressive Era* (Chicago: University of Chicago Press, 1964); Judith A. Merkle, *Management and Ideology: The Legacy of the International Scientific Management Movement* (Berkeley: University of California Press, 1980); Thomas P. Hughes, *American Genesis: A Century of Inven-

tion and Technological Enthusiasm, 1870–1970 (New York: Viking, 1989); Sanford Jacoby, ''Union-Management Cooperation in the United States: Lessons from the 1920s,'' *Industrial and Labor Relations Review* 37 (October 1983): 18–33. For Lenin's assessment of Taylorism, see Vladamir Lenin, ''The Immediate Tasks of the Soviet Government,'' *Izvestia* (28 Apr. 1918), translated in *Selected Works*, Vol. 2 (Moscow: Progressive Publishers, 1967).

8. Richard Walton, *Up and Running: Integrating Information Technology and Organization* (Boston: Harvard Business School Press, 1989).

9. Eric K. Jacobson, *NUMMI: A Model in Human Relations* (BSIE thesis, General Motors Engineering and Management Institute, 1986).

12

Team Concept at CAMI

**JAMES RINEHART, CHRIS HUXLEY, and
DAVID ROBERTSON**

Both advocates and critics of lean production in auto assembly transplants view team concept as central to this mode of manufacture. In *The Machine that Changed the World*, Womack, Jones, and Roos depict cross-training, multi-skilling, and job rotation, which take place within the medium of teams, as key organizational features of lean production. "It is the dynamic work team," these authors declare, "that emerges as the heart of the lean factory." It goes without saying that this camp regards team concept in general and work teams in particular as beneficial to workers, providing them with challenging opportunities for participation and skill development. Kenney and Florida offer a more sweeping assessment in *Beyond Mass Production*. "Team organization and increased worker input," these authors argue, "not only increase productivity but also reduce certain aspects of worker alienation."[1]

Critics Parker and Slaughter treat team concept as a package that includes (1) a philosophy of cooperation, (2) interchangeability of workers, (3) reduction of job classifications, (4) de-emphasis of seniority as the basis for job bidding, transfers, and so forth, (5) standardized jobs, (6) workers' participation in increasing their workloads, (7) more worker responsibility for production problems without more authority, (8) an ideology that stresses cooperation between plants and personnel, and (9) a shift toward enterprise unionism in which the union views itself as a partner of management. At its most concrete level, "team concept tries to break down the solidarity and teamwork of natural work groups that develop on the shop floor by trying—usually unsuccessfully—to channel that sentiment into formal, highly controlled, company-designed team structures."[2]

Research conducted at CAMI, a lean production, team concept plant, furnishes a basis for a concrete evaluation of these divergent views. CAMI is a joint venture between General Motors and Suzuki that makes the Geo Metro subcompact and the GM tracker and Suzuki Sidekick four-wheel drive sports utility vehicles. It is located in Ingersoll, Ontario, midway between Toronto and Detroit in what the company refers to as the heart of the Canadian automotive supplier community. The company began production in April 1989, and is now operating two shifts with a shop-floor workforce of twenty-one hundred. Workers at CAMI are members of the Canadian Auto Workers union (CAW), making this the only unionized transplant or joint venture car factory in Canada and one of only four such organized plants in North America.

After much pressure from the union, CAMI agreed to give our CAW research team access to the plant in order to clarify the dimensions and implications for workers of this new management and production system. Our group was comprised of two CAW researchers from the national office, three local CAW representatives, and two academics. We spent one full week at CAMI at four regular intervals between March 1990 and the end of November 1991. During our first visit the plant was not yet in full production. By our second visit in November 1990, the plant was at full line speed and operating with a second shift on the car side. At each of the four visits, we interviewed a random sample of one hundred workers (give or take a few due to illness, quits, promotions, etc.), ten to fifteen team leaders, an equal number of managers from all levels and departments, and a handful of maintenance associates and local union representatives. Interview schedules consisting of fixed-choice and open-ended questions were administered to workers. Interviews with the other employees were open-ended, and most of them were taped. While the original sample of workers was interviewed each time, with the exceptions noted above, other employees interviewed were not always the same persons. Another component of our study was repeated observations of work stations on the shop floor. Technology, job content and cycles, line speed, work loads, and so forth, were recorded, and we talked informally with team leaders and workers. This paper is grounded in all these sources of information.[3]

Team Concept at CAMI

CAMI emphasizes and posts throughout the plant its four values—open communication, empowerment, *kaizen*, and team spirit. That the Japanese own half of this company is obvious. Japanese words spelled out in English are used and posted everywhere. *Poka-yokes* (devices ensuring fail-safe operations) are located throughout the plant, and a *kanban* system is being perfected that will move operations closer to stockless (or "pull") production. Employee suggestions are called *teians*. Workers are expected to do pre-shift calisthenics called *taiso*, and are prepared for lean production through *nagare* training. The manual used to train recruits has its text in both English and Japanese.

CAMI is a lean factory not only because it tries to implement quick die changes, just-in-time parts delivery, and other attributes of a flexible production system, but also because it operates with a lean, bare-bones workforce. Most jobs at CAMI are highly standardized, with a prescribed sequence of operations that workers are expected to follow without deviation. These standards are posted at virtually every work station in the plant. Cycle times for assembly jobs range from ninety seconds to three minutes, requiring only a few hours to learn the basics and a day or two more to reach line-speed. Management encourages workers to cut these cycle times through participation in the continuous improvement of operations, or *kaizen*.

At the most general level, team concept at CAMI refers to a collaborative partnership between management and workers. Every employee, from the top to the bottom of the organization, is regarded as a member of one big team that pulls together to attain company goals and beat the competition. This element of team concept is expressed in the CAMI value of team spirit and is symbolized by CAMI's egalitarian exterior—common uniforms and cafeterias, the absence of time clocks and special parking spaces, and so forth. At a more concrete level, team concept entails organizing the workforce in teams to carry out production under the direction of a team leader. Production workers in each of CAMI's four departments (stamping, welding, paint, and assembly) are organized into teams, as are electricians and millwrights in the skilled trades and stockers in material handling. Team concept on the shop floor is built into the CAMI/CAW collective agreement, which states: "CAMI will utilize team concept, with employees organized into teams determined in accordance with the nature of an operation or process. All members of a team share responsibility for work performed by the team and for participation in quality and productivity improvement programs."

Team concept also refers to small groups of employees who engage in improvement activities, including *kaizen*. Team members are expected to pass on their improvement ideas to team leaders, and teams, operating as QC circles, are encouraged to issue formal proposals for reducing costs and non-value added activity. Teams, then, take on some of the functions of industrial engineers.

A central CAMI guideline is to "be a good team member," and management has gone to considerable lengths to recruit people who have the ability to communicate and cooperate with others. Among the attributes of an ideal CAMI worker are those of being a team player and being sensitive to the opinions of others. According to the CAMI guidelines, "A good team member involves others in the decision-making process, considers and utilizes the new ideas and suggestions of others, understands and is committed to team objectives, [yet] understands that the integrity of the line of authority must be maintained to keep an effective team."

Team concept permeates CAMI, and the layout of the plant facilitates its implementation. Teams in assembly, welding, material handling, and the paint shop have assigned work areas, usually consisting of numbered work stations. Near each of these work areas (with the exception of the paint shop) are spaces set aside for the team to meet, take breaks, eat lunch, and hold QC circle meetings. These areas are furnished with tables, chairs, lockers and shelves, bulletin boards and blackboards on which are posted information relating to attendance, rotation schedules, jobs learned by each worker, and *teians* (suggestions). Workers are also encouraged to adopt team names—in assembly, these included "Body Snatchers," "Body Slammers," "Trim Busters," and "Triminators." One team had an elaborately hand painted sign emblazoned above the rest area on which they described their work: "We'll rip your doors off."

Teams at CAMI have various production-related functions. First, the team provides a vehicle for training and job rotation. Teams also absorb indirect duties (housekeeping, some material handling, inspection) performed in traditional auto plants by special categories of individual workers. Second, teams provide a lateral control system in which peer pressure is combined with more traditional supervision. Good team members look out for one another, assist those who fall behind in their work, attend to their jobs faithfully, and are careful to do their tasks in such a way that they do not create more work for others. In team concept plants, even when workers are not committed to company values, peer pressure can operate to boost attendance, job performance, and *kaizen* activities.

Finally, the team serves a direct production function. While work is carried out in teams whose members are cross-trained and rotate jobs, output at CAMI remains a product of individual effort. In a few cases, the cooperation of pairs of workers is demanded by the nature of the task. For example, a real cooperative team effort is required when two workers help each other install the rag-top on a Tracker/Sidekick convertible. But cooperative team efforts like this arise out of the technical nature of a particular task and are not commonly required at CAMI. Real team efforts, like that needed to assemble the rag-top, also exist in plants that do not organize the workforce into teams. At CAMI, vehicles are still put together in the traditional way pioneered by Henry Ford—all major assembly tasks follow the logic and pace of the drag chain. Even sub-assemblies, such as those for the instrument panels, are built on moving lines. Hence, work at CAMI is not, for the most part, a team-based production system, but a system of teams superimposed on a traditional assembly line operation in which output arises from the efforts of individual workers carrying out standardized tasks. The team can support and reinforce individual effort, but for most tasks at CAMI the individual has not been supplanted by the team as the operative unit of production. At CAMI, then, teams are more an expression of social engineering than of a fundamentally new system of production.

As noted at the outset, Womack, Jones, and Roos regard work teams with broad operational responsibilities as an essential component of lean production. Kenney and Florida echo this position, repeatedly describing teams in auto transplants as "self-managing." In contrast, a recent study of automotive components plants in Japan and the United Kingdom (one of whose contributors, Daniel Jones, co-authored *The Machine that Changed the World*) found that plants rated "world class" in quality and productivity were less likely than their lower ranked counterparts to assign broad responsibilities like inspection, rectification, routine maintenance, and quality improvement to team members. These "pivotal" activities were undertaken in the high performance plants by team leaders. "These findings suggest that the role of the 'empowered' operator in world class manufacturing may have been overstated and that the crucial differences are at the team leader level." Certainly, worker empowerment and self-management do not describe CAMI's social organization of production. Pre-shift meetings are little more than brief information sessions relating to daily announcements and production schedules. Such tasks as housekeeping, inspection (involving quick checks to see if previous operations were properly completed), and stocking the line with parts hardly constitute major team responsibilities. Needless to say, team working at CAMI does not entail the kind of worker discretion over recruitment, work methods, and workpace that, for example, characterizes the semi-autonomous work groups in Swedish industry. Jobs are so highly standardized and tightly timed that workers have little choice about how and when they perform them or the speed at which they work. In fact, production demands are so great that workers find it difficult to attend to housekeeping, materials handling, and so on.[4]

That said, CAMI's system for distributing jobs and specifying roles does represent a marked departure from the practice in so-called traditional auto plants. In the latter, a job consists of a single task or a bundle of tasks performed by an individual worker who has acquired the right to the job through the exercise of seniority and transfer rights, or who finds him or herself in a particular job due to low seniority. This traditional concept of job ownership, which was reflected in a multitude of job classifications, has much less emphasis at CAMI where all production workers (or "production associates" as they are called) share the same classification.

How Workers View Team Concept

The company's attempt to instill in workers a feeling of team spirit—that working at CAMI is like being on a baseball or hockey team—has not been very successful. For workers, team concept means neither equality of all employees nor partnership with management, and the CAMI value of team spirit is increasingly regarded as little more than an empty slogan. For example, when survey respondents were asked if working in teams helped them feel like part of CAMI, 63 percent in round one but only 23 percent in round four agreed. For most workers, team concept has an immediate, concrete referent that signifies where and with whom they work day after day. When workers think at all of team concept, then, their image is of their own shop-floor teams.

How do people feel about working in these teams? There is no simple answer to this question, since workers regard teams as a mixture of good and bad elements. This ambivalence is underlined by the survey results. On the one hand, only 17 percent of the respondents in round one and 25 percent in round four felt that working in teams was a waste of time, while the great majority of respondents (90 percent in round four) said throughout the survey that they liked the idea of working in teams "very much" or "somewhat." But when asked, "What do you like about team concept at CAMI," most of those interviewed mentioned social aspects, such as friendship, helping out, and sticking up for each other. It was this social solidarity emerging out of the experience of being part of a team that accounted for workers' generally positive evaluation of team work. In rounds one and four 69 percent and 86 percent respectively of those interviewed said working in teams gave them a chance to get to know people. However, some made the point that this kind of social bond would have developed in the absence of team concept. One worker, who liked the idea of team concept, said he often socialized with team members after work, but this, he added, is "just the same everywhere—there's really nothing different here." Previous research in industrial settings confirms this view. The adaptation of team structure to social purposes parallels what ordinarily happens in most workplaces, where informal work groups emerge naturally and provide similar forms of social support.[5]

These answers suggest that there is a relatively high degree of team cohesion. An index (made by combining answers to several questions on teams) was developed to provide a measure of team unity, and the resulting data showed a steady increase in team solidarity from one set of interviews to the next. The percentage of respondents who scored "high" on the cohesion index started at 37 in round two (the index baseline), rose to 48 in round three, and topped out at 60 in round four. These numbers raise a key question: whose interests are served by team cohesion—the company's or the workers'? There is no simple answer. One worker believed "sticking together" was necessary to "deal with management collectively." Another worker said she liked "working together" with her team but stressed there was no alternative to this in a workplace she described as "a battle between management and employees." Survey results suggest such views were shared by coworkers. Respondents said working in teams gave them the opportunity to raise their concerns (84 percent in round one and 70 percent in round four) and allowed them to act together to express complaints (92 percent in round two, when the question was first asked, and 85 percent in round four).

Nearly all of the survey group mentioned something they disliked about teams. Criticism was more pronounced in the final round of interviews, and there was a more acute sense that teamwork was a means of making people cover for absent or injured workers, show up for work, work harder, and so on. Peer pressure to conform to CAMI's expectations and standards was seen as the downside of working in teams. In round one, 40 percent of the respondents reported that working in teams "is a way to get us to work harder," and by the fourth round fully 70 percent of those interviewed expressed this opinion. Similarly, the percentage of respondents who said working in teams "gets us all pressuring one another" climbed from 19 in round one to 60 in round four. One worker said team concept "pits worker against worker" and believed CAMI deliberately set it up this way.

Although it was not a widespread refrain, some workers did blame "slackers" for undermining the team system. As one worker complained, "Not everyone pulls their weight." This kind of attitude was deeply disturbing to persons who had suffered an injury and were working under some kind of restriction, or had missed work altogether. "When you're sick or injured," as one worker observed, "you feel guilty because they won't replace you." Instead of holding CAMI responsible for understaffing and refusing to provide relief workers, some individuals blamed their heavier work load on injured and absent team members—the casualties of the CAMI system of lean production. Commenting on this blame-the-victim attitude, a former Local 88 president wrote in the union newsletter that team concept "has proved to be no more than a method of using peer pressure to improve attendance and to keep people from leaving the line to report small injuries or pains . . . I am sickened by the flack received from other team members by a worker who is injured and must go on light duty. This is related strictly to the Japanese concept of not having replacements for those injured."[6]

It is likely that escalating peer pressure accounts for workers' growing sense that working in teams benefits the company more than workers. In round one, just over one in five respondents (21 percent) believed working in teams "helps CAMI but not me," but by the final interview over one-half (51 percent) shared this view of the consequences of team work. Asked if teams worked more for the good of the company than for the good of workers, over three-quarters (79 percent) in round one "agreed" or "agreed somewhat." By round four the combined response for "agree" and "agree somewhat" had edged slightly higher (83 percent), with those expressing outright agreement increasing steadily over the four rounds from 17 percent in the beginning to 43 percent in the final interview.

People clearly had strong opinions about what they liked and disliked about working in teams, and over time these opinions took on a more critical tone that was reflected in behaviors. In the early stages of our research, before production reached its peak and as new lines and systems were being developed, there were a series of "leaning" or *kaizen* periods when teams were involved in industrial engineering tasks—reducing idle time, rebalancing jobs, and sending redundant workers to other teams. As time passed, teams increasingly acted together in an attempt to make work easier, safer, and less stressful. Some work teams, especially in the assembly area, used QC circles to increase the rate of job rotation. As a result, it is now common in the assembly area for workers to rotate jobs every two hours. Five team leaders from the truck line "kaizened one job per team" to create an off-line sub-assembly area to allow workers to periodically rotate off the more physically demanding main line. Similarly, teams redistributed their work tasks between jobs to free up a position to carry out off-line duties. These gains, however, proved to be temporary, as management unilaterally eliminated the off-line sub-assembly positions and also transferred workers from teams with floater positions to other teams or areas that were short-handed. A local union leader related an incident on the car line: "They kaizened their area . . . to create a floater among the team. The guy was moving around, helping everybody, unpacking stuff, and then the company turned around and started taking the person away when there were head count problems. The team busted their ass to create the position within the team to make it a little easier for themselves. And then as soon as they did it the company started fucking them by taking it away all the time."

Experiences like these contributed to a growing indifference towards team concept, an attitude at odds with the purposes for which teams were established. A team leader described the transformation in his group. "I see it every day, people pulling together really helping each other out. But then there comes a breaking point where one says, 'Heck with the team concept. This is my job, that's all I'm going to do.' Once this takes hold, then I think we kind of get back into the real traditional kind of factory work." An area leader (first-level management) told a similar story. "When the line goes down for up to half an hour or forty minutes . . . people just stand around. Whereas, when I was a team leader . . . a couple of years ago, everyone kept busy, and they'd do things, improve things."

With the passage of time, more and more teams withdrew from QC circles (56 percent of respondents in round one and 38 percent in round four reported participating). Teams have also acted in solidarity to resist doing *taiso* (pre-shift exercises). Almost all respondents reported having done *taiso* at some time, but by the final round of interviews only one percent said they were still doing it. In assembly, teams organized a collective andon-pull to protest understaffing on the door line—an action that brought two extra workers to the area. Workers began to use the right to refuse unsafe work to protest the threat of injury posed by the rapid pace and inadequate staffing. The June 1991 issue of the union newsletter, *Off the Line*, contained a half-page picture of a team in Final 4 that collectively invoked this right to protest the failure to provide relief, rotation, and replacements for workers disabled by repetitive strain injuries. The title was "Changing the Definition of 'Teamwork,' " and the caption read, "What does teamwork mean to you? To the members of Final 4 YOE Assembly it means SOLIDARITY." The action of this Final 4 team was only one of a number of similar collective protests taken in the plant. Of the multiple uses envisaged for team areas, rest breaks and lunch were the only durable activities, while problem-solving sessions were undertaken only when teams faced a pressing issue. Team names often fell into disuse, were forgotten, or their significance downplayed. Teams now are more likely to use the technical language of the plant to describe themselves, such as Line 2,

Team 5 in the case of car engine sub-assembly—or simply "car engine sub-assembly." Attendance at pre-shift team meetings declined markedly over time. In round one, 83 percent of those surveyed said they always attended these meetings, compared to less than one-half (46 percent) who reported regularly attending in the final round.[7]

Team Leaders

Team leaders, who occupy a position similar in some ways to front-line supervisors and in some ways to lead hands, are union members who are paid $1.00 an hour more than production associates. They are expected not only to do paperwork, such as filling out payroll and attendance forms, but also to maintain and boost production, to help train workers, to fill in for absentees, and to assist those who fall behind in their work. In the daily information briefings at the beginning of each shift, team leaders relay to workers the day's production quota and announce any last-minute changes in the job rotation schedule. CAMI provides team leaders with special training. One course is designed to help the company and the prospective team leader decide if the person is suitable for the job and the job accept-able to the person. Team leaders subsequently undergo training that is geared to developing social and communication skills. Another course, which was attended by both team leaders and area leaders, was described by one trainee as a "mini-course on industrial engineering."

Not many workers aspire to be team leaders. In fact, the percentage of respondents interested in being a team leader dropped from 31 in the first round of the survey to a mere 13 percent by the fourth round. Support for the idea of having team leaders at all declined from a high of nearly 80 percent in round one to 63 percent in round four. Under the plant's initial collective bargaining agreement, team leaders at CAMI were chosen by management following a process of peer review within a team. Survey respondents expressed dissatisfaction with this selection process, with most respondents favoring some form of election. In round four, 79 percent of those interviewed thought that team leaders should be elected. Other op-tions, such as rotating the position, were not considered particularly attrac-tive in the early rounds of the survey. However, by round four over one-half of the respondents supported a system of team leader rotation.

The special responsibilities attached to the role of team leader are not accompanied by any form of managerial authority. A team leader's author-ity is supposed to be the moral kind—to set an example and to advise the team. Discipline is meted out by area leaders, who are the first line of management. While they have no formal power, team leaders can still try to invoke it, and the line between management and the team leader can be quite vague. The position of team leader has the potential to be a focal point of tension and conflict between the company and the union. The company gives the impression that it would like team leaders to identify more with corporate goals and act more in concert with first-line management. On the other hand, the union makes it clear that it wants team leaders to identify with union goals and to act in a manner consistent with their status as rank-and-file union members. Thus the company may want to expand the role of the team leader, while the union does not want the team leader to participate in the exercise of management authority.

If the "foreman" can be described as "the man in the middle," then the middle is often especially muddled for team leaders, who find themselves caught between the conflicting demands of management and workers, and sometimes their own divided loyalties. Team leaders complain that they are often berated by workers for policies and practices over which they have no control, such as not getting replacements for injured or transferred workers. On the other hand, when a team refuses to do *taiso*, participate in QC circles, or hand in *teians*, which are supposed to be voluntary activities, it is the team leader who is most likely to be taken to task by management. Consider the following comments by one team leader: "It would be nice to have a line to define where my job ends and where management starts. You know, you feel kind of uncomfortable sometimes to have to deal with somebody who's in the union, when you're in the union yourself. . . . You don't feel really like you belong with the hourly guys sometimes and yet you feel really caught. You're getting pressure both ways." When asked if she felt closer to management or her team, another team leader said, "Some days I might say the workers, other days I might say management. I don't know." A third team leader observed, "I really don't get the respect from the union, and I don't get the respect from management either. I'm somewhere in between. I have a problem with that because I'm a brother just like the next guy."

In the early days at CAMI, there was no clear line demarcating the duties of team leaders and area leaders. Eventually, some of the ambiguities of the team leader role were removed with Local 88's issuance of a set of union guidelines for team leaders. In early 1990, four hundred workers attended Local 88's meeting to discuss the role of team leader. Some months later the local produced a short handbook of guidelines for team leaders. The handbook says it is "intended to be used as a guide by all team members" and has been designed "to help team leaders in performing their team leader functions and be good union members." The guidelines stress that the team leader is a unionized production worker who is a "technical advisor, not a personnel manager." The distinction between team leaders and managers is summed up by the statement that the function of the team leader "is to support production," while that of the area leader "is to manage people."

Most respondents reported a good relationship between their teams and team leaders, and on an individual level most were favorably disposed toward their own team leader. Over time there was some improvement in certain aspects of the relationship. In the first round 42 percent of respondents reported that their team leader thought more like management than one of them. By the second visit the proportion thinking this way had fallen to less than one in three (29 percent), with little change occurring over the next two rounds of interviews. Workstation observations provided additional insights as to the role of team leader. Workers are liable to take strong exception to a team leader if he or she acts too much like management or displays favoritism or discrimination towards particular team members. The most common complaint concerned team leaders who "act like supervisors." On some teams workers maintain a strong feeling of loyalty and solidarity towards other team members but dislike their team leader. One worker in welding was particularly blunt: "Mind you, there isn't anything I wouldn't do for members of my team, but if my team leader tries to tell me to do something I shouldn't have to do, I just tell him to fuck off."

Over time, there was a sharp decline in the proportion of interviewees who felt that their team leader was placing pressure on them to submit suggestions. Between round one and four the percentage of those who reported being pressured "all the time" or "often" fell from 25 to just 6. It is likely that team leaders backed off as a result of the local union's clarification of the role of team leader and its assurance that individuals could refuse to participate with impunity.

The relationship between team members and team leaders is viewed by workers as defined by and confined to work-related issues. In the fourth round 76 percent of respondents reported that they talked to their team leader about work "all the time" or "often." However, in the same round over half (52 percent) said that they never talked to their team leader about personal matters. Team leaders at CAMI generally are regarded by workers as neither counselors nor social conveners.

Many workers feel they should be able to count on the team leader to help the team act together to realize workers' goals. For example, workers frequently enlist the support of their team leaders in the struggle to make work safer and less hectic. Team leaders inevitably become involved whenever workers take the initiative on issues pertaining to the pace and intensity of work. Real, albeit temporary, gains have sometimes resulted, such as when teams and team leaders have acted together to obtain line floaters. On the truck line a team leader divulged how his team had benefited from a mistake made by the time study engineer, who accidentally counted a work station from an adjoining team as part of his team's workload. The error resulted in a welcome reduction in the burden of work for the team. It never occurred to the team leader to report the miscalculation to the area leader. This team leader had no doubt that his loyalty was to the team.

Confronting Team Concept

On September 14, 1992, Local 88 members began a strike that was to last five weeks. This action assumed historical significance in that it was the first time workers had struck a North American transplant or joint venture. Among the gains won by the union several directly addressed team concept and working in teams. CAMI agreed to a one year "experiment" in which team leaders would be elected by team members, and the duties of team leaders are now spelled out in the contract. The new agreement also encroaches on a central objective of lean production, to operate with the absolute minimum number of workers. Before, workers were not only expected to continuously search for ways to reduce "waste" (*kaizen*) and handle work loads that, ideally, entailed working sixty seconds of every minute, they also had to cover for team members who were late, absent, or hurt. Because large teams provided management greater flexibility around work assignments (for example, covering for absentees) the new agreement sets an upper limit of twelve on the size of teams. It also establishes production support groups to provide all departments with pools of relief workers to fill in for people who are absent or injured. This represents a significant modification of lean production's skeletal staffing policy and undermines one important purpose for the establishment of work teams, which is the use of peer pressure to discourage absenteeism and promote rapid, diligent work performance.

From management's viewpoint, certain of these changes in team dynamics may have gone too far. The team leader selection experiment mandated in the new contract was scheduled for evaluation on February 1, 1994, at which time it could be continued "by mutual agreement." CAMI unilaterally shelved the new procedure in June, 1994. While management rationalized this decision by reference to possible violations of Ontario equity legislation, we suspect the company was unhappy with the 90 (out of a total of 240) team leaders who were chosen while the experiment was in force.

Conclusion

Teams at CAMI constitute a major terrain of struggle. Workplace observations and survey responses indicate that group solidarity can produce behaviors, such as helping out and keeping up with the work, that are consistent with CAMI objectives. Even so, teams are not operating entirely as management might like. Research results point to the presence of a growing team-based resistance to some of management's more excessive demands and policies.

The relationship between teams and team leaders is a complex one. In helping to define the role of team leader, the initiatives taken by workers and their union have made a difference. While there are aspects of team working that are not in workers' interests, such as peer pressure on injured or absent workers, there is a tendency for more and more workers to use the team as a lever to advance their demands. The extent to which teams will continue to operate as a tool of management or as a medium for pushing a workers' agenda is not clear. What is clear, however, is that team actions will continue to influence the manner in which lean production operates at CAMI.

Notes

This project was funded by Labour Canada and the Canadian Auto Workers Union (CAW). In addition to the authors of this essay, the CAW Research Group on CAMI consists of Steve Benedict (CAW Local 112), Alan McGough (CAW Local 27), Herman Rosenfeld (CAW Local 303), and Jeff Wareham (CAW Research Department).

1. James Womack, Daniel Roos, and Daniel Jones, *The Machine that Changed the World* (New York: Rawson Associates, 1990), 99; Martin Kenney and Richard Florida, *Beyond Mass Production: The Japanese System and Its Transfer to the U.S.* (New York: Oxford University Press, 1993), 37.

2. Mike Parker and Jane Slaughter, *Choosing Sides: Unions and the Team Concept* (Boston: South End Press, 1988), 45.

3. Some sections of this essay appear in David Robertson, James Rinehart, Christopher Huxley, Jeff Wareham, Herman Rosenfeld, Alan McGough, and Steve Benedict, *The CAMI Report: Lean Production in a Unionized Auto Plant* (Willowdale, ONT.: CAW-Canada Re-

search Department, 1993). Team concept is one of many facets of lean production at CAMI discussed in this report.

4. Jones quoted in Andersen Consulting, *The Lean Enterprise Benchmarking Project* (London: Andersen Consulting, 1993), 14. On the Swedish model see, Christian Berggren, *Alternatives to Lean Production: Work Organization in the Swedish Auto Industry* (Ithaca: ILR Press, 1992).

5. On the social support of informal work groups see Harvey Krahn and Graham Lowe, *Work, Industry, and Canadian Society* (Scarborough, Ontario: Nelson Canada, 1993), Ch. 8, and James Rinehart, *The Tyranny of Work: Alienation and the Labour Process* (Toronto: Harcourt Brace Jovanovich, 1987), Ch. 5.

6. Rob Pelletier, "President's Message," *Off the Line* (Feb. 1991): 3.

7. Under Ontario legislation workers have the right to refuse jobs they believe are unhealthy or unsafe. For a discussion of Canadian health and safety laws and their effectiveness, see Krahn and Lowe, *Work, Industry, and Canadian Society,* 277–282.

13

Whose Team?
Lean Production at Mazda U.S.A.

STEVE BABSON

The nature of lean production as it defines shop-floor relations is substantially determined by the nature of its team organization. If production teams are genuinely ''worker centered,'' then team members have the authority to deploy resources and meet company goals in ways that incorporate their collective needs. If, on the other hand, teams are ''supervisor centered,'' then management can manipulate team dynamics and peer-group pressure to ensure conformity with company standards. These distinctions cannot be drawn in absolute or categorical terms: in its extreme form, ''team syndicalism'' would jeopardize the minimum necessary coordination and standardization of practice necessary for volume production; likewise, management domination of teams would preempt worker initiative and inspire conformity instead of innovation. Rather than make categorical distinctions between ''worker centered'' and ''supervisor centered'' teams, suggesting that either of these can exist in a pure and unambiguous form, it makes more sense to measure any particular team organization against a spectrum of possibilities, from maquiladora plants where there are no teams and supervisors wield considerable authority, to the middle range of team organizations found in transplant and Big Three operations in the United States, to the self-directed assembly teams pioneered by Volvo at

Uddevalla. Many factors determine where a particular team organization falls on this spectrum, but a key determinant is the role of the team leader. An examination of the conflicting claims made on the loyalties of team leaders at Mazda's plant in Flat Rock, Michigan provides an opportunity to specify how team dynamics can change in a workplace where an independent union pushes the organization towards "worker-centered" teams.[1]

Work Teams and Supervisory Units

Mazda began production at Flat Rock in 1987 and added a second shift in 1988, producing the Ford Probe and the Mazda MX6 and 626 models. The UAW won a representation election in 1987 after a campaign in which management remained neutral, and the newly chartered Local 3000 negotiated a collective bargaining agreement the following year that codified the plant's "team concept" structure. The base of the organizational pyramid rested on nearly three thousand UAW members organized into teams of five to ten people, each led by an hourly worker who earned a fifty-cent premium as team leader. The next step upwards on the organizational chart was the unit, led by the first-line supervisor, or unit leader. Most units contained two or as many as four teams, with unit boundaries defined by process parameters (i.e., "Underbody welding, Mazda line") or, where there were no obvious process boundaries (e.g., final assembly), by ad hoc administrative divisions. Above the unit-level supervisor, the management hierarchy ascended through more conventional layers of area, departmental, and plant administration, matched at the last two levels by the UAW's elected representatives on the plantwide Bargaining Committee and departmental District Committee. This conventional UAW structure was modified, however, by the addition of a third layer of representation, the "UAW coordinator," who served a role akin to that of the traditional line-stewards found in Big Three plants during the UAW's early years. Coordinators worked a full shift building cars, but were paid two additional hours a week for investigating grievances and communicating union concerns to the local's members and leaders. With one coordinator for every two units, each of the roughly seventy coordinators in the plant represented about forty workers.

On paper, the plant's formal organization appeared to warrant the designation "team concept," with all its connotations of joint decision-making and worker participation in day-to-day operations. In practice, the actual operating procedure during the term of the first contract, 1988–1991, had little to do with teams. Decision-making was decentralized at Mazda, but the actual base of its production system was the unit, led by the first-line supervisor. It was the unit leader, not team members, who wielded routine authority. "Teams" existed primarily as a rhetorical device, as in the oft cited "team approach" to problem resolution "through understanding and mutual respect while preserving a harmonious environment." Some team leaders made the best of a difficult situation and tried to win the support of their team, but many spent less time leading than they did following the unit leader. In the eyes of many workers, they became "junior foremen."[2]

This was not how it was diagrammed on the organizational chart. In fact, the negotiated process for team leader selection seemed to incorporate sufficient union input and hourly participation to avoid the subordination of the team leader to the unit leader. Applicants for a team leader opening were to be drawn from the unit where the vacancy existed and interviewed in seniority order by a panel composed of the unit leader, the incumbent team leader(s) of that unit, and a designee of the applicant. The company and the union negotiated the criteria (attendance record, knowledge of unit tasks, participation in quality circles, etc.) and a point scale for unit leaders to apply to each candidate, with the position going to the first applicant whose rating exceeded a specified minimum point value.[3]

As hourly workers and UAW members, team leaders who participated in this evaluation process could (in theory) serve as guardians of their fellow workers' interests, preventing unit leaders from dominating the proceedings. In practice, they often failed in this role—at least in the eyes of many of their coworkers. Since incumbent team leaders owed their position to the unit leader's previous assessment of their worth, many apparently deferred to the same supervisor when it came time to evaluate subsequent applicants. According to union critics of management, when the unit leader did not want a particular candidate to get the job, such candidates received fewer points than the necessary minimum. Even when these judgment calls were valid, the unit leader's decision inevitably confirmed perceptions of favoritism among the disappointed and the skeptical.

Those who were favored by this selection process soon found there were few formal guidelines to help them define their role as team leaders. The contract only specified that a team leader was "a resource available to the Unit Leader in the accomplishment of unit goals," with the responsibility to coordinate team activities "through a spirit of team work and cooperation, not direct supervision." All direct supervisory responsibility was to remain with the unit leader. Conceivably, then, the team leader's role could have been operationalized in terms that transposed the role of a skilled trades' work leader to the production line: a combination of tasks that includes set-up, coordination between work stations, relief, repair, and training. At Mazda, this "work leader" role included the team leader's responsibility for monitoring quality and, if serious problems arose, to stop the assembly line by pulling the red cord.[4]

While many of these tasks in a mass-production factory are the responsibility of supervision, there is nothing intrinsically corrupting in the delegation of such duties to an hourly worker. The boundary between workers and managers is historically determined: little more than a century ago, responsibility for quality and control of the job were routine features of industrial labor for artisan and journeymen workers in the metal trades. When management at the turn of the century took control of the shop floor and staked its claim to "scientific management" of the enterprise, it removed those responsibilities from the factory and centered them in newly constituted planning departments far removed from the shop floor. That management now seeks to reintroduce certain elements of responsibility and discretion to production work is a measure, among other things, of how top-heavy these management structures have become.

But at Mazda, the team leader's role accrued more than these coordination and support functions. In many cases, unit leaders also transferred such tasks as distributing paychecks, offering overtime, and taking attendance. Some of these duties—distributing paychecks, for example—were little more than symbolic trappings of managerial power, but others— notably, taking attendance—gave the team leader genuine influence in matters that potentially involved disciplinary action. Team members were all the more likely to see their team leader as an agent of management if he/ she was too aggressive in rebalancing work loads; in such cases, it was easy to assume that the team leader was acting on the unit leader's authority, including the power to determine job assignments, time off the job, and discipline. Membership resentment of these privileged coworkers was further amplified if the team leader was perceived as a "screw off": hogging the easiest jobs, failing to help when problems arose, and leaving the work area. Finally, since many unit leaders gave their team leaders first shot at robot training, they also benefited as the "able and capable" workers who accrued more voluntary overtime servicing these machines.[5]

For all these reasons, many workers perceived team leaders as junior foremen who served the supervisor, not the team. There was little opportunity for team members to exert countervailing pressure. First of all, the contract contained no provision for recalling or removing a team leader. Equally important, there was no specified connection between a team leader and a particular team of workers. At most points where the contract or company policy defined the boundaries of responsibility for decision-making, it was the unit which was so specified, not the team. The unit leader was responsible for vacation scheduling, not the team or team leader. The unit leader decided who would be trained for robot servicing—usually the team leader. Since the contract defined the unit as the overtime equalization group, it was the unit leader who decided who was "able and capable" for voluntary overtime—again, often the team leader if it was robot servicing. The rotation schedule was also the unit leader's responsibility, and the actual distribution of work assignments had little to do with team boundaries: if the unit leader favored job rotation (and not all did), it was often limited to a two-job rotation or expanded beyond team boundaries to include any job in the unit where the unit leader wished to move people. Break areas near the line were designated by unit, not by team. Weekly meetings at the start of Wednesday's shift were convened by units, not by teams. The unit leader chaired these half-hour meetings, which gave team members the opportunity to ask questions or even challenge the unit leader's decisions, but here as elsewhere, a team leader's relationship to a particular team was far more tenuous than the formal structure would suggest. As "resources available to the Unit Leader," they served primarily as adjuncts to the supervisor.[6]

The Bargaining Survey

Disappointment with aspects of lean production became a prominent issue in local union politics at Mazda, and the ambiguous role of team leaders was only one of several themes. As the 1988 contract approached the end of its three-year term, Local 3000 surveyed the hourly workforce to determine how the members assessed these issues. Conducted in November of 1990, the survey was unique in two respects. First, it not only gave respondents the opportunity to prioritize their demands for a new contract, but also asked them to evaluate their work experience during three years of lean production. Second, instead of mailing the survey or printing it in the local newspaper in the hope some members would respond, it was distributed "one-on-one" to every worker in the plant by union coordinators who made a strong appeal for each member's participation. They collected 2,380 surveys in a plant population of approximately 2,800 hourly workers.[7]

Given the prominent role that unit leaders play in Mazda's variant of lean production, workers' assessment of supervisory practice carries a special weight in evaluating the system's organizational dynamic. The company handbook set high standards for these unit leaders, including a "Basic

TABLE 13.1
Perception of Mazda Philosophy

"In terms of considering workers needs and interests, my Unit Leader can be trusted to implement the Mazda philosophy"

Always: 14%	Sometimes: 44%	Rarely: 28%	Never: 14%

(Valid Cases: 2186)

TABLE 13.2
Program Work Sheet Changes

"My Program Work Sheet has been changed without my consultation"

Many times: 35%	Several times: 38%	Once: 7%	Never: 20%

(Valid Cases: 2039)

"The changes made my job"

Easier: 7%	Harder: 67%	No difference: 27%

(Percentages do not equal 100 because of rounding)   (Valid Cases: 1868)

Philosophy'' that promotes ''warm human relationships and comfortable working conditions'' as well as ''participative management.'' Table 13.1 indicates that for 86 percent of the workforce, their unit leader's commitment to this philosophy was a rare or equivocal thing—''only when it suits him,'' according to written comments on the survey form. Other respondents echoed this lack of trust, as well as a perception that the unit leader's chief motivator was the merit bonus paid to supervisors.

As indicated in table 13.2, high expectations of ''participative management'' had been disappointed by three years of actual operation. Mazda workers had been encouraged to ''continuously improve'' their work procedures through written suggestions and voluntary participation in quality circles, but much of this *kaizen* process also included the intervention of supervisors and middle managers who unilaterally changed the Program Work Sheets (PWS) posted at each work station. As the official guideline for standardized work, the PWS breaks down the job cycle into specific tasks, their sequence, and the number of seconds allotted to each. Team members were not permitted to change their PWS without supervisory approval, but the reverse did not apply when managers decided to rebalance an operation. Nearly three-quarters of the survey respondents indicated their PWS had been changed several or many times without their consulta-

TABLE 13.3
Program Work Sheet Changes: Body Department

"My Program Work Sheet has been changed without my consultation"			
Many times: 46%	Several times: 38%	Once: 5%	Never: 12%

(Percentages do not equal 100 because of rounding)   (Valid Cases: 429)

TABLE 13.4
Health and Safety

"If the present level of work intensity continues"	
I can stay healthy and make it to retirement:	27%
I will likely be injured or worn out before I retire:	73%

(Valid Cases: 2,186)

tion, and two-thirds said the changes made their job harder. Since these returns included skilled trades and quality-control personnel whose work did not follow PWS guidelines, the actual experience of top-down *kaizen* was much higher in certain production departments, as indicated by table 13.3. In Body Assembly, 84 percent reported several or many unilateral changes in their PWS and only 12 percent said this had never happened. The comment lines were also revealing: "No worker input on balancing," "Changes usually eliminate people," "Unit Leader pushing for bonus," and "Every time the line is rebalanced, work is added."

Significantly, in the same month the union conducted the survey, the company newsletter acknowledged the very same problem in a frank article titled "Kaizen—Friend or Foe." Reporting on discussions between company president Masahiro Uchida and selected plant employees, the article included a telling summary of complaints about "front-office" *kaizen*: "One participant admitted that these same [management] people who are supposed to support the process are now commonly viewed as 'the enemy.' 'Every time we see someone from the front office, it seems that something negative results.' 'The more kaizen that came from up front, the worse it got. There was no participation or buy into the changes.' "[8]

The perception that management was unilaterally intensifying the workpace no doubt contributed to the somber assessment of future injury indicated in table 13.4. Nearly three-quarters of the survey respondents agreed with the statement that they would be "injured or worn out before retirement" if the present level of work intensity continued. While many factory workers might express similar sentiments about their industrial en-

TABLE 13.5
Team Leader Selection

"Team Leaders should be chosen according to"

Present System: 16%   Election: 48%   Seniority: 16%   Rotation: 14%   Other: 7%

(Percentages do not equal 100 because of rounding)   (Valid Cases: 2,244)

vironment, there is corroborating evidence for the widely held belief among Mazda workers that their jobs were unsafe. According to a detailed study of Michigan's workers' compensation records conducted by the *Detroit Free Press*, Mazda's rate of serious injuries (those resulting in loss of limb or function, or requiring at least seven days' lost work) was triple the rate for GM and Ford in 1988, the last year for which such information was publicly available. At 4.1 injuries per 100 workers, it would take less than twenty-five years for such injuries to equal one hundred percent of the workforce.[9]

Survey results strongly indicated that many Mazda workers held their team leaders accountable for heavy workloads and high rates of injury. Table 13.5 measures the dissatisfaction that survey respondents voiced with the team-leader selection process: 84 percent favored alternatives to the (then) present system dominated by unit leaders, with nearly half favoring election and the balance preferring rotation or seniority as the basis for selection. Cross tabulation of these results with questions concerning workload and health indicate a significant link between a negative appraisal of working conditions and a negative appraisal of the team-leader selection process: 24 percent of those who said their workload was properly balanced favored the current system of team-leader selection, compared to only 9 percent of those who said their workload was too heavy; likewise, while 28 percent of those who expected to stay healthy favored the present system of team-leader selection, support fell to only 11 percent among those who expected to be injured or worn out. This association between perceived working conditions and preferred selection process indicates that many workers held their team leader at least partially responsible for the intensified pace of lean production. They therefore favored a selection process that would make their leader answerable to the team rather than the unit leader.[10]

Worker Centered Teams

The new collective bargaining agreement negotiated in 1991 addressed these and many other issues concerning the Mazda production system. Of

TABLE 13.6
Team Leader Responsiveness

Survey of UAW-Mazda coordinators, production departments, November 1992

"Has election and recall of team leaders made them more or less responsive to the needs of team members?" (N = 57)

More: 37   No change:15   Less: 5

"Do team members use the threat of a recall petition to pressure team leaders?" (N = 59)

Frequently: 12   Sometimes: 28   Rarely: 12   Never: 7

interest here, the union pushed for a new team-leader selection process and the company agreed to substantial changes. Under the terms of the new contract, team leaders would henceforth be subject to election and recall by team members, with the number of eligible candidates limited only by minimum criteria that included good attendance and past service in the respective unit. Team leader incumbents were grandfathered into their positions, but every six months they (as well as those elected to subsequent openings) would be subject to recall if two-thirds of the unit petitioned for their removal. The team leader was still defined as "a resource available to the Unit Leader," but the contract also specified that "it is the responsibility of the Unit Leader to take attendance, to administer the payroll process, to offer overtime, and to update the overtime equalization lists." In short, rather than serve their supervisor as de facto "junior foremen," team leaders were to serve their team as relief workers, trainers, and troubleshooters. In practice, the role still included the continuing obligation to take direction from the unit leader. When a "good" unit leader enlisted genuine participation in decision-making, the team leader had a better chance of surviving the job's pressures; when the supervisor was a pusher, the team leader would feel the contradictory obligations of the position. Yet even when "caught in the middle," the team leader would now more likely ask the UAW coordinator for help, particularly if his/her "constituents" pressed for such action.

Subsequent evidence suggests that the new selection process did affect the behavior—or tenure—of team leaders. Table 13.6 presents the results of a survey conducted in November of 1992 among UAW coordinators from Mazda's production departments. Two-thirds believed that election and recall had made team leaders more responsive to team members, and an equal number believed that team members used the threat of a recall petition to remind team leaders of their obligation to serve the team. When the threat failed, the real thing could happen: in the first round of recall petitions in September 1991, team members gathered the necessary two-thirds support for removing their leader in 33 of the plant's 257 teams, representing 13 percent of the total.[11]

In subsequent rounds, the recall petition took on a variety of meanings. In some teams, members decided to rotate the team leader position, making the petition a routine device for implementing the succession. In some teams, however, the petition played a more divisive role when opinion was closely divided and the recall process forced members to *publicly* align themselves either for or against an incumbent team leader. To eliminate this kind of corrosive factionalism, the union negotiated a new procedure in the 1994 contract which eliminated the petition and provided for an annual election open to any qualified team member (including the incumbent team leader) who wished to put his or her name on the ballot.

It is a measure of how weak the team system had previously been at Mazda that when it came time to conduct the first elections under the 1991 agreement, there were some units in final assembly where no team boundaries had previously been drawn—to conduct the election, in other words, it was necessary to specify which workers were to vote in which team. Certainly in these cases, the union's advocacy of "team democracy" pushed Mazda's team concept further along the continuum towards worker-centered teams, but the company's production system still retained many features that favored unit leader control. Comparison with the team-concept agreement at the Ford Escort Body and Stamping plant in Wayne, Michigan, underlines the point. As specified in the Modern Operating Agreement negotiated by UAW Local 900, the roughly fourteen hundred union members in this plant elect their team leaders for six-month terms; meetings are convened by team and chaired by team leaders; vacation scheduling, rotation, and training are scheduled and evaluated by the team; and overtime equalization is the responsibility of an elected UAW coordinator (one per area, the equivalent of the Mazda supervisor's unit), who works a production job during the shift but is paid the same premium as a team leader.[12]

Many other factors define a team-based system as more or less worker-centered, including the technical configuration of the production process (permitting more or less intervention by shop-floor workers), the nature of the inventory system (providing more or less of a buffer for team activities), and the range of jobs included in the teams (offering more or less rotation through off-line jobs). Given this complexity, there can be no fixed menu for categorically distinguishing a worker-centered team system from a supervisor centered system. But relative comparisons are possible, and on this basis the evidence from Mazda's Flat Rock plant is that an independent union can push a system from a point on the spectrum closer to supervisor-centered teams to a point that lies closer to worker-centered teams.

Notes

1. Data is drawn from the UAW-Mazda membership survey conducted in November 1990 described below, and from informal conversations, formal interviews, and classroom exchanges with Local 3000 union officers, committee members, coordinators, and members from 1990 to 1993. Particular thanks are due to local president Phil Keeling and bargaining chairman Greg Drudi. For a more extensive review of the survey and the issues surrounding the events described here, see Steve Babson, "Lean or Mean: The MIT Model and Lean Production at Mazda," *Labor Studies Journal* 18, no. 2 (summer 1993): 3–24. In 1992, Ford Motor Company, which bought a 25 percent interest in Mazda in 1979, bought a half share of the Flat Rock plant; the new joint venture was renamed Auto Alliance International.

2. The quote is from UAW-Mazda, *Collective Bargaining Agreement*, 7 March 1988, Article X, 1(4), 17.

3. Ibid., Article XI, 6, 25.

4. Ibid., Article XXI, 2, 25–26.

5. The robot operator's job requires a modest amount of skill and experience to perform effectively. The "RO" starts the robot, checks flow rates, dresses the welding tips or cleans the paint-spray heads, changes jump lines, and realigns the program when necessary. It is considered a good job because it's off-line, is more varied and challenging than assembly work, and often entails Saturday overtime cleaning and servicing the machines. Training for this and every other production job was supposed to be universal, as stipulated in the contract (Article XVI, 3 [3], 41). In fact, Mazda only trained about 25 to 30 percent of the work force in any aspect of the robot operator's job, and completely trained only about 15 percent of the work force—most of them team leaders.

6. 1988–1991 *Collective Bargaining Agreement,* Article XVIII, 3, 48–49 (vacations); Article XVI, 3, 41–42 (overtime and training); rotation, break areas, and Wednesday meetings were defined by company policy.

7. A one-day training session for coordinators conducted by Wayne State University's Labor Studies Center stressed the importance of collecting valid returns; badgering or preaching to respondents was discouraged as inimical to the union's need for a true reading of the members. Survey results were tabulated by the Survey and Evaluation Service of Wayne State University's Center for Urban Studies.

8. "Kaizen—Friend or Foe," *New Horizons* (Oct.–Nov. 1990): 3.

9. "Danger Rises in New Auto Jobs," *Detroit Free Press, Special Reprint Section* (7–9 July 1990), 2. Company and union efforts have since addressed these health and safety hazards, but the results weren't statistically evident until 1990, and the union contends that Mazda now systematically under-reports injuries. See Babson, "Lean or Mean," 14.

10. Gamma for these two cross-tabulations equals .353 and .514 respectively. For a detailed discussion, see Babson, "Lean or Mean," 15–16, and tables 6–8.

11. Figures on the number of team leaders removed in the first round of 1991 recall petitions come from a union document, ''Team Leader Selection Process as of 9/6/91 (am),'' in author's possession.

12. UAW Local 900 and the Ford Motor Company, Wayne Body and Stamping, *Local Agreements, Letters of Understanding, and Rates* (Sept. 1990), 12–13, 16–17, 25. In the initial 1990 agreement, the team leader's term was three months. The term was lengthened to six months in the 1993 contract.

14

Lean Production in a Mexican Context

HARLEY SHAIKEN

The intense debate over the North American Free Trade Agreement has focused considerable attention on Mexico's manufacturing base. The ratification of NAFTA will likely accelerate the already considerable economic integration between Mexico, the United States, and Canada, and foster new production linkages between industries in the three countries. In this essay, I examine the use of lean production in Mexican manufacturing. In particular, I explore three questions. First, how extensively is lean production utilized in Mexico today? Second, and at the heart of the discussion, to what extent can advanced manufacturing be successfully sited in Mexico? And, finally, what does lean production look like in a Mexican automobile assembly plant?

Lean Production in Mexico

Little empirical data exists on how extensively lean production is utilized in Mexican manufacturing. Clearly, the presence of many transnational corporations and the enormous attention lean production has garnered in the industrialized economies has generated considerable interest in Mexico. Discussions at innumerable industry conferences and in academic publications often center on lean production, but widespread discussion is not adoption. Overall, a number of obstacles—from a poor transportation network wreaking havoc with just-in-time deliveries, to high turnover undermining worker participation schemes—have slowed the diffusion of lean production in Mexico. Moreover, many firms have either done well or at least grown accustomed to a combination of low wages and traditional Fordism and see little incentive to change.[1]

One area where empirical data does exist concerning the use of lean production is among Japanese firms in Mexico. These firms accounted for about 180 plants in the late 1980s, including some 70 *maquiladoras* or export assembly plants. The plants ranged from Nissan's sprawling $1 billion automotive complex in Aguascalientes, to huge television assembly plants operated by Sony, Sanyo, Toshiba, and Matsushita in Tijuana. Given that such lean production techniques as quality circles, work teams, continuous improvement, and just-in-time inventory were developed in Japan, one might expect to see them widely used among these Japanese-owned firms in Mexico. Surprisingly, few such firms employ any lean production methods at all. In a study of thirteen Japanese plants located throughout Mexico in industries ranging from electronics to auto suppliers, Harry Browne and I found little evidence of "Japanese" techniques. In fact, in some critical areas such as *kaizen*, or continuous improvement groups, very few plant managers or industrial relations managers (outside of a major auto firm) were even familiar with these programs. In a later study of Japanese-owned maquiladoras, Kenney and Florida found that "the labor process in Tijuana was typical of that performed by part-time and temporary workers in Japan. There was scarcely any use of teams or rotation."[2]

Instead of lean production, Japanese transnationals employ traditional Fordist techniques, with mass production assembly lines and little worker input. The production operations are significantly different than comparable U.S. firms, but the differences tend to be at the level of managerial practice or product design, not work organization. Browne and I found that, as with their counterparts from the U.S. and Europe, Japanese firms locating in Mexico were motivated primarily by the prospects of low labor costs. Kenney and Florida concurred, arguing that "the first and foremost factor driving the Japanese maquila investment is labor costs, specifically the availability of inexpensive labor."[3]

Although Japanese firms generally do not pay less than the prevailing wage in an area, they are unwilling to raise wages much above that level. As a result, high turnover proved to be a considerable problem. In the *maquiladoras* we visited, annual turnover ranged from 66 percent to 168 percent, and in Nissan's massive auto complex it hovered at about 100 percent annually. While this level of turnover is typical of the maquiladora industry, it limits management's ability to institute employee participation techniques, which rely on a stable workforce. The president of a Japanese supplier firm commented that much of the *maquiladora* workforce "we consider the turnover zone. So, we do not even listen to them. . . Listening to [those in] the turnover zone just confuses the operation."[4]

The lack of lean production among Japanese firms in Mexico highlights an intriguing feature of mass production. Many observers see traditional mass production as a static system, when in fact it is a dynamic process driven by significant pressures to reduce staffing, increase output, and improve quality. Japanese firms in Mexico modify that system by stressing managerial flexibility, compliant unions or no unions at all, and lower inventory levels. In many cases, Japanese firms might prefer to use more lean production techniques but find it economically rational to place a heavier emphasis on low wages, even if the consequent high turnover disrupts quality circles and other lean production techniques. Implicit in their explanations for this behavior are cost-benefit calculations based on wages that are one-eighth to one-tenth those of their operations in the United States and Japan.[5]

Lean production is present in the Mexican automotive industry, but to date it seems largely limited to a few striking examples among U.S.-owned automakers. The lack of lean production today, however, does not preclude the diffusion of more of these techniques in the near future. But, in the meantime, Japanese firms have achieved important successes in terms of quality and productivity through combining low wages with a driven, somewhat modified version of traditional Fordism.

Mexico and Advanced Manufacturing

Underlying the issue of lean production's diffusion in Mexico is the more fundamental question regarding the extent to which advanced manufacturing can be sited there successfully. Popular and scholarly perceptions of Mexican manufacturing portray a stereotype of low technology, low productivity, and low-quality production. Several years ago, when GM was first contemplating exporting Mexican-built cars to the U.S., executives consulted their legal department to find out if they had to label the vehicles as "made in Mexico." As one executive admitted, "my own bias was that Mexican assembled vehicles were likely to have more 'fit-and-finish' problems than American vehicles and that the buying public would absolutely think this, even if it wasn't so.''[6]

During the NAFTA debate, much was made of problems with industrial production in Mexico. The *Wall Street Journal* ran a widely-cited front page story headlined "Illusory Bargain: Some U.S. Companies Find Mexican Workers Not So Cheap After All, Low Productivity and a Host Of Other Woes Undercut Americans' NAFTA Fears." Not to be outdone, the *Washington Post* ran a subsequent story entitled "On Closer Look, Firms See Less to Mexico." The story began by contending that "as Mexico's low wages emerge as a major issue in the debate over the North American Free Trade Agreement, U.S. businessmen and Mexican officials here are arguing that problems of infrastructure and a range of other economic factors make Mexican labor far less of a bargain than it first appears." Writing in a more scholarly vein, Kenney and Florida observe that "generally speaking, in terms of the regional configuration of production and distribution for North America, the low skill labor intensive aspects of the production process (especially in price competitive product areas) will continue to be located in Mexico, while the capital intensive parts of the production process will continue to locate in the United States." Nora Lustig adds that "even if U.S. firms were to transfer to Mexico their modern technology along with their investment, productivity would still not be equal because Mexico's infrastructure is so much poorer than that of the United States."[7]

Much of the industrial base in Mexico is, in fact, characterized by low volume, low productivity, and often low-quality production. Alongside this older industrial sector, however, a newer manufacturing base is developing, geared for the export market. In areas such as consumer electronics and automobiles, Mexico has seen the rapid growth of more sophisticated production in the last decade, and this trajectory will likely accelerate under NAFTA. Mexico, for example, exported over six million color televisions to the U.S. in 1992, which represented over half of the color televisions imported and almost 30 percent of total sales in the U.S. market. Moreover, Mexico exported automobile engines worth $1.2 billion, making it one of the larger exporters in the world of this complex product, and the Mexican government expects this level to double to $2.4 billion by the end of 1994.[8]

Some of the most impressive export gains have been in finished automobiles. Mexico was the third largest exporter of cars to the U.S. (after Japan and Canada) in 1993, exporting a total of almost 280,000 passenger cars between December 1992 and November 1993, a spectacular increase from total exports of 14,000 vehicles little more than a decade ago. Mexico is now the principal source of Ford Escorts for California as well as Mercury Tracers for the United States, and will also ship Ford's new world car—the Ford Concours and Mercury Mystique—north of the border. Some analysts predict that Mexico will export 1,250,000 passenger vehicles per year in less than a decade.[9]

The most dramatic example of this new export capability is the Ford Hermosillo plant, a state-of-the-art $500 million assembly and stamping plant that began production in 1986. Engineering for both the factory and the car was initially done by Ford's Japanese partner, Mazda, with state-of-the-art robots and programmable machinery built and debugged in Japan before installation in Mexico. The car was a proven Mazda design, rebadged for sale in the U.S. as the Mercury Tracer, with two-thirds of its parts (including engine and transmission) sourced from Japan. The plant brought together advanced manufacturing technology—including about one hundred robots and thirty computer systems—with workers who had never been in an auto plant before and whose average age was twenty-three. Most workers were new to manufacturing because the surrounding economy was based largely on agriculture and services. On the other hand, the region's unusually high concentration of colleges and technical schools (three major colleges in Hermosillo alone) meant that nearly a third of the initial workforce had completed university training, and over 90 percent had a high school education. By 1989, the plant was operating on two shifts, employing sixteen hundred hourly workers and producing 135,000 Tracers.

The start-up of the Hermosillo plant amounted to a test of the ability to site advanced production under the most difficult of conditions, with no experienced workers and little comparable industry to draw on. Since the plant's total output was targeted for the hotly competitive U.S. and Canadian markets, the ability to build high quality cars in a short time-frame was paramount. Contrary to the expectations of many, Hermosillo achieved high quality production almost immediately and within three years was producing the second highest quality small car sold in the U.S. market, trailing the Honda Civic by a heartbeat and leading all other Japanese nameplates (let alone its U.S. competitors) in this segment of the market. After a $300 million changeover to produce a more complex vehicle and implement a more demanding two-shift operation, the quality of the plant's output remained very high. At the end of 1992, it tied for fifth out of forty-six car assembly plants in North America, according to the J. D. Power survey. Quality (measured as defects per hundred vehicles after three months in the field) ranged from 71 in the best plant in North America to 250 in the worst. Hermosillo came in at 97, surpassing the score of 105 at a Detroit-area plant that also produced the Ford Escort. In fact, the Mexican plant came out ahead of five Japanese-owned assembly plants in the U.S.— some by a wide margin—and narrowly trailed the top three.[10]

The productivity of the Hermosillo plant was also very high. The International Motor Vehicle Program at MIT concluded that "the Hermosillo plant [was] near the world average in productivity despite a considerable scale economy penalty due to its small size." The productivity of the plant—now capable of producing 165,000 cars a year—ranked twelfth in North America in 1992, according to a study carried out by Harbour and Associates.[11]

While similar in terms of quality and productivity to the best plants in the U.S. and Canada, the wage rates at Hermosillo are far different. In 1992, hourly wages were about $2.40 an hour in the Mexican plant compared to about $18.50 an hour in Detroit, while total compensation—wages and benefits—were $4.50 in Mexico compared to about $40 an hour in Detroit.

How important are wage costs in high-tech production? The answer to this question proved unusually contentious during the NAFTA debate. Proponents were anxious to prove that Mexico's low wages would not prove to be a lure for U.S. businesses. An oft-quoted article in the *Washington Post* was entitled "In the NAFTA Fight, Rages Over Wages Are Irrelevant." Former U.S. trade representative Carla Hills, among others, was quoted as saying that "if wages were the only factor, many developing countries would be economic superpowers." In other contexts, however, observers readily admit that wages are pivotal in making location decisions. In discussing BMW's decision to buy British-based Rover, for example, the *New York Times* reported that "At $24 an hour, labor costs in the German car business are double those in Britain, where social welfare levies on employers are lower and unions are not so strong as in Germany. That is forcing many German companies to build or acquire new production capacity abroad." If a wage differential of two-to-one can motivate German firms to move production, presumably the Mexico-U.S. difference of eight-or ten-to-one could prove important to U.S. firms.[12]

A quick calculation highlights the importance of wage costs, even in highly automated production. Assume a U.S. auto assembly plant employs two thousand workers, and that a Mexican plant employs three thousand (a conservative assumption given Hermosillo's productivity). Assume also that the U.S. plant works four million labor hours per year (fifty weeks times forty hours times two thousand workers) and the Mexican plant works six million hours. Using total compensation of $40 an hour for a U.S. auto worker, the cost for hourly labor in this high-tech assembly plant would be $160 million a year. In Mexico total compensation is $5 an hour, which translates into a $30 million annual wage bill—a savings for hourly labor alone of $130 million a year.

Hourly labor, of course, is not the only cost of production, but the magnitude of this gap underscores how important hourly labor costs can be in making production-location decisions. Other costs such as salaried labor expand the gap between the cost of production in the United States and Mexico even further; some costs such as transportation narrow the gap, but not enough to compensate for a differential of this size. Overall, the high quality and productivity serve to translate the low cost of labor into low unit costs of production, a powerful driver for investment. The consulting firm A. T. Kearney estimates that final assembly costs for automobiles in Mexico are only 53 percent of U.S. costs, in large part because of Mexico's low labor costs.[13]

Despite significant productivity gains in the automobile sector and throughout Mexican manufacturing in the 1980s, real wages in Mexico have declined. Productivity has gone up by about 40 percent in the last decade for all of Mexican manufacturing, while real wages have declined by about 40 percent. Increasingly, productivity in key parts of the export sector is at world-class levels, rivaling the best plants in Japan, while compensation remains at Third World levels. Wage rates are artificially depressed because state policies to attract investment and a government-dominated labor movement have decoupled earnings from rising productivity. The flip side of these low wages is low purchasing power, which undercuts the growth of the Mexican consumer market.[14]

Work Organization on the Shop Floor: A Case Study

Low wages are not the only attraction for locating production in Mexico. Firms are also attracted by the prospect of operating with a substantial degree of shop-floor flexibility. In fact, when it comes to defining work organization and labor relations, plant managers in Mexico enjoy a far wider latitude than in the United States. This flexibility stems from an industrial relations environment in which worker rights are limited and unions are either weak, government-dominated, or nonexistent. How is this flexibility different than the situation in nonunion plants in the U.S.? During a trip to Japan in 1992, I asked a Toyota executive why certain labor relations practices widely used in Japan, such as pay based on seniority and merit, were not exported to the United States. He immediately answered, "Because of the UAW." Even though the Toyota plant in Kentucky is not a UAW plant, it must comply with certain labor market standards or risk the possibility of a union organizing drive. Managers are well aware of this and act accordingly.

In Mexico, such standards are far less determining. The Hermosillo plant is organized by an affiliate of the Confederation of Mexican Workers (CTM), the principal labor federation in Mexico, but the union has virtually no presence on the shop floor, and had little input in setting up the plant in the first place. Moreover, although the CTM is the predominant union among Mexico's five principal automakers, neither industry-wide or even company-wide bargaining takes place. The three major Ford plants in Mexico, for example, are all organized by the CTM but bargain separately. As Mexican industry moves north, lured by low wages and proximity to the American market, the standards that prevailed in the older industrial centers are further eroded.

The first labor agreement at the Hermosillo plant was only twenty-four pages long and had virtually no language that protected seniority rights, regulated overtime, or specified a grievance procedure. In this context, management was free to install one of the most extensive applications of lean production methods in North America, let alone Mexico. This is not, however, a "fragile" system based on worker commitment and loyalty to the firm—in fact, there have been periods of considerable conflict in the plant, including three major strikes since 1986, mass firings, and a turnover rate that averages 20 to 40 percent annually. Despite all this, the productivity and quality performance of the plant, as we have seen, has been exceptional.[15]

Initially, all workers belonged to a single classification, work was organized into teams in which team members frequently rotated jobs, each team elected a facilitator to coordinate production for two-month stints, team members were consulted on selecting supervisors, workers could stop the line for quality problems, and a modified form of just-in-time inventory was used. Ford also placed a heavy emphasis on training to counter the potential power of skilled workers in a greenfield plant located in a nonindustrial part of Mexico. If an electrician quit, it would be difficult to find a replacement in the local labor market, giving a relatively small number of skilled workers considerable leverage over how the plant was run. To minimize this potential, the company developed a training-intensive form of work organization. All shop-floor workers were trained in maintenance and repair skills normally associated with the skilled trades, providing the company a much broader skill base and reducing its dependence on a key group of workers.

Workers received four months of intensive classroom instruction before they even started on the job, with special attention focused on such topics as machine-shop practice (one hundred hours), arc welding theory and practice (thirty-six hours), basic electronics (thirty-six hours), group work (thirty-five hours), and group problem-solving (sixteen hours). This training was the same whether someone was ultimately going to be repairing complex, state-of-the-art robots, or installing seats on the final line. In fact, when training began, it was not clear which workers would be assigned to production jobs and which would become maintenance workers.

Work in the plant was organized into teams of eight to twenty-five "technicians." The teams initially elected a team leader for two months, after which the leader rotated back onto the line. The teams also had an unusual amount of authority, selecting members for additional training classes and meting out discipline for absenteeism or poor performance. In fact, there were virtually no "skilled trades," as such. Instead, "technicians" took on dual responsibility for direct labor tasks as well as low-end maintenance, and teams selected full-time maintenance workers from their own ranks. Each team in the body shop, for example, assigned two workers to repair machines for nine-month stints, after which they returned to the line and the team selected two additional people for maintenance. The result was a considerable depth of skill and repair experience throughout the plant. Many workers on the line knew how to overhaul complex auto body transfer equipment or to troubleshoot the electronics on sophisticated robots. When a breakdown did occur, those formally assigned to repair the machinery were assisted by workers in the area who often had just returned to the line from their turn at maintenance.

Within these work teams, decision-making was guided by a variety of factors. While in theory the teams decided how often workers rotated between production jobs, in practice the rotation schedule was strongly influenced by the preferences of area managers. In the body shop, formal rotation occurred every two months, but some teams informally rotated certain jobs every few hours. In stamping, the rotation schedule varied between three and six months, depending on the job, while in final assembly management eliminated rotation altogether for teams on bottleneck jobs. Peer pressure was integral to the system but operated differently throughout the plant. In the body shop, for example, team members complained that absenteeism (averaging about 8 percent) was disruptive, forcing added work on the rest of the team or disrupting training schedules, since the facilitator had to fill in for the missing worker. Departmental management permitted the teams to punish absent workers by denying them training opportunities. On the final line, in contrast, workers generally were quite lenient and excused most absenteeism, and when they failed to punish their absent coworkers, management reasserted its disciplinary prerogatives.

High skills combined with low wages fomented considerable tensions in the plant. Although Hermosillo paid among the highest industrial wages in the region, workers were well aware that other plants in the area were not nearly as productive or as advanced technologically. The constant exhortations to achieve world-class quality and productivity and the frequent comparisons to auto plants throughout the world raised inevitable comparisons to wage levels in industrial countries. Workers did not aspire to parity but felt that they were significantly underpaid. This frustration contributed significantly to high turnover and, at times, flared into open conflict. In 1987, Ford rejected worker demands for a 70 percent wage increase, precipitating a two-month strike and a settlement based on the company's offer of a 35 percent raise. When a militant slate swept the local union elections the following year, winning by a 4–1 margin on their promise to improve working conditions, management fired the new leaders and their supporters (forty people in all), charging them with responsibility for sabotage and wildcat job actions. A compliant CTM put the local in receivership as a result.

Despite this flareup, Ford embarked on a complete transformation of the plant's product line, supplier system, and work organization. The company spent $300 million to expand and retool the plant for two new models that marked a significant departure from previous practice: both models were more complex (the new Tracer having 30 percent more parts); both were brand new and would have to be debugged on the Hermosillo line (in contrast to the time-tested and debugged model the plant initially built); and production of both would complicate model-mix variations in the production process. Moreover, both models drew their parts and components primarily from North American rather than Japanese suppliers.

Personnel policies changed as well. In response to high turnover, for example, Ford amended its hiring profile to include older and less educated workers with experience in other work environments. For the same reason, the company reduced the preparatory round of training from four months to two, with the balance of the compulsory training commencing only after the worker had been on the job six months and then continuing over several years to discourage turnover.

The plant has also moved away from some of its more participative features while retaining considerable shop-floor flexibility. The trend is towards a management-dominated model that tolerates the union only so long as it subordinates itself to enterprise goals. On the shop floor, the team facilitators are now selected by the supervisor rather than being elected by the team. In fact, the plant seems to have moved from a model of self-managed teams to one in which the supervisor is central. The supervisor passes on corporate directives to the shop floor and is responsible for soliciting ideas on how to improve productivity and quality from team members. A joint study group of managers and union leaders from Ford's Dearborn Assembly plant visited Hermosillo in mid-1992 and described the character of the teams' weekly thirty-minute meetings in their subsequent report. "One week, the Product Specialist [supervisor] uses the time to transmit information and data to the team. On alternating weeks, Team members have the opportunity to provide their Specialists with information and lists of needs."[16]

Conclusion: The Future with NAFTA

A central part of most discussions concerning ways to create high-skilled, high-wage jobs in the U.S. economy is a strong emphasis on improving training. This strategy certainly has many desirable dimensions to it, but the Hermosillo experience underscores the fact that training costs, as well as wage costs, are far less expensive in Mexico. With a literate workforce and an investment in state-of-the-art training, new skills to successfully staff advanced manufacturing can be developed in a relatively short period of time.

Hermosillo is an atypical example, though hardly an isolated one. The experience of manufacturing in the 1980s indicates the extent to which sophisticated production techniques, in industries from automobiles to electronics, can be located in Mexico. The Hermosillo plant does illustrate the ability to deploy lean production in Mexico, despite the fact that these methods have diffused slowly to date. The expansion of both advanced manufacturing and lean production takes place against a backdrop in which union rights are constricted and the Mexican government continues to follow a policy of holding wages down to attract investment. The North American Free Trade Agreement provides few mechanisms to address these underlying labor problems. In an age of unprecedented global integration, unless alternative means are found to harmonize the social, labor and environmental standards upwards, the promise of the future will be sacrificed for all three member countries.

Notes

1. Jorge Carrillo and Jordy Micheli, "Organizacion flexible y capacitacion en el trabajo: un estudio de caso," working paper (Mexico City: Friedrich Ebert Stiftung, 1990).

2. Gabriel Szekely, ed., *Manufacturing across Borders and Oceans* (La Jolla: Center for U.S.-Mexican Studies, University of California, San Diego, 1991); Harley Shaiken and

Harry Browne, "Japanese Work Organization in Mexico," in *Manufacturing across Borders and Oceans*, ed. Gabriel Szekely (La Jolla: Center for U.S.-Mexican Studies, University of California, San Diego, 1991), 25; Martin Kenney and Richard Florida, "Japanese Maquiladoras: Production Organization and Global Commodity Chains," *World Development* (July 1993): 14.

3. Shaiken and Browne, "Japanese Work Organization in Mexico," 46; Kenney and Florida, "Japanese Maquiladoras," 11.

4. Shaiken and Browne, "Japanese Work Organization in Mexico," 46; Kenney and Florida, "Japanese Maquiladoras," 15.

5. Shaiken and Browne, "Japanese Work Organization in Mexico," 49.

6. Quoted in James Womack, "A Positive Sum Solution: Free Trade in the North American Motor Vehicle Sector," in *Strategic Sectors in Mexican-U.S. Free Trade*, ed. M. Delal Baer and Guy Erb (Washington: The Center for Strategic and International Studies, 1991), 47.

7. Bob Davis, "Some U.S. Companies Find Mexican Workers Not So Cheap After All," *Wall Street Journal* (15 Sept. 1993): 1; Tod Robberson, "On Closer Look, Firms See Less to Mexico," *Washington Post* (29 Sept. 1993): A1; Kenney and Florida, "Japanese Maquiladoras," 44; Nora Lustig, "Let's Take the Drama Out of NAFTA" (Institute of International Economics, NAFTA Summit, Washington, D.C., 1993).

8. Gustavo Saavedra, "The Mexican Government's Perspective on NAFTA" (paper presented at the Seventh Annual Conference of the Society of Automotive Analysts, Mexico City, 11–14 May 1993), 28.

9. United States International Trade Commission, "The U.S. Automobile Industry, Monthly Report on Selected Economic Indicators," USITC Publication no. 2732 (Jan. 1994), 2; Mauro Leos, "Mexican Auto Industry Outlook under NAFTA: 1994–2003" (paper presented at the Seventh Annual Conference of the Society of Automotive Analysts, Mexico City, 11–14 May 1993).

10. Harley Shaiken, *Mexico in the Global Economy: High Technology and Work Organization in Export Industries* (La Jolla: Center for U.S.-Mexican Studies, University of California, San Diego, 1990); J. D. Power and Associates, "1992 Early Buyer New Car Initial Quality Study," unpublished data.

11. Womack, "A Positive Sum Solution," 14; James Harbour and Associates, "The Harbour Report: Competitive Assessment of the North American Automotive Industry, 1989–1992," (Troy, MI: James Harbour and Associates, 1992).

12. James Glassman, "In the NAFTA Fight, Rages Over Wages Are Irrelevant," *Washington Post* (10 Sept. 1993): B1–2; Richard Stevenson, "BMW Will Buy Rover of Britain," *New York Times* (1 Feb. 1994): C1.

13. James Mateyka, "Advantages and Disadvantages of Mexican Production" (paper presented at the Seventh Annual Conference of the Society of Automotive Analysts, Mexico City, 11–14 May 1993).

14. Instituto Nacional de Estadistica, Geografia E Informatica, "Indicadores de Competitividad de la Economia Mexicana," no. 3 (Mexico City, 1993), 8; Instituto Nacional de Estadistica, Geografia E Informatica, "Cuaderno de Informacion Oportuna," no. 243 (Mexico City, June 1993) 47.

15. Fieldwork at Hermosillo began in 1988–1989 with seven visits to the plant and intensive interview sessions with dozens of managers, union representatives, and over two hundred workers. Subsequent visits have updated this data base. For details cited in this article on the Hermosillo case, see Shaiken, *Mexico in the Global Economy*, 21–85.

16. "Dearborn Assembly Plant Visit of the Hermosillo Assembly Plant, June 2–5, 1992, Summary Report," mimeograph (Dearborn, MI). Ford uses the Hermosillo plant as a

model for lean production practices, frequently bringing managers and union leaders from its U.S. and Canadian plants on tours. The company had the rare opportunity to implement lean production with few constraints and has sought to diffuse this experience throughout its plants, much as General Motors has used its joint partnership with Toyota at NUMMI in Fremont, California as a prototype for more widespread changes. This doesn't mean that visiting delegations necessarily adopt the company's favored model; union members of the delegation from Dearborn Assembly, for example, did not endorse the Hermosillo approach.

15

Can *Maquilas* Be Lean?
The Case of Wiring Harness
Production in Mexico

SUSAN HELPER

Among the salient trends in the North American auto industry, two in particular stand near the top of any observer's list. First, many automakers and parts suppliers are introducing new forms of workplace organization emphasizing "lean," team-based decision-making and just-in-time inventory systems; these innovations are said to improve productivity and quality while also engaging a committed workforce in a wider range of responsibilities and tasks. Second, many auto companies are transferring parts-making operations to Mexico and other low-wage economies where unions are weak or nonexistent; *maquiladora* factories along Mexico's northern border are especially prominent in this regard.

The question posed here is whether these two trends are complementary or contradictory. My preliminary answer is based on an investigation of *maquila* supplier firms manufacturing wiring harnesses—the bundles of wires that distribute electrical signals throughout the car. The study is based largely on interviews conducted in Mexico and Texas in August 1992 with two dozen managers employed by two American maquila firms: one an automaker division that I will call "Brookline," the other an independent supplier that I will call "Solon." These interviews were supplemented by fieldwork conducted at the Brookline Division operations in the U.S., and at assembly plants served by both firms.[1]

Maquilas and Lean Production

Since the early 1980s, Mexican automotive parts production for export has increased dramatically, much of it centered in *maquila* operations along the northern border. The Mexican government initiated the Border Industrialization Program in 1965 to attract foreign investment to the region with incentives that included special exemptions from tariff and investment laws, and low wages. The number of maquilas grew steadily through the 1970s and more rapidly thereafter, reaching an estimated two thousand factories employing nearly five hundred thousand workers by the early 1990s. *Maquila* employment in the auto parts sector grew apace, from zero in 1977, to seventy-eight thousand in 1988, to an estimated one hundred thousand in 1992. General Motors, now the largest private employer in Mexico, had twenty-five thousand employees in *maquilas* in 1989; GM's Packard Electric Division alone had twenty-six plants along the border by 1992. Independent parts producers with *maquila* operations include Trico (a maker of windshield wipers), United Technologies (wiring harnesses), and Eaton (valves).[2]

While NAFTA eliminates or phases out the incentives that initiated the *maquila program*, the *maquila economy* will continue to grow as investors exploit its demonstrated advantages—proximity to the United States, and a pro-business polity that discourages enforcement of labor and environmental regulations while suppressing wages to levels well below prevailing standards elsewhere in Mexico. Rates of absenteeism and turnover in the border plants are extremely high—in the range of 10 to 15 percent for absenteeism, and as high as 30 percent monthly for turnover.[3]

At first glance, this would not appear to be the appropriate environment for lean production strategies, which emphasize worker empowerment and heavy investments in human capital. Advocates of lean production prescribe continuous improvement in product and process, to be achieved by a committed, highly skilled group of workers and suppliers who are separated by few buffers and who are in close communication with each other. However, *maquilas* are over one thousand miles distant from most U.S. assembly plants and are staffed by workers who literally speak a different language from their U.S. counterparts, have sixth-grade education on average, are paid less than $2 per hour including benefits, and change employers more often than once a year.[4]

Looking at results, however, one sees a different picture. Several auto-parts *maquilas* have won quality awards from their customers, and the ten Japanese-owned *maquilas* surveyed by Shaiken and Browne reported quality levels close to or better than their parent's highest quality plant in Japan. One of the *maquilas* I visited supplies an Ohio assembly plant with harnesses arranged in the sequence in which they will be assembled into cars, and the assembly plant carries less than one shift worth of inventory. No other suppliers to this assembly plant deliver in-line sequences of parts; instead, many of them deliver to a consolidation point near the plant where the parts are repacked into small, sequenced batches. Another *maquila* plant that I visited had received an award from its Japanese transplant customer for having no delivery errors for a year. In yet another case of superior performance, a GM-owned *maquila* that was having recurring problems with one of its suppliers in New Jersey brought the managers from the American plant to Mexico for a look at the *maquila's* operations; by adopting the small-batch techniques used in the *maquila*, the supplier increased its quality and saved five million dollars.[5]

Reviewing similar cases in a 1992 cover story aptly titled "Detroit South," *Business Week* proclaims a "startling discovery" to its readers: "Mexican auto workers, it seems, not only are dirt cheap but can also deliver quality."[6]

Literature Review

Presumably the reason that U.S. automakers are pursuing both *maquilas* and lean production is that they believe it will maximize their profits. Can these strategies be combined? That is, can leanness at *maquilas* be profit-maximizing for automakers?[7]

As indicated in table 15.1, there are four possible relationships between leanness and profitability at *maquilas*, each corresponding to a particular school of thought. The hidden cost theory holds that firms which source from *maquilas* are misled by their direct-labor based accounting systems. If these firms correctly took into account such hard-to-measure costs as extra inventory and poor quality, they would see that it is more profitable to source domestically. For example, Quick, Finan and Associates, in an analysis done for the National Tooling and Machining Association, find that including these hidden costs can raise the "true cost" of a

TABLE 15.1
Leanness and Profitability

	Profits	
	Low	High
Leanness		
Low	Hidden costs	Contingency theory
High	Excess missionary zeal	Fresh start

foreign supplier's bid by 40 percent. This analysis can be restated in terms of the above framework by saying that use of *maquilas* is not profitable because it is difficult to make them lean. Reasons include long supply lines, lack of infrastructure, and a poorly trained work force.[8]

In contrast, contingency theory holds that different conditions call for different managerial techniques to maximize profits. Morris and Pavett have taken this approach in their comparison of the organizational characteristics of a Mexican plant and a U.S. plant belonging to the same multinational. The product (a disposable plastic item) and the process (a labor-intensive, operator-paced system) were nearly identical in the two plants, and productivity was similar. However, the authors found that Mexican managers used an "authoritative" system, while U.S. managers used a "consultative" system. The authors believe these different styles to be appropriate, since Mexican workers "expect . . . an authority figure to make decisions and assume responsibility," while Americans "desire participation in decision-making and have the training (via the US educational system) to make those decisions."[9]

Another variant of the contingency view holds that due to low skills and high turnover in Mexico, the production process (not just the management style) requires closer supervision and a more minute division of labor. In contrast to the "hidden cost" view, a contingency theorist would argue that use of *maquilas can* be profitable. However, given differences in culture, infrastructure, skills, and workers' options, companies achieve high profits by using a traditional Taylorist ("low lean") system. That is, lower wages for direct labor offset lower productivity and higher supervision costs.[10]

Similarly, those who worry about excessive missionary zeal believe that too much leanness can lead to low profits. For example, spending a lot of money training workers who soon quit will dissipate profits quickly. This view was held by many of the American executives I interviewed at Brookline, who worried that their Mexican plant managers had gotten carried away by a desire to ''raise up'' their countrymen and women at corporate expense.

Finally, the fresh start thesis holds that *maquilas* are as good as, or better, than traditional U.S. plants at adopting lean production methods. According to this view, *maquilas* can compensate for their production workers' lack of technical skills because they do not need to unlearn mass-production attitudes, and because management has a free hand, unencumbered either by old ideas or the need to negotiate with unions, to organize and reorganize production as it sees fit. This argument is made by Shaiken in his study of a northern Mexico engine plant operated by a U.S. automaker, and in his study of Ford's Hermosillo assembly plant included in this volume. In the former, he quotes the rationale given in the engine plant's training manual for prohibiting transfers from the company's older Mexico city plant, namely ''to avoid inflated wages/benefits and old work practices.'' He notes that ''shop-floor flexibility was purchased at the cost of inexperience,'' but finds that machine uptime and quality was comparable to U.S. and Canadian levels within two years.[11]

Case Study: Wiring Harness Production in Mexico

A wiring harness consists of plastic-covered copper wire, terminals, connectors, and tape. In the lead prep stage, the wire is cut to pre-determined lengths, and a terminal is crimped to one or both ends. In the assembly stage, the terminals are inserted into connectors, tape is wrapped around bundles of wires to hold them together, and the completed harness is packed into boxes for shipment. Much of the lead prep stage is still done in the U.S., especially at Brookline. Much of the assembly, however, is done in Juarez, ''the wiring harness capital of the world.'' The assembly process consists of a conveyor staffed by about twenty people. On the conveyor are large peg boards with many posts to guide the routing of leads, and holders for attaching the connectors; for a simple harness, the capital cost of such a conveyor system is little more than one thousand dollars. As the build board moves down the line, each worker attaches a few connectors as it passes her station. While no part of this assembly process is technically difficult, a finished harness is complicated, containing up to a mile of wiring and hundreds of connectors. There are many opportunities to create a defect; common problems include insertion of the wrong connector, and leads incompletely inserted into connectors.

The key differences between doing business in the U.S. and Mexico are, first, that wages are very low, and second, that distances to customers and suppliers (both geographical and cultural) are very long—and made longer by poor infrastructure. The impact of these factors on wiring harness production is evident in the two Mexican cities where I conducted my research: the border city of Juarez (across from El Paso) and Chihuahua (about two hundred miles south).

Low Wages and Turnover

Since the 1982 collapse of the oil boom, wages have been very low in Mexico. The average real wage fell 50 percent between 1982 and 1988, giving Mexico by far the lowest wages of any industrialized or semi-industrialized nation in the world. While wages have recovered somewhat since then, a "basic operator" (the job classification of the vast majority of employees) in the plants I visited received hourly pay of about $.50 in Chihuahua and $1.00 in Juarez. This amount was so low as to produce a shortage of workers, evident in the huge banners reading *"Estamos contratando"* ("We are hiring") which hung from most buildings we saw in two Juarez industrial parks and the frequent comments from managers about the difficulty of hiring workers. In turn, the labor shortage produced a number of management challenges, the principal one being high quit rates; each of the plants visited reported turnover of 90–100 percent annually. Turnover was particularly bad in December and January, since workers would go to visit their families in the interior over Christmas, and then not return. The result of this seasonal labor shortage was a corresponding spike in defect rates. Management's response was to build up inventory in preceding months, a practice Solon's Japanese customer complained about.[12]

Another problem, particularly in the border town of Juarez, is getting workers with the desired demographic characteristics, that is, women in their late teens and early twenties. While 90 percent of the workers in the Chihuahua factory fit this profile, in the three Juarez plants I visited almost half the workers were men and one-third looked to be over thirty. When asked why he preferred women workers, the Mexican manager of one of the Brookline plants in Juarez replied without hesitation: "Because they are more docile to administer." This comment contradicts the lean production model of self-managing workers who make suggestions about the process; indeed, the same manager complained that his Mexican engineers allowed mistakes to be made because they would not challenge the decisions of their superiors.

Management's response to the labor shortage has been non-wage competition. To attract and hold workers, *maquilas* have routinely provided a range of benefits and services: free transportation to and from work; a high-quality and subsidized lunch (at the Brookline plants, management and workers ate the same lunch in the same room); subsidized food for home preparation; attractive *batas* (jackets to wear over work clothes); and sports teams. The cost of these benefits pushes total compensation to about $2 per hour. Firms also competed by having clean, well-lit factories—the Chihuahua plant even took the unusual step of installing potted plants and tanks with tropical fish along the main aisle.

One managerial problem commonly associated with labor shortages is that workers in a seller's market are more likely to reject an intensive workpace and impose their own, more leisurely, pace. I did not hear mention of this problem by management, though the pace of work in the two Mexican plants I visited did not seem onerous in comparison with U.S. auto components plants. One manager (who had also worked for Brookline's parent company in Matamoros) indicated that the lack of disciplinary problems stemmed from the employers' practice of carefully investigating the references given by job applicants; in his words, "the employers all stick together" to warn each other of problem employees.[13]

To escape the labor shortage, American managers favored an approach of moving to towns further and further south in search of a captive labor force. The only problem, they told us, was that as soon as one company identified a town with a hard-working labor force, other companies would soon follow. Once the workers had alternatives, the turnover problem would begin anew.

When asked why it wouldn't be more profitable (given the hidden costs of turnover) to raise wages to the point where the labor supply curve intersected the labor demand curve, *maquila* managers gave a variety of answers. One was that the turnover problem was cultural: Mexicans would always place family over job, regardless of the wage. A more common view was that raising the wage would only reproduce the turnover problem at a higher level of cost: "Everybody else would just raise their wages also, and we'd be back to the same situation—except at $4.00 per hour instead of $2.00." When it was suggested that this reasoning would not apply to rewards given to workers with long tenure, since productivity should also rise with wages due to reduced turnover, the response was that American *maquilas*, as large foreign employers, were highly visible "guests" in the country; as such, it wouldn't be a good idea for them to be seen as bidding up the price of labor. Also, they worried that Mexico was already becoming too expensive; both Solon and Brookline were exploring the possibility of setting up operations in Malaysia and Thailand.

Whatever the reasons, there seemed to be a highly effective employers' cartel in place in both Chihuahua and Juarez. Almost all the workers were in the "basic operator" category, which paid an amount equal to the government-set minimum wage. The cartel did provide for a category called "universal operator," which paid a wage 80 percent higher than the basic rate; but acquiring the necessary skills to achieve this rate of pay took about one year at the same firm, and this incentive was not attractive enough to motivate many workers to hang around. However, efforts to maintain the cartel seemed to be eroding. Several Mexican managers at Brookline had recently begun trying what they called an "underwater" (i.e., under the table) approach to raising wages. At one plant, for example, management had reorganized work so that more people did some set-up operations on wire-cutting machines, which meant they could qualify for the higher pay allowed for set-up people, even though set-up was a minor part of their job. Another manager had just implemented a pilot project he called an "unbalanced assembly line," in which the most experienced operators were given somewhat higher pay and much more work to complete within a given cycle time than their junior coworkers. In effect, he was using a liberal interpretation of the rules to create intermediate steps along the way to becoming a universal operator. A third plant organized workers into teams and promised continual training in general problem-solving skills. Management said that the courses were quite popular, and that workers had applied the principles they learned to resolving family problems as well as work-related issues; in the few months the program had been in operation, turnover had declined to 60 percent, although absenteeism remained at 4–5 percent per day.[14]

Why the difference in approach between these Mexican managers (who wanted to work with the people they had) and U.S. managers (who wanted to continually seek out new workers)? One reason seemed to be nationalism: consistent with those American managers who expressed a fear of "excessive missionary zeal," the Mexican managers were interested in "developing workers as people," as one training document put it; this sentiment was echoed frequently in our interviews with Mexican managers. Another reason is that turnover more directly affected the Mexican managers' quality of life. It was they who had to continually recruit new workers and train them, find substitutes for absent workers, and so forth; altogether, I would estimate that dealing with turnover and its effects absorbed as much as 50 percent of management time.

High turnover seemed to entail additional hidden costs in terms of labor productivity. The pace of work on conventional (balanced) lines, for example, was deliberately kept at relatively low levels to match the capacity of inexperienced workers. The ratio of supervisors and trainers to operators was also quite high—in one plant it was almost 1:2. Here, especially, the contrast with the lean production model is evident.

Both the plant with the unbalanced assembly line and the plant with work teams had cut the number of supervisors significantly (by 25 to 50 percent), but high turnover limited the effectiveness of the plant's extensive efforts in training. While both firms worked to continuously improve their processes, high turnover (with the exception noted below) meant that almost all of this *kaizen* was done by managers and engineers without, as prescribed in the lean production model, the input of production workers. At the one plant with production-worker teams, weekly meetings were held for the purpose of *kaizen* and workers elected team leaders who took minutes of the meetings. These minutes were quite short; probably three-quarters of them were something like "We all agreed to work hard to avoid defects." (The one suggestion of an irreversible countermeasure had to do with better separation of two similar-looking components, so that one would not be mistakenly installed in place of the other.)

Ironically, although turnover hampered efforts to provide training, it did promote diffusion of good practices. One Solon worker had suggested that a roll of bright orange tape be placed at each board on the rotating assembly line so that operators who didn't have time to fix a defect could at least mark it for future repair. This system is a direct copy of that used by Brookline, where the operator who made the suggestion had apparently worked before coming to Solon. Another potentially beneficial effect of turnover may be to reduce the incidence of repetitive stress injuries, which none of the Mexican managers we interviewed had heard of, and which the U.S. managers felt was largely an ailment invented by "[U.S.] workers who just don't want to work."[15]

In any case, management at the two firms seemed to have designed quality control systems that compensated quite well for high turnover. Both firms had defects delivered to assembly plants in the range of one hundred or so parts per million. Management attributed the performance on this measure to rigorous inspection and re-inspection, which was possible because labor was so cheap. First-pass yields (the percentage of harnesses which were assembled correctly the first time) were also quite high, in the range of about 95 percent. Some of the Mexican managers worried that it would be hard to improve on this record without shifting to lean production methods, which would require more training—and hence, less turnover—to be cost-effective. They stated that there is a limit to how much quality one can achieve through inspection, since the probability of damage increases every time the harness is handled.

Long-Distance Manufacturing

The second key feature of *maquila* production is the substantial distance from established centers of auto production. There are two corresponding effects on performance: a negative effect due to long supply lines (consistent with the hidden cost view), and a positive effect due to distance from traditional ways of thinking (consistent with the fresh start view).

Long supply lines require extra inventory at the supplier plant, as well as in transit. However, as described above, distance did not prevent one of the Brookline plants from being a pioneer of just-in-time sequential delivery to one of its customers, with a total elapsed time of about four days from the time a harness was assembled in Mexico to the time it was installed in Ohio. Perhaps the greatest negative impact of long supply lines was to complicate and increase the expense of problem-solving between the wiring plants and their customers. Wiring is a lot easier to change than other parts of the car (for example, changing a metal part usually requires redesigning a die, at a minimum cost of several thousand dollars). Therefore, engineers try to solve problems by changing wiring, if possible. The result is many engineering changes—at GM's Packard Electric Division, harnesses for even a mature car had an average of two major engineering changes and dozens of minor ones every year. These changes involve modifications to the production process and require constant communication between the assembly plant and the supplier plant. Solon maintained an office and consolidation center in the midwest, located less than two hours from its two principal customers. Engineers stationed there served as a liaison between the customer plants in the midwest and production in Mexico. Brookline also had liaisons, called "cooperative involvement engineers," stationed at division headquarters in the midwest. The managers I talked to felt that this system worked well, though it was expensive compared to the alternative model of customer-supplier liaison when the two operations are close together. The expense of travel definitely reduced face-to-face communication—especially in times of budget crisis, since travel was a large and visible expense with an intangible payoff. In at least one instance in 1992, distance hampered quality enough to knock Solon out of the running for a quality award from its major customer. The problem was in a branch of a harness that had to meet a tolerance of five millimeters (if it was too short, it pulled out of its connector; if it was too long, it interfered with another part). The problem recurred several times before the parties (communicating by telephone and fax rather than seeing the problem) realized that they were not interpreting the specification the same way. The distance was supposed to be measured from the middle of one connector to the middle of another; given ambiguity about what the "middle" was, and the slight stretchiness of the harness, it was easy to get measurements of even the same harness that were more than a few millimeters different.[16]

Although distance complicated problem-solving between customer and supplier, it seemed to facilitate problem-solving *within* the supplier's operation. Gillett describes how Brookline went from being one of the lowest-quality suppliers to a Japanese transplant to being one of the highest-quality suppliers. The source of learning was six months of technical assistance provided by the transplant's Japanese supplier of wiring harnesses. It included assistance in such matters as designing visual controls (for example, the problem of damaged harnesses was dramatically reduced by drawing a line six inches off the floor below the shelf where harnesses were kept, and decreeing that no part of a harness could fall below the line). Also, work stations were redesigned so that components to be attached to the harness were conveniently located for the operator. (In the old system, still in evidence at some of Brookline's U.S. plants, components were located behind the work station in no logical order, forcing operators to turn around and select components.) Adopting the new system required moving to in-plant JIT, since there was room for only small bins near the operator.[17]

These changes (visual control, JIT, and *kaizen*) seemed well-integrated into the thinking of the managers we spoke with in Mexico. Each of the Brookline plants I visited had active study groups, in which managers and engineers would meet to discuss books and articles on production management (a particular favorite was Eliyahu Goldratt's *The Goal*). Consistent with lean production principles, the production process at all four plants was in a state of flux: managers were constantly experimenting with new layouts of work and locations of components to achieve a smoother flow of production. However, in contrast to the principles of lean production, almost all of these changes were initiated by management; workers were largely uninvolved.[18]

In contrast, a commitment to continuous improvement was not particularly evident in the midwestern Brookline plant I visited. While much data on defects was recorded, there seemed to be little attempt to use the data to improve the process. There was little attention paid to maintaining a smooth flow of production., and there were no study groups for engineers or managers. Gillett argues that this difference in attitude between the Mexican and midwest plants is due to the Mexicans' ability to start fresh, without the baggage of mass production, and to the Mexican nationals' desire to prove that they were just as good as the Americans when it came to managing a plant. Distance itself contributed to the ability to try new things, since headquarters was less likely to meddle in the day-to-day affairs of plants one thousand miles away.[19]

Conclusion

The analysis presented in this section on the effects of low wages and long distances provides support for the hidden cost thesis. To illustrate, we can examine the wiring-harness cost data presented in 1992 by the Office of Technology Assessment. For a harness priced at $250, the difference in direct labor cost between an independent nonunion supplier (at $18 per hour) and a *maquila* is estimated to be at most $11. (This figure assumes that U.S. and Mexican workers are equally productive—i.e., that they each take forty minutes to assemble a harness, an assumption challenged by the managers I interviewed. For example, a Solon plant in the U.S. had three times the productivity of the Juarez plant.) The $11 direct labor saving is offset by a $7.50 increase in inventory and shipping costs, leaving a net savings from Mexican production of $3.50—less than 2 percent of the estimated total cost. Even this amount is overstated, however, since it apparently does not take into account such additional hidden costs as increased travel and communications (including, for example, maintenance of a private telephone system).[20]

Yet Mexico does offer benefits compared with production in the US—the benefits of a fresh start and a free hand for managers—and these benefits are particularly large if, as at Brookline, the U.S. managers and workers are uninterested in continuous improvement. Mexican wiring-harness production combines, in varying degrees, JIT production and "*kaizen* from above," with the close supervision and control of wages characteristic of Taylorism. This approach appears to be viable, and Mexican wiring-harness production has expanded rapidly. However, the Mexican model does contain significant internal contradictions that stem from its emphasis on keeping wages low; low wages cause high rates of turnover, and high turnover undermines training efforts and reproduces a low-skill, inexperienced workforce; inexperienced workers, in turn, are less productive and less capable of making suggestions that could improve the production process.

Mexican success appears to be based on a unique combination of the elements described above. Because of hidden costs, low wages by themselves do not give Mexico much of a cost advantage. Therefore, part of Mexico's advantage comes from the willingness of *maquila* managers to continuously tinker with the production process—a capacity for adopting

271

lean production methods ascribable to Mexico's "fresh start." However, as predicted by contingency theory, high turnover makes it difficult to adopt those lean production methods (quality circles, team production, etc.) that enlist line workers in the process. These internal conflicts suggest that Mexico's hybrid model is not the only profitable approach to manufacturing automobile parts and components (let alone the one which maximizes social welfare). For example, the Solon plant mentioned above, which pays the U.S. minimum wage, is profitable, while the Juarez plant is not.

The bottom line is that even higher-wage workers can compete—at least for now—if they and their management engage in serious efforts at continuous improvement.[21]

Notes

1. Thanks to Steve Babson, Thea Lee, and Arthur MacEwan for helpful discussion, and to Sylvia Brandt, Michael Robek, and Patricia Clifford for research assistance; I'm grateful to Frank Gillett for many fruitful discussions about wiring. Interviews with Mexican personnel were conducted in Spanish; all translations are my own. Except for a brief discussion with team leaders at one plant, all interviews were with management. In the future I hope to talk with workers as well. For much useful information on "Brookline," see Frank Gillett, "The Integrating Supplier: A Study of an Auto Industry Supplier's Relations across Several Customers" (master's thesis, MIT, 1992). Almost all of Solon's production was supplied to Japanese assemblers in the United States.

2. For comparison, there are about seven hundred thousand workers in U.S. auto parts production. See U.S. Congress, Office of Technology Assessment (OTA), *US-Mexico Trade: Pulling Together or Pulling Apart?* ITE-545 (Oct. 1992), 134; and James Rubenstein, *The Changing U.S. Auto Industry: A Geographical Analysis* (New York: Routledge,1992), 248–249. For background on *maquilas* and Mexican production, see Mary Teagarden, Mark Butler, and Mary Ann Von Glinow, "Mexico's Maquiladora Industry: Where Strategic Human Resource Management Makes a Difference," *Organizational Dynamics* 20 (winter 1992): 34–47; Tom Barry, ed., *Mexico Info Pack*, loose leaf (Albuquerque, NM: The Resource Center, 1992); Dan La Botz, *Mask of Democracy: Labor Suppression in Mexico Today* (Boston: South End Press, 1992); "Detroit South. Mexico's Auto Boom: Who Wins, Who Loses," *Business Week* (16 Mar. 1992): 98–103.

3. Even after Mexico's interior was opened to *maquiladoras* in 1972, more than 80 percent of these operations remained at the border, according to Teagarden, Butler, and Von Glinow, "Mexico's Maquiladora Industry," 35. On turnover and labor conditions, see Teagarden, Butler, and Von Glinow, "Mexico's Maquiladora Industry," 41–44, and La Botz, *Mask of Democracy*, 161–183.

4. Steven Herzenberg, "The North American Auto Industry at the Onset of Continental Free Trade Negotiations," U.S. Department of Labor, Bureau of International Labor Affairs, Economic Discussion Paper 38 (Nov. 1991), 40; OTA, *US-Mexico Trade*, 133–150.

5. Shaiken and Browne are cited in Herzenberg, ''The North American Auto Industry,'' 41.

6. ''Detroit South,'' 100.

7. In this essay, I will not address the question of whether leanness and/or *maquilas* maximize social welfare.

8. Quick, Finan, and Associates, *Hidden Costs in Offshore Sourcing* (Washington: National Tooling and Machining Association, 1987).

9. Tom Morris and Cynthia M. Pavett, ''Management Style and Productivity in Two Cultures,'' *Journal of International Business Studies* 23, no. 1 (1992): 169–179. Quality and delivery reliability data are not provided.

10. See for example William Baumol and Alan Blinder, *Economics, Principles and Policy: Macro Economics* (New York: Harcourt, Brace, Jovanovich, 1991), ch. 7.

11. See Harley Shaiken, ''High Tech Goes Third World,'' *Technology Review* 91, no. 1 (Jan. 1988), and ''The Universal Motors Assembly and Stamping Plant: Transferring High-Tech Production to Mexico,'' *Columbia Journal of World Business* 31, no. 2 (summer 1991).

12. As two of Brookline's Mexican managers pointed out, the wages paid in their plant were sufficient to enable a worker to buy a car after two years—provided that she had no other expenses, and that the car was a cheap used model from Texas. The reader should remember that this description of wages and turnover is based on a small sample of plants in only two cities. Even along the border, conditions vary greatly from location to location. For example, in Matamoros, wages were lower, and so was turnover and the cost of living. Although we saw some environmentally questionable practices (unvented fumes), we did not see anything that could be called a sweatshop. Since there are many published reports of squalid conditions, there must be wide variation among working conditions in different plants. It is interesting to note that even those plants offering relatively good working conditions still suffered problems with recruitment and turnover. In terms of the high turnover rate during December and January, I did not ask how Brookline managed to maintain its daily in-line delivery to Ohio. Stockpiling would have been difficult, since the Mexican facility received only fifteen days' notice of the schedule. Since the in-line operation was only a small part of the plant's production, perhaps management was able to keep it running by shifting workers away from other customers.

13. Regarding the possible link between working conditions and turnover, the managing director at Solon did complain that his firm's work was viewed as relatively undesirable because it required workers to stand up. He attributed this attitude to a weak Mexican work ethic, rather than low wages.

14. We heard less about such approaches at Solon, possibly because they were less used, or possibly because we had less access to Mexican managers in the absence of their American superiors.

15. Thanks to Frank Gillett for pointing out the identical use of orange tape at Brookline. Note that in contrast to the principles of lean production, the line is not stopped when defects are found; the problems are merely noted so they can be fixed later.

16. On the number of engineering changes at Packard Electric, see Geoffrey Gill, ''General Motors: Packard Electric Division,'' Case Study, Harvard Business School (3 Jan. 1992), 3.

17. Gillett, ''The Integrating Supplier.''

18. See Eliyahu Goldratt, *The Goal: A Process of Ongoing Improvement* (Croton-on-Hudson, NY: North River Press, 1984), who advocates a management-driven process of continuous improvement consistent with Brookline's ''*kaizen* from above.''

19. Gillett, ''The Integrating Supplier.''

20. OTA, *U.S.-Mexico Trade*, 147. The reason given for the higher productivity of So-

lon's U.S. plant was that it had lower turnover, and could therefore operate at a faster pace with fewer supervisors and trainers. The superior performance was not attributed to differences in capital/labor ratios; the equipment used was similar.

21. Frank Swoboda, ''Cooperation Worth Copying?'' *Washington Post* (13 Dec. 1992): 13, shows how Xerox and members of the Amalgamated Clothing and Textile Workers Union have modified the production process to keep wiring harness cost and quality competitive with Mexican producers.

PART 5 | EUROPE

16

Are Assembly Lines Just More Efficient? Reflections on Volvo's "Humanistic" Manufacturing

CHRISTIAN BERGGREN

Are we living in an age with no viable alternatives to the Japanese model of production design and work organization? That is certainly the conclusion advocates of lean production want to establish. In their view, the Toyota system is not simply the most productive form of industrial organization, it is the *only* form worth considering among the several alternatives. One such alternative, the Volvo assembly plant in Uddevalla, Sweden, draws especially vigorous criticism following the company's decision to close the operation in 1993. According to advocates of the Japanese model, the closing marks the failure of this experiment in "humanistic manufacturing," leaving lean production as the sole benchmark of international best practice—a conclusion that does not give much leeway for independent union or government action.

In fact, contrary to these assertions, Uddevalla was a remarkable success in terms of productive performance and commercial potential. This chapter, first, summarizes and analyzes Uddevalla's achievements, second, outlines the reasons for its closure, third, discusses the theme of organizational learning, fourth, criticizes superficial comparisons of worker satisfaction, and fifth, highlights some of Uddevalla's contributions to a system of "reflective production."

Uddevalla and Its American Critics

In 1989, when Volvo inaugurated auto assembly operations at Uddevalla, the plant manager boasted that "this isn't just new production technology. It is the death of the assembly line." The plant design was, indeed, conspicuously different from standard car plants. Instead of one long moving line, forty parallel teams built complete cars at stationary "docks," producing three or four cars per team each shift. At the normal production pace, individual cycle times ranged from 1.5 to 3.5 hours—a stark contrast with the one-minute standards on a moving assembly line. In the absence of foremen, team members (roughly ten per team) took responsibility for coordination of whole-car assembly as well as three major sub-assemblies: engine dress, doors, and instrument panels. Team members also managed the monthly rotation of job assignments through such indirect tasks as maintenance and quality control. Wages for individual workers rose according to a pay-for-knowledge system, with the top rate corresponding to "whole-car competence"—a status attained after working a minimum of sixteen months in the plant, and passing a test requiring whole-car assembly in twenty hours or less with a maximum of four minor defects. A team bonus also pegged compensation to the productivity and quality performance of the group. The assembly teams were supported by a partially automated materials handling process that used four AGV "taxis" per car to deliver the body, major components, and "kits" of from thirteen hundred to seventeen hundred parts. Vocational training and technical information were redesigned to sustain a new assembly culture, characterized by functional understanding and combined product and process knowledge. New technical aids made assembly work ergonomically superior to traditional forms. This included an ambitious project to develop new hand tools adaptable to different sizes and strengths, as well as tilted-assembly docks enabling team members to work in an upright position for nearly all operations.[1]

The plant aroused enormous international interest and inspired at least partial emulation by several automakers, with Daimler-Benz in particular incorporating some elements of Uddevalla's approach into its design of the new Rastatt operation in southern Germany. Many American academics were enthusiastic, others sharply critical. Womack, Jones, and Roos disparaged the concept, arguing that the "productivity of the Uddevalla system is almost certain to be uncompetitive even with mass production, much less lean production." A long report in the *New York Times* also concluded that the plant was doomed to failure, since "assembly lines are just more efficient." In the same article James Womack asserted that "Uddevalla is not in the ballpark. . . . It's not even in the outer parking lot of the stadium. Frankly it's a dead horse."[2]

In November 1992, Volvo officially announced that it would close its Uddevalla operation in 1993 and its Kalmar plant in 1994. (The Kalmar plant built the top-of-the-line model, Volvo 960, and represented an earlier stage in Volvo's trajectory of production innovation.) All of Volvo's Swedish assembly will henceforth be concentrated in the main factory in Gothenburg, where headquarters, design, and engineering departments are also located.

Were the critics right after all? Was Uddevalla, as the *New York Times* said, just a "noble experiment in humanistic manufacturing," a passing response to the industrial labor crises of the 1980s (when Swedish manufacturers had so many difficulties recruiting and keeping production workers), now doomed to failure in the hard times of the 1990s? Some critics believe the closing is reason enough for self-congratulation. Paul Adler and Robert Cole adopt a more sophisticated approach, stressing in a 1993 article in *Sloan Management Review* that "these plant closings should not close the debate over the significance of their innovations. . . . Whether the advocates of work reorganization within Volvo will be able to refocus their efforts on reforming Volvo's other facilities remains to be seen. Whatever the case, there is much to be learned from the Kalmar and Uddevalla experience." However, in a comparison of Uddevalla and NUMMI, they draw the same conclusion as the MIT team: "There is little doubt as to which production system is capable of delivering the greatest efficiency and quality; it is NUMMI. . . . Uddevalla was not within striking distance of NUMMI's productivity and quality." According to Adler and Cole, NUMMI is very strong on organizational learning, whereas Uddevalla could not translate its impressive individual learning to organizational performance. This is a neat theory, but to substantiate it requires long-term comparative studies of the plant-wide learning processes in these two operations—something Adler and Cole have not attempted.[3]

Performance and Politics

Uddevalla's actual performance contradicts the negative claims of both the business media and the academic partisans of lean production. On closer examination, it is evident that Uddevalla's rate of improvement (or "learning") in productivity and quality performance was particularly high in the second half of 1992, demonstrating that it had nowhere reached the limit of its possibilities. In October 1992, after only three years of operation, the plant equaled the productivity of Volvo's line-assembly operation in Gothenburg, Torslanda and surpassed it in quality. Indeed, at the time of its closing, Uddevalla had emerged as Volvo's internal benchmark of market responsiveness and customer satisfaction.

This achievement can be analyzed and measured in four dimensions: productivity, quality, flexibility, and customer orientation.

Productivity. During its first year of production, as teams were trained and new operations brought on line, final assembly time per car at Uddevalla averaged seventy hours, including materials handling, maintenance, and other indirect activities, but no salaried positions. By the last quarter of 1990, plant performance had improved to fifty-nine hours per car, and from then on assembly time was reduced by an average of one hour per car every month, until November 1992 (in the last days before the closure decision was announced), when this figure was down to thirty-three hours—50 percent below the start-up rate. Already by 1991, this rapid improvement had brought Uddevalla to the same productivity level as Gothenburg's assembly line, something MIT and the *New York Times* had ruled out of the question. Admittedly, at this time the Gothenburg plant was not very productive in European terms, a main reason being the drastic fall in Volvo's sales and the consequent decline in capacity utilization. Inspired by Japanese methods, a new management eliminated Gothenburg's overstaffing and launched a comprehensive productivity program that overtook Uddevalla in early 1992. But in the second half of that year, Uddevalla upped its performance and in the month prior to the shut-down decision the two plants competed neck-to-neck, with Uddevalla taking the edge in worker hours per car. None of Uddevalla's managers doubted that the plant had abundant potential for further improvement, with a target of twenty-five hours per car well within range for the middle of 1993.[4]

Quality. In 1990, Uddevalla's quality rating reached 890 on Volvo's internal index, in which 1,000 equals a perfect car; Gothenburg's rating was basically the same. In 1991 the target was raised to 910 and Uddevalla achieved 907, slightly ahead of Gothenburg. Best in class was Kalmar. Originally, management had expected Uddevalla's highly skilled and motivated teams to attain superior quality more or less automatically. It was only in 1992 that the plant introduced and trained workers in the rigorous quality control procedures already installed at Kalmar. New forms of team-based self-inspection were also implemented—for example, having workers check each other's jobs when shifting positions within the teams. The result was an improvement in the plant's quality performance to a level of approximately 920–925 points on the old index system. According to J. D. Power surveys for model year 1992, U.S. customers reported 124 problems per 100 vehicles produced at Uddevalla within ninety days of purchase, while for Gothenburg cars the corresponding figure was 144 (the average for European cars in the U.S. was 158). In the second half of 1992 both Uddevalla and Gothenburg reduced these figures significantly, as indicated in the J. D. Power statistics for model year 1993. The 940 model improved from 132 to 87 complaints, and Uddevalla and Kalmar improved most rapidly of all.

Flexibility. Parallel assembly at Uddevalla meant that cars were built in many places simultaneously. Before the plant came on-line, it was generally expected that this would result in considerably higher tool costs and a corresponding disadvantage implementing the minor adjustments specified in the annual model change. In practice, the opposite was true. The three model upgrades in the years 1990–1992 were introduced with between 25 and 50 percent lower costs per car than at Gothenburg, and Uddevalla returned to normal productivity in only half the amount of time it took at the line-assembly plant. Several factors contributed to this superior performance. One was the plant's deliberate low-tech strategy for the assembly process: simple, flexible tools were substituted for complex dedicated equipment, allowing modification rather than replacement when the new model year commenced. While process engineers at Volvo's other plants accepted the product designers' assembly specifications, Uddevalla's engineers required designers to standardize and modify technical requirements in order to minimize the need for extra tools. In that way the annual model upgrade became a much more interactive process, resulting in considerable cost savings. The same applied to the role of production workers. To retool the Gothenburg plant, industrial engineers and sub-foremen relocated materials, adjusted equipment, and provided new tools; assembly workers were informed of the changes, but seldom participated in shaping the outcomes. By contrast, the assembly teams at Uddevalla implemented the changes, studied the new instructions, and rearranged their workplaces. The system of providing parts and components in programmed kits also accelerated the learning process for assemblers. The head of the plant's industrial engineering department was emphatic on the advantages this gave Uddevalla: "Our cost for training and preparing people for new models has been only half that of the Gothenburg plant. The main reason is the enormous competence and skills of the assembly workers and materials handlers."

This superior flexibility is all the more noteworthy when compared with the recent performance of the Japanese model. Contrary to the claims of MIT's International Motor Vehicle Program, lean production does not always produce the desired flexibility. In fact, the severe recession in Japan's auto market in the early 1990s has produced the opposite trend, as

Japanese auto companies strive to cut costs and reduce the number of variants and options; commonization of components across the model range has become the order of the day. The proliferation of models that occurred during the 1980s caused a lot of problems for Japanese manufacturers, including uneven work loads and poorly balanced lines as the model mix varied. These problems are one of the reasons for Toyota's experiments in new assembly designs and work patterns at the Tahara plant.[5]

Uddevalla's radically parallelized production design offered a way out of these balancing problems. (In their treatment of this aspect, Adler and Cole confuse line balancing with setup times, an altogether different thing.) When the plant had concluded the official breaking-in phase and reached its performance targets in mid-1993, it planned to take further advantage of this flexibility by adding special vehicles, such as police cars, extended wagons, and other "quixotics," to its production of regular cars. Preliminary tests demonstrated that Uddevalla could assemble such cars in half the time it took at Gothenburg, where "raw versions" were first put together on the line and then partly disassembled and customer-equipped in a separate special-vehicle shop. The gains in lead time by building these cars at Uddevalla would have been even more impressive.[6]

Customer Orientation. At Uddevalla, there was an early awareness of the importance of fostering close contacts with the market, but Volvo's system for evaluating plant performance concentrated on narrowly defined production parameters, such as assembly hours and quality indices. Initially, therefore, Uddevalla had to focus on improving its assembly performance, and nothing else. In 1991, however, a study of lead times revealed that the average interval from customer order to delivery of an individually specified car in Sweden was two months, with a range from one to four months! The company's rigid planning system, the functional specialization and high barriers between production and marketing, and the complex product structure with its high option content all contributed to this prolonged delivery process. At this time, only 20 percent of Uddevalla's volume was custom-ordered, the balance representing "plan cars" assembled according to the company's market forecast and central scheduling system. For these "stockers," total cycle time was even worse—on average they spent twelve weeks after production waiting to be sold and delivered in a depressed auto market.

All of Volvo's plants responded to this problem by refocusing on direct delivery of customer cars to the dealers, but Uddevalla was first off the mark in October 1992, when it began to assemble cars for the Swedish market on customer orders only. One month later this principle was extended to the whole European market—the plant would still produce "plan cars" with no guaranteed delivery date, but delivery of any custom-ordered car would henceforth be guaranteed within four weeks. Basically, Volvo Uddevalla had realized what Toyota tried but failed to accomplish in the 1970s, that is, to establish direct links between customers and factory scheduling.[7]

Within Volvo, it was the Uddevalla plant that pioneered this very lean principle. The reasons for its successful implementation of this approach are evident when its flexible production system is contrasted with the operation of a conventional assembly-line plant. In the latter, truly customized production inevitably creates uneven workloads. A stream of highly specified and labor intensive cars might be succeeded in unpredictable ways by cars which have a low option content, producing wide variations in work intensity among assemblers assigned to job-cycles of only one or two minutes. Such variation is difficult to accommodate at a conventional plant, "lean" or not. In order to maintain a steady work flow on the long assembly lines, it is vital to sequence and even out production (for example, every second car a turbo, every third an automatic transmission, every fourth a sixteen-valve engine, etc.). Thus it was difficult for Volvo's Gothenburg plant to accomplish a complete custom-order assembly system without impeding productivity and jeopardizing its targets for reduction of assembly hours. At Uddevalla, in contrast, the many parallel teams and materials handlers did not require any specific, planned sequencing of cars with different option contents. Whole-car assembly and long work cycles made rebalancing a relatively easy matter as team members responded to the program and "kit" for each car. Indeed, the introduction of customer order-planning provided an additional motivational advantage, for the teams now knew that the cars were not to be stored in a warehouse somewhere, but delivered directly to individual customers.

By November 1992, on the eve of the shut-down decision, Uddevalla had expanded the proportion of custom-ordered cars from 20 percent of its total output to 70 percent. The corresponding figure at Volvo Gothenburg was 35 percent. In one year Uddevalla had reduced the total lead time by half, from sixty to thirty days. The plan was to cut it by half again, to fourteen days, in the next few years.

Future plans also called for a radical break with the previous practice of installing radios, telephones, tow hooks, and other options at the dealerships. To customers, this division of labor between plants and dealers means high costs, less reliable quality, and extra delays. Uddevalla's flexible assembly would have no problem producing fully equipped cars, including all the features traditionally handled by dealers. Such an integration would result in substantial advantages: lower installation cost, reduced handling and warehousing, higher and more consistent quality, and shorter lead times. For example, it is much more efficient to mount a tow hook, including necessary wire connections, when the car is being assembled, than to do it afterwards when several components first must be dismantled. This dismantling entails the risk of damaging other components, and quality procedures in dealer shops are seldom of the same caliber as the factory standards. Beginning in mid-1993, Uddevalla's market and delivery planners had advanced plans to integrate almost all of these traditional "dealer installations" in the factory process, and as a result would be able to produce cars that could be delivered directly to customers. At Gothenburg-Torslanda, there were no such plans—for good reasons. Its assembly lines could not cope with additional variation.

Why, then, did Volvo decide to shut such a productive operation? Management's official answer referred to depressed markets and dismal capacity utilization. Indeed, the automaker was in deep trouble. In only three years, from 1989 to 1992, its total sales of big cars dropped by 30 percent as the Swedish market, Volvo's second most important, virtually collapsed. Volume at the main assembly plant in Gothenburg fell by half between 1988 and 1992, from 150,000 cars to only 80,000. In 1992, the Volvo Group's operating loss was estimated to be 2.6 billion SEK (approximately $350 million U.S.); of this Volvo Cars accounted for half. Awash in red ink, management became preoccupied with immediate measures to reduce capacity, and Uddevalla and Kalmar were targeted despite their superior performance. Theoretically, the two assembly-line plants in Ghent and Gothenburg have the combined capacity to produce 300,000 cars—50 percent greater than then-current sales. In addition, Gothenburg is the center of Volvo's car-making capacity, with stamping and body plants as well as engineering and design facilities. Uddevalla and Kalmar, as small and incomplete plants (only final assembly, with no body or paint shops) were at a fatal disadvantage. Uddevalla's per-shift capacity of 40,000 cars a year was redundant; as the market slumped in 1992, it was already operating well below that potential, producing 25,000 units of an older model that was losing market share. Management turnover also played a role, as the old CEO, a champion of Uddevalla who was also responsible for Volvo's failure to speed up its inefficient product development process, gave way to a successor with no personal ties to the Uddevalla plant. In the internecine struggle for survival between Volvo's Swedish plants, the powerful unions in Gothenburg sided decisively with the new management, saving local jobs at the expense of the branch plants.

Productivity Comparisons and Organizational Learning

With this overview of Uddevalla's achievements and the reasons for its closure, let us now analyze its capacity for learning in more detail. As we have seen, Adler and Cole argue that Uddevalla was not even within "striking distance" of NUMMI's productivity. This alleged performance gap is attributed to the Swedish plant's emphasis on individual, as opposed to organizational, learning.

If we want to analyze organizational learning, it is essential to distinguish between *absolute performance* and *rate of improvement*. Adler and Cole are quite correct when they report that the NUMMI plant consumes fewer assembly hours to build a car than Uddevalla, or any other Volvo plant. The problem is the next step, their attempt to establish a direct link between this performance gap and the capabilities of organizational learning at the two plants. As emphasized by Karel Williams and his colleagues in their study of productivity in the auto industry, it is very difficult to compare data from plants belonging to different companies, producing different products, using different component suppliers, and so forth. Rather than focus on the absolute number of assembly hours required, the more fruitful approach is to interpret the differences between two plants, and their rates of improvement.[8]

In the case of NUMMI and Uddevalla, the performance gap is influenced by a number of factors outside the control of the final assembly process. First, there is an important difference in product manufacturability—NUMMI workers would certainly appear much less productive if they had to assemble Volvo cars. Second, the quality of the components supplied are by no means the same. This is not only true for external deliveries, but also for components supplied by previous processes within the company. Third, as Williams et al. have demonstrated, capacity utilization must be included in any serious comparison of plant productivity. Since Uddevalla barely utilized 50 percent of its one-shift capacity in 1991–92, whereas NUMMI operated much closer to optimal efficiency, Volvo's plant is again at a disadvantage. Fourth, the two plants are differently positioned on their respective learning curves. NUMMI adopted a mature, fine-tuned concept, developed for decades in Japan; Uddevalla, on the other hand, had just established its learning curve for a qualitatively novel concept, and needed much more experience for developing its potential.[9]

Here I will focus on Uddevalla's rate of improvement, rather than its absolute productivity. Considering that worker hours per car declined by 50 percent from 1989 to 1992, and by 26 percent in 1992 alone, it is difficult to maintain that Uddevalla did not have a significant capacity for systematic, organizational learning. Moreover, the accelerated productivity progress in the fall of 1992 was combined with a 20 percent improvement in quality and the almost complete conversion to custom-order assembly. In fact, the plant had never before made such broad progress as it did in the nearly twelve months before the decision to close it.

Adler and Cole emphasize the importance of organizational learning, but analyze the organization of the two plants in a very simplistic way. Thus, under the heading "organizational design" there is only a description of the assembly teams at Uddevalla. For students of management and administration, it should be obvious that management policies and administrative hierarchies have some impact on productivity, and cannot be conflated with shop-floor structures.

A paradoxical aspect of the Uddevalla story is that the plant's advanced structure of assembly teams coexisted for such a long time with a basically traditional management apparatus located in a detached and secluded office building. The plant demonstrated its superior potential despite this anomaly, but in early 1992 there were clear signs that Uddevalla needed a congenial plant organization and a managerial structure that could maximize the strengths of its team system. Accordingly, in mid-1992 a new plant manager (supported by the unions, and previously successful in reorganizing the pilot plants belonging to Volvo's development and product engineering departments) installed a very different, process-oriented organization at Uddevalla. In the new structure there were only two hierarchical levels, shop and plant management. As before, the roughly six hundred workers in the assembly and materials shops were organized in teams with rotating, hourly team leaders. They communicated directly with the shop managers (five assembly and four materials), who in turn made up the bulk of the plant's new management committee. This participation of first-line managers in Uddevalla's central governing body reflected a very strong emphasis on process and process development (including organizational learning!) in the new structure.

For the new plant manager, the flattening of the hierarchy was only the first step. Next, he planned to empty the office building completely, and relocate all managers and administrative officers in facilities directly adjacent to the production process. "Some of the functional heads did not believe me," he admitted when interviewed about this plans, "but I intended to move first, and then the others would have no choice but to follow suit."

A third aspect of this focus on process was a series of initiatives to involve salaried employees in direct production activities in order to build an intimate knowledge of manufacturing problems across the plant. To gain first-hand experience, the new managers of the assembly shops started to learn how to assemble cars—not complete cars (that was in most cases too daunting a task), but at least fairly complex sub-assemblies. The remaining industrial engineers, who had been relocated from the office to the assembly and materials shops, were expected to spend half of their time building cars in the assembly teams. To bridge the still existing gap between white- and blue-collar workers, the head of manufacturing assigned other managerial staff, such as accountants and systems analysts, to assist the teams for a shorter period (normally one week). Initially, this program encountered vehement opposition, but in the end the reactions were very positive.

Far from being a mere cultural exercise, these initiatives served several well-defined purposes, one of the most important being to develop and diffuse best-practice methods throughout the plant. Aggressive perform-ance demands provided the impetus, while the presence and participation of the support staff (engineers, etc.) provided the opportunity to elaborate and spread best-practice procedures as swiftly as possible. As a part of this drive there was also a very successful introduction of a plant-wide *kaizen* program in the fall of 1992.

Adler and Cole quite correctly emphasize that both organizations, NUMMI and Uddevalla, are capable of learning and evolution. Nonethe-less, they tend to interpret their impressions from a 1991 visit to the Swed-ish plant in a very static way, presuming that conditions at a particular point in its development constituted the indelible essence of the Uddevalla concept. "At Uddevalla," they write, "work teams were left to their own devices. In the very early days of Uddevalla, managers gave workers the procedure documents from the [Gothenburg] Torslanda plant. But these procedures were not very well designed. . . . As a result, the Uddevalla workers quickly discarded them, and, along with them, the very idea of detailed methods and standards. . . . This management philosophy sounds more like abandonment than empowerment." It is true that there was an interregnum at Uddevalla when the traditional standards did not work and new standards had not been developed. This interregnum was not an inher-ent feature of the Uddevalla concept, however. In fact, at the time when Adler and Cole visited the plant, this period was coming to a close, new procedure documents had almost been completed, and their introduction to the assembly teams started.[10]

The problem of finding effective means for diffusing methods and practices outward from higher-performance teams—that is, organizational learning—had been a management preoccupation since the start of the plant. Thus, Adler and Cole are wrong when they argue that "a third as-sumption built into the Uddevalla approach . . . is that an increase in indi-vidual learning automatically leads to an increase in organizational learning. This is a fundamental fallacy." Uddevalla had no problem ac-knowledging the need for organizational learning. The challenge was to organize it in effective and congenial ways, and in 1991 and early 1992 the managerial answer was to strengthen the hierarchy and expand the role of technical expertise. The new process-driven organization represented a very different solution, combining radical decentralization, participative management, and a strong performance orientation. The *kaizen* program was one approach to developing and diffusing best practices. To accelerate the process of knowledge transfer, the plant manager also envisioned a comprehensive system of personnel exchange within and between assembly shops, and eventually also between the assembly department and materials handling. According to managers interviewed as part of my evaluation study, it was only in 1992, three years after its inauguration, that Uddevalla had acquired an overall organizational form that fitted the team structure and production design. As the plant's former personnel head, a shop manager in the new organization, pointed out: "We had to learn so many things from scratch, starting with a process of un-learning, getting rid of previous conceptions and behavior. Only in September 1992 had we found on organization suited to our production concept. We also introduced a new program for leadership development, which was essential for all shop managers, and the new management board. The first session of the program took place in November, on the same day as the close-down decision was announced."[11]

Working Conditions under "Reflective Production"

The IMVP researchers attack Uddevalla not only for its alleged performance deficiencies, they also argue that its vaunted "humanistic manufacturing" does not mean any real improvement or change in the nature of assembly work. For Womack, Jones, and Roos, lean production does that job much better than whole-car assembly, since "simply bolting and screwing together a large number of parts in a long cycle rather than a small number in a short cycle is a very limited version of job enrichment." Whereas long work cycles only provide satisfaction from "reworking and adjusting every little part so that is fits properly," lean production represents the intellectual challenge of constant problem-solving. This summary account forgets the fact that during most of the day lean production is not about problem-solving, but the constant pressure to perform highly repetitive tasks at an intensified pace. (Incidentally, issues such as physical and mental stress, workplace injuries, and cumulative trauma disorders are never mentioned in the IMVP book.) Whole-car assembly at Uddevalla certainly was not conceived to offer workers the dubious satisfaction of reworking and adjusting parts. On the contrary, a basic rationale of the concept was to give workers the possibilities, the competence, the tools, and the authority to do a high-quality job without any subsequent adjustment. This was combined with an extended scope for intellectual challenges. The plant's kaizen program represented only one example. Another, more advanced form was the dialogue and interaction between product engineers and production workers during pilot runs of the annual model changes. Interviews with Gothenburg's engineers, whose experience included all of Volvo's assembly plants (including the Belgian plant in Ghent, and the small Canadian plant in Halifax), indicated that discussions with skilled workers at Uddevalla, especially the whole-car assemblers, were especially productive. These problem-solving sessions were not constrained by the rigid sequencing and interdependencies of the assembly line system; Uddevalla's workers could question the proposed assembly methods and develop innovative solutions. As one product engineer observed: "In 1992, when the last model change took place, their skill level was really high. We had a very good response at the pilot run, the assembly workers were more competent and more curious than at any of the other plants. What the plant lacked, as a consequence of its short time of operation, was a more advanced professional knowledge." In this respect, Kalmar was the best of all Volvo plants, according to unanimous interviews. "If they (Uddevalla) had been allowed to exist and develop their competence, they would have been outstanding and our dialogue with them truly professional."[12]

Adler and Cole are more low-key and sophisticated in their discussion of working conditions at Uddevalla and NUMMI. They admit that Uddevalla probably had a human advantage, but contend that "NUMMI's quality of worklife, although not ideal, is in the 'acceptable' range as far as workers are concerned." At the same time, they argue that the difference is not large, and to support this they cite a survey of worker satisfaction at Volvo in which Uddevalla reportedly did not score much higher than Volvo's traditional Gothenburg plant. Now, surveys of worker satisfaction are notoriously difficult to interpret since they are so heavily influenced by worker expectations, individual histories, and the precise wording of the survey questions. Most surveys which ask workers to indicate their level of job satisfaction have a positive bias, since work normally comprises an important part of a person's self-identity, and respondents are therefore predisposed to report favorably on their jobs. An exception to this rule, however, occurs when the work process has undergone the kind of reorganization that occurred at Uddevalla: here, positive expectations tend to outrun actual experience, producing a negative bias. As a result, differences between workplaces with "good" and "bad" conditions tend to be understated. In 1985–87, in a study of organizational changes within the Swedish auto industry, I developed an assembly survey to measure physical, mental, and social aspects of working conditions, using methods designed to minimize the inherent bias found in most attitude surveys. In a five-plant comparison, this instrument was used to study the impact on working conditions of different production designs, ranging from two-minute work cycles on traditional car assembly lines, to advanced team assembly comprising eight- to ten-hour work cycles. The results of these comprehensive studies were unequivocal. The further from traditional line assembly a plant moved, the better the outcomes in terms of variation, prospects for personal growth, the assumption of responsibility, and the opportunity to use one's skills. The Volvo assembly lines at Gothenburg-Torslanda had the lowest values, while bus factories where teams were responsible for the assembly of complete vehicles consistently had the highest scores. The same broad pattern applied for physical strains and occupational injuries. Asked about desires for change, workers at all the line plants criticized the repetitiveness of their work and viewed holistic assembly as the only real solution.[13]

Unfortunately, the decision to close Uddevalla halted plans to apply this instrument at the plant. I will therefore confine myself to quoting the comments of three Uddevalla workers who had previously been working on the assembly line at Saab. They may not be representative in a statistical sense, but they are supported by numerous observations by other Swedish researchers visiting the plant.

"There, at Saab, the foreman drove you with the whip. Motivation was only negative, you worked in order to avoid criticism and hassles. Here work is hard, but it is so interesting that you are prepared to put in more effort."

"You cannot find a better manufacturing job. Here we are trying to do as much as possible as good as possible. At Saab, it was the opposite way. Here you have an overview, and don't learn just about parts and details. And our shop managers are very different from the supervisors on the line."

"This place is pure paradise, in spite of the heavy production pressure. You have the responsibility, and the possibilities to influence and change things. We are the masters and face the consequences."

The day of the close-down decision, a woman assembler told a journalist: "When I left previous jobs, I missed the work mates, but that was about all. Here I will miss both my team members and friends, and the job itself."

Notes

1. Plant manager quoted in Jonathan Kapstein and John Hoerr, "Volvo's Radical New Plant: 'The Death of the Assembly Line'?" *Business Week* (28 Aug. 1989): 92–93. For a

comprehensive analysis of Uddevalla and other workplace innovations in Sweden, see Christian Berggren, *Alternatives to Lean Production: Work Organization in the Swedish Auto Industry* (Ithaca, NY: ILR Press, 1992), esp. 146–166. Unless otherwise indicated, performance figures provided by Volvo and interview quotes from workers and managers are drawn from my study of Uddevalla and Kalmar, "Excellence or Disaster: An Analysis of Volvo's Assembly Plants in Uddevalla and Kalmar" [translated], *Arkiv* (1993).

2. James Womack, Daniel Jones, and Daniel Roos, *The Machine that Changed the World* (New York: Rawson Associates, 1990), 101; Steven Prokesch, "Edges Fray on Volvo's Brave New World," *New York Times* (7 July 1991).

3. Paul Adler and Robert Cole, "Designed for Learning: A Tale of Two Plants," *Sloan Management Review* (spring 1993): 85–86, 88, 91.

4. Productivity figures for Uddevalla are not comparable with the assembly times MIT researcher John Krafcik calculated at various car plants in "Triumph of the Lean Production System," *Sloan Management Review* 30 (fall 1988): 41–52. The aim of Krafcik's study was to compare data across plants and countries. Thus they only registered a standardized subsample of assembly activities at each plant and did not compute total assembly times. Even comparing Uddevalla and Gothenburg, two plants within the same company, is made difficult by a variety of measurement errors (e.g., the allocation of maintenance and other indirect activities) that blur the picture when differences are small.

5. Masami Nomura, "Farewell to 'Toyotism'? Recent Trend of a Japanese Auto Company," mimeo (Department of Economics, Okayama University, 1992).

6. Adler and Cole, "Designed for Learning," 89.

7. On Toyota, see George Stalk and Thomas Hout, *Competing against Time* (New York: The Free Press, 1990), 67–69. Unfortunately, their account is not correct. In the Toyota distribution system, dealers, not customers, order cars, and dealers are manipulated by various factory incentives. As a result, sales outlets in Japan tend to carry a lot of excess inventory. Takahiro Fujimoto, personal communication, 19 November 1993.

8. Karel Williams, Colin Haslam, John Williams, and Tony Cutler, "Against Lean Production," *Economy and Society* 21, no. 3 (Aug. 1992): 321–354.

9. Ibid.

10. Adler and Cole, "Designed for Learning," 90.

11. Ibid., 92.

12. Womack, Jones, and Roos, *The Machine that Changed the World*, 102.

13. Adler and Cole, "Designed for Learning," 91. For a more complete discussion of survey methodologies and bias, see Berggren, *Alternatives to Lean Production*, 184–193.

17

Lean Production and Co-Determination: The German Experience

ULRICH JÜRGENS

While lean production and other variants of the Japanese model found ready acceptance in many parts of the world auto industry, German management and unions were not among the early recruits. They didn't have to be. The 1980s were very successful years for German industry, and there seemed little need to amend the country's unique reliance on skilled labor and upscale markets. In the car industry, on which we will concentrate in the following, employment rose by 12 percent from 1981 to 1990, whereas most car industries in other countries experienced sharp declines in employment.

This positive performance drew attention to a specifically German model of production organization based on a "virtuous circle" of market requirements, skilled labor supply, and co-determination. By focusing the product range toward the upper segments of the buyer market where price elasticity is low, companies could mitigate the pressures to reduce costs, pay wages that met the requirements of the union, and produce high-quality products under working conditions that took full advantage of skilled workers. High wage rates, good working conditions, and co-determination are not only compatible with this model, but are integral elements of it.[1]

Since 1990, with the steep recession in the German economy and with a general crisis evident in the auto industry, lean production concepts now find a growing audience. Indeed, the "German model" is under considerable pressure, with some critics calling for a complete change in management practices. In the following, I will first review the outlines of this debate and the circumstances that are pushing German automakers towards change. I will then describe the basic features of the German system of co-determination and how it influences the organization of work and production. Following this, I will describe the different approaches to lean production that are being implemented at car companies in the West German homeland of the "German model," also with a particular view to the effects of co-determination. After this I will deal with developments on the periphery, especially in "German transplants" located in Eastern Europe, where German manufacturers have until now focused their efforts to realize lean production principles in the spirit of the Japanese model.

Market Crisis and MIT Critique

In retrospect, it is apparent that sales opportunities on the American market were a major prerequisite for the success of the German and, by the way, of the Swedish model. As the situation on the American market changed due to shifting exchange rates, altered tax structures, and the emergence of Japanese competition in the upscale market, sales declined and both models entered a period of crisis. This crisis became evident at just the time when MIT's International Motor Vehicle Program (IMVP) proclaimed that "lean production" was catalyzing a second industrial revolution. (The German edition of *The Machine that Changed the World* was published 1991 with the title *Die zweite Revolution in der Autoindustrie.*) In addition to the Volvo plant in Uddevalla, the IMVP authors focused their criticism of western European production practice on a German plant. When they visited this plant, the authors recall,

> We didn't have to go far to find the basic problem: a widespread conviction among managers and workers that they were craftsmen. At the end of the assembly-line was an enormous rework and rectification area, where armies of technicians in white laboratory jackets labored to refine the finished vehicles up to the company's favorite quality standard. We found that a third of the total effort involved in assembly occurred in this area. In other words, the German plant was spending more effort on fixing the problems it had just created than the Japanese plant required to make a nearly perfect car the first time.[2]

The Financial Times disclosed that this was a Mercedes-Benz plant. "Our advice," the IMVP authors concluded, "to any company practicing 'craftsmanship' of this sort in any manufacturing activity, automotive or otherwise, is simple and emphatic: stamp it out. Institute lean production as quickly as possible and eliminate the need for all craftsmanship at the source. Otherwise lean competitors will overwhelm you in the 1990s."[3]

The critique of craftsmanship does indeed go against the grain of the German model and the widespread conviction that the *Facharbeiter* (skilled worker) is the source of Germany's strength and success in world markets. The criticism of the MIT authors and their "change or die" message would not have had the same impact on this self-certainty if it had come at a different point in time. But in view of the far-reaching restructuring of the German polity and economy following the incorporation of the former East German state, and with the insecurity accompanying that social-political transformation, the ground was well prepared for the acceptance of radical concepts. Concern for the efficiency of German factories grew with the prospect of intensified competition, particularly with low-wage sites in Eastern Europe that are barely fifty miles east of Berlin, but which are directly connected to the know-how of western manufacturers. On top of this came the recession in 1992.

These conditions have created a dynamic for change that influences the co-determination system at just the point where companies are considering and implementing measures that move towards lean production. However, the process is still in its beginning stages and it is too early to make reliable statements about the possibility of an independent, German realization of the lean production concept. On this score, timid assessments even predominate among the practitioners in the field. Even so, it is possible to discern two basic features of this change process. First, the strategies for finding a solution—particularly in defining the contours of a new productivity pact between the companies and the unions—are becoming increasingly radical as the pressure for action increases. Second, despite all the insecurity regarding that future relationship, the realization of the lean production concept is currently taking place *within the framework* of the co-determination system.

Co-Determination and New Production Concepts before the 1990s

Since its establishment in the 1950s, the co-determination system has evolved into one of the central institutions of postwar democratic Germany.

As currently structured, it regulates the relationship between "capital and labor" from micro to macro levels in many areas of society, and its principles are broadly accepted by the major societal actors. In regard to the regulation of work, three levels should be differentiated.

Works Councils. The influence of works councils, exercised through elected officials representing blue- and white-collar interests at different levels within the company, is the foundation of the co-determination system. The Works Constitution Act gives the works council a graduated influence, depending on the subject matter, extending from the right to information concerning economic data and business performance, to the right to consultation, up to the right of co-determination—that is, the right to veto certain measures of management. Although the subject areas for co-determination are limited, they nevertheless play a key role in the negotiation of interests and in the adjustment of other matters. Subjects for co-determination include: (a) the selection of personnel in the case of layoffs, (b) the scheduling of overtime work, and (c) changes in the system and determinants of wages and salaries. Plant agreements between management and the works councils extend or specify further the influence of the elected councilors in defining work organization, the introduction of new technology, the delivery of training, and other matters.

Labor Representation on Company Boards. Through their legally mandated representation on company boards, worker delegates from the union and the works councils can, under certain conditions, exert strong influence on the nomination of the executive board and on strategic company decisions. While the law specifies formal parity on the company board between representatives of labor and capital, the vote of the chairman is usually cast in favor of the capital bench. But a pro-labor coalition can form, as at Volkswagon where the state of Lower Saxony is a major shareholder represented on the capital side. Presently, with the Social Democratic government holding state office, labor positions can gain a majority on VW's company board, as also occurred at the beginning of the 1970s.[4]

The collective bargaining system. Bargaining between national unions and employer associations, with collective agreements reached on this industry-wide level, often provides minimum standards for the regulation of work and road maps for further action at the company level.

The system of co-determination is based primarily on governmental policy and is sufficiently independent of party platforms and alliances that it cannot be attributed to Social Democracy alone. Conservative governments have also shaped and supported this structure. Without a doubt, it was a central element in a cold war strategy of securing a socially attractive capitalism at the most sensitive juncture between the First and Second Worlds in the postwar decades. This global and historic dimension has a concrete relevance for the current debate concerning lean production, expressed in the fear—of many managers as well as works councilors—that Germany will revert to "early capitalist" methods and a stronger emphasis on management prerogatives.

This system of co-determination made a strong contribution to shaping the German production model through the 1980s. As it was generally recognized that Fordist and Taylorist principles of production organization were no longer appropriate, a new model emerged which aimed at the increased employment of skilled workers—*Facharbeiter*—in direct production tasks. This went along with a vision of "computer integrated manufacturing" aiming at high degrees of automation even in final assembly and low-volume production runs where labor-intensive methods have usually prevailed. The skilled worker was regarded as the key figure in the modernized factory, and it was widely held that high-tech work structures would give Germany the competitive edge again, even in segments of the mass production market.

The "qualification offensive" contributed to this technology orientation. The background for this public campaign was the high level of structural unemployment which, by the end of the 1970s, threatened the prospects for young people entering the job market. In order to improve their chances for a decent working life, a broad policy consensus emerged that every youth should have the right to enter an apprenticeship after finishing school. As a result, the actual demand for skilled labor became less of a factor for determining the number of apprentices a company would take. But after finishing the apprenticeship, finding a skilled worker's job became correspondingly difficult. To avoid laying off these young qualified workers, companies deployed them in direct production jobs on an equal footing with ordinary production workers. In anticipation of future automation measures, which were seen by management as the coming trend even in the assembly areas, production managers had an interest in retaining qualified workers. As a consequence, the labor force contained a growing share of skilled workers who had gone through a solid industry-relevant apprenticeship program. If extrapolated into the 1990s, this trend could be expected to raise the proportion of *Facharbeiter* to three-quarters of the direct production workforce.

Focusing on the *Facharbeiter*, therefore, was consistent with the larger focus on automation and "high technology work structures." The *Anlagenführer* (equipment controller) became the new paradigm of industrial work propagated by Kern and Schumann. This is a person who ideally would be a skilled worker with further training for running production equipment and "managing" support work. This preoccupation with automation was also evident in the discussion of group work, which started again (after the pilot projects of the Humanization of Work program during the 1970s) with the debate over how to run complex high-tech equipment in teams that also took responsibility for quality control, maintenance, and such "residual" manual jobs as filling magazines and transferring parts.[5]

The fixation on an automation strategy was almost complete, and left little room for consideration of how to reorganize work in the assembly process. The goal of lengthening individual work cycles on the line, which also dated back to the Humanization of Work program, bore only modest fruits when compared with Sweden. Nevertheless, cycle times of between two and five minutes on conventional assembly lines had become common in German manufacturing by the middle of the 1980s, and represented a far cry from the cycle times of one minute or less which were commonplace in American factories. Even where new production concepts which partially did away with assembly lines were introduced—as at Opel, GM's German subsidiary—this was seen as a preparatory step for future automation. In these sub-assembly/module areas with stationary work positions, there were longer work cycles of between fifteen and forty-five minutes.

Under the combined influence of the co-determination system and this strategic orientation towards high-tech production of upscale models, a specific model of future-oriented work emerged in Germany that differed from both the Swedish and Japanese models in important dimensions. The basic features of these three models are compared in table 17.1.[6]

In the German case, the automation strategy did not bring about the economic effects which were originally expected. It led instead to recurring breakdowns of the equipment, grossly increased personnel requirements in the indirect areas of the plant, and large buffer areas before and after the automation equipment, which, in turn, absorbed capital and floor space. The IMVP authors characterize Western production organization as "robust-buffered" (compared to the "fragile-lean" system of Japanese manufacturers), but even this misrepresents the practices that prevailed in parts of the Western economy, where the complex technology created a "buffered-fragile" system that was very risky for companies facing growing competition. In the performance comparison of the IMVP, which determined an average of thirty-six hours per vehicle for European manufacturers in European plants, the German mass manufacturers (as one heard in off-the-cuff assessments) were no better than average, and were certainly well behind the figure of seventeen hours per vehicle for Japanese manufacturers in Japanese plants.[7]

TABLE 17.1
Models for Production Organization

Swedish	German	Japanese
semi-skilled workers with high initial training (quasi-apprenticeship)	skilled worker deployed on direct production jobs	semi-skilled workers with generally high starting qualifications
work completely uncoupled from production cycle	work partially uncoupled from the production cycle	work tied to the production cycle
wholistic tasks with long work cycles above one hour	job enlargement with work cycles below one hour	highly repetitive work; cycle times around one minute on the assembly lines, around five minutes in the machining areas where multimachine work is the norm
homogeneous groups	mixed teams of "specialists"	homogeneous groups
high partial autonomy for teams through process lay out	little partial autonomy for teams through automation and module production	no partial autonomy for the teams through JIT design
de-hierarchization with elected speaker and self-regulation of group affairs	controversial role of group speaker/leader and of degree of self-regulation	strong hierarchical structures, group leader appointed by management, no group self-regulation

Embracing Lean Principles in the Early 1990s

While the general claim that lean production represents global "best practice" has strongly influenced German thinking, there is little clarity as to what lean production or "lean management" actually is. Two interpretations predominate, the first focusing on the system's organizational characteristics and structural prerequisites, the second on performance.

Organizational characteristics and structural prerequisites. According to this definition, lean production is a set of new practices and new forms of work and process organization. In the early 1990s, German observers focused on five key measures: (a) the introduction of team work and project organization; (b) the decentralization of management structures and the flattening of hierarchies; (c) continuous improvement activities; (d) integration of product and process development to include suppliers (simultaneous engineering); and (e) a reduction in the degree of vertical integration achieved by the creation of systems suppliers and increased just-in-time deliveries.

Performance. By this standard, lean production is defined by the benchmark results of the best-practice companies. "Lean production is 'lean,' " according to the IMVP authors, "because it uses less of everything compared with mass production," including half the labor required in a conventional plant. According to this interpretation, lean production is the definite and determined effort to achieve the quantum leap in productivity and quality improvements required to catch up with the best-practice companies.[8]

The ambiguity in these alternative definitions helped the concept of lean production to gain a wide degree of acceptance. But the split in the tectonics can break open easily. After all, we are dealing with the crucial question: Is a reduction of personnel in the dramatic magnitude of 50 percent (ceteris paribus) the necessary *prerequisite* for setting off the functioning principles of lean production, or can the introduction of key organizational characteristics set off a self-sufficient process of rationalization that could be supported by all participants and make it easier to socially cushion the personnel reductions *over time*? The collective actors have been temporarily spared this difficult decision by the impact of the recession—companies like Volkswagon and Mercedes-Benz have reduced their German work forces by around 15 percent in 1993. (In 1994 plans to dismiss another thirty thousand VW workers were forestalled by a joint agreement to introduce a four-day work week for two years.)

The lean production debate has also, for the time being, made it easier for union and management in Germany to at least agree on a diagnosis of the problem. In particular, the new emphasis on workplace organization has supplanted the *Standort Deutschland* (production site Germany) discussion which employers have been pushing for years. Here, management has complained about the great burdens placed on economic activity through governmental and union policy: high wages, short working times, co-determination rights, taxes, and governmental regulations. The message of the IMVP study, which implies that it is not the state with its taxes or the unions with their demands, but rather primarily the management and the system of production organization they created which make up the core of the problem, shifts the focus of debate to shop-floor practices and management policies. Management and the union can proceed from this common starting point. (However, this dividing line between the production site discussion and the lean production debate is also precarious and by no means stable.)

The attempt to define a common agenda for change is expressed in the recommendations which the Arbeitgeberverband Gesamtmetall (Employers' Association for the Metal Industries) presented to its associated companies in 1992. These recommendations are also positively emphasized by union representatives. The basic principle is formulated as follows: ''At the center of our concept is the ability and willingness of the workers to deliver performance. The workers are of highest importance for the competitiveness of companies in the metalworking and electronics industries. It is therefore necessary to strengthen and use these human resources and to change everything which impedes their being developed.''[9]

The twelve recommendations put forward by the employers association to its member companies could indeed be shared by many unionists: (1) design work content and work organization in such a way that they increase the motivation of employees; (2) use the benefits of teamwork; (3) integrate the tasks of planning and executing work and speed up product development through ''simultaneous engineering''; (4) deploy technology so as to take into account efficiency as well as the needs of employees; (5) maintain and increase the qualifications of employees; (6) increase the quality of the work; (7) make work time flexible; (8) design a system of remuneration that supports performance as well as cooperation; (9) design work to promote the health of employees; (10) keep employees informed and let them participate; (11) co-operate with your works council on the basis of trust; and (12) practice leadership.

A key focus of this lean production strategy is the introduction of group or team work. The debate over group work has continued since the 1980s, when the orientation was more strongly directed toward the Swedish model. At the beginning of the 1990s the debate turned to overlapping and hybrid forms of team organization, with a growing emphasis on objectives that favored Japanese transplants. In the meantime, all German manufacturers (except Porsche) have introduced group work, at least in certain areas. In particular, Opel and Mercedes-Benz have given concrete time-frames within which they want to introduce team organization in all of their plants. In all these cases, company management and works councils negotiated plant agreements regarding the introduction of group work, and established steering committees with an equal number of members from management and the works council to oversee the process and evaluate the results.

Works councilors were guided in these negotiations by previous debates within the labor movement. The discussion about group work began in the ''Industriegesellschaft Metall'' (I. G. Metall, the metalworkers union) in the second half of the 1980s, leading to the formulation of structuring criteria and minimum requirements for group work. In a brochure published by the works council of Mercedes-Benz's Bremen plant, the works council and the regional I. G. Metall give an exemplary summary of the requirements which have to be fulfilled before agreeing to the introduction of group work:[10]

- Works council and I.G. Metall support the introduction of group work if manning levels within the groups are sufficient;
- if a common task exists which is well-known to every group member;
- if older workers and workers with health limitations are fully integrated;
- if the works council is involved in decisions on the composition of the group;
- if performance control is based on group performance;
- if the groups are provided with time and space for the group meetings;
- if tasks are integrated; if performance targets are agreed to by the group and the works council;
- if the group is authorized to deal with fluctuations in the production schedule and with breakdowns;
- if the group members participate in the planning and design of their working conditions;
- if the new tasks stimulate personnel development and further qualification on the job.[11]

There were several controversial issues in the initial design of group work (in some cases called team work—I use group or team as synonyms here).

First, the role of the team speaker or group leader—should he or she be elected by team members or nominated by management? The answer varied by company and even within companies. At Volkswagon, leaders in some pilot group areas are elected by the group and the function rotates every two weeks (the rotation scheme is different in other areas); at Opel and Mercedes-Benz, group leaders are elected for a longer term, normally one year, and there is no policy of rotating this role; at Ford, the group leader position is a semi-supervisory role; at BMW, there is no group leader below the *Meister* in most group areas. The union had to address an additional problem raised by the group leader position: it was afraid that the function of representing the group members' interests could hollow out the function of shop stewards, the front-line union representatives on the shop floor. At first, the union put forward the demand that shop stewards should become the group leaders, but it was subsequently decided that it was best to let team members decide whether or not they elect shop stewards as group leaders. Actually, the percentage of shop stewards elected as group leaders was low (in one major plant about 30 percent).

A second controversial issue was the degree of homogeneity or functional specialization within the group and, as a consequence, the differences in pay levels, qualifications, and possibilities for learning on the job within the group area. In most cases, this question was suspended or left to plant-by-plant resolution.

A third issue focused on the question of technical or process layout prerequisites for the introduction of team work. This was not a controversial issue in the case of automation areas, but group work was not regarded as compatible with assembly line operations. While work planners and unionists have favored the Swedish model, especially the system implemented at the Uddevalla plant, the demand to eliminate the assembly line as a precondition for introducing group work has not been given priority attention since the economy turned down and the Swedish plants were closed.

These and other controversial issues have been addressed within the framework of co-determination, but negotiating a mutually acceptable solution often takes much time. In the case of Volkswagen, for instance, it took four years before an agreement was reached just to try group work in selected pilot areas. At Mercedes-Benz, the timetable for fully realizing team structures in all plants will stretch over several years, from 1992 to 1995. The time-frame for some issues is even longer, particularly the key question of introducing a wage system that is supportive of group work. This issue cannot be decided at the company level, but requires negotiation at the level of industry-wide collective bargaining.

In many respects, this wage issue highlights both the opportunities and the risks of the co-determination system. Viewed from the standpoint of lean production, the traditional wage system's differentiation between direct and indirect labor, with blue- and white-collar workers each compensated according to different criteria, is no longer up to date. This is also the case for incentive systems, which are only geared to efficiency and ignore or downplay quality performance, readiness for deployment, cooperation, and improvement orientation. Under the Works Constitution Act, as we have seen above, the works council has far-reaching co-determination over the methods and, in part, even over the standards for regulating performance. But it has little influence on wage determination for indirect blue- and white-collar employees. Removing the distinction between the two now raises the question whether the co-determination rights of the works council should also be extended to indirect tasks or, conversely, whether its influence in the direct area would be reduced to the low level of the indirect area. The bargaining partners in Germany have bogged down on this critical question. The union demand for the extension of co-determination to also include white-collar tasks, in exchange for implementing parts of the lean production model, appears too high for many employers. However, the fact that leading companies in the automobile industry have signaled that they are willing to make this exchange indicates the obvious high regard of leading managers for the system of co-determination. The exchange is now being blocked by the fact that these companies are bound to collective bargaining systems which also include small and middle-sized companies, and companies from other metal industries. In the discussions within these regional employers' associations, large companies with an interest in lean production have not been able to assert themselves. They will negotiate further and a compromise is more likely. In the meantime, strategies for introducing lean production have been making a detour around this question.

Just as the works councils supported an increase in productivity as a main objective in exchange for participation in the design of group work and the process of introducing groups, they are also willing to support the realization of lean production principles in exchange for expanding the co-determination rights to personnel staffing levels and thus performance standards in the white-collar area. These proposals have not always won easy or unanimous support from employers, but there is no indication that disagreement on this or other issues concerning lean production cannot be contained and ultimately resolved within the co-determination system. On the union side, even though there is also some grumbling about lean production concepts, there is no opposition group comparable to the New Directions Movement in the United States. The German system of co-determination thus also seems to be capable of dealing with the "lean revolution."

Internationalization and the Future of Co-Determination

To this point, we have only considered developments in the core of the German automobile industry. However, the previous picture of a solid and, with respect to lean production, quite sovereign co-determination structure is changed considerably when we turn to developments on the periphery of German automaking. Of the new plants which are currently in the starting-up phase or will be opening in the near future, only the Mercedes-Benz plant at Rastatt is located in the core area and, therefore, subject to the internal dynamics described above. In contrast, the new plants located on the periphery are clearly subject to different pressures and opportunities.

These start-up facilities include two new Volkswagon plants, Martorell in Spain and Mosel in eastern Germany, and a General Motors plant at Eisenach in eastern Germany. Volkswagon has also modernized Skoda plants in the Czech Republic and established a joint venture with Ford to build a plant in Portugal.

The difference between the newest (and last?) core plant at Rastatt and the new plants on the periphery could not be greater. The planning for the Rastatt plant was modeled after the Swedish example, especially the Uddevalla plant. Like Uddevalla, Rastatt is a pure assembly plant without a body shop or paint operations. Unlike Uddevalla, Rastatt does not follow the radical course of completely abolishing the assembly line in favor of whole-car assembly by a production team. But the break with traditional methods is quite evident, with the assembly line eliminated for about half of the work operations, and significantly modified in other areas. Throughout the plant, efforts to achieve integral, long-cycle work content have extended cycle times to as much as two hours in stationary work areas, and between fifteen and forty-five minutes on the assembly line. Group work has been introduced as a universal principle at Rastatt, with the fine-tuning and evaluation carried out by a steering committee made up of an equal number of representatives from the works council and management. Rastatt's hybrid combination of German and Swedish organizational elements is supplemented by a touch of Japanese practice through the introduction of a "continuous improvement" program, with the corresponding visualization and communication forms.

The new plants built on the periphery of the German auto industry clearly took their inspiration from the Japanese model, as mediated through Japanese transplants in North America and Great Britain. The term "German transplants" suggests itself, as these are largely establishments of German companies (including Opel, GM's German subsidiary) making resolute attempts to realize the Japanese model outside of the auto industry's traditional core area. Despite considerable differences between them, it suffices here to look at the Eisenach plant to clearly show the main features of the new organization. The model for this plant was a hybrid of GM's experience at NUMMI and CAMI; in recruiting upper management, Opel indicated a clear preference for people who had worked at these two plants. As at NUMMI and CAMI, the team principle is universal and all employees wear the same uniform. The assembly line is conventional, as in the transplants, with short cycle times; but there are pull cords planned to permit assembly workers to stop the line—the first time ever in a German plant. In keeping with the Japanese model, the plant uses a *kanban* system for parts supply. Despite the fact that virtually all of the production workforce has *Facharbeiter* training, no internal maintenance department is planned—this function, to the extent that it is not done by direct production workers, is to be contracted out to external firms.

This new approach to production organization corresponds to manning policies that target the best-practice benchmarks among the transplants. Built on the site of the now defunct state-run factory that built 70,000 Wartburgs a year for East Germany, the new plant is designed for a yearly capacity of 150,000 units, staffed by two thousand employees screened and recruited from the eight thousand who worked in the old plant. The industry press is already comparing Eisenach to plants in western Germany: while Opel's Bochum plant produces forty-three cars per worker annually, Eisenach is slated for seventy-five per worker when it reaches full production. At that time, management anticipates that it will take less than twenty hours of labor to produce the Corsa model, compared to the roughly twenty-five hours it takes in Opel's other plants.[12]

For the Eisenach plant, as for Volkswagen's Mosel plant since 1991, the previous West German system of co-determination is in force, but not the customs and practices which have developed in the core plants over the years, and not the very substantial volume of plant agreements reached between management and works councils. As both Eisenach and Mosel are independent according to corporate law, they are not included in labor's company-wide board representation as mandated by co-determination in the core industry, and their works councils are not included in the company-wide works council. There are some continuities—the works council chairman of the Volkswagen plant at Mosel was previously on the works council in one of the core plants in Germany, for example. But the system of co-determination in the plants in eastern Germany is just beginning to develop and still has to prove itself.

This will now take place under different conditions than prevailed when the core industry developed its co-determination practices. The new conditions arise from the internationalization of production, the intensification of competition in Europe and worldwide, and the problems arising from the integration of East Germany. Signs of intensified competition between the plants are already conspicuous, and the union is criticizing whipsawing practices that were largely unknown in Germany until the 1990s. These pressures on individual plants to ''change or die'' will likely increase in view of a growing surplus capacity caused not only by short-term market fluctuations but also by the long-term restructuring that accompanies the consolidation of a European market, the arrival of Japanese transplant competition, and the consequent modernization and rationalization of European manufacturers. These conditions create a permanent challenge for the system of co-determination.

Unions have anticipated this problem by forming Euro-Works Councils. But without a legal basis, which can only be established at the European political level, the formation of such transnational councils remains dependent on the willingness of company management to recognize these institutions. Few companies are so willing, and the exceptions—Volkswagen is one of the pioneers—have only accepted a diluted form of co-determination. VW has had a Euro-Works Council since 1990, but its competence area is not comparable with that of German works councils. Its rights are limited to periodic access to information; it does not have co-determination and corresponding veto rights over company measures in the production network outside the Federal Republic.

Summary and Conclusions

The foregoing leads to four theses concerning the German environment for adopting lean production:

First, the German system of co-determination has demonstrated its capacity to accommodate change. The realization of lean production principles thus takes place within the system and in agreement with its basic principles. Up to now there has been no organized group among employees or employers which has openly questioned this basis for the exchange relations between capital and labor.

Second, while the co-determination system remains part of the "long term orientation" in the German economy, it could be that the benefits of this approach have to be questioned more closely in a context where "time based competition" defines the rules of the game for success. In these circumstances, we have to expect more rapid reaction times from social-organizational structures. The well-balanced negotiating systems of co-determination do move very slowly when we are dealing with fundamental innovations, as we have seen with the introduction of group work. It is also to be expected that no radical solutions will be reached within this framework.

Third, with the "German transplants," management is clearly pursuing a different strategy. These new plants are seen as the opportunity to experiment with and learn about new production and organization systems. The possibility that management could purposely use these new plants to spur competition with its older facilities represents a latent threat to the standards and achievements which were negotiated in the framework of the co-determination system. For the foreseeable future, an extension and internationalization of the system of co-determination through Euro-Works

Councils does not have much of a chance in the European political arena; in any case, the strong co-determination structures evident in the German model are not to be expected there.

And fourth, the challenges to the German co-determination system have increased dramatically in the 1990s as previously latent conflicts are becoming more and more clear. Co-determination will experience its true test as the site competition in Europe intensifies and the Eastern European peripheral countries enter this competition. Even so, to cast co-determination on the rubbish heap of history as an outmoded model would be just as premature as to proclaim it without reservations as the model for future success.

Notes

1. Arndt Sorge and Wolfgang Streeck, "Industrial Relations and Technical Change," Wissenschaftszentrum Berlin fuer Sozialforschung, discussion papers IIM/LMP 87-1 (1987); Wolfgang Streeck, "Successful Adjustment to Turbulent Markets: The Automobile Industry," in *Industry and Politics in West Germany: Toward the Third Republic*, ed. Peter Katzenstein (Ithaca and London: Cornell University Press, 1991), 113–156.

2. James Womack, Daniel Jones, and Daniel Roos, *The Machine that Changed the World* (New York: Rawson Associates, 1990), 90.

3. Kevin Done, "Sophistication May Not Suffice," *Financial Times* (3 May 1991); Womack, Jones, and Roos, *The Machine that Changed the World*, 91. The IMVP critique confuses the type of craftsmanship Volvo was aiming at in its Uddevalla plant with the German type of craftsman, the *Facharbeiter*.

4. Eva Brumlop and Ulrich Jürgens, "Rationalization and Industrial Relations: A Case Study of Volkswagon," in *Technological Change, Rationalization and Industrial Relations*, ed. Otto Jacobi, Bob Jessop, Hans Kastendiek, and Mareno Regini (London and Sydney: Croomhelm, 1986), 73–94.

5. Horst Kern and Michael Schumann, *Das Ende der Arbeitsteilung? Rationalisierung in der Tindustriellen Produktion: Bestandaufnahmen, Trendbestimmung* (Munich: Verlag C. H. Beck, 1984). In more recent publications of the *Sozialforschungsinstitut Göttingen* the equipment controller is called the *Systemregulierer* (systems regulator). According to 1992 data, the share of systems regulators in the production workforce in German car companies is 8 percent, but 25 percent in press shops, 27 percent in machining operations, 6 percent in the body shops, and 1 percent in final assembly areas. See Michael Schumann, Volker Baethge-Kinsky, Martin Kuhlmann, Constanze Kurz, and Uwe Neumann, "Der Wandel der Produktionsarbeit im Zugriff neuer Produktionskonzepte," in Soziale Welt, Sonderband "Umbrueche gesellschaftlicher Arbeit," 1993, 17.

6. For an extended discussion of the Swedish model, see Christian Berggren, *Alternatives to Lean Production: Work Organization in the Swedish Auto Industry* (Ithaca, NY: ILR Press, 1992).

7. Womack, Jones, and Roos, *The Machine that Changed the World*, 92.

8. Ibid., 13.

9. Arbeitgeberverband Gesamtmetall, "Mensch und Unternehmen: Mit qualifizierten und motivierten Mitarbeitern die Wettbewerbsfaehigkeit staerken," 1992, 11.

10. For an English-language account of the union's discussions in the 1980s, see Lowell Turner, *Democracy at Work: Changing World Markets and the Future of Unions* (Ithaca and London: Cornell University Press, 1991), 112ff.

11. Betriebsrat Mercedes-Benz, Werk Bremen, Gruppenarbeit bei Mercedes-Benz in Bremen (Bremen: Scholz Druck & Co. Verlag, 1990), 20.

12. *Automobil-Produktion* 6 (Oct. 1992): 3; Karen Lowery Miller, "GM's German Lessons: Will the Eisenach Plant's Lean Production Transfer to the U.S.?" *Business Week* (20 December 1993).

PART 6 | TRAINING

18

Lean Production and Training: The Case of a Japanese Supplier Firm

JAMES JACOBS

Proponents of lean-flexible production argue that the increased training prescribed in the Japanese model provides workers with ''the skills they need to control their work environment.'' The substantial commitment to training not only makes the system more efficient than mass production, but also more ''humanly fulfilling'' for workers. Examination of worker training in a recently opened Japanese auto supplier in Michigan provides the opportunity to test these claims. Rather than simply describe the train-ing, the purpose of this investigation is to determine the *role* that training plays as lean production is implemented in a nonunion environment. Does it provide workers, as many proponents argue, with the conceptual tools to not only understand and adapt to the intensified work process, but also to thrive within it? Based on a single case, this study can only draw tentative conclusions, but the evidence suggests that training in North American transplant operations emphasizes firm-specific procedures and conservative methodologies that facilitate accommodation rather than empowerment.[1]

Training-Intensive Manufacturing

There is little doubt that Japanese manufacturers place a heavy emphasis on training, measured both in hours of classroom time and breadth of instruction. Beyond the narrow competencies required for a particular job, a lean-flexible production system cross-trains workers to perform a wide variety of tasks, including simple machine repair, quality control, materials ordering, and problem-solving. While training for a newly hired worker averages only 46 hours in an American auto plant, a new hire in a Japanese auto plant can expect to receive between 370 and 380 hours of instruction, according to MIT's International Motor Vehicle Program.[2]

Toyota, the exemplar of lean production, has already implemented the new system in its American operations, with positive results claimed for both bottom-line performance and worker morale. In addition to job-specific technical instruction, the Toyota Motor Manufacturing plant in Florence, Kentucky provides all hourly workers a 40-hour introduction to "understanding Toyota and its operational philosophies," as well as 91 hours on quality circles and problem-solving. Managers receive an additional 154 hours of training in interpersonal communications and leadership, while skilled workers go through a seven-year progression of advanced technical training requiring 1,680 hours in the classroom to obtain full certification. At Toyota's joint venture operation with GM in Fremont, California Japanese managers have also installed what Paul Adler describes as a "learning oriented" approach, where "instead of circumventing user intelligence and initiative, the production system is designed to realize as much as possible of the latent collaborative potential between the workers and the system." Adler argues that the systematic training of workers not only prepares them for lean production, but establishes a process by which the system is improved through the continuous input of workers.[3]

Robert Cole, in an article primarily concerning human resource policies in Japan, extends the analysis to Japanese transplant operations in North America. To illustrate the commitment to training of Japanese corporations, he describes, without attribution, a discussion between plant management and a local community college regarding training in nine fundamental new manufacturing technologies (including robotics, CAD, and CNC). "The official in charge of the local community college responsible for training employees for the new plant asked the plant manager: 'How many of the 400 production workers would you like to have trained in which of the nine production technologies?' The answer stunned him. The Japanese wanted all 400 employees trained in all nine production technologies.'' As Cole argues, if the company had only wanted engineers to do the sophisticated work, they would have no reason to undertake such training with these workers. Without confirming whether this training did, in fact, occur, he speculates that the Japanese ''aim to create a large cadre of middle level technicians with broad flexible skills.''[4]

The growing interest in Japanese training methods persuaded the United States Office of Technology Assessment (OTA) to conduct an examination of U.S. and Japanese training practices in the automobile industry. OTA researchers found that Japanese transplants not only conduct more hours of entry-level training, but the annual hours of training per employee are 50 percent higher (from thirty hours in US plants to forty-five hours in Japanese transplants). The OTA report also noted that ''in their pre-employment screening, Japanese automakers value willingness and ability to learn more highly than previous experience or specific skills. Their training programs emphasize individual and group responsibility along with job skills. U.S. automakers look for more experience and their training tends to stop with narrow technical skills for craft workers, and brief on-the-job sessions for unskilled workers.''[5]

Issues of Training

These studies suggest that lean production does more than simply increase the hours of training and education for the hourly workforce. Beyond this quantitative distinction, it is the content and goals of the training that make lean production unique. For a system that requires intense concentration from its workers and imposes highly structured norms on their behavior, the training in a lean production factory provides a specific understanding of the organization and aligns the workforce with its intensified demands. The relevant question then becomes: can this be understood as training that enhances the worker's economic value, or is it best described as a process of socialization that attunes the worker to firm-specific norms? The question can be broken down into four specific issues of skill, credentials, selection, and pedagogy.

Training and Skills. A cursory examination of the training conducted at Japanese plants indicates a significant emphasis placed upon understanding company practices and strategies as opposed to the learning of new technical skills. Indeed, as Robert Cole has suggested, much of the training in U.S. transplants concentrates upon team work and group dynamics, which are not taught in Japanese schools as subjects—because they are embedded in the culture. Thus, it might be argued that much of the increased training does not represent technical skill development, but the promotion of group dynamics specific to lean production.[6]

Training and Credentials. A second and related issue concerns the existence of externally validated credentials. For most Japanese firms, the training is done only on their processes and equipment, utilizing company-developed strategies and methods. Thus it could be argued that the increased hours of training in company-specific processes does not necessarily raise the skills of workers, since these "skills" are not portable to other jobs. Significantly, some of the education proposals made by the Clinton administration have called for the creation of national standards and some form of public credential system as a means of promoting a more trained workforce. There may be a conflict between such a federal human resource development policy and the approach utilized by the Japanese.[7]

Training and Selection. Few if any of the Japanese plants offered courses in basic skills, literacy, or remedial training. However, as noted by the OTA study, great care was taken in the selection of the individuals to be employed. Japanese firms use very complex selection standards to hire workers within their facilities. At Mazda's Flat Rock assembly plant, for example, over 108,000 people applied for 3,000 jobs, and that number was whittled down through psychological screening, formal testing, and evaluation of problem-solving skills. The practice of locating plants in rural areas of high unemployment aids Japanese firms in insuring a large pool of workers from which they can skim new hires. Consequently, these firms are not faced with many of the basic skill problems found within the American workforce, and their approach to training cannot be easily adopted by firms that already have a workforce with skill deficiencies in place.[8]

Training and Pedagogy. One of the most important issues raised by Japanese training methods is their overall effectiveness in terms of the learning process. In process and in delivery, the Japanese system relies on an "empty vessel" analogy that sees students as unfilled containers to be "filled up" with information. Much the same approach is found in the military training offered by the American armed services. Current educational research suggests that individuals learn in vastly different ways, and it is the gifted instructor who can combine alternative learning strategies that will enhance performance. This diversity in learning strategies combined with an emphasis on job performance contrasts with approaches that emphasize academic tests and other formal procedures. For example, the work conducted by Sylvia Scribner suggests that beyond any formal training system there are informal systems by which workers learn from each other. Effective training capitalizes upon these systems. The training performed by the Japanese is based upon methodologies that are often considerably more disciplined and conservative and less likely to produce empowerment effects.[9]

Case Study: A Japanese Auto Supplier In Michigan

What do the training practices of a Japanese auto supplier in Michigan tell us about the implementation of lean-flexible production in a nonunion environment? Before describing the specific case study, a few words of caution are necessary.

First, this is a start-up facility that, despite its operation over two years, has not yet reached full production. Indeed, during the month of April 1993, when the main interviews were completed in the plant, management was busy introducing a new assembly line and hiring more workers. Thus, lean production as *routinized behavior* has not been fully achieved in this plant. However, based on discussions with plant management, I believe the structure is now in place to initiate a mature lean production system.

Second, the interviews were conducted only with American management and some American training vendors in the facility. None of the Japanese management was interviewed, though the highest ranking American manager believed he was able to speak about their interests and concerns. Perhaps more important, there was no attempt made to systematically interview any workers at the plant—thus their perceptions of the training and activities are absent from this report.

Third, as with any case study, visits to the plant and collection of data through interviews permits only tentative conclusions. Thus, these findings should be considered with some care.

The Setting

Michigan Automotive Compressor, Inc. (commonly referred to as MACI) is located in the rural community of Parma, Michigan, directly west of Jackson. It is within a ninety-minute drive of Detroit. MACI is a joint venture between two Japanese companies, Toyota Automatic Loom Works and Nippondenso. It manufactures compressors and magnetic clutches used in air conditioning units for original equipment manufacturers (OEMs) in the automobile industry.

While the plant does have the capacity to cast and machine many of its own parts, MACI also buys from outside suppliers and sources key sub-components from its Japanese partner facilities. The parts-making operations are highly automated (for example, four-axis robots insert the aluminum castings into the turning centers for boring). Most of the hourly workers are concentrated in assembly and sub-assembly operations, which are performed in minimum lines of twenty workers. While the principle customers for the two basic clutches produced at the plant are both Japanese (Toyota) and American (Chrysler), the company's goal is to increase market penetration on this product among American OEMs.

The plant began production with about 240 hourly workers in 1989, and now has increased the total workforce to over 400 workers. The original contingent of thirty-eight Japanese associates who started with the plant will eventually be reduced to twenty-nine. Most of these Japanese workers are from the two parent companies, and they are rotated back to Japan every three to six months. The president of the company is an executive from one of the Japanese partner companies, and the highest ranking American is the human resources director. The plant is nonunion, though the rotating Japanese technicians and managers do bring their union representatives into the plant to inspect their working conditions.

The plant was established near Jackson, Michigan for three reasons, according to the personnel manager. First, there was a desire to be located in an area where unemployment was high enough to insure a large pool of workers from which to hire. Jackson was a regional center of the screw industry, hit hard by plant closings in the early 1980s. In addition, the community experienced the closure of Clark Manufacturing, a heavy equipment manufacturer that had employed four thousand people. As a result, unemployment in the Jackson area for the past ten years has been one of the highest in the state of Michigan.

Second, there was the existence of a reliable training institution—Jackson Community College—which won a state grant of $700,000 to provide initial training. Jackson Community College initiated the first major United States community college training program in Statistical Process Control (SPC) in 1984, coordinated through a state grant, and has acquired a reputation for its ability to conduct customized training.

Third, the community's Chamber of Commerce has developed a fairly sophisticated community infrastructure to provide support mechanisms for the Japanese and their families. Learning from the experience of Battle Creek, a Michigan city about forty miles west of Jackson, which had attracted a number of Japanese manufacturing firms, the program recruited American families who would adopt Japanese newcomers and ease their transition to American surroundings.

Selection of the Workforce at MACI

Proponents of the Japanese training system often overlook the significance of workforce selection as the principle precondition for the successful implementation of lean production. The goal of Japanese management in the formation of the MACI workforce was the development of a ''homogenous'' workforce, that is, a workforce capable of thinking and reacting to production problems in a predictable fashion. The company did not select workers for their technical expertise or their creative ability. They selected people who would fit within their system. From this perspective, a rural, nonunion economy was more likely to provide suitable recruits than a unionized urban economy—a fact not lost on employers in many other sectors of American manufacturing.[10]

The eight thousand applicants for work at MACI had all successfully completed the psychological and attitude tests used by the Michigan Employment Security Commission. Each of these individuals then took an extensive exam that measured their math, reading, and writing skills—projected at eighth-grade levels to weed out those who were not qualified—followed by a one-hour interview, which focused on the significance of work in their lives. Prospective employees were asked to respond to such questions as ''What are good reasons for not coming to work?'' If a worker answered by saying ''going hunting,'' or ''taking my child to the dentist,'' this would not be considered a positive response. From these tests and interviews, the group was whittled down to about twelve hundred prospective employees.

This group was then divided into teams of four people each and put through a forty-five minute exercise observed by four senior managers of the company. As the prospective employees worked in their team to solve a problem, the management observers carefully noted their body language, eye contact, willingness to take leadership, and willingness to follow leadership. If the four assessors could not agree on an individual, he/she was not passed on to the final set of personal interviews with top management. The American human resources director sat through each of these interviews to make the final determination. Those who survived this process were then hired—but only as employees of a temporary agency to work on a three-month trial basis at the plant. If that trial was completed successfully (and for 99 percent of the selected workers it was), the workers became MACI ''associates, '' entitling them to the $8 hourly starting wage.

These methods were considerably modified in the selection process for supervisors and technical staff. Instead of group skills, the initial supervisors were evaluated for their manufacturing experience as well as their willingness to put in long hours to solve problems. In addition, the engineering and professional staff were hired fresh from college, especially those from small-town backgrounds who might be convinced to stay with the company. They were interviewed extensively by senior management before selection, but in general they were not given specific tests to determine their personal or technical qualifications, as the Japanese believed their successful completion of college programs was evidence of these capabilities.

While many of the details of the above procedure were developed and implemented by the Americans, Japanese managers were involved in the final selection process and also monitored the actual hires. While voicing concerns about some of the prospective employees, they never overruled the decision of the American managers. In one instance, the American managers were able to bend some of the selection rules when they secured a group of skilled workers from a local firm that was going out of business.

This selection process was very time-consuming and costly—in fact, it took over five months to get the first group of 240 people to start up the plant. Much of the time and energy of local plant managers was focused on this activity, and the technical and design issues of the plant were left very much to the Japanese associates. Currently, the selection process is conducted by a local temporary agency using the guidelines specified by MACI. This same time-consuming approach to screening and hiring a new workforce has been characteristic of many, but not all, Japanese plants in manufacturing.[11]

Three general comments can be made about this process. First, it is highly reliant upon formal aptitude tests and other standard measures to select the initial group of hourly workers. These tests, all formulated in the United States, have been subjected to criticism within educational circles as predictors of occupational success. It appears the Japanese are willing to accept test scores as indications of successful work at the job, when most American educational theory suggests quite the opposite: those who perform best on tests may be the worst on the job. This reliance on testing represents a very limited approach to determining the skills of workers. It is also of some interest that these tests were used only among the hourly workers, not the technical and management staff.

Second, the assessment process is an extremely costly operation, representing an enormous investment of time by the company. Rather than seeking out workers who already possess specific technical *skills*, the company selected less experienced workers who possessed the proper *attitude*. The assumption was that training moneys would be spent to "fill in" the knowledge of the workers with the MACI training system. It is interesting that there was no "training budget" for this phase of the operation. It was assumed by the Japanese that whatever it took, the cost was acceptable. Granted, the state of Michigan provided a generous training subsidy. But even so, given the relatively low wages of the plant, imposing considerable start-up costs on the operation is a risky human resources strategy.

Finally, this process can only work if there is a large pool of people from which to draw new hires. In the training field, this approach is called "creaming." Since it can only be successful when there are large numbers of potential applicants, it is not a viable strategy in labor markets close to full employment. Thus, it is somewhat ironic that lean production for a firm might work best when there is high unemployment in the community.

Training at MACI

The training at MACI can be divided into technical instruction focused on particular jobs, and general instruction focused on the MACI production system. Technical training for most MACI associates is based upon the application of the Seven Steps, a strategy widely used by one of the parent partners, Nippondenso. Each step defines a specific part of the training process.

1. Describe The Job In General Terms
2. Demonstrate What To Do And How To Do It
3. Find Out What The Associate Already Knows About The Job
4. Discuss The Job With The Associate
5. Allow The Associate To Practice While You Watch
6. Allow The Associate To Work Alone
7. Check Back To Determine The Associate's Progress

These steps can be utilized only in the training of specific assembly or sub-assembly tasks that can be discretely separated out and mastered through performance. The transmission of the information in the training process is one dimensional. While points three and four appear to indicate the impact of the worker on the process, observation of the actual training indicates that this merely provides an opportunity for associates to relate their previous training experience in the plant. This does not mean, for example, "based on your knowledge as an assembly worker, how would you undertake the job?" but "what have we already taught you?"

All of the hourly associates were sent to an eight-week technical training class run by Jackson Community College. The classes introduced employees to basic mechanical concepts and electrical controls. The course material was from the Japanese partners and developed by community college instructors. Its main feature was the development of an "open entry, open exit" process by which workers could be "promoted" through basic training if they were able to perform specific functions in the process. The goal of the training was to bring all workers up to a similar standard of technical knowledge. Specific on-the-job training using the Seven Steps was given to each associate in the department.

Training for the skilled trades and engineers is a mere elaboration of the Seven Steps. Skilled-trades tasks are taught through the application of a step-by-step process for determining the "root cause" of a problem. Individuals are not encouraged to skip steps, or deviate from the memorization of specific written processes developed by the parent companies. Many of the skilled trades individuals were sent back to Japan for weeks of specific training on machines that were operated first in Japan, then torn down and brought to the plant by the skilled workers. For engineers, the process was even more time-consuming and costly. Each American engineer was assigned a Japanese mentor who taught the processes and standards of the company to the associate one-on-one. Many of the American engineers were expected to spend time in Japan to master the specific processes of the firm through job-shadowing their mentors.

This type of training is the logical extension of the selection process. If workers are not selected for their technical skills, then at best they are trained to perform their tasks, not develop the skills that would make them marketable outside of the specific firm. Indeed, because of the joint ownership of the plant by two Japanese partners with slightly different training approaches, American associates were often given slightly different training depending upon the "parental" background of the Japanese associates. This system at MACI fits the needs of the present workforce: training for the simplified operations of parts making and assembly. The MACI plant is more of a "branch facility" of the Japanese parents, and thus the technical expertise and training remains in the hands of the Japanese.

This dynamic can be observed in such projects as the installation of the new production line. Despite the corporate assertion that "Our associates are our most important asset," all of the installation of new machinery was performed by Japanese associates who discussed all of their work in Japanese. All materials and manuals were in Japanese—and only operating instructions and maintenance instructions were translated. There have been complaints in the plant by some of the American associates that Japanese associates are unwilling to resolve problems with the machinery at the plant. Several times, according to an American plant manager, Japanese associates would wait until the Americans went home to fix particular equipment—and when asked how the repair was accomplished, they would say it was "magic." Given the fact that all the equipment in the plant is from the parent company, the training and skills learned are primarily those which will make one successful within the company.

The other major component of the training was an orientation to the basic concepts of the MACI system. The five "S"'s (separation, simple sequence, spotless, sanitized, and systematic) and *kaizen* (continuous improvement) drew the most attention. There was an emphasis also upon the team system used at MACI. Most of the twenty team leaders were hired from the outside rather than chosen from their teams or from the shop floor. They are required to know how to operate all of the machines in their work area, and are also responsible for the production and quality in their work team. Most of the teams also have an assistant team leader responsible for the maintenance of the quality records kept by the teams.

It is through the team leaders and their assistants that further training needs are determined. There are team meetings each shift, and all team leaders meet once a day to determine priorities and schedules. The team leaders are paid about 16 percent more than the hourly associates and serve as the first-line supervision for the plant. Assistant team leaders are not paid more, but the role is considered the recruiting grounds for team leadership in the future. Since it is through the team leaders that job assignments are made, management monitors all complaints from workers about favoritism among team leaders: indeed, the number one complaint of workers, according to management, is favoritism in assignments. The goal is to ensure that the team leaders conduct their work groups fairly, but the company apparently has difficulty applying consistent standards. Some American managers report conflict with their Japanese counterparts over how much job rotation should be permitted, with the Japanese favoring far less rotation than the Americans, claiming the need to master the jobs is more significant.

There are also quality circles which meet independently of the work teams. One member of every team is involved in monthly meetings to discuss ways of improving productivity in the plant, and these workers constitute quality teams to undertake continuous improvement. Some of the associates have made presentations to the customers of MACI, which has aided in building team spirit and dedication to quality.

The plant has a relatively modest "training center"—one large room—primarily to accommodate the skilled trades and the Japanese associates who are installing the new machines. It appears that most of the production associates are trained on the job or within the conference rooms of the plant. There is a human resources director and two trainers, one of whom is devoted solely to skilled trades. The human resources director would like to implement more general training—such as a class in economics—but the demands for production (the plant normally works ten hours a day, six days a week) make that difficult to accommodate. The amount of money spent on training is now budgeted in the normal operations of the plant, but most of the early training and development were part of the initial investment by the Japanese partners.

Analysis

Training at MACI is clearly unlike what prevails in most small-to-medium manufacturing establishments. First, as pointed out by Adler and others, there is a "training system" in place. This means that training and development is a central part of the production process, and is internalized as part of the culture of the plant. Second, it is a comprehensive and planned process, not ad hoc, and clearly not subjected to much alteration by the local management. Every associate goes through the training, from hourly worker to plant manager. Third, training is central to the particular strategy of the plant. Indeed, conflicts among the Japanese managers over specific training strategies indicates how seriously the parent companies take training as part of their competitive edge.

There is no question that this training has paid off in a number of ways. The plant is exceptionally clean (to highlight the cleanliness, a potted plant sits in the middle of the alumina casting department), and very well organized in terms of minimizing in-process and parts inventories (no "sleeping money," as the Japanese say). Moreover, during in-plant interviews, several of the skilled-trades trainers indicated how impressed they were with the willingness of the company to provide them with training, including trips to Japan to learn specific features of the machines. There is also the typical suggestion box, and the highlighting of contributions workers have made to the overall production process.

In addition, the investment in training is paying off for the company as it begins to slowly introduce the process of total preventative maintenance (TPM). This will require hourly workers to undertake some of the low-end maintenance work now assigned to the skilled trades. There is little reported resistance from the trades since most skilled workers are absorbed with the challenges imposed by the introduction of the new production line.

However, the claim that training at MACI represents the "hub" of an empowerment system appears to be unfounded. Rather, the training conducted at MACI fits the needs of a batch supplier and assembler of mature products for the auto industry. Most of the technical training is directed at the skilled trades and engineers, while hourly people are "taught" to perform their specific jobs. There is little attempt to learn from workers, outside the narrow confines of five-minute meetings and monthly quality circles. While the normal information on parts production and rejects is shared with workers, there is little information distributed on the financial standing of the plant or future budgets.

All of the training is delivered in a conventional process that assumes little or no input from the workers. The assumption is that management implements work-load changes, job re-design, and equipment alterations, while workers respond with suggestions. In no real sense do they have the power to control the process. The content of the training reinforces the reality that this is a top-down organization in which the power to run the plant is centered in Japan, and nowhere near the shop floor.

Moreover, there is a clear recognition that the Japanese associates in the plant are the sources of technical knowledge and expertise. Indeed, the initial assumption that the Japanese associates would be the teachers of the American associates was replaced with the assumption that the Japanese associates would continue to work "alongside" their American counterparts. This suggests that the parent corporations provide the technical expertise to run the plant—and that advancement from the ground up will therefore be difficult. Given the unusual selection process, there are many workers in the plant with college degrees, but the relative lack of advancement opportunities may make it difficult for the plant to retain this high quality workforce.

Finally, the absence of a union means that none of the rights associated with worker training and retraining in a collective bargaining environment are found at MACI. There is a tuition reimbursement plan for workers who wish to attend college on their own time, but only for courses management approves. There is no credentialing process for the training used within the company, and management is uninterested in apprenticeship or any outside certification of their workers. Breaks, job rotation, changes in shift and all other job-related decisions are the prerogative of management. It is likely that the company would not only discourage a union, but actively fight any attempts to bring about representation of the associates.

Conclusion

There is a training system in place at MACI, but its primary goal is to insure a stable production system, not the success of a particular "learning organization.'' The system is based upon a very rigorous selection of appropriate individuals who are willing to memorize their jobs and adapt to management's unilateral changes in the work process. This is an efficient system, and compared to other mid-sized batch manufacturing facilities, MACI has successfully incorporated a concern for training within the overall production process. However, within a nonunion setting, where workers lack an independent voice to assert their interests, the training system does not mitigate the intense pressures that lean production creates for the hourly associates. Nor does the system appear to be a ''learning organization'' in terms of skills development, since the Japanese associates appear reluctant to turn over the highly skilled technical work to their American counterparts. The organizational structure is more like the branch plant operations found in many other parts of the world.[12]

Notes

The author would like to thank the management of MACI for permitting interviews and a tour of the plant. Management at MACI is not responsible for any of the following description or evaluation of the plant's training program.

1. James Womack, Daniel Jones, and Daniel Roos, *The Machine that Changed the World* (New York: Rawson Associates, 1990), 100–102.

2. Ibid., 92, 99.

3. Sam Heltman and Kiyoshi Furuta, *Workforce Quality: Perspectives from the United States and Japan.* International Symposium Report (Washington, DC: U.S. Department of Labor, 1991), 28; Paul Adler, ''Time and Motion Regained,'' *Harvard Business Review* (Jan.–Feb. 1993): 104. For a description of the specific organization of the training at Toyota's Kentucky plant and the corporate philosophy behind it, see John Allen and John Breakes, ''Toyota's Camry, Toyota's Training,'' *Technical and Skills Training* (Oct. 1992): 41–45.

4. Robert Cole, ''Issues in Skill Formation in Japanese Approaches to Automation,'' in *Technology and the Future of Work*, ed. Paul Adler (New York: Oxford University Press, 1992), 207–208. Cole is discussing the plant visited in this study. His information comes from a conversation with Nippondenso executives before the actual training system was implemented. This approach of only discussing training in general, as opposed to more careful analysis of actual training practices, is also taken by two other researchers who focus on Japanese supplier plants in the United States. Kenney and Florida discuss training and selection practices at the Nippondenso facility without interviewing workers, examining training documents, or visiting the training center. They depend solely upon interviews with top management. See Martin Kenney and Richard Florida, *Beyond Mass Production: The Japanese System and its Transfer to the U.S.* (New York: Oxford University Press, 1993), 126–154.

5. Office of Technology Assessment, *Worker Training: Competing in the New Economy* (Washington, DC: U.S. Government Printing Office, 1990), 15.

6. Cole, ''Issues in Skill Formation,'' 207.

7. The Japanese are very serious about their specific forms of corporate training. In a

major community college in Arizona that has two different auto company service technician programs, not only did each Japanese company demand their own separate facilities be constructed by the college, but that restrictions be imposed to make sure that students could not enroll in both programs. Even tools and major pieces of equipment could not be shared by the two programs. The separation of auto service technicians in community college is not unusual in American programs, but the extent to which the Japanese companies insist that there be no crossover of students is highly unusual. Concerning federal training policy, the administration introduced and successfully passed through Congress legislation that calls for national certification of skills. This measure will begin the process of developing skill standards for all industries.

8. My understanding of the Mazda selection process is drawn from conversations with participants, and from Mike Parker and Jane Slaughter, *Choosing Sides: Unions and the Team Concept* (Boston: South End Press, 1988), 175–185.

9. The Department of Defense is the single largest trainer in the United States, and one of the major innovators in training technologies and techniques. DOD funding for training and technology averaged $56 million a year in 1990. As the federal government downsizes the military, it is anticipated that much of this training will become available for civilian use. See OTA, *Worker Training*, 63–67, 259. The alternative approach to learning is derived from certain insights of cognitive science. The late Sylvia Scribner has applied them to specific areas of manufacturing training. See Sylvia Scribner, *Technical and Symbolic Knowledge in CNC Machining—Draft* (New York: City College of New York, 1990). Her work has also been summarized in Sue Berryman and Thomas Bailey, *The Double Helix of Education and the Economy* (New York: Columbia Teachers College, 1992). This is not an issue of a structured learning environment versus a non-structured learning environment, but the type of learning structure selected. For a discussion of a particular structure that is not based on the Japanese approach, which taught skilled workers in multiple trades, see Gary Saganski, "A Worker Centered Approach to Education and Training," in this volume.

10. Obviously, this can be viewed as a means of excluding African-Americans and others from these plants. While there are African-Americans at MACI, and the plant has fulfilled EEOC hiring requirements, the selection of Jackson County (black population in the 1990 Census was 8 percent) is a choice that would place the plant in a predominantly white area. For a discussion of these practices see Robert Cole and Donald Deskins, Jr., "Racial Factors in Site Location and Employment Practices of Japanese Auto Firms in America, *California Management Review* 31, no. 1 (fall 1988): 9–22.

11. A more recent Japanese plant in Jackson, TAC, did not undertake this intense screening and hired some of the people rejected by MACI. Ruth Milkman, in her study of Japanese plants in California, found little assessment or screening for jobs. Significantly, she also found little evidence that these Japanese plants used lean production methods. Ruth Milkman, *Japan's California Factories: Labor Relations and Economic Globalization* (Los Angeles: Institute of Labor Relations, 1991), 52–54.

12. This finding is similar to the conclusions drawn by Ruth Milkman in her study of Japanese owned manufacturing facilities in California: "I found that most of the Japanese owned plants in the state closely resemble American owned nonunion firms." Milkman, *Japan's California Factories*, xiv.

19

A Worker-Centered Approach to Education and Training

GARY SAGANSKI

As new technology and new forms of work organization redefine industrial practice, questions about workers' skills are revisited on a daily basis by management and unions alike. Unfortunately, few companies develop the necessary organizational strategy for technology-based education and workforce development. More often, training is prescribed in isolated doses and with standardized content, with the result that much training is ill-defined and cannot possibly deal with larger educational and organizational issues. Colleges are often called on to immediately implement educational activity in such a context. As a public sector institution in metropolitan Detroit primarily involved in applied technical skills training and education, Henry Ford Community College (HFCC) responds with an approach that analyzes skills and educational issues from the worker-learner's perspective. Presented here is a case study of one such training program developed for an auto supplier undergoing significant work reorganization. In this and other programs of the college, HFCC draws on a humanistic tradition that imbeds technical training within the development of the whole person, an approach that contrasts sharply with training practices in most workplaces, including lean production environments.

Training and Lean Production

Most advocates of lean-flexible production systems place a heavy emphasis on training. They acknowledge that such practices as job rotation, just-in-time delivery of parts, quality control, and "productive maintenance" put added pressure on workers, but they argue that a matching system of work-based education compensates for the increase in responsibility and skills required of each worker. This commitment to training seems to address the concerns held by those workers' advocates and conscientious managers who stress the need to empower the workforce. It appears that the management strategy of lean production can close the gap between the rhetoric of worker development policies and the experience of workers.

Yet, in working with self-declared large and small "lean producers," we have yet to encounter any company that considers itself successful or fully realized in employing the techniques indicated above. This is due in part to the fragmented organizational context into which each of these separate processes and related skills are developed, not to mention multiple problems in operationalizing these techniques. To a greater extent this failure is due to the imposition of these new skills by others rather than their being seen as viable solutions to production and quality problems identified by the workers themselves.

Indeed, many lean production operations employ workforce development strategies that *increase the contradiction* between what those in control of human resource development policy say about workforce development, and the training resources and activities that in fact materialize. In large firms, lean or otherwise, the maintenance and skilled trades workforce is often challenged beyond their level of skill and often overlooked when it comes to issues of new technology and changing processes. And in smaller enterprises, where operators experience pressure to contribute the new skills needed to cope with radically changing production processes, long-term training for human resource development rarely takes place. When businesses adopt elements of lean production, often including extremely narrow staffing levels, the tight schedules, limits on training time, and the draining of workers' physical and mental energy all create added barriers to effective skill development.

When training does occur, the type of systems approach utilized in most lean production strategies is mechanistic in nature. The individual worker is clearly not seen as the foundation and the center of the factory operating system; rather, the individual is a replaceable component into which new information and techniques are placed and then expected to be utilized. Little if any concern is placed on the perspective of the worker. There is a heavy reliance on learning aids—including work-station visual aids, SPC charting and interpretation formats, problem-solving methods, and self-paced computer instructional aids—to boost the skills and knowledge base of the individual worker, but these types of training appear to be successful only in the development of rudimentary work skills. They typically fail when the desired competency approaches a higher level of technical and organizational skills or an understanding of the systems that govern an operation. Further, these efforts will continue to fail until the current process is modified to create an organizational strategy for workforce development and education that addresses the needs of the individual, as well as the individual within the organization. Lean operations appear even less likely to embrace this kind of "non-production" related human resource and educational strategy.

A Worker Centered Approach

Our experience serving the training needs of auto and steel companies in southeastern Michigan indicates the relevance of a worker centered approach to education and training. The key questions—what kinds of education or training, and for whom?—can only be addressed when the work experience and knowledge of the workers is known, as well as *their* perspective on the training needs associated with specific production technologies, areas of skill building, the organization's processes, and the related workforce development demands of the operation.

Before turning to the more detailed case study of this training agenda, a brief review of the Trade and Apprentice Education Revision process HFCC has participated in over the last several years will illustrate the worker-centered approach. In this project, workers analyzed current and future skill needs and created educational solutions collectively. Discussion groups organized by electrical, maintenance, and manufacturing trades were convened to help clarify a skills outlook for apprentices entering a rapidly changing work environment. The groups wrestled with the reality of adding new technical and conceptual skills to the traditional educational core of general industrial apprentice skills. In the context of Detroit's automotive steel, vehicle manufacturing, and parts supplier sectors, the skills discussed indicated a need for increasing trade specialization as well as expanding the basic applied technological foundation of each trade. This analysis was based on the workers' perceived need to cope with the increasing complexity of manufacturing technical systems as well as a growing inter-dependence of trades.

In this process, major insights were contributed by a group we came to call "the old salts"—that is, trades people working daily in their trades for at least twenty to twenty-five years. The depth and breadth of their knowledge and experience provided insights into how the factories actually work and helped clarify a perspective on what constitutes the core of various trade apprenticeships. The more recent skilled trades within our groups, with ten to fifteen years of experience, appear to have been more dramatically affected by the rapid computerization of mechanical and electrical processes. Their perspective on the needs of future trades tended to be rooted in the mastery of complex specific technical systems. The combined contributions of these two groups led to a comprehensive idea of how the trades are changing, and how educational strategies for the trades need to be revised.

For the workers, managers, and college faculty involved in the process, such a comprehensive approach, based on trade inclusion, profoundly affected the ways in which skills and education issues will be framed for future apprentices. This reliance on a critical dialogue between the trades, and between workers and faculty, differs from the usual approach in which educational specialists define what skills are needed and then deliver the training "package" to the workplace. In contrast, a worker-centered approach originates from the perspective of the workers themselves, and draws educational specialists into their dialogue.

Case Study

Our recent work at a major steel company with unionized workers provided an opportunity to explore some of these strategies involving workplace education and "leaner" production methods. In this project, over one thousand skilled trades at Rouge Steel, an automotive steel supplier in Dearborn, Michigan, were to take part in 480–600 hours of projected training over a two-to-three year period. With hundreds of the tradespeople taking twenty class and lab hours weekly, the program was to become one of the largest in the country.

In preparing for such an ambitious undertaking, what presuppositions should or should not guide the "retooling" of a skilled workforce? A recent publication of the National Council on Vocational Education lists five "wrong assumptions" about how people learn:

1. People readily transfer learning from the classroom to other "real life" contexts.
2. Learners are best seen as passive vessels to be "filled up" with knowledge.
3. The process of learning is essentially the strengthening of bonds between stimuli and response (i.e., a classic behaviorist process).
4. Learners are blank slates onto which knowledge is inscribed.
5. Skills and knowledge should be acquired independently, outside of any social context.[1]

One of the more popular training strategies based on these wrong assumptions is the Develop a Curriculum (DACUM) method, a variant of task analysis favored by many companies, colleges, and private-sector training consultants. This educational strategy also surfaced in the initial stages of the Rouge project. The DACUM method divides complex work skills into discrete *tasks*. From there, curriculum development is the process of building up independent modules which eventually lead to the mastery of the job skills. This view of training skills development—creating clusters of elementary tasks—is strikingly compatible with the management theories of Frederick Taylor. While this is currently the dominant approach in developing work-based education, this method consistently eliminates the context of higher order cognitive and organizational skills. It also de-emphasizes the approach of looking at the totality of an occupation in the social or organizational context. Some skills can be adequately defined through the use of a modified DACUM, but they are not framed within the learning context of the future operator. Indeed, the individual learner is systematically de-emphasized within DACUM.

With the completion of the DACUM process, the exploration of topics for the future curriculum content ends. Little attention is paid to the future students other than an evaluation of reading, math, and writing ability—skills that are essential in the classroom but do not indicate the pre-existing informational or subject-matter knowledge of the student. The resulting courses and curricula then are often based on an ineffective listing of skills which are unrelated to the experiential and content knowledge of the future students. This invariably leads to overall low assimilation of the marginally relevant content.

If it is assumed that the learner is an empty vessel without a relevant experiential and knowledge context, there is clearly no role for the learner or the learner's organizational peers in the design process. From the beginning of the Rouge Steel project, the plan was to use skilled tradespeople as *peer instructors* who would eventually lead all instruction in the project, but in the initial phases of program development the peers were viewed as secondary in the learning process and were not involved in discussions concerning course content, design, and method. Experienced community college faculty found this DACUM process and the subsequent learning modules a hindrance to the communication necessary for learning— between student and teacher, and between student and student. Also, experienced tradespeople and front-line management were insulted by the way elementary material was presented in the "blank slate" approach during the joint labor-management committee sessions which reviewed the initial curriculum. It became clear that the peers had much more to offer than serving as warm versions of video-scripted presentations.

This initial phase of curriculum development demonstrated that we could not be bound to traditional behaviorist education theory, and that the development process had to be participant driven. In spite of deadline pressures, faculty, peers, and joint committee members began to develop a fundamentally new approach. First, we agreed on the basic assumptions on which the training program was to be grounded, reflecting both our educational views and the real-world constraints that we faced. The experience and knowledge of the trainees, the equipment available, the budget, and the needs and interests of the principal stakeholders were all considered key factors:

1. The experience and knowledge of the tradespeople varied greatly in both depth and subject area. Although all of the tradespeople to be trained had journey-card status, actual experience and knowledge ranged from virtually no advanced industrial technology background to twenty years of intensive experience.
2. Although both cross-training and upgrade-training were central goals of the program, the rapid advancement of electronics technology made the latter the real challenge. There were many skilled tradespeople who wanted more than just basic training and, given these needs, would resent being put through a course that did not assist them in challenging the technology.[2]
3. Hands-on and theoretical learning were equal goals of the training and needed to be integrated. There is a tendency to view theory as the opposite of practical or hands-on training and minimally relevant to "less educated" people working in blue-collar occupations.
4. The curriculum had to be worker-centered: the priority goal of the training team should be the provision of learning tools for the skilled tradespeople.
5. The ability of the joint union-management committee to access shop-floor expertise and resources should be more fully utilized.

With these assumptions in mind, we began to draft the electrical and mechanical curricula. First we examined other training programs for the industry and found one in particular that provided several key ideas for the Rouge Steel program. Our model of learning developed as we began to generate the curriculum, and later sections more consciously used the worker-centered model, especially in the area of the electrical curriculum.[3]

By way of contrast, consider the approach of a traditional course in electronics technology. The training is divided into classroom and laboratory sections, with the classroom portion typically organized around lectures heavy on theory, solving electronic problems mathematically, and perhaps some class discussion. Students move into the lab for carefully structured exercises that supposedly demonstrate the classroom theory using just the exactly prescribed equipment and supplies. There is often a lot of record keeping. The classroom portion is taught using a building block approach. First the blocks of basic theory are established, followed by the next blocks of higher level theory. The material is taught in a logical sequence, increment by increment, usually assuming the learner masters the increments as the basis for proceeding. However well this approach is executed, it treats learners as passive vessels or blank slates. In fact, as Paulo Freire suggests, the method may require the teacher to *project* absolute ignorance onto the learner.[4]

Respecting the Framework of the Learner

Our model of learning suggests a different way of handling the links between theory and practice, and the prerequisites for learning. We believe that one of the most important—and most ignored—determinants of learning is what we call the *learner's framework* or *internal context.*

Whether and how well a person can hold and use a piece of information depends on the framework the learner has in place for accommodating the information. This framework is a combination of the way the learner has organized previous experiences and the working method for filtering, understanding, and integrating new information. There are similarities between this notion of connecting learning to a framework, and the step-by-step logical foundation approach to training. The difference is that the logical progression implicit or explicit in the traditional step-by-step approach is that of the *curriculum designer or the instructor.* This is the way a student *should* learn; or the way the instructor learned; or some distant person's view of *the* logical progression to teach someone who is committed to learning the field but starts out with no knowledge; or the way to teach someone willing to suspend his or her framework. In contrast, our model begins by respecting the *learner's* framework. After all, we are designing the curriculum for tradespeople—people who have worked in the field for years. Many of these people are the "experts" about their job and a small piece of the electrical field. Some have taken additional courses, are self-taught, and may very well know more about some topics than the curriculum writer or instructor. Adult learners, particularly people learning more about their own trade, already have a framework with its own holes, points of contact, and hooks. Why should we ask such people to completely put aside their framework and adopt ours? The truth is that there is probably no reason why our framework is any better than theirs.

But how do you create a curriculum around the thousands of potentially different frameworks that can exist in the workplace? *By allowing the learner maximum control of the learning process.* The learner needs to determine what she or he will learn and how to learn it. The curriculum should be structured to provide an overview to let the learner know what is available, and then let the learner choose to dig in at her points of interest and to go in as deeply as she wishes.

Learning situations vary greatly and therefore so does the relevance of this approach. Building the training around the learner's framework rather than assuming or supplying the framework makes more sense where: (1) the learners have developed frameworks; (2) the learners have different frameworks; (3) the learners have no special motivation or reason to discard their framework for a new one. These are all critical factors in assessing and developing new technology training for the skilled trades.

There is support for this framework idea in fields outside of education. For example, psychologist Gisella Labouvie-Vief cites one study which presents a logical problem of the following type. In this study, different audiences are asked to evaluate a living situation in which the sitting room is in the front of the house and the kitchen is in the back. Traffic noise is very disturbing in the front rooms. Mother is in the kitchen cooking and grandfather is reading the paper in the sitting room. Who is most likely disturbed by traffic noise? College students almost invariably answer "grandfather," whereas older adults give a variety of answers. Some researchers take this as a sign of the decline in ability to process information logically. But as Labouvie-Vief points out, the mature respondents could simply be refusing to limit the information and logic to what is presented, and are adding their own experience. For example, the respondent might reasonably assume from age and gender that grandfather is likely to have poorer hearing; or, grandfather cannot possibly have been disturbed because, had that been so, he would have moved. Labouvie-Vief argues that

younger people tend to think within a single system, whereas mature think-
ers tend to redefine the "space" of problems from the perspective of multiple systems.[5]

The concept of multiple learning frameworks also sheds light on the
issue of hands-on training. There is an almost paternalistic tendency in
some educational approaches to believe that non-college educated people
have a limited ability to deal with abstract reasoning and subjects—
therefore the physical objects of hands-on learning are necessary. But being
able to deal with concepts hands-on also means the ability to deal with the
richness and subtleties of the system. This does not necessarily have anything to do with the sense of touch or even the question of abstraction, but
with the reference point from which one starts. The "logical" approach
starts with a simple abstraction and forces information to conform; the
"hands-on" approach can start with the object or situation and bring to
bear several relevant models. This becomes a less biased jumping-off point
for the participant in both theoretical and applicable areas of learning.

To implement this approach, the peer instructors helped select the appropriate applications and examples for class exercises and discussions.
These skilled trades workers gave the instructors tours of the plant pointing
out areas where electricians and instrument people had the most common,
or the most difficult, work. In addition, they were able to propose exercises
and examples that paralleled specific applications with which tradespeople
worked in the plant.

Our learning model meant that the course would need to constantly
change to meet the needs of different participants and changing technology. Since the peers would be making these modifications, it made sense
that they thoroughly understood the reasoning behind the initial curriculum.

Union and Skilled Trades Involvement in Program Performance

We see union involvement as decisive for the development process and
training model described here. The union, both the leadership and membership, represents the worker's interest in maintaining the approach of
worker-centered education. This increases the relevance of long-term training goals and facilitates the transfer of power to the worker in the classroom. Since so much of the experience of education is a cultural
phenomena, alternative practice must be continuously reinforced before the

new standards become learner expectations in the classroom. Thus, the involvement of the union is crucial at several different levels, including organizational and political policy-making, identifying curriculum topics, developing the actual curriculum, defining classroom protocol and presentation, and monitoring the overall learning experience.

The union members of the joint program development committee, or Training Team, acted as a coordinating medium. They kept the union leadership for the skilled trades unit informed on training issues related to contractual or operating policies. They also communicated concerns about training content or practices from the various skilled trades to the joint committee and the union unit leadership. As a result, the skilled trade's unit leadership remained integrally involved in the development and implementation of the entire program, and individual worker's rights were advanced through the process.

With a participative process enhancing individual and collective rights in the workplace, the skilled trade's unit and their Training Team representatives gained access to the knowledge and experience of the entire unionized workforce. This dramatically improved the collection of shop-floor data and enhanced the overall relevance of the curricula. With this process made operational, the relevance of the curriculum continuously improved the longer the program was in operation.

With the learner placed at the center of the design, the role of the union-designated peer trainers greatly expanded. Instead of being script readers as originally planned, the peer instructors played a significant role in conceptualizing, developing, and applying the model. The peer trainers also helped to set the standard for classroom protocol. There was a natural recognition of the shop-floor group dynamics in the classroom, with activities focused through the naturally evolving peer work groups.

The Role of Instruction

A worker-centered approach demands that instructors play a new role and utilize a broad range of skills in the classroom. First, the instructor needs to command a much larger body of material because the class could take the discussion in different ways. In particular, the instructor needs a solid understanding of theory to be able to teach in a process of classroom discovery. Second, it takes a greater commitment of time and creativity to develop quality classroom experiments, since more material, equipment, and exercises need to be prepared than will probably be used by any single participant. Finally, instructors need to develop the personal self-confidence and teaching skills to maintain leadership in the classroom, since discussion of unplanned topics will often expose a lack of knowledge by the instructor or superior knowledge by some participants.

Adjusting to these methods was difficult for those instructors accustomed to traditional classrooms, and peer instructors faced these same difficulties with less to fall back on in terms of teaching experience and theoretical knowledge. They were also on "front street" with people they would continue to work with for years, and revealing ignorance to peers is rated no more highly in industrial culture than anywhere else. Indeed, some peers at least initially preferred a reduced role, the security of the script, and assurance that every possible question would be answered in the manual. This set of problems necessitated a special training program for peer instructors that began with a general orientation and discussion about the aims and methods of the program and proceeded through measured stages of peer involvement in classroom teaching. As indicated, peers were involved in conceptualizing parts of the course and developing the necessary equipment, as well as trying out exercises and evaluating the curriculum. The initial classes were then taught by experienced instructors selected by Henry Ford Community College, with peer trainers participating as student-assistants responsible for handling small-group exercises. As they developed confidence in teaching and their ability to deal with the content, the peers took over portions of the course with college faculty observing and coaching. In the final stage of this process, peer instructors took over the full course with an HFCC instructor present for consultation.

In addition, various support activities helped sustain the development of both the peer instructors and the curriculum. These included regular meetings between peer instructors and the HFCC faculty to discuss problems with subject matter as well as handling of classroom situations. (I should note here that often it was the peer instructors who gave each other or the HFCC instructors excellent guidance in handling difficult classroom situations.) Special teaching skills classes were designed and provided for the peers, who were also encouraged and supported in getting outside training (vendor or community college) in areas that would be helpful to the curriculum. In addition, special classes were organized on topics that would give the peers a better understanding of technical subjects—for example, a mathematics course designed to fill in knowledge gaps and take the peers through the basics of calculus.[6]

Finally, everyone involved, from the joint union-management training coordinators to the HFCC instructors, worked to create a supportive atmosphere where there was no shame in an instructor not knowing everything and where a good answer is "I don't know but I'll find out and get back to you tomorrow."

Reaction to the Program

Training began in 1990, when approximately two hundred skilled workers went through Electrical Module I. In the fall of 1991 the program was suspended pending resolution of some contract disputes between the union and the company not necessarily related to the training.

Our assessment of the program is that the learning experience in the classroom exceeded our expectations. We received a positive response from skilled tradespeople often cynical about training programs. Indeed, contrary to expectations that older tradespeople would resist training, we found enthusiasm and assistance forthcoming from older as well as younger workers. From participant feedback and direct observation of how the training impacted the shop floor, we believe that this process has potential in three ways.

1. It is a successful method of improving and adapting skilled trades workers to meet the demands of new technology.
2. It is potentially an ongoing solution to the problems of changing technology. Peer instructors with both teaching and technical skills can readily adapt to changes in plant equipment and work organization.
3. The role of peer instructor adds a new level of skill to the shop floor workforce, which in turn adds pride and confidence to those jobs. Impressionistic evidence suggests that this can result in impressive improvements in the work process if management allows it.[7]

Conclusion

Both the efforts at Rouge Steel and the on-going Trade and Apprentice Education Revision project are based on a worker-centered approach that challenges the traditional power relations in workplace education. The learning process described here puts into practice the currently popular axiom that the person doing the job is the expert on that job. Therefore, when it comes to learning, the worker brings to the classroom important knowledge as well as a sense of what additional information she or he needs. But the learner can become a driving force in workplace education only if the worker is also a driving force in shaping the work environment. From this perspective, lean production's strategy of expanding the responsibility of workers becomes feasible to the degree that the power of organizational change also lies with the workers. A strong and well-defined union role is essential for this to happen. After all, workers seeking alternatives to the current organization of work and workplace training must contend with the existing hierarchy of workplace management as well as the authority of institutional education experts. Educators and managers must be persuaded, and if need be pressured, to share the process of goal setting, design, and implementation of educational and organizational change. Unions, as well, must use these activities to reflect on how work is changing and how new skills and responsibilities can be formalized into a just and equitable system of industrial practice.

Notes

This article is possible due to the work of the UAW/Rouge Steel Joint Training Committee and the faculty and staff of Henry Ford Community College. It is based upon a previous work, entitled "Technology Transfer: Transferring Control to the Learner," co-authored by Mike Parker and myself. Mike Parker's dedication to fair and honest workplace education and his ability to bridge the worlds of technology, education, and workplace politics have been crucial in realizing the theory and practitioner insights proposed herein. The views expressed in this paper are those of the author and not those of Henry Ford Community College, the United Auto Workers, or Rouge Steel Company.

1. See Sue Berryman, *Solutions* (Washington, DC: National Council on Vocational Education, 1991).

2. Cross-training is often associated with combining classifications. There is considerable disagreement about the issues of classification lines and the meaning of the current contract language. The distinction between *understanding* the basics of other trades in coordinating work and *performing* the basics of other trades is at the root of one dispute. I do not intend to get into these issues except to note that they are an important part of the backdrop for the training.

3. Our thanks to Stan Briggs of HFCC who generously shared his insights into the "discovery method" of teaching electronics, and such techniques as the creative use of bench signal boxes.

4. Paulo Freire, *Pedagogy of the Oppressed* (New York: Continuum, 1993), 58.

5. See Gisella Labouvie-Vief, "Intelligence and Cognition," in *Handbook of the Psychology of Aging*, ed. J. E. Birren and K. W. Shaie (New York: Van Nostrand, 1985), 500–530.

6. A contract dispute between the union and management caused suspension of the training program during the calculus course, so I am not yet in a position to evaluate it.

7. The Mechanical Power Transmission curriculum taught new methods of computerized shaft alignment which immediately proved their value across the mill. For examples of skilled worker contributions in another industry see Daniel Marshall, ''Unions and Work-Based Learning: The Rediscovery of Apprenticeship,'' *ILR Report* 28 (fall 1990).

PART 7 | PUBLIC POLICY

20

Lean Production, Labor-Management Cooperation, and the Future of the NLRA Paradigm

WILLIAM GREEN

The Clinton administration put labor issues squarely on the political agenda when Secretary of Labor Robert Reich announced the establishment of the Commission on the Future of Worker-Management Relations in May 1993 with a mandate to examine the current state of labor law. The Reich Commission (also known as the Dunlop Commission after its Chairman, John Dunlop) has since conducted an extended scrutiny of the National Labor Relations Act, the legal foundation for American labor relations since 1935. The NLRA model, as defined by the Wagner Act and its amendments and by decisions of the National Labor Relations Board and federal courts, establishes the rights of workers to freely choose a union and bargain collectively with management over wages, hours, and working conditions, including grievance rights and procedures. The NLRA paradigm otherwise leaves in place exclusive managerial control over strategic decisions and, until recently, a shop-floor system defined in terms of a Fordist model of work organization and adversarial labor-management relations.[1]

The rapid growth of both cooperative labor-management relations and of new production systems based on lean production raises important legal and political questions which are the focus of this chapter. As a production method, the technical aspects of lean production—just-in-time inventories, elimination of buffers, and job rotation—do not necessarily raise any NLRA issues. But the system's social and organizational dimensions, particularly cooperative labor-management relations in a union setting and management's use of work teams in a nonunion setting, do have implications for the NLRA's continued relevance.

The NLRA and Labor-Management Cooperation in Union Firms

Between 1983 and 1985, the UAW reached pre-recruitment agreements with NUMMI and Saturn that provided for labor-management cooperation in making plant location decisions, worker recruitment decisions, and, once the assembly plants were operating, a wide spectrum of strategic and shop floor decisions. The UAW-GM Saturn Labor Agreement became the test case for measuring the impact of this brand of labor-management cooperation on the NLRA paradigm. The National Right to Work Legal Defense Foundation challenged two provisions of the agreement: preferential hiring rights for GM's UAW-represented employees, and pre-hire recognition of the UAW. The National Labor Relations Board found that neither provision violated the NLRA. The preferential hiring clause was a "lawful byproduct of mandatory effects bargaining" and the pre-hire recognition of the UAW merely provided for future recognition if the UAW acquired majority support from Saturn employees. The UAW was subsequently recognized and negotiated Consensus Guidelines that currently govern Saturn labor-management decision-making from the strategic level to the shop floor. While this Saturn model appeals to many who favor labor-management cooperation, the agreement also specifies a purposeful blurring of company-union leadership roles (pairing union and management counterparts, giving them the same titles, and permitting management and the union to veto each other's appointments) that make the Saturn local a somewhat anomalous "enterprise" union within an industrial organization.[2]

What needs to be done to foster genuine labor-management cooperation? To begin with, the Supreme Court's distinction in the *Borg Warner* case between mandatory and permissive collective bargaining subjects needs to be eliminated. Extending collective bargaining to strategic-level subjects will not be enough, however, if there aren't additional protections that legally mandate this expanded scope for joint decision-making. The Clinton administration is said to be enamored of the German co-determination model, but the political and social context that defines this labor-relations system suggests that it is only possible where a strong labor movement with nationally unified organizations is backed by a tradition of "corporatist" pattern bargaining, and supported by both a political party and by labor laws that provide an independent basis for worker participation in decision-making. These social and political conditions are absent in the United States. The American labor movement is smaller, is often fragmented into competing organizations, and is divided internally over the virtues of adversarialism and cooperation. Traditions of corporatist pattern bargaining and political party support are weak, and the NLRA does not provide the legal foundation for organized labor's independent participation in decision-making. Simply put, the United States is not Germany.[3]

Therefore, to argue that the UAW should abandon its adversarial tradition and cooperate in the process of managerial decision-making is only one half of the equation. Without labor law reform, organized labor has much to fear from labor-management "cooperation" on management's terms. Without labor law reform, organized labor also has much to fear from those who advocate cooperation on the shop floor and adversarialism at the bargaining table. As described below, the Supreme Court's decision in the *Yeshiva* case suggests that adversarial bargaining may be a moot point should a federal appellate court decide that workers are managers when they cooperate in deciding matters that have traditionally involved strategic-level subjects.[4]

The NLRA and Nonunion Transplants

The NLRA paradigm faces its toughest challenge from the nonunion Japanese transplants—Honda, Nissan, Toyota, and Subaru-Isuzu—and from the newly arriving German transplants: BMW, Mercedes, and, once again, VW. The nonunion Japanese transplants have taken full advantage of the limitations of the NLRA paradigm to thwart union organizing. These transplants selected their greenfield locations, in part, to have virtually unqualified strategic control over the selection of a workforce with minimal or no union work experience. Their recruitment processes screened in lean production players and screened out applicants with pro-union sympathies. Their training and lean production practices have so far assured managerial control of the shop floor and discouraged union organizing. Nissan selected a Tennessee site not only for these reasons, but also because the state had enacted a right-to-work statute which the automaker believed would discourage UAW organizing. Nissan, Toyota, Honda, and Subaru-Isuzu have been enormously successful in keeping the UAW out of their wholly-owned assembly plants. In sum, lean production, however it may be practiced, is firmly in place at these four U.S. transplants, and employee participation is limited to the shop floor where it is defined on management's terms.[5]

What needs to be done to advance transplant labor organizing activities and to promote organized labor-management cooperation? Many changes have been proposed in the NLRA, including shorter union certification campaigns, recognition of union authorization cards as an alternative to elections, and repeal of Section 14(b), the so-called "right to work" provision that allows states to ban contracts making union membership a condition of employment. Shorter certification campaigns and recognition of union authorization cards may be helpful, but it should be noted that even though the Canadian Auto Workers (CAW) can rely on card-checks to demonstrate majority support, the CAW has not succeeded in organizing Honda, Toyota, and Hyundai. Only CAMI, a GM-Suzuki joint venture, was organized by a pre-hire agreement similar to those at Mazda, NUMMI, and Saturn. Repealing Section 14(b) would eliminate a safe haven for nonunion transplants, but only Nissan is located in a right-to-work state. The German transplants have located in Alabama and South Carolina, both right-to-work states, and represent additional cause for concern, but the current prospects for removing this Taft-Hartley provision from the NLRA are nil.

The more likely reform agenda, and the single most important change that needs to be resisted, is a rewrite of the NLRA's definitions of a labor union and of management's unfair labor practices related to the formation and operation of a labor organization. In this context, the legal question is whether a lean production team is a Section 2(5) labor organization and, if it is, does management commit a Section 8(a)(2) unfair labor practice by dominating or interfering with its formation and operation? No one can answer the question in the abstract. Even if one could get inside a Japanese transplant and find out how management uses teams, there is no judicial consensus on whether these uses would violate the NLRA. A federal court applying the Supreme Court's *Cabot Carbon* decision would broadly define a labor organization under Section 2(5) and find that an employer's conduct violated Section 8(a)(2) even if it merely created a potential for domination of teams. However, this traditional analysis, which is clearly protective of union interests, has lost favor with two federal courts of appeal, which have adopted a more cooperative view of the NLRA. If, for example, a federal court followed the Sixth Circuit decision in the *Streamway* case, it might well find that work teams in a nonunion transplant were not Section 2(5) labor organizations because they do not "represent" other employees, but instead involve mere "participation" by all members of the plant. If a federal appellate court did find that a nonunion transplant team was a labor organization, it would turn to Section 8(a)(2), but might well find, as the Seventh Circuit did in the *Chicago Rawhide* case, that employer involvement does not constitute actual domination, but mere cooperation with employees. These rulings of the Sixth and Seventh Courts of Appeals could be politically influential, since Saturn, all of the Japanese transplants, and the Big Three-Japanese joint ventures except NUMMI, are located in these two circuits.[6]

In this regard, what does the *Electromation* case have to say about nonunion teams? The NLRB's decision followed Cabot Carbon's traditional judicial view of the NLRA and found that the employee committee was a Section 2(5) labor organization and the company dominated the organization and functions of the committee in violation of Section 8(a)(2). What the *Electromation* decision means for the NLRA paradigm is unclear, however, because the holding is limited to the specific facts of the case: Electromation, a nonunion employer, organized, funded, and directed employee committees that dealt with management about working conditions. In the event that the case is appealed to the DC Circuit and then, perhaps, to the Supreme Court, the transplants might turn to the *Yeshiva* case for legal support. In this case, the Supreme Court overturned an NLRB decision that university faculty had an NLRA right to engage in collective bargaining, and ruled instead that they were managerial employees because they exercised decision-making powers over class schedules, admissions, and graduation requirements. Using *Yeshiva*, the nonunion transplants might well argue that team members are not covered by the NLRA at all because they are managerial employees. If so, organized labor has much to fear from federal judges who are swayed by management's siren call of cooperation and competition.[7]

Conclusion

If organized labor has a prayer of playing an active role in a post-Fordist world, it needs to organize the nonunion transplants, and strengthen its hand in truly cooperative actions from the strategic level to the shop floor. These tasks will require a legal and political solution, but the Supreme Court and federal appellate court decisions do not provide an encouraging avenue for action. Labor law reform is, therefore, the only meaningful option. Here the question is not whether labor law reform is possible, but whether the UAW and organized labor will be satisfied with the Reich Commission's proposals. In this regard, there are two recommendations the Reich Commission did not make. First, there will be no whole-sale scrapping of the NLRA in favor of state labor relations legislation, since Section 14(b) already satisfies a large part of that regressive interest. Second, the Reich Commission may offer some form of co-determination babble, but it does not support genuine labor-management co-determination. Business opposition is too great, union power is too weak, and, once again, the United States is not Germany. As a consequence, the Reich Commission's recommendations will likely lead to only minimal changes in federal labor law. Clinton administration apologists will, no doubt, claim that these reforms establish a more level playing field for labor and management. In reality, however, they will merely advance the administration's primary goal of assisting American business in becoming more competitive in a global marketplace, not in meaningfully advancing the interests of union labor.[8]

In that case, will it make any real difference how the Clinton administration tinkers with the NLRA? The answer seems to be no. Since labor law is defined in terms of the vector of national political forces, while corporations operate in a highly mobile manner on an international economic stage, American business can leave the NLRA paradigm behind and move manufacturing operations not just to a right-to-work state, but to Mexico. German business can also leave the co-determination paradigm behind and move manufacturing operations not just to Hungary, but to the right-to-work states of Alabama and South Carolina.

Given these political, legal, and economic realities, how can organized labor meaningfully negotiate the future from a position of strength? Labor has been chasing capital for years and has widened its organizational reach accordingly, from single-site locals, to city-wide organizations and multi-employer agreements, to national bargaining. So the answer for organized labor probably lies in strategies that further widen its agenda to include international alliances with unions and workers in other countries. Extending solidarity across international borders is difficult in its own right and doubly so when national pattern bargaining is under attack. Still, preliminary efforts are under way, including the exchange of delegations and information between the UAW's Mazda (Auto Alliance) local and its CAW counterpart at CAMI, and the worker-to-worker delegations that link locals and UAW regions with workers in Mexico's maquiladora auto plants. Only when these tentative alliances multiply into a genuinely international movement linking workers in all of North America with workers in Europe and Asia, will unions be able to propose global standards that genuinely empower labor.[9]

Notes

1. Lindley Clarke, Jr., "Yet Another Clinton Commission—on Unions," *Wall Street Journal* (6 Apr. 1993): A-14; Mike McNamee and Christina Del Vale with Aaron Bernstein, "Reich's Return to Those Thrilling Days of Yesteryear," *Business Week* (12 Apr. 1993): 45.

2. "Advice Memorandum Issued by NLRB on GM-UAW Saturn Agreement," [Text] 110 *Daily Labor Reporter* (9 June 1986): E-1; Michael Powers, "The GM-UAW Saturn Agreement," *Virginia Law Review* 74 (1988): 93. For a favorable assessment of the Saturn agreement, see Irving Bluestone and Barry Bluestone, *Negotiating the Future: A Labor Perspective on American Business* (New York: Basic Books, 1992), 191-201. For a critique of the Bluestones' book, see Dana Frank, "Sleeping with the Enemy," *The Nation* (8 Mar. 1993): 310–13.

3. NLRB v. Borg Warner Corp., 356 U.S. 342 (1958). On co-determination and comparison of U.S. and German conditions, see Lowell Turner, *Democracy at Work: Changing World Markets and the Future of Unions* (Ithaca, NY: Cornell University Press, 1991), 29–171.

4. NLRB v. Yeshiva University, 444 U.S. 672 (1980).

5. Doron P. Levin, "What BMW Sees in South Carolina," *New York Times* (11 April 1993): F-5; Martin Kenney and Richard Florida, *Beyond Mass Production: The Japanese System and Its Transfer to the U.S.* (New York: Oxford University Press, 1993), 101–105.

6. NLRB v. Cabot Carbon Co., 360 U.S. 203 (1959); NLRB v. Streamway Division of Scott Fetzer Co., 691 F.2d 288 (6th Cir. 1982); Chicago Rawhide v. NLRB, 221 F.2d 165 (7th Cir. 1955).

7. Electromation Inc., NLRB No. 163, December 16, 1992; "NLRB Cites Electromation for Illegal Domination," *Labor Relations Week* 6 (23 Dec. 1992) 1229–30; "Labor and Management Assess Impact of Labor Board *Electromation* Ruling," *Labor Relations Week* 7 (6 Jan. 1993): 19–20; NLRB v. Yeshiva University.

8. "The Same Old Song," *Wall Street Journal* (6 Apr. 1993): A-14. See also Richard B. Freeman and Joel Rogers, "A New Deal for Labor," *New York Times* (19 Mar. 1993): A-17, and a critique of this article by Alexander Cockburn, "Clinton and Labor: Reform Equals Rollback," *The Nation* (17 May 1993): 654.

9. David Brody, "The Future of the Labor Movement in Historical Perspective," *Dissent* 41 (winter 1994): 57–66; Mike Parker and Jane Slaughter, "AFL-CIO May Trade Away Law Against Company Unions," *Labor Notes* (Dec. 1993): 7–9, 11; Lowell Turner, "Beyond National Unionism? Cross-National Labor Collaboration in the European Community," paper presented at the annual meeting of the American Political Science Association, Washington, DC, 2–5 Sept. 1993.

21

Public Policy and the Evolution of Change in Industrial Relations

IRVING BLUESTONE

Catch-phrases and acronyms are commonly used to invoke a universal pre-scription of what ought to be. In the current world of business management, the term "lean production" has become this kind of generalization. The fact is, no two companies, even companies in the same industry, are admin-istratively or operationally identical. Even within the same multi-facility company, significant differences exist, plant by plant. Therefore, I hesitate to use the term "lean production" as if there is some kind of universal operational application of that phrase. There is simply too much variation in the prescriptions for change that different managements and unions are pursuing to apply a catchy generalization to their respective or joint efforts.

For some years now, a "joint action process" has been developing in various sectors of the industrial relations arena, undertaken in a spirit of equality between organized labor and management, with commitment on both sides to find common solutions for common problems. Thus, in an atmosphere of mutual understanding and within the precepts of collective bargaining, the parties seek jointly to plan, design, and implement pro-grams and processes that meet shared objectives, such as improved quality of the product and/or service, enhanced efficiency, assurance of employ-ment security and income for the workforce, and profitability for the firm.

Whatever title is applied to this joint endeavor, in a unionized setting it is not a unilaterally imposed management prescription for "lean production." Rather, it is a process jointly developed in a co-equal setting, determined and decided upon through collective bargaining procedures. Intensive research has established that such a joint union-management approach, if backed by a genuine commitment to the objectives described above, can improve productivity in greater measure than management-driven programs in nonunion settings.[1]

Given the established track record of the joint-action process and its evident advantages for the advancement of the national economy, what role should pubic policy play as a constructive force in the adoption of this joint practice in labor-management relations? Moreover, what impact should these recent developments have on the practices of the labor movement in its efforts to organize the unorganized?

The Union Challenge

This latter question brings to mind an experience the UAW had in its organizing efforts at new General Motors plants in the 1970s. During that decade, GM embarked on a vast expansion program to enlarge its productive capacity, investing billions of dollars in constructing new facilities located primarily in the southern United States. The UAW called it GM's "Southern Strategy," an attempt to maintain these new plants as union-free. In 1976, after considerable discussion in national contract negotiations, GM pledged in writing that it would maintain a neutral position in UAW organizing drives at any GM facility covering the types of workers normally represented by the union. Three years later, as 1979 national contract negotiations at GM were scheduled to open, UAW organizers at the new GM assembly plant in Oklahoma City discovered that plant management was directly involved in distributing anti-union literature to the workers. This breach of the corporation's signed commitment to remain neutral in such union organizing drives became the first issue for discussion on the opening day of 1979 national contract negotiations—and was the first issue resolved that same day. The corporation agreed in writing that "any new plants opened by the Corporation in the United States to produce products similar to those now being produced at plants in which the Union is currently the bargaining representative of the production and maintenance employees will involve a 'transfer of major operations,' " and, pursuant to existing contract provisions, such facilities would automatically come under union representation. This resolved the issue for future new plants.[2]

As for the Oklahoma City plant, since it was already operational prior to the 1979 provision, the union still faced the problem of organizing the workers. When the plant first opened, management introduced a manufacturing system which, in today's parlance, would be called "lean production." Management established work teams. The foreman in each case was the team leader or coordinator and gave overall direction to the group. The system was controlled by management, which invoked its authority through instructions to the work teams. The union organizers' efforts were directed toward convincing the workers that, as long as the system was initiated, planned, designed and implemented by management, subject solely and exclusively to management determination, there could be no guarantee that the workers would have any realistic control of the process. Management held all the cards. Management could change the process at will or even eliminate it if it so decided. The only assurance of true workers' empowerment in workplace decision-making, the organizers admonished, is to establish the union as the counterbalance to management's otherwise unrestricted authority. Basing its campaign on this appeal, the UAW won the representation election and the Oklahoma City plant was certified as a UAW-represented facility and placed under the terms of the UAW-GM national agreement.

As this experience indicates, the lean production model challenges the labor movement to find new and effective ways of organizing workers, building solidarity, and promoting democratic values in the workplace as the counterbalance to management's otherwise unilateral control. This challenge encompasses more than just the UAW. In fact, the AFL-CIO is now in its second stage of a Special Committee on the Evolution of Work, chaired by Tom Donahue, the secretary-treasurer of the AFL-CIO. One of the major purposes of the Committee is to explore and develop new ideas and new organizing techniques for the labor movement to adopt in advancing its organizing efforts.

The Public Policy Challenge

As the labor movement and its constituent unions seek innovative ways to strengthen unionism and rehabilitate its progressive role in society, public policy must be reviewed and refashioned with the aim of creating a "level playing field" in labor-management relations. It is no secret, to be sure, that in the period of the 1980s and into the 1990s, the national administrations of Presidents Reagan and Bush gave encouragement to the advocates and practitioners of anti-unionism. The Clinton administration has now signaled the need for change in the current labor law, and change as well in the administration of existing labor law.

The creation of the Commission on the Future of Worker-Management Relations under the joint sponsorship of the U.S. Departments of Labor and Commerce, and chaired by the highly respected Harvard professor, John Dunlop, points to the recognition that a comprehensive review of the status of labor-management relations and labor law in our country is overdue. The instructions to the Commission set forth the following areas for exploration and recommendation:

1. What (if any) new methods or institutions should be encouraged, or required, to enhance workplace productivity through labor-management cooperation and employee participation?
2. What (if any) changes should be made in the present legal framework and practices of collective bargaining to enhance cooperative behavior, improve productivity, and reduce conflict and delay? And
3. What (if anything) should be done to increase the extent to which workplace problems are directly resolved by the parties themselves, rather than through recourse to state and federal courts and government regulatory bodies?[3]

As for the composition of the National Labor Relations Board, President Clinton will have the opportunity during his first term in office to fill three seats on the five-member Board and appoint a new general counsel. As Professor Charles J. Morris has noted, the Clinton appointments could represent the ''most promising opportunity to provide meaningful protection for the employee rights which the [National Labor Relations] Act is supposed to guarantee.'' Professor Morris sets forth certain suggested ''non-legislative procedural reforms'' as well as ''new substantive interpretations of the law.'' His recommended procedural changes include:

1. Further expanding the use of substantive rule making.
2. Reorganizing and streamlining Representation procedures, including (a) broad promulgation, through APA rule making, of a comprehensive set of appropriate bargaining unit rules; (b) the use of show cause orders and summary judgment procedures in ''R'' case hearings; and (c) shortening the standard time period between the direction of an election and the holding of that election.

3. Greatly increasing the use of Section 10(j) injunctions for temporary relief in the United States District Courts, especially in Section 8(a)(3) discharge cases, and also reorganizing Section 10(j) procedures in order to facilitate the handling of such cases.
4. Seeking and obtaining temporary injunctive relief under Sections 10(e) and 10(f) in the appellate courts at the time the Board petitions for enforcement of many of its orders, especially orders in Section 8(a)(5) and 8(b)(3) duty-to-bargain cases.
5. Reorganizing Administrative Law Judges' operations so that ALJs will function more like traditional judges, including (a) assigning them to a case immediately following the issuance of the complaint; (b) providing them with authority to act upon all motions relating to the case, including motions relating to discovery, summary judgment, and initiation of Section 10(j) interim injunctive relief; and (c) further decentralizing their geographical home-base locations.
6. Making discovery available when required, including pre-complaint discovery.[4]

Over and above the opportunities for a reconstituted NLRB to interpret and administer the National Labor Relations Act, there is the issue of reforming current labor law. On this score, there is little doubt that the Dunlop Commission's recommendations will be a continuing focus of political debate. The controversy over the striker replacement bill, subject to forceful opposition by the Republican members of Congress and against which business engaged in a vigorous lobbying campaign, previews debates that will arise as the reform agenda takes shape and substance.

The need to guarantee "a level playing field" in labor-management relations is self-evident. Example after example has been cited, for instance, in which open violations of employee rights by management during union organizing drives have been used to defeat the union. Equally pernicious are the long delays in NLRB procedures and court litigation, sometimes stretching over several years, which are used to block and negate unionization. Moreover, union-busting tactics, even where the union has already won representation rights by majority vote of the employees, have been used increasingly by some managements bent on maintaining a "union-free environment."

These practices can be addressed by several of the reform proposals considered by the Dunlop Commission. First of all, the current license allowed for anti-union managements to interfere with the right of workers to choose to be represented by a union should be substantially restricted. Time and again, managements have employed abusive tactics against their employees in order to discourage support for the union. Misinformation about the union, predictions of dire consequences resulting from collective bargaining, the threat of plant closure, the one-on-one interviews with employees, and other coercive actions—many of which clearly violate current law—must be prevented.

In Canada, the law provides that a "card check" suffices to establish union representation. This practice puts a halt to the almost endless delaying strategies commonly used by management to thwart a swift election for union representation—delays that often kill an organizing drive after it begins with high hopes. Having a card-check recognition provision in the law would expedite the process and establish that the legitimate signing of union authorization cards by a majority of the employees in a designated bargaining unit automatically establishes bargaining rights for those employees.

Even after a union has been legally declared the bargaining agent for the employees, time and again the employer will sabotage negotiations for a first contract with deliberately unreasonable demands and actions. Flagrantly unacceptable proposals, refusal to agree to commonly used language governing grievance procedures and grievance arbitration, and deliberate flaunting of "red flag" contract provisions are used to prolong the bargaining process and demoralize employees. One reasonable solution is for the law to require, after a designated period of fruitless negotiations between the parties, mandatory arbitration of all unresolved contract issues in first-time labor contracts. Thus, the current law's "bargaining in good faith" requirement would more likely be adhered to through the normal bargaining process if a legal mandate for "compulsory issues arbitration" was the inevitable consequence of failed negotiations.

Another important proposal for labor law reform addresses the slow-moving administration of current law. The discharge of union supporters is illegal. However, investigations into charges of such illegal acts are too often long-delayed and the penalties for violating the law are, to say the least, a mere slap on the wrist. A legal provision that would expedite the decision-making process in such cases, coupled with a requirement for the appropriate representative of the NLRB to seek a court injunction to have the employee(s) reinstated, would go far to dissuade managements from abusing the legal rights of employees. Indeed, under current law, a mandatory injunction is called for if a *union's* conduct (illegal picketing, for instance) causes irreparable harm to the employer. No less an action should be mandated when the employees' exercise of their legal rights are thwarted by management's illegal actions.

Reform efforts must also focus on the penalties assessed against employers who habitually violate the law. The current legal sanction imposed against an employer is an order to post a notice in the workplace promising not to commit similar infractions in the future. The "mildness" of the penalty is hardly conducive to stopping the continuing anti-union behavior of the employer. Consideration should be given, therefore, to introducing harsher penalties which would more likely convince management to refrain from its illegal actions.

Empowerment and the Law

Consideration of labor law reform will no doubt include the subjects related to both the *Yeshiva* decision and the *Electromation* decision. Both cases bring to the forefront the broad issues concerning employee empowerment and employee participation in decision-making. The ever-widening introduction of employee involvement processes, including "self-directed" work teams with varying degrees of decision-making authority, inevitably raises legal questions—particularly in nonunion settings—about company unionism and the delegation of managerial authority to employees. It seems clear that the presence and involvement of the union as a direct participant with management in joint action processes presents no particular problem with the law. Moreover, there is ample evidence that the successful joint action process in planning, designing, and implementing the employee involvement process results in enhanced efficiency and improved quality of product and/or service. In this regard, the research study by professors Kelley and Harrison at Carnegie Mellon University is persuasive. The Kelley-Harrison study covered more than one thousand large and small firms in a variety of metalworking and machinery industries, both union and nonunion, with special note taken of the differences between union and nonunion subsidiaries of the same firm. The conclusion was that "nonunion work places with labor-management problem-solving committees are significantly less effective" than comparable unionized plants. Based on these results, Kelley and Harrison observe that "for collaborative problem-solving to succeed, it must be possible for employees to achieve outcomes that also empower them. In management-initiated schemes, the narrow focus and limited objectives for which these programs were designed are quite possibly frustrating these aspirations, undermining the trust and commitment so necessary to success."[5]

In light of these and other findings on the positive role of union "voice" in the efficient operation of the enterprise, one of the major issues the Dunlop Commission has considered is the decision-making mechanisms used in the employee and union participation process—from the workplace up through the hierarchy to the top level of the enterprise. Defining what is legal and what is illegal—in terms of power and control in the context of true industrial democracy—will likely be the focus of continuing intense debate. In particular, the key question of employee independence in the decision-making process will doubtless be the subject of careful review and discussion.

The fostering of joint efforts by management, labor, and the government is yet another salient factor in determining the future direction of industrial relations in our nation. Recall, for instance, that there existed in the U.S. Department of Labor a Bureau of Labor-Management Relations and Cooperative Programs. The Bureau's mission was to bring labor, management, and government together for the purpose of exploring ways to meet the competitive challenges facing the nation. This did not mean bowing to management's needs or necessarily bowing to the workers' needs. Rather, the Bureau created a forum in which labor, management, and government could meet on common ground, identify the key problems, and, with appropriate research, determine what works and what doesn't in terms of the joint action process. Its resulting publications were widely read. The accumulated experiences of the participants were lessons for the uninitiated to absorb and use when they undertook their own joint action initiatives.[6]

The Bush administration eviscerated the program. However, shortly after assuming office, the Clinton administration's Department of Labor, under the leadership of Robert Reich, reconstituted the program by establishing the Commission on the American Workplace. This rejuvenated body will bring together labor and management at various levels in our society, along with government, to explore the kinds of joint responses to global competition that will serve the interests of workers, companies, and the community at large.

Clearly, the Clinton administration is giving recognition to the long-neglected need for "reinventing" labor-management relationships. Included in this urgent reexamination is the employer-employee relationship in the government itself. Thus, President Clinton's Executive Order 12871, "Labor-Management Partnerships," signals the administration's support for the joint-action process in the management of the federal government. To advise the president and promote labor-management partnerships throughout the executive branch, the Executive Order establishes a National Partnership Council comprised of ten members, four of whom represent the AFL-CIO and public-employee unions, and the balance drawn from the relevant executive branch departments dealing with labor and labor relations. "Only by changing the nature of Federal labor-management relations," as stated in the Order's preamble, "so that managers, employees, and employee's elected union representatives serve as partners will it be possible to design and implement comprehensive changes necessary to reform Government.'' The Order goes on to set forth procedures for achieving its purposes, with specific emphasis on provisions to: (a) create labor-management partnerships by forming labor-management committees or councils at appropriate levels, or adapting existing councils or committees if such groups exist, to help reform Government; and (b) involve employees and their union representatives as full partners with management representatives to identify problems and craft solutions to better serve the agency's customers and mission.[7]

These initiatives by the federal government can serve as a model for establishing similar partnerships in the private sector. The government can also promote these outcomes through the more active involvement of agencies such as the Federal Mediation and Conciliation Service (FMCS) and equivalent services at the state level. The FMCS is generally known for its role as mediator, taking the lead in resolving issues of controversy between management and labor. But the agency also devotes its energies to promoting, in a non-adversarial setting, the concept of joint action and conflict resolution as a vehicle for labor and management to solve problems of mutual interest and concern. It may be anticipated that the current national administration will arrange for the FMCS staff to play a more vigorous role in initiating joint action processes.

At the Crossroads

Labor-management relations in the United States are moving simultaneously in two opposite directions. On the one hand, the anti-union, arms-length adversarial mode has been increasingly embraced by the business community, aided by professional anti-union consultants. On the other hand, within the still-unionized sectors of our economy there has been a growing trend that favors labor-management joint-action processes and practices directed towards achieving mutually desirable objectives. The opportunity is ripe for changes in the law that will reinforce this latter trend and discourage the union busting that impoverishes workers and enfeebles our economy. Indeed, the opportunity is ripe for government to act as a catalyst to bring labor and management together and help create the benign climate in which healthy relations will grow and prosper.

This happy outcome would not bring the total elimination of workplace conflict or of adversarial bargaining. The equitable adjustment of wages as against profits will continue to be a subject for tough negotiations. Likewise, the issues surrounding benefits and working conditions will continue to be bargained in the heat of the negotiating process. However, there is a lengthy list of issues for the negotiating parties to address about which there is "more in common than in conflict," as Walter Reuther used to say. It is in these areas of mutual concern that the joint action process can help the nation's economy and its individual industries develop a healthier competitive posture.

True, there are those in the labor movement who insist, "Don't use the word 'competitiveness.' That's a slogan used to get workers to cave in to management—a one-sided gimmick for management to achieve its objectives with little or no favor to the employees." In the joint action context, however, in which employee representatives and management representatives act in co-equal partnership, resorts to gimmickry must be out of the question. The employees' interests will be amply protected while the effort to build a healthy organization will serve the interests of all.

It is equally true that many business managers view the joint action concept as an unwelcome invasion of their managerial authority. There is need for a vigorous orientation process to bring these managers to genuinely embrace employee empowerment principles within a joint action process. There is ample evidence to justify the need for change. The U.S. economy is beset with persistent problems, not the least of which is its low productivity growth rate—one vital factor in measuring the health of the national economy. Increasing the productivity growth rate creates expanding wealth to be distributed as equitably as possible in an economy in which unions can organize and democracy prevails. Yet, even during the 1929-1939 period of the Great Depression, the average annual rate of productivity growth was 1.6 percent, while for the decade 1979–1989, the annual productivity growth rate was only 1.3 percent. Today, the U.S. is the largest debtor nation in the world, struggles with the largest budget deficit in its history, suffers an ever-present heavy trade imbalance, and faces a decline in real median family income, with over thirty-five million living at or below the poverty line.[8]

The global economic challenge is self-evident and formidable. In the relationship between management and labor, the answer is not for workers and their unions to bow and announce: "Mr. management, what do you want? We'll give it to you." Quite the contrary. The need is for management to say: "We recognize the importance of employees as a force that can find answers that help solve our mutual problems. We recognize the importance of the union movement as a constructive force in the economy and in society. Working together on these issues of common and mutual concern can pave the way to a healthier economy with employment security and a rising standard of living.''

In this context we may look to a brighter future, not by invoking the short-sighted ''lean and mean,'' ''slash-and-bash'' strategy, but by embracing everyone's capacity to find solutions that assure long-term success. Above all, there is the need for serious commitment to change, a commitment that is visible and tangible. It is not a commitment in which the CEO makes a laudable speech and then disappears into the walnut-paneled office. It is a commitment accompanied by active involvement and participation by the leadership, with the appropriate investment in orientation and training, generating the sense of sincerity and integrity—with no hidden agendas and gimmicks. It is a commitment that guarantees co-equality between management and labor in planning and implementing employee involvement in the decision-making process. It is translating EI— Employee Involvement—into EI—Endless Improvement.

Toward this end, public policy can and must play a significant role. It can and should be a catalyst that helps to propel and protect the joint action process. Management and labor will continue to deal with controversial issues, and flareups will occur. Even so, the future health of the nation lies in their mutual recognition of shared interests, and their commitment to jointly address them as co-equals.

Notes

1. A growing number of studies demonstrate the positive results of the joint action process and the empowerment of employees in decision-making. The intensive research study by Maryellen Kelley and Bennett Harrison, ''Unions, Technology, and Labor-Management Cooperation,'' in *Unions and Economic Competitiveness*, ed. Lawrence Mishel and Paula B. Voos (Armonk, N.Y: M. E. Sharpe, 1992) is widely cited. See also William Cooke, *Labor-Management Cooperation: New Partnerships or Going in Circles?* (Kalamazoo, MI: W. E. Upjohn Institute, 1990).

2. Letter of Understanding signed by GM vice president and director of labor relations, George B. Morris, Jr., and included in the UAW-GM contract settlement agreement, 1976; Letter of Understanding signed by GM vice president and director of labor relations, George B. Morris, Jr., and included in the UAW-GM national contract settlement agreement, 1979. Some years later, the corporation agreed to accept the results of a card check and grant recognition to the union in those new plants which had opened prior to the 1979 contract and were not, therefore, covered by the 1979 recognition agreement.

3. U.S. Department of Labor and U.S. Department of Commerce, ''Commission on the Future of Worker-Management Relations: Notice of Establishment'' (4 May 1993), 1–2.

4. Cited in the Bureau of National Affairs, Inc., *Daily Labor Report* (28 May 1993),

from a speech delivered by Professor Morris at the Los Angeles and San Francisco meetings of the labor and employment law section of the State Bar of California, 21 and 28 May 1993.

5. Kelley and Harrison, "Labor-Management Cooperation," 277.

6. In passing, the term "joint action" is preferable to "cooperative." "Joint action" sets a tone of equality between labor and management in the decision-making process. The application of this joint action process is not a matter of unions or workers "cooperating" with management or vice versa. It is a matter of both parties reviewing jointly the problems that are of common and mutual concern and resolving them within the climate of co-equality.

7. Office of the President, Executive Order 12871: Labor-Management Partnerships (1 Oct. 1993), Section 1(a) and Section 2(a) and (b).

8. Paul Krugman, *The Age of Diminished Expectations* (Cambridge: MIT Press, 1990), 12; Bureau of Labor Statistics, P-60 Series, "Annual Earnings in 1991 Dollars."

Index